It's About That Time
Miles Davis On and Off Record

Richard Cook edits the magazine *Jazz Review* and is the co-author, with Brian Morton, of the *Penguin Guide to Jazz on CD*, which is now in its seventh edition. He is also the author of *Blue Note Records: The Biography* and *Richard Cook's Jazz Encyclopedia*.

RICHARD COOK

It's About That Time

Miles Davis
On and Off Record

OXFORD
UNIVERSITY PRESS

2007

OXFORD
UNIVERSITY PRESS

Oxford University Press, Inc., publishes works that
further Oxford University's objective of excellence
in research, scholarship, and education.

Oxford   New York
Auckland   Cape Town   Dar es Salaam   Hong Kong   Karachi
Kuala Lumpur   Madrid   Melbourne   Mexico City   Nairobi
New Delhi   Shanghai   Taipei   Toronto

With offices in
Argentina   Austria   Brazil   Chile   Czech Republic   France   Greece
Guatemala   Hungary   Italy   Japan   Poland   Portugal   Singapore
South Korea   Switzerland   Thailand   Turkey   Ukraine   Vietnam

First published in Great Britain by Atlantic Books 2005

Published by Oxford University Press, Inc.
198 Madison Avenue, New York, New York 10016
www.oup.com

Oxford is a registered trademark of Oxford University Press

Library of Congress Cataloging-in-Publication Data
Cook, Richard, 1957–
It's about that time : Miles Davis on and off record / Richard Cook.
p. cm.
Includes bibliographic references, discography, and index.
ISBN-13: 978-0-19-532266-8
ISBN-10: 0-19-532266-5
1. Davis, Miles—Criticism and Interpretation I. Title
ML419.D39C66 2007
788.9'2165092—dc22
[B]   2006050694

9 8 7 6 5 4 3 2 1
Printed in the United States of America
on acid-free paper

Contents

List of Illustrations | vii

Abbreviations | ix

Introduction: Hello, Miles | 1

Birth Of The Cool: 1926–52 | 9
   Birth Of The Cool

Steamin': 1952–6 | 31
   Steamin' With The Miles Davis Quintet

Like Nobody Else: 1956–7 | 61
   Miles Ahead

Scales And Tones: 1957–8 | 83
   Milestones
   Porgy And Bess

So What?: 1958–9 | 105
   Kind Of Blue

I'm Going Out To Hear Miles: 1959–62 | 123
   In Person Friday Night At The Blackhawk
   In Person Saturday Night At The Blackhawk

All The Rockets Taking Off: 1963–6 | 145
   The Complete Live At The Plugged Nickel

A Fine Madness: 1966–7 | 175
  Nefertiti

A Portion Of The Music Inadvertently Gets Repeated: 1967–9 | 189
  In A Silent Way

He Didn't Erase Anything: 1969–70 | 211
  Bitches Brew

Dark, Dark: 1970–75 | 231
  Agharta

Tais-Toi Some Of This!: 1975–85 | 263
  You're Under Arrest

White, Yellow, Orange, Red ...: 1985–8 | 285
  Aura

They Offered Me A Lot of Money: 1989–91 | 305
  Live At Montreux

Outro: Goodbye, Miles: 1991 | 321

Acknowledgements | 329
References | 330
Discography | 333
Index of Recordings | 354
General Index | 362

List of Illustrations

Bebop lives: Davis with Charlie Parker, Lee Konitz and Kai Winding
(Herman Leonard/Redferns Library)   ii

Miles Davis, 1949 (Popsie Randolph/Frank Driggs Collection)   8

Miles Davis and John Coltrane, 1950s (Al Avakian/Sony BMG Music
Entertainment Inc.)   30

Davis with Gil Evans, the great alliance, 1957–8 (Don Hunstein/
Sony BMG Music Entertainment Inc.)   60

Pensive Miles (Michael Ochs/Redferns Library)   82

Davis and Bill Evans in the studio (Don Hunstein/Sony BMG Music
Entertainment Inc.)   104

One of Don Hunstein's classic portraits of Davis from 1958
(Don Hunstein/Sony BMG Music Entertainment Inc.)   121

Outside the Blackhawk, San Francisco, 1961 (Leigh Wiener/Sony BMG
Music Entertainment Inc.)   122

Miles in the 1960s (David Redfern/Redferns Library)   144

Miles Davis in profile (Gai Terrell/Redferns Library)   171

The last phase of Italian suits, late 1960s (Michael Ochs/Redferns
Library)   174

The new look to end the 1960s. Miles at the Paris Jazz Festival, 1969
(Guy Le Querrec/Magnum)   188

Miles in the early 1970s (Paul Hoeffler/Redferns Library) 210

The Miles Davis band with Chick Corea and Dave Holland (David
Redfern/Redferns Library) 212

Miles in 1975 (David Redfern/Redferns Library) 230

Sartorial Swagger: Miles in the 1970s (David Warner Ellis/Redferns
Library) 259

The standard playing stance of the 1980s (Charlyn Zlotnik/Redferns
Library) 262

Surprisingly muted: Miles in the 1980s (Alain Dister/Redferns Library)
283

Thoughtful in the 1980s (Paul Bergen/Redferns Library) 284

Nice jacket plus the hair weave. Miles Davis in concert, 1991
(Guy Le Querrec/Magnum) 304

An untitled sketch by Miles Davis, drawn in the presence of the author,
1985 (courtesy R D Cook) 319

Miles Davis in concert, 1986 (Ebet Roberts/Redferns Library) 320

List of Illustrations

Abbreviations

af	alto flute	*g*	guitar	
arr	arranger	*hmca*	harmonica	
as	alto saxophone	*hp*	harp	
b	bass	*ky*	keyboards	
bcl	bass clarinet	*ob*	oboe	
bs	baritone saxophone	*org*	organ	
bsn	bassoon	*p*	piano	
btb	bass trombone	*perc*	percussion	
cel	cello	*picc*	piccolo	
cl	clarinet	*ss*	soprano saxophone	
cond	conductor	*syn*	synthesizer	
cor	coranglais	*t*	trumpet	
d	drums	*tb*	trombone	
euph	euphonium	*tba*	tuba	
f	flute	*ts*	tenor saxophone	
flhn	flugelhorn	*v*	vocal	
frhn	french horn	*vib*	vibraphone	

Introduction:
Hello, Miles

The Prince of Darkness, the Evil Genius of Jazz, the Man with the Horn, the Master Magician, the Picasso of Jazz . . . or, simply, just plain Miles. No other jazz musician has been mythologized so completely as Miles Davis. Some fifteen years after his death, he remains the embodiment of 'modern jazz' as a mysterious, exotic, faintly chaotic music – most casual listeners, after all, find the idiom baffling. A lot of jazz music is these days serviceable as background sound or hip easy listening, but Miles obliges his witnesses to pay attention (even though he made the hippest easy-listening record of them all, *Kind Of Blue*), simply through an enduring force of personality. His career spanned close to a half-century of music-making and he was prominent during the most extraordinary upheavals in twentieth-century music. He started as a sideman to the coolest musician in jazz, and five decades later the coolest players in popular music still wanted to play with him, or at least be seen with him. His life was sensational, too: long before the excesses of over-indulged rock stars took the fancy of a voyeuristic audience, Davis had, unwittingly or otherwise, courted many kinds of scandal.

He was a past master at resisting archetypes. Before Davis, black musicians had largely been seen as untutored, 'natural' geniuses, in the mould of the first great trumpet virtuoso, Louis Armstrong. Davis, who despised the showbiz mugging of Armstrong and was openly hostile to his 'Uncle Tomming' for white audiences, was a middle-class black who had no poor background to live down and who spent most of his adult life in affluence and with prestige. Like any performer, he enjoyed applause and acclaim, yet he saw no need to acknowledge them, implying that the audience's appreciation for his work was better acknowledged by a quiet mutual respect. Anything more would have been to reduce himself to the level of Armstrong. Even in his artistic old age, when he would sometimes take on a more antic persona and pose onstage for photographers or speak in mono-syllables to an adoring crowd, he could still seem like the most distant of presences. He was a small man, slight of build, but with a lifelong interest in the boxing ring, who – as long as he was able to dance around a gym canvas – kept himself fit with sparring practice and encouraged his sons to do the same. He had a dapper dress sense and a city slicker's wardrobe and carried himself with a delicacy which suggested to some, men and women alike, that he was gay; yet he conducted a long series of often brutal relation-ships with women, regularly resorting to physical violence, and he could display a cold machismo even towards a partner in one of his warmest liaisons.

He studied at Juilliard when he came to New York, and though he later spoke of the experience as if it were a waste of time and taught him little that he needed to know, the period of study there seems to have instilled in him a sense that his playing and the milieu he would work in were ultimately as serious as anything else in the business of making art, and as much as he would later seem to act according to the dictates of commerce rather than music, an underlying intuition about music for its own sake stayed with him till the end. Sometimes he was puritanical about what he ate and drank: at the start of the bebop era, when many followed Charlie Parker's example of substance abuse, he distanced himself from it, and in his later years he often spoke of the merits of a good diet, vegetarian food, and drinking water and juice. Yet he also spent much of his life as a heavy drinker, an obsessive consumer of drugs and stimulants of all kinds, and a sex addict who couldn't resist physical gratification.

His music displayed many contradictions, too. Miles was never either hot or cool: he could be both, or neither. When bebop trumpeters were loud, fast and high, he was quiet, steady, hovering in the middle register. He softened his trumpet with a device – the Harmon mute – which gave his sound a sneaky, inward-facing timbre which could seem tremulously vulnerable one moment, mockingly acerbic the next. He played ballads better than most other musicians, but he never gave his listeners the easy option of a simple, romantic identification with a poignant lyric: whether it was 'My Funny Valentine' or 'Time After Time', he simply adapted the setting to his own inscrutable delivery: 'What you think, is yours.' He turned away from categorizing anything he did, unwilling to accept even the word 'jazz', yet he refused to admit the anarchy of free jazz and its supposed liberations from imposed rule. He is often thought of as a restrained musician, but he could be bitingly expressive, frequently sounding sour and aggressive, and at many points in his career he played the trumpet with something approaching venom: he made sure that his sound was always the one that cut through to the audience.

In his later years, nurtured by decades full of fawning admirers, iron-clad by an overwhelming legend, he seemed to settle, perhaps too worn out to do anything else, into the frame which was just what everyone expected him to be inhabiting. During a conversation late in his life, when told that such-and-such was a remarkable position to adopt, his response was, 'Well, I *am* remarkable.' At this point, so many people had credited him with so many superhuman achievements – that he had changed the course of music several times, that he was a figure on a par with the great philosophers and thinkers and cultural innovators of his time, that he had remained vital and ageless in his outlook throughout his many years of creativity – that he might well have felt invincible, even as he had also suffered decades of indifferent health, pain and a longing for withdrawal from human contact, the strange other face to his more familiar, performer's persona. Legends in their own lifetime have a hard time handling themselves. Miles enjoyed his unmatched fame, but it was blemished by too many ghosts and demons to ever really satisfy him.

For a taciturn and difficult man, he came up with an uncommonly large number of quotable quotes over the years, and by far the most regularly cited one is 'I have to change, it's like a curse.' How much Davis really changed over time is as much a moot point as anything else about him. It's true that many jazz musicians, having decided on their style and matured it to the point where they know pretty much what they're doing every time they play, are content to revisit the same climes over and over, seeking points of detail as their means of varying the pace or freshening the result. Davis did much more than that. He moved from bebop to modal playing to a kind of jazz-rock, a journey nobody else took in quite the same placidly inevitable way, even though each evolutionary step often seemed like something that happened through Miles rather than because of him. In later years, he always claimed that he disliked looking back, that he didn't want to return to the old material, and it was hard to argue with him when he reminded you that he had musicians such as John Coltrane beside him then, and how could anyone try to emulate them? But Davis often 'changed' only slowly and reluctantly. He liked the style of many other kinds of music, but only rarely the substance: he knew that there was only so much he could do, and only so many kinds of music that would work for him.

Now that he is already long gone, there is nothing left but the records, a modest library of video and film footage – given his long and high profile career, a surprisingly small amount – and no chance for any present or future listeners to attend one of his performances, to bear witness to an artist whose charisma and magnetism ensured him an audience even among those who didn't really care about what he was playing. The records present a prodigious and often painfully revealing body of work, though, and they continue to speak to contemporary listeners in a bewilderingly powerful way. *Kind Of Blue*, his landmark 1959 recording, remains, year after year, present in the best-selling jazz record lists around the world. There are still new listeners discovering music as diverse as that on *Miles Ahead*, *On The Corner* and *You're Under Arrest*. While most of his early contemporaries have faded into a history which is usually visited only by jazz aficionados with a nose for tradition, consigning even such giants as Charlie Parker, Dizzy Gillespie and Bud Powell to specialist ears, Miles Davis persists in attracting a different audience.

Anyone reading this far may have guessed already that this is not an attempt to set down yet another piece of Davis hagiography. The author does not come to either praise or bury Davis. The trumpeter has already been the subject of several well-researched and thoughtful biographies, which attempt to portray the man at least as much as the music. What *It's About That Time* attempts to do is disentangle, perhaps, the mythology of Miles from his music, to rehear and consider his marvellous oeuvre as it was documented by the record industry with which he conducted an embattled relationship over many years. It is often said that jazz is a living art, which record albums demean and reduce, but while anyone who's attended an outstanding jazz event will understand that judgement, it tells only a part of the story. Records long ago began to be more than mere replays of some musical performance: they have been shaped and retooled as stand-alone works of art, produced under a variety of conditions, for decades. One of the striking things about the Miles Davis discography is the many fascinating differences between his studio and live performances, how his approach varied between a late-night club set and a temperate studio treatment. Caught as he was by both unofficial and authorized microphones throughout his career, he left a formidably comprehensive collected works, which, at a point where everyone who has an interest seems to realize that they would do well to keep it available, is today remarkably accessible to anyone interested.

The reader can interpret this as an attempt to 'make sense' of Davis's enormous output if they choose, although that suggests that a musician's path is based around logic and a preordained plan, rather than the happenstance which creates most opportunities to move on and up in something as volatile as a career in music. More than any other jazz artist, Davis is an intimidating musician to approach, if only because of the diversity of his work. It can seem scarcely credible that the same man was responsible for leading such different records as *Birth Of The Cool*, *'Four' And More* and *Bitches Brew* – in the space of not much more than twenty years, to boot – yet these were simply staging posts in a recorded output surpassed only by that of Duke Ellington in the jazz realm. Davis came to despise the word 'jazz', but there is little or nothing in his music which strays outside that idiom, and no disrespect to either artist or music should be implied in using it throughout this book. Following his story on record is hard work, if only because there is so much of it, and the narrative has been divided into fourteen chapters, each of which focuses on a particular record, with various 'satellite' albums spinning round the central selection in each case. It shouldn't necessarily be implied that these are absolutely the best records which have Davis's name on them, but they do seem to me to exemplify certain aspects of his work at the time each was made.

These are all official releases. Davis spent most of his career on record under contract to either Prestige, Columbia or Warner Brothers, and the bulk of his work was issued by these three companies. Inevitably, though, there were many other unauthorized recordings made at concerts or via radio broadcasts which have found their way on to LP or CD pressings and into collectors' hands. I have attempted to discuss as many of these as is possible alongside the official records, although some have been released in such tiny quantities (and in such close to unobtainable circumstances) that they have proved too elusive. As to the merits or otherwise of this kind of activity, that judgement is left up to the individual reader.

Miles Davis left behind him an inexhaustible fund of music. While his own playing offers an absorbing journey in itself, he also had his name out front on dozens of records which feature many of the finest musicians of his time. As a single window on to the jazz of the bebop era and everything that came after it, they are unrivalled. But the most effective way to approach them is on their own terms: what do they tell us about their creator, and what he was trying to do? Records may only be, as one of Scrooge's ghosts had it, shadows of things that once were. But in reviving that unique trumpet sound, and the cracked whisper of the voice that went with it, they have much to tell us.

Birth Of The Cool

1926–52

M iles Davis and bebop didn't really go together. Among bop trumpeters, he was always an uneasy fit. The musical language and style of bebop was, from the beginning, bitterly demanding on a musician's technique: that was part of its nature, devised by its principal architects – Dizzy Gillespie, Thelonious Monk, Kenny Clarke – to keep lesser players in the shadows, and leave the stage to the real champions. When Charlie Parker came along, the idiom gained its most particular voice, a virtuoso whose musical grasp and intensity of delivery personified bop itself. Young musicians such as Davis were dazed and spellbound.

Davis was only eighteen when he first played with Parker. Like many young American blacks, he had grown up fast. Born into a comfortable middle-class family in St Louis, he had started on trumpet at thirteen, and by the time he was fifteen he was good enough to play in local bands, and could boast of earning $85 a week as a musician. He was one of the numerous young musicians given encouragement by the local star, Clark Terry, who suggested a fundamental of the Davis style, playing without a pronounced vibrato. The St Louis scene was busy but unremarkable, and when Billy Eckstine's band came to town in July 1944, and Davis was asked to fill in for one of the absent trumpeters, he had his first taste of bebop: Parker and Gillespie were in the band, and it must have been an overwhelming experience for a young and inexperienced performer. Eckstine himself remembered Davis as a dunce who could hardly play at this point, although the trumpeter saw himself somewhat differently, and claimed that he could handle the band's book with few problems. But it was over in two weeks. Nevertheless, the experience must have decided Davis on a move to New York, where Parker and his circle held regular court.

In 1945, Davis's father sent the young man to study at New York's Juilliard College, with a regular allowance, and he made a point of seeking out Parker, the two men eventually rooming together, even though Davis was by this time a family man: though he never married his girlfriend Irene, they already had a baby, Cheryl. Davis mixed his Juilliard studies – little of the teaching there either impressed him or taught him much that was new – with hanging out with other musicians, spending hours in the company of Dizzy Gillespie, and taking his first few gigs on 52nd Street, the central strip for the city's downtown jazz clubs. By 1945, bop had moved well past the experimental stage and out of the black clubs of Harlem, and Parker and Gillespie were the music's corner-men. While they regularly worked together in a quintet, Parker's behaviour, sullied by his heroin addiction and gargantuan appetite for food and drink, led to his becoming so unreliable that Gillespie eventually decided to go his own way. Parker's response was to engage Miles Davis as his trumpeter. On 24 April 1945, Davis had made his first record date, an innocuous group of titles by a band led by Herbie Fields with the vocalist 'Rubberlegs' Williams, but he already had plenty of live work with Parker behind him when he recorded as part of Charlie Parker's Reboppers on 26 November. Of the six titles made at what was also Parker's debut as a leader on record, Davis played on three and Dizzy Gillespie (who also played piano on two titles) handled the trumpet parts on the remainder. The most famous piece is 'Now's The Time', illuminated by a characteristic piece of Parker brilliance on the master take, but a track on which Davis's clear sound and careful phrasing leave their own mark. On 'Billie's Bounce', recorded at the same date, Davis was reputedly so nervous that he improvised a solo which may have been fashioned out of phrases that were a familiar part of the playing of Freddie Webster, a contemporary of his whose playing Miles particularly admired (Webster died in 1947, and the extent of his influence over the young Davis remains enigmatic). But if he was inevitably overshadowed by Parker, then coming to the height of his powers, the trumpeter's particular style was already beginning to be formulated.

He continued to work with the saxophonist nicknamed 'Bird' or 'Yardbird', a name derived from Parker's taste for eating chicken (although Davis insisted to the author in 1985 that 'he used to squeak on his reeds a lot, that's why we called him Bird'), but Davis actually spent much of the next eighteen months in other playing company: he worked on the West Coast with Benny Carter's big band, played with Charles Mingus and Billy Eckstine again, and spent two months with Dizzy Gillespie's big band before returning to Parker's small group in April 1947. Between then and the end of 1948, it was his most regular association, even though he was by then sharing the distaste for Parker's behaviour which many of the saxophonist's associates experienced. Davis had previously played on a septet session with Parker, Lucky Thompson and Dodo Marmarosa, which produced a sensational version of 'A Night In Tunisia', but it was the sessions for the Savoy and Dial labels that Parker recorded during 1947–8 (*The Complete Savoy And Dial Studio Recordings* [1]) that demonstrated the trumpeter's insidious, thoughtful way of interleaving the momentous passions of Parker's idiom. For many years, nay-sayers complained that Davis wasn't up to the technical demands of Parker's music, and how these sessions might have sounded with the ebullient Gillespie, by now working to his own agenda with a big band, is a tantalizing jazz what-if. Instead of trying to match Parker's pyrotechnics, as Gillespie would have done, Miles chills out the music. He plays soberly and sensibly within the middle range which gave him most of his best tones. There is a peeking, behind-the-hand quality to some of his improvising, although the idea that he is a bumbler is scarcely borne out by most of the evidence: he commits fewer fluffs than the Olympian Parker himself on the various rejected takes of the pieces they played. Occasionally, as on the 17 December 1947 date, Davis reverts to a more perfunctory, note-spinning bebop style, and on a much superior date recorded four days later, where the highlights are the themeless 'Klaunstance' and 'Bird Gets The Worm', he sounds oddly detached, as if the jam session feel of that kind of bebop date was simply uninteresting to him. Yet it is the piquancy of his contrasting approach to that of Parker which spices and lifts so many of these titles. His sparser improvisations throw the outpourings of Parker into a sharper relief. His spindly, almost nondescript blues playing – next to Miles, Parker sounds like an angry behemoth in this situation – has its own peculiar wistfulness. It would be wrong to make too much of his contributions to what are indisputably Parker's achievements. But Davis plays his inimitable part.

The full flavour of Davis's take on bebop comes out most clearly on the one date where the trumpeter himself took the leader's role, the four titles by the Miles Davis All Stars, made for Savoy on 14 August 1947. Here Parker plays tenor saxophone, a very rare example of his setting aside his customary alto, and while his solos exude his usual mastery, it is Davis whose temperament settles the way the music emerges. 'Sippin' At Bells' is a blues marked by a criss-cross forest of chord changes, and it has sometimes been revived in the modern era: Stan Getz recorded it for one of his Concord albums in the 1980s. 'Milestones', which is not the same tune as the much more renowned theme which Davis recorded in 1958, is an easygoing original that has a very different feel to nearly anything else in the Parker Savoy sessions. 'Little Willie Leaps' is a deceptively tricky variation on 'All God's Chillun Got Rhythm', and 'Half Nelson', which sounds almost uncomfortably close to Tadd Dameron's 'Lady Bird', was a theme that Davis would return to in his 1950s recordings. Given the limelight of the leader's role, he is not so much a different man but one whose playing has gained in stature through the sifting of context. Harmonically, this material is strikingly different to most of the raw matter of 'standard' bebop sessions. The presence of the feline-sounding John Lewis at the piano, himself an urbane contrast to the percussive approach of Monk or Bud Powell, helps firm up Davis's position: the music feels like a collaboration between, primarily, Lewis and Davis.

By the time Davis left Parker's group for good at the end of 1948, he had something over three years of regular and intense work in bop behind him. At that point, bop itself was petering out. The raw intensity of its first period, which had shocked and dismayed as many musicians as it had enthralled, had been smoothed and mollified: boppers were working in the more forward-looking of the big bands, such as those of Woody Herman and Stan Kenton, and the saxophonist Charlie Ventura had even formed a band he called Bop For The People. In a few years, though, the core jazz audience had changed, from a mass market of listeners who liked swing music for dancing to a coterie of young metropolitans willing to haunt the clubs and spend hours sitting and listening. Davis, who had rarely shown any interest in playing for audiences anyway and would probably have preferred to work in some sort of commerce-free environment of pure music, nevertheless found that he had a following. In 1948, he managed to front a dramatic move away from bebop into a place that promised a new world.

Birth Of The Cool

CAPITOL

Move; Jeru; Budo; Godchild.
Miles Davis (*t*); Kai Winding (*tb*); Junior Collins (*frhn*); Bill Barber (*tba*);
Lee Konitz (*as*); Gerry Mulligan (*bs*); Al Haig (*p*); Joe Shulman (*b*);
Max Roach (*d*). 21/1/49.

Venus De Milo; Rouge; Boplicity; Israel.

Miles Davis (*t*); J. J. Johnson (*tb*); Sandy Siegelstein (*frhn*); Bill Barber (*tba*);
Lee Konitz (*as*); Gerry Mulligan (*bs*); John Lewis (*p*); Nelson Boyd (*b*);
Kenny Clarke (*d*). 22/4/49.

Deception; Rocker; Moon Dreams; Darn That Dream.

Miles Davis (*t*); J. J. Johnson (*tb*); Gunther Schuller (*frhn*); Bill Barber (*tba*);
Lee Konitz (*as*); Gerry Mulligan (*bs*); John Lewis (*p*); Al McKibbon (*b*);
Max Roach (*d*); Kenny Hagood (*v*). 9/3/50.

The Miles Davis nonet was another uneasy fit with bebop. It sounded light, smooth, purged of undue passion: the music seamed from one incident to the next, a direct counter to the jaggedness of bop's momentum. Suffused with low brass, buoyed up on almost feathery rhythms, it might have sounded effete, if the playing hadn't projected a different sort of intensity. Davis was fronting an experimental group which helped lay the groundwork for much of the small-group jazz of the next twenty years.

Not that it was all his idea. Several composing and arranging hands were involved, and the concept was itself midwifed over the course of many months of discussion, theorizing and practice. Much of it stemmed from a tiny apartment on West 55th Street in Manhattan, where Gil Evans, an arranger and pianist, held informal court with seemingly dozens of other players, who dropped in to talk, sleep or otherwise partake of an atmosphere which resembled a cooperative bohemia. Evans had been an arranger with Claude Thornhill's orchestra for a number of years, before departing in 1948, and his work had attracted the attention of many inquiring musicians. Thornhill had one of the strangest books which any of the big bands of the era could muster. Among his studio and transcription recordings are versions of 'Pop Goes The Weasel', 'O Sole Mio', 'La Paloma' and 'Royal Garden Blues', a mixture which the leader seemed to find no paradox in. Many of his records point towards the mood music which would be a dominant force in American record-making in the 1950s. He had used tuba and french horn in his instrumentation, and he gave Evans scope to use the band as a kind of sound-palette: there wasn't much one could call 'impressionism' in jazz at this point, but if anyone was getting close to it, it was Evans in his work for Thornhill, particularly in such scores as 'La Paloma'.

Evans, a Canadian by birth, was a gentle soul whose soft voice and unassuming modesty went with a home-made approach to arranging and composing: he had very little in the way of a musical education, and found his way through his work more by intuition than anything else. There was nothing he liked more than to talk about musical ideas, and as he was the informal head of the circle which developed around his apartment, his influence seeped into the work of several of the participants. The music collected as *Birth Of The Cool* has often been credited primarily to Evans, as the conceptualist at least, but that judgement is unfair on several others – in particular, Gerry Mulligan and John Lewis.

Mulligan is in some ways the most significant influence behind the music. It chafed with him in later years that he didn't get as much credit as he might have expected for the music, and it was he who created a *Re-Birth Of The Cool* recording project many years later. A year younger than Miles Davis, Mulligan was a baritone saxophonist whose red hair matched his fiery temperament. At twenty-one, he was already a veteran of several big bands and had, like Evans, provided arrangements for the Thornhill band. The difference was that, where Evans claimed little in the way of executive instrumental ability, Mulligan was a fine saxophonist and an impassioned improviser – and, at this point, a brilliant talent with nowhere to go. A few years later he became something of a star in his quartet with Chet Baker on the other side of America, but in New York he was hustling for attention like every other young musician. Although the gestation of the scores for the nonet is hard to pin down, Mulligan remembered later that he and Evans 'spent the better part of one winter hashing out the instrumentation' of the group, and the saxophonist was in the end responsible for six of the dozen items collected on the original

Capitol twelve-inch LP. John Lewis arranged three pieces, the composer John Carisi scored his own blues 'Israel', and Evans ultimately contributed only two charts to the final result.

The sound of the nonet was akin to a reduction of Thornhill's idiom. By halving the size of what would have been Thornhill's instrumentation, and emphasizing brass over reeds – note that the tenor saxophone, one of the dominant sounds in the jazz of the time, doesn't figure at all – Davis's group secured a more limber and fluid music than anything Thornhill had created. The group is routinely described as a small ensemble, but with nine musicians involved it's more like a little big band. Tuba and french horn play a vital role, but they're not used as improvisers: instead they follow lines of counterpoint and harmony which give the ensemble a tonally hollow, almost lugubrious timbre which is alleviated by the spring in the solos and the rhythm section. On the slower pieces, the group approaches the mood music which Thornhill himself was probably happiest making, although here it is more like the sunken melancholy which Davis in particular would investigate in some of his recordings ten years hence.

There could hardly be a better example of how important records are to the course of jazz history than *Birth Of The Cool*. By the time the first session was recorded, the group no longer existed other than as a recording group. If Davis was far from being the guiding hand behind the music, he was certainly the leader-figure who actually made the group happen. Gerry Mulligan's much-quoted remark that Davis 'called the rehearsals, hired the halls, called the players and generally cracked the whip' demonstrates how the band probably wouldn't have got further than the discussions in Gil Evans's apartment if it hadn't been for impetus given by the trumpeter. After a lot of talk and plenty of rehearsal, the nonet secured an engagement at the Royal Roost, one of the more adventurous clubs in the city. They played as a support act to Count Basie (who liked what he heard) for two separate weeks during September 1948 – and that amounted to the group's existence as a live group. Fortunately, two broadcasts made from the club featuring the nonet have survived, originally released as *Cool Boppin'*, [2]. The trombone player on the gigs was an eighteen-year-old named Michael Zwerin, given the job by Davis after the trumpeter heard him at a jam session; otherwise the personnel is drawn from the nucleus which made the studio sessions. While inevitably rougher and less finessed than the material would become, the music is otherwise a close match for what would later be set down for Capitol. There are also two charts which didn't make it into the studio sessions: 'Why Do I Love You', a feature for Kenny Hagood scored by Evans, and 'S'il vous plait', a fast and exciting piece which has been variously credited to Mulligan, Lewis and Davis as the arranger.

The polite applause which greets the music suggests that the Davis group was scarcely creating a storm of interest. It was fortunate that the arranger Pete Rugolo, then acting as something of a talent scout for the independent Capitol Records, heard the band at the Royal Roost and offered Davis a deal to make some records. It wasn't until the following January that a studio session finally took place, and even though the first eight tracks were cut only three months apart, there were no fewer than five changes of personnel on the second date, which hints at how 'flexible' the circle of players in the nonet was. At the first session, arranging credits were split between Mulligan ('Jeru' and 'Godchild') and Lewis ('Move', 'Budo'), and it would be interesting to discover why these pieces were chosen over anything by Evans: it might be because these are the catchiest tunes in the group's slim book, and Capitol wanted to get off to a good start with the best numbers. At any rate, the results were a quietly spectacular success.

'Move' is a composition by the drummer Denzil Best, an interesting figure in bebop who only rarely got much attention either during or after his career (he died young, after a fall, in 1965). The basic line is a typically convoluted bop melody with a clever accenting of irregular beats, and in the opening chorus it is played by Davis and Konitz, while two different counterpoints are offered by two other pairings: baritone and tuba, and trombone and french horn. Lewis's score is a beautiful piece of dovetailing, rhythmically and harmonically: on the opening chorus he has each pair of horns execute a different variation on the basic pulse, and on the final ride-out he reverts to the introductory idea but subtly evolves each of the three parts. This makes it seem like an ensemble piece, yet in a sense the music also works as a framing device for two central solos, the first by Davis, the second by Konitz. The trumpeter opens with a pair of two-note phrases, and he squeezes the second one in such a way that it sounds like he's about to execute an awful clinker – then rights it, and from there simply flies. Konitz picks him up imperturbably at the start of his chorus, and then hustles his way through a typically inscrutable improvisation: with his needle-fine tone and almost clenched style of phrasing, he cuts through his surroundings rather like a spill of acid. Lee Konitz was a particularly interesting member of the nonet's gathering. A New Yorker who had been studying with the Svengali-like pianist Lennie Tristano, Konitz already had a kind of kinship with Davis: like his leader, he was a bebopper who could deliver within the idiom but was fundamentally working at a remove from the familiar dialect of the style. Konitz's lean, almost nerveless phrasing and pinpointed manner were a striking contrast to Davis, even as his dialogue with the trumpeter was generously sympathetic.

The two solo choruses then lead to a fourth where Max Roach executes what is in effect a kind of chase chorus between himself and the ensemble. Roach's playing is the real line back to bebop. If anything, he sounds a little clattery on this piece, but elsewhere on this and the subsequent session he finds a way of playing bop rhythms but keeping them light and almost airily swinging, a marked contrast to the almost furious intensity of vintage bop timekeeping. One of the main differences between the studio tracks by the nonet and the material broadcast from the Royal Roost is in Roach's playing: on the live gig he is more like the archetype of the bomb-dropping bop drummer, whereas in the studio he sounds much more guileful.

Mulligan's original 'Jeru' is the most individual piece of the date. The composer scores the theme in such a way that the horns voice a thick carpet of harmony which unfolds and shifts around the soloists, Davis and Mulligan. Instead of the dialogues of 'Move', this is more like a continuous speaking role for the entire group. Lewis's other piece is different in ambition. 'Budo' is closer to a conventional bop record. The theme was originally a collaborative effort between Davis and the pianist Bud Powell (who also recorded it under the title 'Hallucinations'), and the ensemble plays its serpentine melody line as a bookend for the solos. Davis plays a brilliant improvisation here, entirely at ease on the chords, his phrases flickering over the pulse of the rhythm section. He is just as masterful on the final track cut at this date, George Wallington's tune 'Godchild', but in a different way: this is the Davis who is aiming most clearly at a way forward from bebop. He all but abandons the short-note values which were a staple of bop improvising, and plays a careful but not cautious, lyrical solo where each measure seems to breathe. Mulligan's score is another thing of beauty. He twins baritone and tuba for the opening melody (and the opening phrases might have given him the idea for his subsequent tune 'Walkin' Shoes') and ends the record in the top register with alto and trumpet leading.

Capitol Records must have been impressed with the results they got on that day. The four titles were out within a few weeks, coupled as a pair of ten-inch 78s, and were soon enough among the hippest records on jazz jukeboxes on the East Coast. But it took three months to get Davis and his men back into the studio. In the interim, the trumpeter had been back working with Parker's quintet, and in a larger group led by Tadd Dameron, where he was subbing for the ailing Fats Navarro. Eventually, the nonet reassembled in April, though with five substitutions for the previous team. If anything, though, the music was even more impressive in the four titles produced. Mulligan's 'Venus De Milo' is cast at the steady mid-tempo which always seemed to bring out the best in the composer-arranger, and the melody is sweetly put across by the horns, much of it based around a see-sawing two-note motif. Davis repays the favour of getting his name in the title by playing a handsome solo. John Lewis's 'Rouge' is a very demanding piece which here and there sounds as if it could have used a little more rehearsal on the day, but again the ensemble plays it with fearless commitment and there is a particularly apposite solo by Konitz.

The most renowned pieces, though, are the other two recorded on that April day. Evans finally got his name on the session-list with 'Boplicity', credited to 'Cleo Henry', but actually a collaboration between Evans and Davis. In some ways this is the most enigmatic music of all three sessions. While it acts as a kind of fantasy on a conventional bebop line, Evans carefully mixes together the horns and comes up with an elusive texture which has a curiously disassociated feel. There is a particularly eerie passage where the bridge between improvisations from Davis and Mulligan seems to float in from another piece altogether. And just when the horns seem ready to return after the baritone solo, they do not – and there is an unexpected piano break. Davis himself named this as his favourite piece from the three sessions, and it certainly embodies much of what he and Evans had been pursuing.

If anything, though, it is surpassed by the amazing 'Israel'. Carisi's blues is so densely packed with ideas and details that the simple root source is scarcely evident at first, but the feel of a blues eventually emerges as Davis solos against the chords. This follows a series of interacting melody lines which evolve so fascinatingly that one's first reaction is to return to the start to try to detect just how they have been sewn together. As fine as Davis's solo is, Konitz then outdoes him. Some might complain that the saxophonist's shift into double-time at half-way is a reversion to a bebop cliché – but what a thrilling demonstration of saxophone playing! Davis had originally wanted Sonny Stitt to take the alto chair in the band, and fine as that saxophonist was, it's hard to see how his more conventional bop approach could have come close to Konitz's ideas and delivery. In all, 'Israel' lasts a mere two and a quarter minutes, but there is enough packed into it to make it seem twice that length.

'Israel' and 'Boplicity' were doubled up as a single 78 release (probably one of the best records one could buy in 1950), but 'Rouge' wasn't released until 1954, and there were still more titles to make to fulfil the contract with Capitol. By the time the nonet came together again, almost another year had gone by. The nonet had begun to recede into history: Davis never reconvened the band for any live work, and it must have seemed almost like ancient history to some of the participants at this point. Little wonder that the final four titles, cut in March 1950, seem like something of a hangover after the brilliance of the previous session. 'Darn That Dream' is set up as a feature for the vocalist Kenny Hagood, a now forgotten exponent of the Billy Eckstine school of romantic baritones, and while he does a respectable job, it does feel like a piece which has strayed in as an afterthought. Mulligan's chart has some thoughtful touches, but the net effect is to make Hagood sound like more of a bewildering intrusion into the group's music, simply because he is such a conventional performer. 'Rocker' is a Mulligan original which the composer liked enough to revive again for his own groups subsequently, and though its inbuilt humour is perhaps untypical of the nonet's introverted streak, the playing is fine enough. 'Deception' is almost an interloper. Though credited to Davis, it is much the same piece as a George Shearing composition, 'Conception', which the British pianist had only recently premiered with his own group, in between the second and third nonet sessions. (Many years later, Shearing recalled: 'Miles didn't do it right, God rest his soul. I think he didn't get the bridge right.') Still, Mulligan's chart has its own ingenuity, although there is a sense that he wasn't sure how best to make it work as a three-minute record: the band actually play the introductory sequence twice all through before solos by Davis and, stepping up for his principal spot on these sessions, the impassive-sounding J. J. Johnson.

Which leaves 'Moon Dreams'. Why Gil Evans picked out a fairly obscure and not especially interesting composition by Chummy McGregor, who played sweet music with Glenn Miller and Charlie Spivak, is hard to say, although the feel of the piece does chime in with many of his assignments for Claude Thornhill. Here, the nonet work to an almost entirely prescripted agenda, with only a brief passage by Mulligan and even shorter breaks by Davis and Konitz to insinuate a little improvisation into what is otherwise a lugubrious and entirely becalmed piece of music – all Max Roach has to do is swish at his ride cymbal. The six horns move through the intricacy of Evans's chart patiently, but the overall effect is of torpor, the sonorities more enervating than uplifting. Evans would do this sort of thing much more effectively in his Prestige albums and particularly in the memorable 'Sunken Treasure' from *Out Of The Cool* (1961).

Even so, 'Moon Dreams' fits in with the sound of a band that had no real precedent in jazz, despite the various pre-echoes in Thornhill's music and elsewhere – in 1950, there was already little that was completely new under the sun. (It helped that the music was very cleanly recorded by the producer on the dates, Walter Rivers, who secured a remarkably clear and lucid mix of what was a tricky instrumentation to balance. For decades, listeners had to put up with a third-generation master of the music, which was the source of the 1957 LP, until in 2000 the original tape masters were finally remastered by Rudy Van Gelder for the latest CD issue. His work underscores the exemplary diligence which Rivers brought to the task of recording the music.) Davis and his group looked forward and back at the same time. After the Herculean improvising which dominated bebop, the nonet's carefully codified playing distilled such elements as bop rhythm and its abstruse melodies into a smoothly tailored package, still fresh, but with prearranged structures displacing spontaneity. Yet in other ways, the nonet presented a *departure* from form. Where bop's demarcation of bar lines and chorus lengths was always very explicit, the writing of Mulligan, Lewis and Evans displaced expectations as to where one section would start and another end. The discourse between the different elements of the band had a flow to it which was strikingly at odds with the cut-and-dried roles of the bop small group. The 'light sound' which Davis was in search of was a much better match for a musician whose approach was always, as it turned out, going to be about paring away and winnowing down to some kind of essence. The tuba and the french horn, which played such a vital part in making up the nonet's ensemble sound, didn't become modern jazz instruments overnight, and a nine-piece band wasn't suddenly going to become any kind of norm as the size of a group – in the end, Davis's band played for only two week-long engagements and left less than forty minutes of studio music. It was the example they set that was most profound. Mulligan, Konitz and

Lewis moved on from here to distinguished and high-profile situations which built on their endeavours in the Davis circle. The tenor of the nonet seemed to drift across America, to the West Coast, where throughout the next decade bandleaders and studio regulars such as Shorty Rogers and Shelly Manne established a sound which borrowed many of the tenets of Davis and his arrangers – even though 'West Coast jazz' came to be almost a pejorative term for music that many saw as too white, clean and neat.

There's an irony about Davis being associated with a style that was perceived as a jazz which wasn't black enough. At that point, though, he had long since moved on. By the time of the final date for Capitol his personal and professional situations had changed dramatically from how they had been at the outset of the first. In the meantime, Capitol continued to market the results of the three sessions. Although they were at first issued only as a series of single 78s, in 1954 the label combined eight of the twelve tracks on a single ten-inch disc in the new long-playing format. By another irony, the record was titled *Jeru* (the nickname which Davis had bestowed on Gerry Mulligan). It wasn't until 1957 that all twelve tracks were brought together on their first twelve-inch release, by which time Capitol were emboldened enough to title the results *Birth Of The Cool*, using at last the term which had in the interim become the principal buzzword for the style of jazz which these sessions had, perhaps, ushered in.

The fourteen months covered by the nonet sessions was eventful for Davis. In December 1948, he had left Parker's quintet behind, tired of the leader's behaviour, although relations between them remained cordial enough if at a distance. The following May, only a few weeks after the first of the Capitol dates, he was in Paris with Tadd Dameron's group, playing opposite Parker at the Paris Jazz Fair. Like so many other Americans who visited Europe during this period, Davis was astonished at the reception he received: he was treated like visiting royalty and acclaimed as one of the stars of the event. Surviving material from the event, released as *Festival International de Jazz Paris 1949* [3], finds him playing in a more familiar bebop style, and far more aggressively than on his recent American recordings: excited perhaps by the occasion, he takes surprising chances and sometimes fluffs his way through a solo. On his return to the US, however, the reality of his working life came home to him: there was little to do, no regular band or gig to work, and adrift from Parker and not yet established as a bandleader following the lack of interest in having the nonet perform he kicked his heels. Which led, he later claimed, to his becoming hooked on heroin, a move brought on more by boredom than anything else.

Throughout his association with Parker, Davis had kept his distance from hard drugs. Never much of a drinker and proud of his appearance, he seemed to be trying to set an example which countered Parker's addictions. The saxophonist's notorious appetite for substance abuse had created a culture of hard drugs within the bebop circle: aspiring players wanted to copy Bird, and that meant copying his habits too, or so it seemed to many. Though Parker's example left Davis unimpressed, he found himself mixing with addicts such as Gene Ammons, Sonny Rollins, Jimmy Heath, Jackie McLean and Stan Getz, and eventually he was turned on to the habit himself. It turned out to be a major setback in a career which might then have started to blossom.

In 1950, 52nd Street was in decline and several of what had been hardcore jazz clubs a decade earlier were changing their policies. But there were new clubs, too, on Broadway, including Birdland (named for Charlie Parker) and Bop City. A February 1950 broadcast from WNYC featured Davis and Getz sharing the front line of a sextet with J. J. Johnson, and Tadd Dameron, Gene Ramey and Max Roach in the rhythm section. A surviving airshot from the engagement, *All Stars Recordings* [4], suggests a band that had done a significant amount of preparation, since the tunes are handled as more than just blowing vehicles, and there is the prototype of the arrangement of George Shearing's 'Conception' which would become 'Deception' at the final nonet Capitol session. But the surviving music is all that remains of the potentially fascinating collaboration between two of the master lyricists in jazz, Davis and Getz. A further broadcast made at Birdland in May 1950 (also [4]) has Davis sharing the stand with Johnson and Fats Navarro, a young master of bebop trumpet who was then only weeks away from his death, his once large frame shrivelled through the effects of both tuberculosis and heroin addiction. Not much enjoyment can be gleaned from a shabby recording, but there is some lively bebop played nevertheless. The ad hoc nature of these survivals suggests something of the waywardness of Davis's career path at the time. By the end of 1950, his addiction beginning to take a toll, he was more or less hustling for work instead of being feted as a leader. He backed Billy Eckstine and Billie Holiday in touring engagements, but was picked up on a heroin charge while in Los Angeles, and even though he was subsequently acquitted, it was very bad publicity. In January 1951 he played on what turned out to be almost his final meeting with Charlie Parker on record, a studio date for Norman Granz's operation. The quintet play four tunes which hark back to the old music the two horns cut when they were recording for Savoy, and, as then, Davis is content to take a modest role, leaving Parker to make the major impression with some ferocious improvising. But it was a momentous day altogether for Davis, since later in the evening he was booked to cut his debut recordings for the young jazz independent Prestige Records.

Bob Weinstock, who owned Prestige, had heard and admired the nonet material, and had been seeking out Davis for some time. Eventually he signed the trumpeter to a year-long contract and had engaged him to make the first of three sessions on that day, 17 January 1951. Davis had settled on Sonny Rollins and John Lewis as sidemen, and in addition there were Bennie Green (trombone), Percy Heath (bass) and Roy Haynes (drums) (released as *Miles Davis And Horns* [5]). But the music proved to be confused and unremarkable.

Lewis's 'Morpheus' mixed some dissonant ensemble passages with shrill bebop solos, and although Davis's blues 'Down' was an agreeable theme, Rollins outplays the trumpeter in the solos and Green turns in a merely faceless plod. The only other pieces recorded consisted of a slog through two standards, 'Blue Room' and 'Whispering', and on both Davis is notably below par. Perhaps he was simply tired at the end of a long day; whatever the reason, it was an inauspicious debut.

In March, Davis turned up as a sideman on a Lee Konitz date for the label, *Ezz-Thetic* [6]. Reunited with his former colleague in the nonet, the trumpeter seems subdued. Konitz dominates the four titles (two of them by George Russell, including his vivid original 'Ezz-Thetic') and Miles is given very little space to himself. The timbre of this session appears to fit in with the desultory nature of Davis's working life at this point. Various broadcast performances from Birdland have survived from this period, gathered on *Birdland 1951* [7], and they make up a dispiriting and haphazard lot, even through what are mostly very low-fi recordings. A June session features Davis with Rollins, J. J. Johnson, Kenny Drew, Tommy Potter and Art Blakey, and considering the stellar personnel, the results are rambling and sometimes barely coherent. A September date with the improbable line-up of Eddie 'Lockjaw' Davis and Big Nick Nicholas (tenor saxes), Billy Taylor (piano), Blakey and Charles Mingus (bass) was rather better, although it seems sad to hear the freshness of 'Move', which two years earlier had been a step forward for jazz, now turned into a routine jamming vehicle.

On 5 October, Davis returned to the studio for his second session for Prestige as leader (*Dig* [8] and *Conception* [9]). Besides Rollins, Potter and Blakey, the line-up included the young alto saxophonist Jackie McLean and Walter Bishop on piano. The most immediate matter of significance is the duration of the tracks. Hitherto, all of Davis's records had been conceived with the three-minute single-side format of the 78rpm record as their medium. The long-playing record, though, was quickly taking over as the industry's preferred format. While it had been launched in the 1940s and marketed as a sophisticated new medium for, primarily, classical music (finally allowing an entire symphony to be contained on one disc), within a few years it had begun to impact on jazz. Instead of one- or two-chorus solos, improvisers could begin to stretch out; performances could start to approximate the more loose-limbed feel of a live setting; the quieter surfaces of long-playing vinyl enabled subtleties of tone and texture to emerge; the engineer began to assume a much greater importance as the intricacies of microphone placement began to assert themselves. The bassist, in particular, began to be heard with some clarity on jazz records for the first time.

Rudy Van Gelder, who would go on to become the most renowned of all jazz engineers, was in charge at this session, although the results were on this occasion not that impressive from a sonic viewpoint (even Van Gelder was still finding his way). Davis usually takes the opening solo and on most of the tracks plays a closing one as well. Although there are three horn players involved, there is little attempt to create interesting settings or contrapuntal interplay: the tracks generally follow a head–solos–head format. But Davis plays so much better than he did on his previous Prestige sessions that Weinstock must have been relieved. His blues playing on 'Bluing' is exceptionally imaginative, a return to Shearing's 'Conception' is capably handled by the band, and Davis draws some ear-catchingly lyrical ideas out of the standards 'It's Only A Paper Moon' and the ballad 'My Old Flame'. Nevertheless, the music can't evade the rote feel of so much late bebop. McLean and Rollins, still young men learning their vocation, have little to offer other than agility at this point, and Blakey sometimes seems to be paying little attention: he drifts off altogether at the end of 'Bluing', only to be audibly admonished by Davis. That Prestige left this intact on the record goes to show how the new LP idiom was as much a novelty for the labels as it was for musicians and audience.

At the beginning of 1952, Davis was getting close to rock bottom. He began taking money from prostitutes as their informal pimp, although with characteristic self-belief he looked back on the episode as a vindication of what a pleasant and sweet-natured man he could be, claiming he was 'like a family they like to be in'. An addicted man will, though, do most things to suppport his habit, and that included immoral earnings as well as stealing from fellow musicians (Clark Terry remembered putting Davis to bed one day, only to return and find his belongings gone). He was sometimes in New York, some-times not, often playing with whatever band he could find. Weinstock gave up on him and didn't renew his contract. One surviving memento of an out-of-the-way engagement was caught in St Louis in early 1952, where Davis sat in with a group led by the saxophonist Jimmy Forrest (*Complete Sessions* [10]). Forrest, a reliable tenor player with a big sound and an ability to play strong R&B licks as well as bop-oriented material, was the sort who could turn out professional sets to order. He easily outdoes Davis here, even though the recording doesn't help either of them and the local players in the band are second-rate. Another

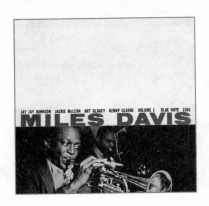

broadcast caught Davis and McLean leading a group on successive nights at Birdland in May (*Sextet With Jackie McLean* [11]). The music again suggests little more than a routine bebop assignment, with older pieces such as 'Wee Dot' and 'Confirmation' mixed in with 'Conception' . If any player shines, it is McLean, who has come on considerably since the studio date for Prestige.

A few days later, though, Davis was himself back in the studios. Blue Note had contracted him for a session (*Miles Davis: Volume 1* [12] and *Volume 2* [13]), and he enlisted an interesting group including McLean, J. J. Johnson, Gil Coggins (piano), Oscar Pettiford (bass) and Kenny Clarke, for a session which turned out to be a compromise between a blowing date and a more considered series

28

of ideas. Davis probably had the idea of doing 'Dear Old Stockholm' after Stan Getz had played the tune (an old Swedish folk melody) some time earlier. He sets up the melody so that the trumpet parts follow it through while the ensemble plays an arranged backdrop. 'Yesterdays' sounds a like a dry run for the more affecting ballad style he would secure later in the decade, and 'How Deep Is The Ocean?' is in a similar though less intense vein. But three other tracks by the sextet have a sometimes lifeless feel to them, as if Davis can't see the point of the music itself – a bad situation for a man who wanted to be a musician rather than any kind of entertainer.

Motivation was surely Davis's great problem at this point. While he was still regarded by the jazz audience at large as one of the princes of the music, he had no regular band or work and his addiction was eating into him physically, mentally and financially. Within two years, he would turn the situation completely around, and set the stage for an extraordinary comeback.

The Other Records

1 **Charlie Parker, *The Complete Savoy And Dial Studio Recordings*** (Savoy, eight CDs)

2 *Cool Boppin'* (Fresh Sound)

3 *Festival International de Jazz Paris 1949* (Sony Jazz)

4 *All Stars Recordings* (Definitive)

5 *Miles Davis And Horns* (prestige)

6 **Lee Konitz, *Ezz-Thetic*** (prestige)

7 *Birdland 1951* (Blue Note)

8 *Dig* (prestige)

9 *Conception* (prestige)

10 *Complete Sessions* (Jazz Factory)

11 *Sextet With Jackie McLean* (Fresh Sound)

12 *Miles Davis: Volume 1* (Blue Note)

13 *Miles Davis: Volume 2* (Blue Note)

Steamin'

1952–6

Jazz is sometimes seen as a history of great individual voices, instrumental soloists whose sound has the indelible singularity of a fingerprint. Ever since Louis Armstrong began to burst out of his musical surroundings in the early 1920s, jazz progress tended to be defined by the evolution of the improviser's approach, from Armstrong's generation to the swing masters and from there through the bebop era. Studies of 'jazz giants' have tended to revolve around a lineage of such names. For the most part, though, the sound which lingers in listeners' memories is of *groups* of players. Armstrong's Hot Five, the orchestras of Goodman, Ellington and Basie, the Jazz Messengers, the Modern Jazz Quartet, the bands of Cannonball Adderley and Ornette Coleman, and on into the fusion era of Weather Report and Return To Forever: all these bands could boast star soloists, but it was their ensemble sound which lent them their distinction, and settled on them an enduring kind of listener loyalty.

Miles Davis was a star soloist at the end of 1952, but as a bandleader his career had entirely stalled. The nonet had enjoyed a considerable reputation but little commercial success or even awareness: for many bebop fans, Davis was most likely best known as Charlie Parker's long-term front-line partner. On his first record date in 1953 (*Collectors' Items* [1]), he was, somewhat unexpectedly, reunited with Parker, in their very last recording together. Bob Weinstock had decided to give Davis a second chance, and he re-signed him to Prestige: on 30 January Davis went into a New York studio with Sonny Rollins, the pianist Walter Bishop, bassist Percy Heath and drummer Philly Joe Jones, and, in what was effectively a guest-star role, Charlie Parker. The situation was complicated by Parker's decision to play a King tenor saxophone, which he had apparently acquired only days earlier, and his usual ill-considered way of warming up: by the time the first take of the first number was ready to be made, he had already downed a quart of vodka.

The music played at this date seems characteristic of the way Davis's career as a leader had drifted. Ira Gitler's sleevenote for the original issue of these

tracks (he was also credited as 'supervisor') contains a testy remark that the engineer 'hadn't helped much', although one can forgive the exasperation of a professional with a band which had, across an afternoon's work, managed to finish only three complete takes of two pieces. Davis brought two tunes of his own, 'Compulsion' and 'The Serpent's Tooth', and the group stumbled through Thelonious Monk's 'Well, You Needn't' without getting a decent result. In the final minutes of the date, they did at least manage to complete a version of 'Round Midnight'. The resulting music is roughly exuberant but badly lacking in focus or direction. The two originals belong to a bop era which had all but passed away, and the playing of all three horns veers between hamfistedness and genuine insight: one hardly expected Davis, Rollins and Parker to play like dunces, but they rarely approach their peak form, and Parker's grey-sounding tenor doesn't fit with the other two horns. Davis sounds enfeebled by 'Round Midnight' and fluffs his way through his solo. It doesn't help that the studio balance is poor, with Bishop barely audible at times. If anyone emerges with modest honours, it's Jones, making his debut with Davis but already fast friends with the trumpeter: his mix of brashness and supportive playing points a way ahead.

Weinstock must have blanched when he heard the results, and there wasn't enough for a record here. On 19 February, Davis went back to the studios with a team chosen by Weinstock himself: Sonny Truitt (who plays trombone on one track), the twin tenors of Zoot Sims and Al Cohn, John Lewis, Leonard Gaskin (bass) and Kenny Clarke. Perhaps the label boss thought that the perpetually sunny music of Sims and Cohn would have brightened up Davis. The four tracks which came out of the date (released on *Miles Davis And Horns* [2]), all Cohn originals and arrangements, certainly bowl along in the composer's witty style, and Davis sounds like he's playing with excessive care, as if afraid to blot his work in such failsafe professional company. Beyond that, the music is nice but forgettable, and again marred by a very poor studio balance which has Kenny Clarke's cymbals set at a deafening level.

This session was surprisingly followed by another date for Blue Note (*Miles Davis: Volume 2* [3]). Davis reassembled some of the cast of the previous session for the label, including J. J. Johnson and Gil Coggins, but the saxophonist Jimmy Heath, his brother Percy and Art Blakey made up the rest of the team. Everything went much better than it had done at the previous date. Six complete numbers were set down, including originals by Johnson and Heath, and everything is crisply despatched, the ensembles tight and on the button, the rhythms lit up by Blakey's typically assertive drumming. The most interesting piece is probably Johnson's 'Enigma', a ballad cast to feature Davis's trumpet in a kind of storytelling role, while tenor and trombone fill in the background. The only real solo is a brief linking passage by Coggins. Doug Hawkins, the engineer at WOR Studios (Van Gelder had not yet assumed overall responsibility at Blue Note sessions), got a fine sound and these were some of the clearest records to date as far as catching the timbre of Davis's trumpet sound is concerned. But most of the session consists of fast bebop lines – Bud Powell's 'Tempus Fugit' among them, which elicits some of the trumpeter's most assured playing on both the issued takes – and the playing has the sheen of dutiful and perhaps clockwatching professionalism. Jimmy Heath's 'C.T.A.' (reputedly named after the three things he liked most about women) sets Davis a modest challenge with its downshifting chords, and Miles starts his solo on the issued take with spaced single notes that suggest someting interesting about to happen. But he resolves it into familiar bebop phrases soon enough. 'I Waited For You', a ballad feature for the leader, is pleasing enough, but marred by Coggins's clumsy comping.

There was only one further studio session to come in 1953. Davis made another quartet of titles for Prestige on 19 May, with the rhythm section of John Lewis, Percy Heath and Max Roach (*Blue Haze* [4]), although Charles Mingus replaced Lewis at the piano for some reason on one of the four titles (Ira Gitler's sleevenote says that Lewis had to leave 'because of an emergency'). That tune, 'Smooch', sounds a bit like the opening measures of 'Round Midnight', and runs moodily through three minutes. The other pieces sound much more like

Davis finding a new voice. 'When Lights Are Low', a familiar Benny Carter tune, receives a strangely poignant reading. 'Tune Up', a theme which Davis would use many times in the years to come, makes its debut here, and though it is patterned after a fast bebop style, Davis actually works his way cleverly into a busy solo while laying back on the brisk pulse from Max Roach. 'Miles Ahead' is even more interesting, since it recasts his earlier 'Milestones' in a sparser, more elliptical set-ting. The tempo is a medium lope, and Davis takes an unhurried path over the ingenious comping by Lewis, who again suggests what an apposite foil he could be for the trumpeter. There's an extraordinary moment on the bridge of the second chorus when Miles squeezes out what might have been an outrageous fluff but which sounds like a dramatic exclamation point, a startling piece of colour.

Strong as this session was, it still amounted to only four brief titles, and underscored how transient Davis's path as a leader on record was becoming. Away from the studios, he was no nearer to any kind of breakthrough. His addiction continued to interfere with his career, and he roamed the country with Philly Joe Jones or Jimmy Heath, playing local gigs with pick-up groups and making the best of his aimless situation. On more than one occasion, he retreated to his parents' farm in St Louis, but even there he was sought out by local dealers and fellow junkies. In August, Max Roach and Charles Mingus visited while en route to California, and when they left Davis departed with them, eventually staying on the West Coast for several months. While there, he turned up at a jam session recorded at the famous Lighthouse club, one of the premier venues for the new style of West Coast jazz which had been growing up around the likes of Gerry Mulligan, Chet Baker, Shorty Rogers and Shelly Manne. In the event, Davis's desultory contributions to *At Last!* [5] are scarcely worth hearing.

He returned to his parents' home in November, where he attempted to get himself off heroin through the process of abstension usually called going 'cold turkey'. In his autobiography, he manages to romanticize this dismal ordeal: 'One day it was over, just like that. I felt better, good and pure.' In fact, he hadn't yet left the addiction behind. He went to Detroit around Christmas and worked with some regularity at a club called the Blue Bird Inn: Detroit was an almost undiscovered jazz community at that point, even if it included many front-rank musicians, and though Davis still had an air of stardom around him, he was also a damaged soul who drifted on and off its local scene like a spectre. Eventually, in March 1954, Davis returned to New York. He had long since become estranged from his common-law wife Irene, and was wary of being too visible in the city since she had begun to hound him over child support. Staying at the Arlington Hotel on 25th Street, he got to know a young pianist who was also resident there, Horace Silver. On 6 March, Davis took a rhythm section which included Silver, Percy Heath and Art Blakey into Rudy Van Gelder's Hackensack studio. The six tunes they recorded [3] marked a notable advance on anything he had recorded over the previous year. The trumpet playing is finally leaving bebop behind, even though, on 'The Leap' and 'Take Off', he still falls back to some extent on fast bop phrasing. On the other, more easygoing, tracks, the style which would become familiar as the decade wore on was asserting itself: conversational, the notes logically but unpredictably spaced, the tone precisely judged to make the most impact with the least palpable effort. On the ballad 'It Never Entered My Mind', which Davis plays with a cup mute, one can witness the first appearance of the ballad player who could silence noisy rooms and provoke tears, even though he had yet to acquire the slightly preening delivery which would, again, be perfected later. On Monk's 'Well, You Needn't', assured where the version with Parker and Rollins a year earlier had failed to even reach a completed take, Silver's contribution comes to the fore. Horace Silver

would be one of the architects of the hard-bop movement which dominated black jazz in the later 1950s and early 1960s, and like John Lewis he was a fine foil for Davis without drawing much attention to himself. Here, he does Monk as well as anyone from that period, and on the originals credited to Davis he plays in a more personal style, the blues and gospel touches which colour his playing deftly suggested. Of those new pieces, the standout is 'Weirdo', a tune which Davis later revised as 'Sid's Ahead', and which is in turn derived from a tune Davis would record a few weeks hence, 'Walkin''. As 'Weirdo', it sounds like not much more than a single phrase, from which Davis and Silver spin lucid solos.

Nine days later, Davis was back in the studio with the same group, this time for Bob Weinstock and Prestige. Only three tunes came out of the date (issued as part of [4]). One was the first appearance of 'Four', destined to be part of Davis's regular repertoire for many years and claimed by him as an original, although the saxophonist Eddie 'Cleanhead' Vinson later insisted that he had written both this and the earlier 'Tune Up'. Here, 'Four' gets a somewhat perfunctory treatment, the catchiness of its main line rather tossed off. 'That Old Devil Called Love' is earthbound by the decision to switch between a vamping stop-time feel and a swinging four during each chorus. Weinstock must have been

disappointed that again Davis hadn't managed very much over a whole session and was rewarded only with one further, final, piece, 'Blue Haze', where Davis improvised a blues over a ponderous bass part which Percy Heath spelled out for two choruses before the leader came in.

On 3 April, the same group minus Blakey but with Kenny Clarke and the alto saxophonist Davey Schildkraut returned to make four more titles for Prestige. One, 'I'll Remember April' is included on [4], while the other three turned up on *Walkin'* [6]. It's not clear what Schildkraut, a Stan Kenton section-player who had just come off the road with that band, was doing on the date, and some of the time he feels almost frozen out of his surroundings. But he doesn't play as indifferently as some have suggested: his solo on 'I'll Remember April', although oddly sandwiched between two Horace Silver improvisations, is a nervily effective pirouette through the chords, and he does some excellent work on 'Solar', even though he gets very little space. Davis uses a cup mute for all four tracks, Clarke employs brushes rather than sticks, and the whole date has a foot-padding feel to it, sprung off the drummer's flawless time. Davis plays concisely and takes nothing in the way of a risk. 'You Don't Know What Love Is', one of the most doleful of standards, here has a strangely wistful feel.

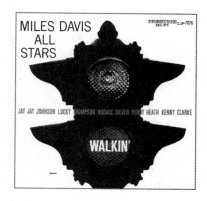

At the end of the month, 29 April, Davis arrived at Van Gelder's with a sextet, including J. J. Johnson and the tenor saxophonist Lucky Thompson, as well as the rhythm section of Silver, Heath and Clarke. The original intention was to record a number of pieces which Thompson had arranged, but nothing went right at first. Davis had actually arrived without his trumpet and had to borrow a battered old horn. The four Thompson charts needed more rehearsal and never made it to a finished take. In the end, the band all but improvised two blues – one at a steady mid-tempo, one at a faster pace. The resulting tracks,

'Walkin'' and 'Blue 'N' Boogie', have ever since received extravagant praise. John Szwed suggests that they started the whole hard-bop era; Ian Carr reckons that 'Blue 'N' Boogie' is 'One of the most dynamic and exhilarating jazz performances ever recorded in a studio'. It would be absurd to fly in the face of all other critical judgements, since these tracks are obviously very fine music, but they're hardly the harbinger of the hard-bop movement: Davis did, after all, operate almost at a tangent to the groove adopted by the hard-boppers. 'Walkin'' is remarkable particularly for the balance between relaxation and intensity. Davis's seven choruses have a poise and calm about them which give what is otherwise a conventional blues solo a meditative, even a timeless quality. Johnson's following contribution is more in a familiar bop vernacular, but arguably both of them are outdone by Thompson in his solo. The saxophonist may have been dismayed that his work on the unrecorded material had gone to waste, and perhaps that put him on his mettle: either way, it's his playing which stands out most, in part because he was a musician who seemed, quite unselfconsciously, to straddle different eras. He had the big, virile sound of the Coleman Hawkins school of tenors, and he inhabited the orthodoxies of bebop phrasing without surrendering the older style he had come up with. The open canvas of a blues at a grooving mid-tempo was meat and drink to him – he would repeat the trick in his beautiful sessions with Milt Jackson for the Savoy label, two years later – and his playing is a wonderful instance of utterly assured though spontaneous blowing. 'Blue 'N' Boogie' is effectively a second helping at a faster tempo, and again the playing feels unusually inspired, a group of fine players suddenly at the top of their game – maybe the mix of youth and experience which the line-up suggested helped make the results what they were. Either way, this was surely Davis's finest hour since the *Birth Of The Cool* sessions. Ironically enough, it was at this point that Capitol chose to gather together most of the tracks made by the nonet and issue them for the first time as *Birth Of The Cool*, on a ten-inch LP, omitting four of the twelve titles (three of them would be added to the twelve-inch version of the album, issued three years later in 1957). It reminded audiences of Davis's bandleading abilities, and it was appropriate that the trumpeter was attempting to solidify his own group at this point.

The trouble was, the players he wanted weren't available as regular sidemen. The group he assembled on a further Prestige date on 29 June, issued as *Bags' Groove* [7]), again included Silver, Heath and Clarke, and added Sonny Rollins as Miles's front-line partner. But none of these players wanted to work full-time with Davis, with Heath and Clarke in particular already committed to their roles in the new Modern Jazz Quartet. Still, it was a remarkable quintet, as the results of this date suggest. Rollins contributed three originals, 'Airegin', 'Doxy' and 'Oleo', and the remaining title was the standard 'But Not For Me'. 'Oleo' offers a bountiful instance of Davis's creative thinking. For the first time, he uses the Harmon mute in his trumpet, a metal cone minus its stem squeezed into the bell of the horn. Rollins's tune sounds like a vintage bebop construction, but it's played at a jaunty mid-tempo and the opening chorus features the two horns together, bounced off Percy Heath's bass line – no piano, no drums. After sixteen bars, the full rhythm section plays the bridge, and then it reverts to the original setting of front line and bass. Davis and Rollins then solo and again Silver sits out except on the middle eight. On the pianist's own solo, Clarke deftly switches to brushes. All the way through this glorious performance, Heath's impeccable note choices mark out the progress of the music, and even though he doesn't play a 'solo', he takes the central role in the group.

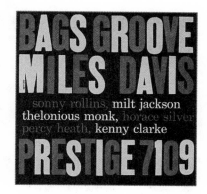

The other pieces are in comparison more conventional, but Davis continues in the illustrious form he had shown on the previous session for Prestige, and in comparison Rollins sounds surprisingly restrained, even though it's his compositions that provide most of the raw material. He was only a year or so away from commencing an incredible year of leadership work on record, for

Prestige and Blue Note, where he mostly stood as the sole horn, and here he seems to be deferring to Davis: the deliberately halting way he starts his solo on 'Oleo' sounds akin to Sonny doing Miles, a skin which he eventually sheds.

Davis closed the year with another extraordinary date. Bob Weinstock assembled a group at Rudy Van Gelder's studio on Christmas Eve which included Davis, Thelonious Monk, the vibraphonist Milt Jackson, Percy Heath and Kenny Clarke, and the released music was billed as *Miles Davis And The Modern Jazz Giants* [8]. The famously unconventional Monk seems to have been in a mood of blithe mischief-making. At the start of the first take of 'The Man I Love', he interrupts Milt Jackson's shimmering prologue with the words 'When am I supposed to come in, man?' Jackson stops and the rest of the

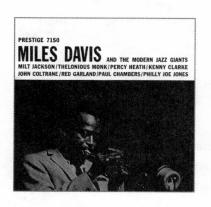

PRESTIGE 7150
MILES DAVIS AND THE MODERN JAZZ GIANTS
MILT JACKSON/THELONIOUS MONK/PERCY HEATH/KENNY CLARKE
JOHN COLTRANE/RED GARLAND/PAUL CHAMBERS/PHILLY JOE JONES

group complain, before Davis barks out to Van Gelder, 'Hey Rudy, put this on the record – all of it' (Weinstock obviously concurred). The two surviving takes are nevertheless full of dazzling playing. Davis contributes an achingly slow chorus following the introduction, before Jackson's solo vaults the music into double-time. Milt Jackson was among the most reliable of jazz musicians: he could play entire sets based around simple blues themes, and create unstoppably swinging, joyful music almost to order. That made him a very different musician to either Davis or Monk, and the piquancy of his inclusion is that his playing here is a glittering riposte to them in its simple eloquence. On the first take, Monk follows Jackson by attempting the audacious feat of spreading the original melody across twice its bar-length, and despite what sound like a few characteristic Monk hesitancies, he makes it work, before Davis returns in a jauntier solo; they finish the final half-chorus by reverting to the slow tempo. A marvellous performance, but more notorious was the second take. After a superb second shot from Jackson, Monk again tries the same slow-motion device and this time appears to lose his way, and he stops dead while Heath and Clarke swing imperturbably on. Davis starts playing on the bridge of the chorus from what sounds like the other side of the studio and Monk, as if he's been guying the leader all along, suddenly bursts back into life and seems to 'find' his place again. Davis picks him up at the close of the chorus and starts his own solo. On the second section, he suddenly screws his Harmon mute into the horn and plays a few needling phrases before the ensemble reverts to the slow pace of the final bridge.

This was actually the final piece on the date. Three other tunes had already been completed. A climate of prickliness seems to have been established between Davis and Monk from the off: the trumpeter had told Monk not to accompany him while soloing, and Monk had responded by getting up from the piano and standing uncomfortably close to Davis when there was a trumpet solo due. 'Swing Spring' is an interesting line by Davis based on a scale which Miles had often heard Bud Powell tinkering with, and though it hints at his later, modal music, this was the only time he recorded it. The surviving take runs for nearly eleven minutes, and is dominated by three long solos from the principals: Jackson is cheerfully buoyant, Davis edgily brooding, and Monk manages to suggest something of both of his predecessors' approaches in a skulking, funny improvisation. Jackson then returns for a second bite before the theme is restated. Monk's own 'Bemsha Swing' is interesting in the way it suggests how Davis and Monk were both close to and remote from each other. Some of Monk's best horn partners turned out to be performers whose temperament was superficially unlike his own, men such as Thad Jones and Johnny Griffin. Davis inhabits the world of 'Bemsha Swing' as an ingenious, urbane outsider. His elegant solo builds into a personal tour of the area, but he sounds oddly cold, even disdainful, as if Monk's renowned eccentricities weren't much to his taste (the pianist responds with some of his best playing on the session). Milt Jackson's blues line 'Bags' Groove' exists in two completed takes, and both were issued as part of [7] rather than [8]. Davis's playing is immaculate in the long solo which opens take one. Blues playing later seemed to bore him, but here he sounds utterly fresh and in perfect control. His string of choruses manage the feat of independence and integration: each sounds like a model solo by itself, but one chorus will hint at a device which he will then elaborate on or transcend in the next. He squeezes some notes to pick out a vocal effect, and his changes of volume are beautifully subtle. After this, Jackson's solo, good though it is, sounds almost plain, and it's left to Monk to play one of his characteristic departures. He gnaws away at a single phrase, creating strange pools of silence and stuttering fingerings which somehow knit into a remarkable statement. The second take is perhaps not quite as exalted: Davis is a shade less impeccable, but Monk this time plays an entirely different sort of solo, practically swarming around the keys in comparison to what he tried on the first take.

Whatever griping had gone on in the studio, it hadn't detracted from the music, and it might be fair to say that the tension had actually improved the results. Certainly Davis could look back on the date as one of his best achievements. It was surely a dazzling way to round off the calendar year which had gone a long way towards revitalizing his career. As 1955 began, Davis was still looking to bring together a new working band, but the world of modern jazz briefly halted in its tracks altogether when it was announced that Charlie Parker had died on 12 March. Parker's career hadn't exactly gone into a tailspin, but his appetite for substance abuse had finally wrecked his body and, at times, reduced him to a shadow of the player he had been, and although any number of things might have killed him, the official verdict of lobar pneumonia seems the likeliest one. As the vanguard figure of bebop, his death created a sense of a vacant throne, which Davis, whether he aspired to it or not, was the most suitable candidate to seize.

It was something of a problem for him that he was tied to Bob Weinstock's Prestige, a leasing that at present was scheduled to last through 1957. Prestige was an important independent, but Davis itched to find his way to a major label. In the meantime, on 7 June he recorded the six tracks that were eventually released as *The Musings Of Miles* [9], a quartet date with Red Garland (piano),

Oscar Pettiford (bass) and Philly Joe Jones. Garland's presence offered a significant change, and aired some new preoccupations for the trumpeter. Davis's affection for the music of the Pittsburgh pianist Ahmad Jamal has sometimes surprised his admirers: Jamal formed a trio in 1951 which began to win popular acclaim in Chicago and New York clubs, and his style – trilling, spacey improvisations matched with a trim and lucid rhythmical feel – set its face against the more heavily fingered hardbop manner, suggesting economy, lightness, grace. There was a sense of triviality to go with it, as if Jamal treated the keyboard as a

chic, inconsequential instrument, but Davis didn't seem to hear that, and he was intrigued by the pianist's methods. The obliging Garland plays in a style which at least suggests Jamal's basic approach, and the use of a highly unlikely tune such as 'A Gal In Calico', a swing-era standard by Leo Robin and Arthur Schwartz, is explained by the fact that it was also used as one of Jamal's early recordings. The results were rather mixed. Davis plays fitfully on the date, essaying some very appealing melodic work, trying a daringly soft treatment of 'A Night In Tunisia' and writing a sort of answer to Monk's 'Well, You Needn't' in an original titled 'I Didn't'. But the music often tends to droop, lacking any kind of firmness at its centre, and Garland seems to be feeling his way into his accompanying style. Nevertheless, one striking aspect of this record was its use of three standards from the 'American songbook' repertoire. Hitherto, Davis had seemed to dislike the sort of dependence on standards which many of the swing-era players had shown in their choices. From this point, he often dipped into this large pool of material.

A month later, Davis was booked to play at the Newport Jazz Festival, an event which had first been held a year earlier and which, under the shrewd management of the promoter, George Wein, was already on its way to becoming one of the premier jazz events in America. It was held in a bourgeois Rhode Island community which seemed a long way from the seamier New York jazz environment. Wein was an astute pioneer of presenting jazz to an audience which didn't especially relish the thought of staying up past midnight in a dark city club. It was just as percipient of Davis to get himself on to a bill which originally didn't include him: he was actually a last-minute addition to what amounted to a festival band with a front line of Zoot Sims and Gerry Mulligan – two horn players who loved impromptu jamming situations – and a rhythm section of Thelonious Monk, Percy Heath and Connie Kay. The music was caught on a Voice Of America broadcast (and first released as *Miscellaneous Davis 1955–57* [10]) and features Davis playing on Monk's 'Hackensack' and 'Round Midnight', as well as on the closing version of 'Now's The Time'. The recording reveals Davis to have been in strong voice, and he is particulary good on 'Round Midnight', laying bare the melodic detail of a tune which, among trumpeters, Dizzy Gillespie had hitherto claimed as his own. Festival reporters bayed that Davis was the hit of the night, although the recording hardly confirms it, since his playing appears to receive only a modest ovation. Monk certainly wasn't impressed: on a car journey back to the city, he scolded the trumpeter for playing the melody wrongly, and then grumpily chose to make his own way home. But even though Davis himself was outwardly unimpressed by the fuss, he must have enjoyed the attention, and it helped him on another level: he tied for first place (with Gillespie) in the trumpet category of the 1955 *Down Beat* poll, a clear sign of a burgeoning eminence and quite a comeback for a musician who only eighteen months earlier had looked dangerously close to being washed up.

Davis had for some time made it his business to be known to George Avakian, who ran Columbia Records' jazz division. Avakian was present at the Newport Festival appearance and was impressed but uncertain. The group featuring Davis was really only a fill-in, between sets by Count Basie and the small group which had recently been signed by Columbia, Dave Brubeck's quartet. Avakian thought he was on to a commercial winner with Brubeck – and he was right. He probably considered Davis still unpredictable and difficult, and there was the Prestige contract to consider. But the response to Davis was clearly tempting for any record producer. The trumpeter had been making a record for, of all people, Charles Mingus. The tempestuous bassist had established his own label imprint, Debut, in 1952, and engaged Davis to play on a session where the accompanying players included trombonist Britt Woodman and vibes player Teddy Charles, Elvin Jones at the drums and Mingus himself. A curious line-up – Charles wrote the arrangements for the date, Woodman was a Duke Ellington sideman, and Jones was a young drummer just starting to make a name for himself on the scene – and the results (*Blue Moods* [11]) were surprisingly flat and lackadaisical. The group managed to get through four standards, each at a funereal tempo, and the impression was of a date which had been built around the gimcracked idea of Davis as a wounding ballad player. In the event, his playing drifts between feelingful and merely uninterested.

The date was really only a spacefiller as far as Davis was concerned. He had his mind on an upcoming engagement at New York's Café Bohemia, where he was to feature the quintet which he hoped would become his regular working band. In July, the five-strong line-up made its debut at the club: Davis, Sonny Rollins, Red Garland, Philly Joe Jones, and a twenty-year-old bassist from Detroit, Paul Chambers, who was already attracting attention in New York. Two pieces were illicitly recorded from one set, 'Bye Bye Blackbird' and 'Walkin'', but they have thus far not found their way to a CD issue. There was a good turnout to listen, and Davis clearly felt he had a settled band together at last; but the problem was Rollins,

then going through one of his contrary periods, who kept threatening to walk out of not only the group but the jazz scene altogether. In the meantime, Bob Weinstock had Davis make one further 'all-star' date for Prestige on 5 August, with Jackie McLean, Milt Jackson and a rhythm section of Ray Bryant, Percy

Heath and Art Taylor. The music on *Milt And Miles: All Star Quintet/Sextet* [12] is yet another example of the Prestige bop-and-blues blowing date. The tunes are little more than prop sequences for the solos, and while they suit McLean and Jackson agreeably enough, Davis takes a more dispassionate course. His long solo on 'Dr Jackle' is a bluesless blues, the trumpet tone oddly lovely, yet expended on a patchwork of ingenious motifs which might have meant something if only Davis could be bothered to impart meaning to music which he clearly could hardly care less about. Yet it was a tune he would return to in future sets. Thad Jones's 'Bitty Ditty' is much the most interesting piece, and here Davis plays with a graceful sweep. Ray Bryant, a much tougher player than Davis was used to having behind him at this point, plays some piquant rejoinders during the date, but Art Taylor is given a surprisingly muzzy sound by Rudy Van Gelder.

The success of Davis's Café Bohemia dates had encouraged him to prepare for a tour by the quintet in the autumn, but Rollins refused to be considered for the gigs. Davis rehearsed the band with a Chicagoan saxophonist, John Gilmore, who had already begun what would turn out to be an almost lifelong association with the maverick bandleader Sun Ra, but at the recommendation of Philly Joe Jones he instead turned to another saxophonist, John Coltrane, whom the drummer knew well from his Philadelphia days. Coltrane was a year older than Davis but thus far his jazz career had been unremarkable. He had previously played and recorded with Johnny Hodges and Dizzy Gillespie, but had enjoyed very little in the way of limelight, and he was arguably the least regarded of any of the musicians in the quintet's line-up at this point. At first he bothered Davis intensely, asking him numerous questions about the music and the trumpeter's intentions as to where it was supposed to lead, the kind of detail which exasperated Miles more than anything else. The leader still harboured a lingering desire to have Sonny Rollins with him on the stand, but in the end he went with Coltrane: the tour was booked and only days away, and there was no other saxophonist who knew the material. On 28 September 1955, the new Miles Davis Quintet finally made its debut in a club in Baltimore.

Steamin' 1952–6

Steamin' With The Miles Davis Quintet

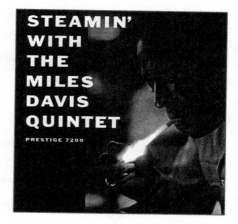

PRESTIGE/OJC

Diane; Something I Dreamed Last Night; Surrey With The Fringe On Top; When I Fall In Love; Salt Peanuts.
Miles Davis (*t*); John Coltrane (*ts*); Red Garland (*p*); Paul Chambers (*b*); Philly Joe Jones (*d*). 11/5/56.

Well, You Needn't.
Same personnel. 26/10/56.

In July, Davis had done a deal with George Avakian and signed to Columbia. Avakian knew that Miles still had his tenure with Prestige to run, but at Davis's own suggestion Columbia's jazz executive had made an arrangement with Bob Weinstock that he would record the quintet but not release any of the results until after the Prestige contract had expired – thus benefiting the independent label by stirring up some free publicity for them. It was a clever idea, which showed again how shrewd an operator Davis himself could be when it came to self-promotion. In the event, Columbia set down the first recordings by what came to be known as 'The Great Quintet' on 26 October 1955. The session yielded four complete titles, released on *'Round About Midnight* [13], which were in the event a feet-finding exercise that harked back to an older era: two were the bebop staples 'Two Bass Hit' and 'Ah-Leu-Cha', one was the *Birth Of The Cool* favourite 'Budo', and the fourth was Jackie McLean's 'Little Melonae'. While the bop pieces elicit purposeful, fast performances, it's the more inquiring 'Little Melonae', a harmonically quite daring line by McLean, which inspires the best music: Davis plays a deep-sounding, plump-toned solo which is countered by a typically spearing improvisation from Coltrane in counterpoint. 'Budo' has the trumpeter following the John Lewis chart from the *Birth Of The Cool* sessions but he plays it with the Harmon mute in, and Coltrane's heavy, uninflected tone is again a striking contrast.

The see-sawing dialogue between Davis and Coltrane fired this group with an extraordinary individuality. As tantalizing as it is to conjecture on what Sonny Rollins would have set down had he kept the tenor chair throughout the Prestige and Columbia sessions, the vividness of the Davis–Coltrane interplay was, in its way, as electrifying as that of Louis Armstrong and Earl Hines or Dizzy Gillespie and Charlie Parker before them. Where those earlier players were, though, compatible in their shared virtuosity, Davis and Coltrane were unalike in almost every way, musically and personally. Davis had already been refining his art to its essentials, always seeking to eliminate unnecessary flab, cutting and clearing away superfluous detail. His adoption of the Harmon mute had become a staple part of his playing regime, and its tight intimacy suited his interest in a style of playing which seemed almost to insinuate itself into the listener's ear. Like Sonny Rollins, whose interest in thematic improvisation on melodies rather than chords was just starting to blossom on his Prestige records, Davis often found ways to paraphrase melodies which left them fresh but not devastated by the sort of pillaging which a standard bebop approach would have delivered.

Coltrane also evaded bop clichés, but he came at the music from a different direction. His saxophone tone had a flat, iron-grey quality, although in the manner of his phrasing and articulation he could suggest immense strength. Where Davis pared away, Coltrane built over the melody and the chords. On club engagements, he would spend his time between sets running through scales, trying one setting after another to go with a sequence of chords. On the quintet's records, his solos typically follow a first statement by the leader, and the contrast is usually almost glaring: Davis will pick at the melody, defty suggesting and paraphrasing, and then Coltrane will come hurtling in – often sounding as though he were standing some way off the microphone, and literally jumping forward into position – and begin piling through phrases which throw out one permutation after another over the chords. It is unlovely and often plain awkward, but as a counter to the leader it's remarkable. And there is already something majestic and implacable about Coltrane, which makes his emergence from a dim obscurity all the more bemusing. While Rollins had a kind of sardonicism about him, vaulting through his improvising with an offhanded bravado, Coltrane plants his feet and sets his face and seems to roll monumentally forward.

It was a stance which continued to bother Davis. Sometimes Coltrane seemed all but oblivious to his surroundings, and he would reel off chorus after chorus. Davis treated his saxophonist to one of his most famous rebukes, supposedly when Trane complained to him that he was often unsure as to how to finish a solo: 'Try taking the horn out of your mouth, man.' A vintage example of their collaborative work is 'Diane', from the 11 May 1956 session which produced most of *Steamin'* as well as the majority of *Workin' With The Miles Davis Quintet* [14]. Davis plays three choruses to open the record: the first is a light, almost skipping process through the melody, which he only modestly strays from, the Harmon mute offering its characteristic plaintiveness. He ends the chorus on a three-note phrase which he later uses again to wrap up the track, and then sketches two choruses of indolent but beautifully coloured lines. Coltrane picks him up for two choruses which are, in comparison, hectic and anxious. There is a spectacular reed squeak around bar ten of the first, and at the close of the second he sounds unsure whether to carry on or not. Red Garland makes his mind up for him by quietly adopting centre stage. As he does so, the mood changes back to an almost breezy good humour. Garland's gift for lightening an atmosphere is matched by Chambers and Jones in the way their rhythms move to a sort of bumptious funk. For Davis they play stealthily, for Coltrane they toughen up and buttress his wanderings, but for Garland they seem to fuse with the pianist, and when he moves to a locked-hands stroll in his second chorus, the feel is perfect. Davis returns for a final half-chorus of melody, and Coltrane joins him for only the final two-note tag. It is in some ways a scrappy, technically spotty track: Davis chokes one note as well as Coltrane, and the joins between the various parts of the performance aren't exactly seamless. On feel and group interaction, though, this is a textbook jazz record – sensitive, quietly exciting, compelling to follow as it unfolds, unfussily lyrical, and uncompromisingly spontaneous. With a suddenness which belied the age it had taken Davis to get to this point, the quintet was the most significant new jazz group of its time.

In a sense, it's a little meaningless to subdivide the five Prestige albums which made up Miles's obligations to Bob Weinstock and his label. After a date on 16 November 1955 that produced the six tracks which made up the

simply titled *Miles – The New Miles Davis Quintet* [15], the remaining four records were made up of tracks taken down at two marathon sessions on 11 May and 26 October the following year. Fourteen pieces were set down at the first session, twelve at the second, and Davis's working methods under studio conditions – a dislike for having to make multiple takes of the same piece, and an improvisational informality when it came to organizing a piece – come through clearly. There is surviving studio chatter on the issued records themselves, as on 'Woody 'N' You' from *Relaxin'*, where Weinstock makes the ironic suggestion that they do another take, an annoyed Davis asks why, and a sleepy-sounding Coltrane is heard to merely ask for the beer opener. The music on *Miles* was a shift from that set down at the

Columbia date a few weeks before, but still suggested a band that was obviously continuing to feel its way forward. Benny Golson's theme 'Stablemates' is probably the best thing on this date, and there is an extended version of 'The Theme', a traditional set-closer from the 52nd Street bebop days, which for once is amplified to allow space for solos by the three principals. Four other standards recorded at the date are slightly marred by Coltrane sounding either confused or uncomfortable with the material – with hindsight, the idea of John Coltrane playing 'Just Squeeze Me', one of Duke Ellington's most frivolous pieces, does seem a little peculiar – and Davis at times seems to have his eye on the clock: he plays 'There Is No Greater Love' in a subdued state of facelessness.

The tracks cut at the remaining two sessions, though, have an intensity and shared inspiration which has survived the half-century since they were recorded with amazing vitality. Part of that is probably down to Davis's taste for immediacy. Some of the fast pieces have a lick of wildness to them which here and there almost results in the music getting away from the players: the best instance might be their version of Sonny Rollins's 'Oleo', on *Relaxin'* [16]. Paul Chambers plays throughout in a walking style, but Garland and Jones feature only on the bridge of each chorus and otherwise offer only brief fillips to the soloists. On Coltrane's second chorus, Jones finally lets go and the music careers forward. But at the close of Trane's solo, the drummer quietens again for Garland's turn. The performance has a kind of controlled recklessness about it which is riveting. On 'Woody 'N' You', Davis plays with a spinning velocity which seems to take him to the edge of his technique, the ascetic tinge heard elsewhere notably absent. But more typical are the mid-tempo tracks which show off the variety of approach the rhythm section could turn on for each occasion. Jones switches between brushes, rimshots and sticks on snare, depending on which soloist is in the chair, but he sometimes simply chooses to shade his dynamics in one setting, as he does on the simple head blues 'Blues By Five', from *Cookin'* [17]. Chambers was quickly becoming recognized as one of the new virtuosos on an instrument which was finally coming into its own in a jazz environment, via improved amplification and recording techniques. He plays arco here and there, and his biting technique as a four-in-the-bar exponent gives the music a very specific lift, to the extent that some thought of Chambers as more of a dialogue man than a supporting bassist in the Percy Heath mould. He finds a medium between those two points on a piece such as 'In Your Own Sweet Way', a Dave Brubeck tune recorded for [14], where the ear is taken by his sound without truly distracting from what Davis and Coltrane are playing in their solos.

Red Garland is the most amenable of the three rhythm-section men. On 'You're My Everything', from [16], he begins what sounds like an ornate introduction, only to be cut off by Davis rasping, 'Play block chords, Red', and he duly obliges. 'Ahmad's Blues' on [14] is the best place to hear his appropriation of the Ahmad Jamal style which Davis liked so much. Jack Maher's original sleevenote suggested that Garland was actively parodying Jamal in the opening chorus before playing in his own style. But there seems little to choose between the two. The principal characteristic which Garland brought to the group was lightness. By voicing most of his chords in the middle and upper parts of the keyboard, he left the deepest sonorities to Chambers and focused the piano sound in a central position which gave the music both buoyancy and brightness. His fingerings seem gentle, even when the music sounds otherwise aggressive. Jones and Chambers can be thundering along, while Red is going his own graceful way.

Prestige approached the packaging of these sessions in a somewhat curious way. After [15] had appeared in April 1956, nothing else was delivered to the public until both of the two long sessions had been completed. *Cookin'* came out right at the end of 1956, consisting mainly of up-tempo pieces, and both [16] and [14] emerged in 1957. The programming of these two is odd, since the first is dominated by ballads and the second seems a complete hotchpotch, including both versions of 'The Theme', 'Trane's Blues' (which is effectively 'The Theme' again in disguise) and 'Ahmad's Blues'. *Steamin'* didn't actually emerge until 1961, and is made up mostly of pieces from the first date with just 'Well, You Needn't' selected as a leftover from the second. 'Something I Dreamed Last Night' and 'When I Fall In Love' are ballad features for Davis where Coltrane sits out. This is the Davis which many of his more sentimental admirers love most: the Harmon mute is in, the horn seems to be only a hair's-breadth away from the microphone, and Miles is the romantic though gimlet-eyed crooner on both pieces. Ballad playing had become a central part of Davis's make-up, and it was an idiom which was a difficult one to master for most trumpet players. Saxophonists such as Coleman Hawkins and Ben Webster were generally considered the leading balladeers in jazz, with the rhap-sodic indulgence of a wide vibrato and a way of feathering a melody which was usually beyond the capa-

bilities of brass players. Davis found a way of tugging at heartstrings which sounded more modern, less obviously sensuous. 'Something I Dreamed Last Night' is a rather rare ballad, seldom featured by jazz interpreters, and Davis handles it with superb aplomb. The Harmon's interiorized sound doesn't so much caress the melody as sing it, with the steely sonority which a saxophonist couldn't duplicate. Davis would later allow this approach to fall into a degree of self-regard, but here he is simply leafing through the melody, choosing points to spotlight. The much better-known 'When I Fall In Love' isn't quite so good, in part owing to its very familiarity, but again it's the soloist's exacting way with his own delivery which impresses.

The outstanding piece on the record is 'Surrey With The Fringe On Top', which runs for just over nine minutes and is one of the longest pieces in the Prestige sessions. The tune, lifted from the *Oklahoma* score, was at this point an unlikely jazz vehicle, although it was another composition that Ahmad Jamal had been playing. The performance is an archetype of the way the group went about their business. A muted Davis introduces a chorus of the melody, and then solos on it. Coltrane follows him. Garland follows Coltrane, and leaves a precipitous gap before Davis returns to take the tune out. There is really no ensemble playing at all, just a team of soloists and the rhythm section. Individually, though, the group are sublime. Davis's exposition is gorgeously drawn. Coltrane charges in, again sounding as if he were loitering at the back of the studio, and twists and gargoyles his way through a meaty solo. Red is all felicitous bounce in his turn. Chambers and Jones pursue their paces without faltering. One could almost say it is a routine the five men have already settled into, and they would indeed take more obvious creative progressions on the later session: but what a routine! 'Well, You Needn't', a Monk tune, is the one track which was included from the October session. This date was rather better balanced – Chambers in particular comes through more strongly, and it is at the least a sonic contrast to the other pieces. For once, Davis sounds to be struggling with the piece, which is taken at a good clip, and Coltrane outplays him this time. Garland is taken a little out of himself too: he plays much of his solo in the lower register, with Philly Joe playing a Blakey-like rattle on his snare rim, and Chambers follows him with a short and formidably executed arco solo, a real rarity in the jazz of that time. It is a piece which suggests a group with the jitters, but in the end they resolve it like masters.

Steamin' 1952–6

The Prestige albums are the ones that tend to be best remembered among the recordings by the quintet, but their music for Columbia, set down in the same period, has claims on being a finer representation of their work. Following the session of October 1955, George Avakian booked Davis in to cut two further dates the following year, on 5 June and 10 September, splitting the two Prestige sessions. In June, Davis recorded three pieces: the standard 'Bye Bye Blackbird', the Swedish 'folk' theme 'Dear Old Stockholm', and Tadd Dameron's 'Tadd's Delight' (originally called 'Sid's Delight'). There is something cleaner and more taut about the group's approach to their tasks. 'Dear Old Stockholm', which Davis had previously recorded at one of his Blue Note dates, was a borrowing from Stan Getz's repertoire, but the quintet develops it into a long and naggingly memorable meditation. A recurring motif, over a harmonic suspension, is sustained by Garland through the passage of the piece, with a further development of it at the close of each chorus. Meanwhile, Chambers – this might be the initial post-bop jazz track where a bassist is the first to take the solo – unexpectedly leads off the improvisations, followed by the looming Coltrane and the muted Miles, who sounds even closer to the microphone here than he does on the Prestige dates, almost piercingly adjacent to the listener's ear. The track ends abruptly after the trumpet solo, with no recapitulation of the theme. 'Bye Bye Blackbird', which would become a staple of Davis's live set that lasted well into the 1960s, is played at a rather stately mid-tempo, and Miles treats it, in both surviving takes, as a blues meditation, alternating long notes with judicious rests, seeming to deliberate no further than the end of each phrase, sustained by the momentum of his rhythm section. Coltrane's inevitable riposte is to charge down the chords, but he sounds at his most controlled too. 'Tadd's Delight' is almost clipped in comparison, with Chambers and Jones at their most boppish, but this is bop with all of Dameron's innate lyricism pushed to the fore, the music touching on a genuine elegance.

The September session includes two masterpieces which need very little qualification. 'All Of You' is Davis at his finest. Cole Porter's melody has often been prized by jazz musicians, but few have configured the kind of decisive yet utterly relaxed variations that Davis draws out of it in his two opening choruses. On the master take (an alternate is only slighty less compelling) he is followed by an equally inspired Coltrane, as differently as he plays: for once the note-spinning that was such a helpless part of his playing here sounds almost as finished and logical as the music of the leader. Garland continues the mood of almost joyful music-making with two choruses of his own, and Davis returns to close proceedings after a typical dead stop by Philly Joe. A little classic, but it is surpassed by the enthralling version of 'Round Midnight' which they cut next. What's immediately striking as this performance unfolds is that, unlike almost everything else committed to tape by the quintet, this one features a particular ensemble arrangement. Davis leads the group through a full state-ment of Monk's melody, with not only the rhythm section but Coltrane, if only dimly, playing obbligati in the background. There is the fanfare which Dizzy Gillespie always emphasized in his big-band arrangement of Monk's tune, here played by the two horns, which leads into a two-chorus improvisation from Coltrane which asks its creator to focus himself almost as never before on these sessions; and he is up to the challenge, for once playing almost as sparely, from moment to moment, as Davis. The final 'movement', if you will, restores Davis and has him pace out the closing measures of the melody. The 'chart' for this tune is really no more than a sketch, and, as noted, it closely fol-lows in its essentials the orchestral version which Gillespie had been playing since the 1940s, but parts of it have been credited to Gil Evans, supposedly working with Davis again for the first time since the *Birth Of The Cool* sessions. One further track, a self-consciously modern treatment of a song dating back to the 1920s, 'Sweet Sue, Just You', was also recorded on the day, as part of a record devised by Avakian in consultation with Leonard Bernstein, tying in with a TV programme on jazz which the American composer had fronted. A young arranger-composer and saxophonist, Teo Macero, had devised an arrangement for the tune in a supposedly ultra-contemporary style, but Davis and Coltrane play only an introductory motif to start their version, and from there go into solos which never refer even remotely to the original melody. Bernstein most likely approved of such radical tactics, but there is a sense that Davis was sending up the whole thing: in a surviving piece of studio chatter, he kids Avakian that for their next piece, which was to be 'Round Midnight', they would take the melody of 'Sweet Sue' as the middle section.

Most of the tracks from these two dates were released as [13], with the addition of 'Ah-Leu-Cha' from the initial session for Columbia (the remaining tracks from that date didn't filter out until, in some cases, the 1970s, on sundry compilations). This album emerged late in 1956, and it was bolstered by a keen marketing campaign by its label. As a result, it reputedly sold more copies than all of the five Prestige albums put together, although its fame and renown among Davis admirers has mostly lagged behind that accorded to the Prestige quintet. What that result proved was that Davis had been, from a career point of view,  entirely correct in hankering after a deal with Columbia. They had paid him what was, for a jazz artist in the 1950s, a handsome advance against future royalties, and were in a position to capitalize on the advantage any major label enjoyed over its independent rivals: vastly superior resources in marketing and distribution. It should have been the start of a golden period for the Miles Davis quintet.

Yet it wasn't. Davis was in charge of a group of junkies and addicts. By 1957, he seemed to have got himself off his heroin addiction, although it isn't clear exactly when he finally managed to leave hard drugs behind. But Coltrane and Jones were both still in thrall to junk, Chambers was a ferociously heavy drinker, and the collective behaviour of the band was almost comically sloppy and unprofessional. Davis sometimes despaired of keeping the band in shape and on the road. While the group played regularly on the American club circuit from those first dates in September 1955 onwards, Davis had to be constantly on his toes in watching his men. There was a camaraderie between the players, but that was in part due to the brotherhood of addiction. Coltrane's habit was becoming so bad that he would often nod out on the stand, his clothes filthy and dishevelled. Chambers would frequently be incoherent with drink, and Jones, in some ways the ringleader, had a bizarre propensity for being almost comatose one moment and fit and ready to play the next. While the hippest members of the jazz audience were probably talking about little other than the Miles Davis quintet, its leader was rapidly becoming sick of his own band and its conduct. After a final New York engagement at the Café Bohemia, where Sonny Rollins replaced Coltrane on the opening nights before both saxophonists eventually shared the stand, Davis disbanded his group altogether. It was November 1956, and he was on his way back to Europe.

The Other Records

1   *Collectors' Items* (Prestige)
2   *Miles Davis And Horns* (Prestige)
3   *Miles Davis: Volume 2* (Blue Note)
4   *Blue Haze* (Prestige)
5   *At Last!* (Contemporary)
6   *Walkin'* (Prestige)
7   *Bags' Groove* (Prestige)
8   *Miles Davis And The Modern Jazz Giants* (Prestige)
9   *The Musings Of Miles* (Prestige)
10 *Miscellaneous Davis 1955–57* (Jazz Unlimited)
11 *Blue Moods* (Debut)
12 *Milt And Miles: All Star Quintet/Sextet* (Prestige)
13 *'Round About Midnight* (Columbia)

14   *Workin' With The Miles Davis Quintet* (Prestige)

15   *Miles – The New Miles Davis Quintet* (Prestige)

16   *Relaxin'* (Prestige)

17   *Cookin'* (Prestige)

| 59

Like Nobody Else

1956–7

As important as the quintet was, there were few attempts at recording it on the hoof: frustratingly little exists of the group away from its studio sessions for Prestige and Columbia. One early fragment which has survived is its appearance on the Steve Allen TV show for NBC (17 November 1955), although it exists in audio only (*Rare Unissued Broadcasts* [1]). The group play fairly brief versions of 'Max Is Making Wax', a bop tune dating back to Charlie Parker days, and 'It Never Entered My Mind'. Allen tries to engage Davis in a little repartee, but is shocked by the sound of his voice: 'Got a cold?'. 'No,' responds Miles, 'I had an operation on my throat.' A month earlier, Davis had indeed undergone surgery, to remove polyps on his larynx. He had never had an elegant speaking voice – it already sounds throaty on the Prestige session where he castigates Monk – and the operation had been meant to alleviate some of the problem. But he had been required not to speak beyond the bare minimum for a period after the operation, and had, at some point, raised his voice in some measure of anger: it may have been at a rehearsal, or in some heated conversation with some industry figure, nobody seems quite sure. Either way, his voice ever after was usually confined to a whispery, almost half-human sound, which seemed to emerge from somewhere very low in his throat. Already self-conscious about a speaking voice which was as gravelly as Louis Armstrong's, Davis became even more taciturn. The rasping sound heard on some of the Prestige records must have shocked listeners who hadn't heard him in person.

The November disbandment was not the first time Miles had split up his group. He had broken up the band early in 1956 following his operation, in order to recuperate. Just prior to this, the quintet played a concert for the impresario Gene Norman at Pasadena Civic Auditorium (18 February), recently given a first release as a bonus in Columbia's newest edition of 'Round About Midnight. The band play bebop on 'Max Is Making Wax', 'Woody 'N' You' and 'Salt Peanuts', and a rather unkempt 'Walkin'', on which Miles throws in a quote from 'It's Magic'. The man Norman introduces as 'Johnny Coltrane' tunnels through the piece and gets barely a ripple of applause.

During Davis's spell of inactivity, he played a single date for Prestige, on 16 March, which produced enough music to fill out the LP which was eventually released as *Collectors' Items* [2], a coupling with the session where Charlie Parker had played tenor. Sonny Rollins returned from that occasion, and Tommy Flanagan, Paul Chambers and Art Taylor made up the rhythm section. It is desultory music: 'No Line' is a themeless blues which might as well have strayed in from some jam session, starting and ending aimlessly, while 'Vierd Blues' is paceless and barely musters a theme. Rollins had his great sequence of Prestige albums under way by this point, but he plays with disarming reserve here, as if trying to duplicate Davis's feel. The mood changes entirely for Davis's first try at Dave Brubeck's 'In Your Own Sweet Way', where the group plays with care and grace. Even so, the music overall amounts to little more than Miles finishing off an obligation.

Between the Columbia date which produced 'Round Midnight' and the final session for Prestige, there was one other record which Davis was involved with. In the aftermath of bebop, modern jazz was moving in more than one direction. The nonet music which Davis had led at the end of the 1940s was something of a template for a number of works involving medium-sized and large ensembles, as well as suggesting musical procedures which were about to blossom on one particular branch. The classical horn player and scholar

Gunther Schuller emerged at this time as a kind of spokesman for a group of composers who wanted to build a practical bridge between jazz improvisation and classical form, and he christened the notion Third Stream music, a supposed blending of these – on the face of it – incompatible elements. It wasn't a case of jazzing the classics – that had been tried extensively in the swing era, and the results were little more than interesting novelties – but fashioning new composed music that somehow found space for improvisation as well as a sense of spontaneity which would permeate even the following of the score. Besides Schuller, John Lewis and J. J. Johnson – both close associates of Davis in the recent past – were looking through the ideas with interest, Lewis having established the Modern Jazz Quartet as a kind of Third Stream band in microcosm, and Johnson seeking to expand his ambitions as a composer. Johnson and Lewis were then engaged by Columbia to record two extended pieces for an album which would be a sort of manifesto for the ambitions of Third Stream. Who better to engage as the principal soloist than the new Columbia signing Miles Davis?

In the event, *Music For Brass* [3], recorded on 20 and 23 October and credited to the Brass Ensemble of the Jazz and Classical Music Society, was all but buried by both its label and the American media. The record was packaged in an unprepossessing design which made only modest play of the presence of Davis, and its portentous titling was scarcely likely to appeal to straight-ahead jazz fans. It is still among the least known of all of the many records Davis played on. Schuller conducted an ensemble with seven brass players, bassist Milt Hinton and drummer Osie Johnson, and the tympanist Dick Horowitz added for John

Lewis's 'Three Little Feelings'. Lewis's composition offers the most productive setting for Davis as a soloist. Cast in three movements, this is one of Lewis's

characteristic pieces of writing, brooding on classical form but imbued, deep down, with the blues, something that Davis lightly touches on in his solos. The second movement, which is sketched almost as a miniature concerto for the trumpeter, finds Davis drawing a poignant solo out of sparse harmonic resources, which the ensemble lays down behind him in a series of sustained, mournful chords. With hindsight, this is a notable pre-echo of what Davis would be doing with Gil Evans only months in the future. One striking aspect of these sessions is that at some points Davis uses the flugelhorn, a larger, more lyrical-sounding horn than the trumpet, which brass players will often employ on ballads to get a warmer and more rounded timbre. On Johnson's 'Jazz Suite For Brass', where Davis is featured on the first section, Miles plays his first recorded solo on flugelhorn.

It is, in sum, an interesting and often lovely record, but it was the sort of interlude which ultimately had little meaning for Davis, prescient though it was of some of his work with Evans. Acting as a bit player in a movement set to be dominated by composers surely held little appeal for the trumpeter, and perhaps he also sensed that Third Stream was destined to go nowhere much: if so, he was right, since it never really got beyond a handful of records and concerts.

Davis's trip to Europe had been organized by Morris Levy, a booking agent who had interests in several New York clubs and who would shortly be one of the directors of a new jazz record label, Roulette. (Levy was in later life honoured as a giant of the record industry, which for many years maintained laughable standards of business decorum in its dealings with artists. In fact, he was a crook who was finally convicted on charges of conspiracy to extort in 1988). The line-up consisted of a package of players including Davis, Lester Young and the Modern Jazz Quartet. Miles toured with this entourage for some three weeks, playing with a French rhythm section led by the pianist René Urtreger, as well as sharing stages with Young and the MJQ. As he had done years before, Davis found the European air much to his liking, and he was in a happy frame of mind for much of the tour. A few airshots have survived. On

12 November, the tour reached Freiburg in West Germany, where four pieces were recorded (released as *Rare Live* [4]). Davis sounds in fine shape on the two numbers with the Urtreger-led rhythm section, 'Tune Up' and 'What's New', and he gamely contributes to a jam on 'How High The Moon' with Young and the MJQ, and a version of Young's old speciality 'Lester Leaps In', which has the Kurt Edelhagen Orchestra filling in for the Basie band. But the music is unhappy listening when it comes to the playing of Lester Young. He sounds as if leaping was something he couldn't even think of doing, his playing shambolic and enfeebled: the drink problem which would eventually lead to his death three years later had crippled his skills. Three other titles were captured at the Zurich stopover of the tour (and can be found on *Miscellaneous Davis* [5]) and here at least Young makes a slightly better fist out of 'Lady Be Good', although if it had been any kind of cutting contest Davis's following solo would have shredded the saxophonist. On the other two pieces, Miles again sounds almost light-hearted: he spins a decorative line out of 'Four' and teasingly suggests other tunes in a brief 'Walkin''. Far away from the hustle of American jazz clubland and the management of a band of problem musicians, he was entitled to feel as if he were on a European vacation.

It was over soon enough. Back in New York, Davis reconvened the quintet, and it played an engagement in Philadelphia's Blue Note club on 8 December which survives (in rather poor audio) in the form of a mere two tracks, 'Tune Up' and 'Walkin'', preserved via a broadcast on the regular radio show *Bandstand USA* (on *Rarities From Private Collections* [6]). Davis's solo on 'Walkin'' is very like the one from the Zurich concert made a few weeks earlier. The main point of interest here is Chambers's fine solo, which starts off-mike but emerges and gets stronger as it goes on.

The quintet was very busy in the first few months of 1957. It played long engagements in Hollywood, San Francisco, St Louis, Chicago and Baltimore, before returning to New York's Café Bohemia, where it performed for most of April. In Miles's home town of St Louis it was at the Peacock Alley Lounge, where two broadcasts were made and have survived, from 16 and 23 February, on *The*

Miles Davis Quintet At Peacock Alley [7]. Both seem to offer what were presumably typical sets, with familiar pieces such as 'Oleo', 'Ah-Leu-Cha' (the announcer inquires if that is some sort of foreign language, and Davis responds, 'Charlie Parker's language'), 'Well, You Needn't' and 'Walkin''. Deprived of the clarity of the studio sessions and preserved as little more than a simple hour's work in the middle of many such occasions, the music is perhaps disappointingly prosaic at times, although it says much about the often exhausting regimen of a band required to fulfil a long club engagement. In St Louis, the group played a matinee between 4 and 7 p.m., then returned from 9 p.m. until 1.15 a.m. Davis was already starting to grow tired of the working conditions prescribed by most club owners, and had taken to cancelling gigs which looked too arduous. The fact that the band was working so consistently during these months says much about its ability to draw an audience, despite having a leader who would have been considered difficult by most club managers.

The behaviour of the players, though, hadn't improved much. At the end of the Café Bohemia stint, Davis was so angry with Coltrane and Jones that he fired both from the band. Backstage at one of the gigs, he had begun to slap Coltrane. The saxophonist was a big man, a good deal taller and heavier than Miles, but his natural meekness and the effects of his addiction left him unable to respond, except to take the punishment. Thelonious Monk had watched this going on, and suggested to Coltrane that the saxophonist should work in his band instead. Coltrane took him up on the offer, and the quintet was over again – for the time being.

Davis had something else on his mind. He had been wanting to renew a working relationship with Gil Evans for some time. Evans had done little of consequence since the nonet sessions of seven years earlier. His name can be found on numerous minor albums by singers made during the early part of the 1950s: perhaps only his collaborations with Helen Merrill, on an excellent 1956 Emarcy record called *Dream Of You*, really offer notable evidence of his talents being used to some purpose at this point. Evans was known to George Avakian – he had done some work on a Johnny Mathis record for Columbia

– and the producer was looking for ways to shift Davis's career in a more productive direction. At this point, several of the Prestige albums had emerged alongside Columbia's own *'Round About Midnight*, and the marketplace looked bloated with Miles Davis small-group records. Avakian needed something new. The *Music For Brass* album had been an interesting setting for the trumpeter's sound: how about another project on at least similar lines, but more specifically featuring Davis?

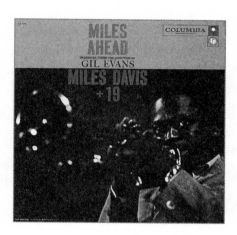

Miles Ahead

COLUMBIA

The Maids Of Cadiz; The Duke.

Miles Davis (*flhn*); Bernie Glow, Ernie Royal, Louis Mucci, Taft Jordan, John Carisi (*t*);
Frank Rehak, Jimmy Cleveland, Joe Bennett (*tb*); Tom Mitchell (*btb*); Willie Ruff,
Tony Miranda (*frhn*); Bill Barber (*tba*); Lee Konitz (*as*); Romeo Penque (*f, cl, bcl*);
Sid Cooper (*f, cl*); Danny Bank (*bcl*); Paul Chambers (*b*); Art Taylor (*d*);
Gil Evans (*arr, cond*). 6/5/57.

My Ship; Miles Ahead.

Same personnel. 10/5/57.

New Rhumba; Blues For Pablo; Springsville.

As above, except Jimmy Buffington (*frhn*) replaces Miranda;
Penque also plays oboe; Wynton Kelly (*p*). 23/5/57.

I Don't Wanna Be Kissed; The Meaning Of The Blues; Lament.
As above except Tony Miranda (*frhn*) and Eddie Caine (*f*, *cl*) replace
Buffington and Cooper; omit Kelly. 27/5/57.

Avakian offered Davis the choice of either Evans or Gunther Schuller to orchestrate his first large-scale record. Evans was the inevitable pick, and it is interesting to conjecture on what Schuller might have done with the same project. Evans, though, was given virtual *carte blanche* over the direction of the project, what material would be used, what the instrumentation would be. Avakian's only stipulation was that there be an original track called 'Miles Ahead', which could be used as the album title and would be a promotional

trailer for the entire album.

Avakian had also worked with Evans when the arranger had been part of Claude Thornhill's staff. He told Gil to go for the Thornhill sound at its most voluptuous: 'rich, fat brass with tuba, french horns, woodwinds ... '. According to Avakian, Evans's response was to ask how far the budget would stretch. In the end, eighteen musicians besides Davis lined up in Columbia's 30th Street Studio on 6 May.

Evans had prepared the way as best he could. For a man who was essentially an autodidact, with very little in the way of real musical training, this was probably the toughest assignment he had ever set himself, arranging for the man who was well on the way to becoming jazz's most eminent soloist, pushing a crack studio team through a difficult set of scores, and in particular, conducting the whole ensemble himself. A tall order, and one which in some senses Evans was not really up to: there were murmurings among a few of the musicians on the dates that Gil's conducting and instructions to the ensemble had an imprecision which could cause confusion, and as fine as much of the playing is, the music here and there is blemished by ensemble flaws which a more skilled director might have eliminated. (Latterly, Evans blamed himself for not holding out for more rehearsal time, although one

doubts whether that would have truly solved the problem. Some of the same difficulties attended the recording of both *Porgy And Bess* and *Sketches Of Spain*.) This is, though, nitpicking. Much of the music is so fine that searching for mistakes is almost perverse: Evans and Davis were seeking a result which was amazingly different to almost any other big-band project yet committed to recording tape.

The first indication of surprise comes in the instrumentation. Lee Konitz is the only saxophonist present. Brass otherwise dominates the ensemble: no fewer than five trumpets, three trombones, bass trombone, a pair of french horns and a tuba. Instead of a reed section, there are three woodwind specialists, who handle either flute, clarinet or bass clarinet. There is no piano or guitar (Wynton Kelly plays only a very brief contribution to 'Springsville'). The only precedent for this kind of line-up, as far as a jazz-associated big band is concerned, would be Thornhill's orchestra, yet Evans went much further here, delineating the group almost as a chamber ensemble. The decision to feature Davis solely on flugelhorn added a further freshness to the textures.

The material offers the next taste of the unexpected. Evans picked all but two of the pieces: the exceptions were 'The Duke', the Dave Brubeck composition which the pianist had premiered on his own Columbia album *Brubeck Plays Brubeck*, and Ahmad Jamal's tune 'New Rhumba'. Both were suggested by Davis. 'Miles Ahead' itself was at first listed as a Davis composition, but Evans was subsequently co-credited and it seems likely that he was responsible for most of it. Otherwise, the material came from a remarkable variety of sources. Leo Delibes's melody 'The Maids Of Cadiz' was a piece which fascinated Evans, and this was his second version of it. 'I Don't Wanna Be Kissed' was a Doris Day hit. Bobby Troup, a pianist who had been working with his future wife Julie London, was responsible for 'The Meaning Of The Blues'. 'Lament' was one of J.J. Johnson's most distinctive originals, and 'My Ship' was a ballad composed by Kurt Weill. 'Springsville' was a composition by John Carisi, the man who had created 'Israel' for the nonet sessions. And there was one other original by Evans, 'Blues For Pablo', which had already been recorded by a group led by the saxophonist Hal McKusick. As an agglomeration of music, it must have seemed unprecedented on a jazz album.

Evans's final conceptual stroke was to fuse these sources into a single entity by creating passages which linked one track to the next. For a music which had hitherto been heard on record primarily via radio or jukeboxes – where even the Capitol records by the nonet had thrived – this was absolutely unheard of. Evans might as well have been overseeing a classical concerto, and in a sense he was. Over all this sonority and steadily evolving orchestration, the flugelhorn of Miles Davis was cast like a plume of smoke.

The first piece, 'Springsville', is a rousing and somewhat uncharacteristic start. Carisi's theme is spread through sections of the ensemble in a boisterous counterpoint to Davis's lead voice. The trumpet–trombone textures must have seemed familiar enough to listeners who had followed the music of such bands as Stan Kenton's, with his massed ranks of horns, but what immediately sounds offbeat is the use of the woodwind section, given a strange, almost gnarled sonority by the use of Danny Bank's bass clarinet in particular. The piece proceeds in a call-and-response fashion, with periods when Davis is alone with just Chambers and Taylor, and it moves to a final note held by the trumpets – where, for the first time, Evans has them use their mutes, a brilliant and unexpected switch in timbre. Chambers doodles a couple of phrases, the music stills its pace, and then Taylor is marking out a very slow tempo with the brushes, and Davis peals out the opening line to 'The Maids Of Cadiz'. The transitions from one piece to the next are some of the most magical music in this album: Evans seems to delight in sleight of hand which has one guessing where one theme ends and another begins.

'The Maids Of Cadiz' offers Davis a perfect opportunity to play in his most golden tone, deftly offset by the low brass. It is ballad playing of an almost celestial order. Just occasionally he is tempted to squeeze a note, and to hint at the tendency to preen which overtakes him on some later records, but the ear relishes the straightforward accuracy of the playing, the notes honeyed but not cloyingly articulated. Rather than apotheosizing Davis as existential soloist, Evans's music is about an overall result, and he must have felt that this was at least as much about him as it was about Miles. From here, the ensemble starts on 'The Duke', Brubeck's oddly harmonized melody given to a quartet of flugelhorn, trombone, alto sax and tuba, over a skipping four from Taylor's brushes. When the theme is reprised for the final time, it is granted a whistling sonority by being handed over to bass clarinet and the two flutes. 'My Ship' is perhaps the most conventional piece of scoring, Evans using the ensemble almost continuously as a backdrop to Davis's thoughtful embracing of the melody, although again there is a shifting of sounds behind the soloist which is never still: it absolves Davis of the need to do much other than follow the contours of the theme. At the close, the arranger has the ensemble follow a descending motif over the tinkle of the drummer tapping on a triangle, a simple but immaculate touch.

'Miles Ahead' itself is an almost jaunty stroll, perhaps the closest echo of the music of the nonet sessions, but it paves the way for 'Blues For Pablo', one of Evans's most exceptional inspirations. Max Harrison identified the source of the music as part Spanish (Manuel de Falla) and part Mexican (a native folk song), and André Hodeir, who wrote the original sleevenotes for the album, pointed out how 'a latent conflict takes shape between the Spanish-type theme in minor and the blues theme in major'. It scarcely feels like a blues at all, even though the blues theme actually dominates most of the piece. Davis opens the track with a motif that sounds as if it might have come straight from the bull ring, and his subsequent entrance sounds almost akin to the opening notes of 'Out Of This World', but he is set aside by the ensemble, which works through Evans's voicings in a hypnotic atmosphere. There are some remarkable rhythmic elements to this performance, which belie the idea that Evans's music is all about texture and never about groove: following the parts given to the brass, the woodwinds, and to Chambers and Taylor opens up a fascinating vista, where what is basically a stealthy ballad tempo is actually given a complex life of internal rhythms. There is an intriguing comparison to be made with what was actually the first recorded version of this piece. Evans had scored his idea for a record date led by the alto saxophonist Hal McKusick a year earlier, which was eventually released on a record called *Jazz Workshop*, one that rather confusingly emerged at the same time as a George Russell date on the same label with the same title. In terms of the formal content, the octet version which McKusick recorded – using trumpet, trombone, alto and baritone saxes, two guitars, bass and drums, plus a bit of tambourine playing (handled by George Russell!) – is startlingly close to that of the *Miles Ahead* version, and it is interesting to hear Art Farmer, one of the few players whose lyricism on the trumpet was a rival to Davis's in this period, handling the brass role. What the orchestral version reveals is how handsomely Evans was able to build on what seems, in the original, like a skeletal idea by comparison. In this treatment, a lush bittersweetness sets the overriding tone.

'New Rhumba' spins off from the riff which permeates Jamal's original version of the tune. As Davis toys with his solo part, Evans offers one orchestration of that motif after another: now the trumpets have it, now the brass, now the woodwinds (with Penque's oboe unexpectedly prominent). Eventually, the music struts forward on Chambers's walking lines. Davis's improvisation drops in quotes from Jamal's own playing on the piece, and it eventually leaps to a concluding slam by the brass. There is a moment or two of silence before 'The Meaning Of The Blues' comes in, with a spectacular unison chord, and it is played as an almost dreamy ballad by Davis, Evans treating the theme as a nocturne. It is barely divisible from the ensuing 'Lament', the one piece moving seamlessly into the next. On both tracks, Davis is at his most pensive, but the playing isn't self-regarding: he seems to be thinking each note out against the harmonies of the ensemble. The slightly off-kilter closer is 'I Don't Wanna Be Kissed', which seems an almost humorous rejoinder to the rest of the music, as if it were a flip encore to the preceding music. Davis doesn't quite nail the melody but the ensemble playing has a real zing, and Evans constructs an outrageous finale: Ernie Royal hits a spectacular top note, which the rest of the brass fill in with a descending chord that would have shocked most arrangers of the period.

Like Nobody Else 1956–7

Miles Ahead isn't a long record. The ten pieces combine to reach a little over thirty-seven minutes. But it could hardly be a more focused, intensely realized project, standing as an almost continuous piece of music which is absorbing from start to end. There are really no weak spots, no filler. André Hodeir, who contributed the admiring essay printed on the back of the original LP cover, later complained about the inclusion of 'Blues For Pablo', saying that it 'only seems so weak because it does not go with the rest of the pieces'. Given the vibrancy of a track which on most records would stand out as exceptional, Hodeir's judgement seems unwontedly harsh, but it does underscore the consistency of Evans's inspiration. The music was put together from a bemusing variety of sources, yet Evans succeeded in shaping every theme without homogenizing them.

It was, though, a difficult record to make. Jazz was at that time recorded with the minimum of preparation, fuss and rehearsal. Most records in the still relatively new long-playing format would be set down on a single day in a studio: witness Davis's Prestige quintet sessions, where five entire albums were recorded in three days. *Miles Ahead* took four full days of studio time, plus a further day where Evans completed some overdubbing. Evans had preplanned the dates to the extent of mailing copies of the individual parts to the musicians ahead of the sessions. In the studio, tracks were completed only slowly: rehearsals went forward at a trudge, and some of the pieces got as far as take nineteen. Avakian, fearful that some pieces might never come out as a satisfactory finished take, began recording some of the rehearsals themselves, another decision which was practically unheard of. Overdubs and tape splices were a comparatively new part of record-making, and were rarely encountered in jazz, but Avakian realized that any procedure to get a perfect result was fair game, and he had already instituted overdubs on a Louis Armstrong record. With Davis, who became frustrated with his own failings on some of the takes, it was clearly going to be a prerequisite to edit together the best of the music to get the finest result.

The Columbia reissue *Miles Davis & Gil Evans: The Complete Columbia*

Studio Recordings [8] includes no less than two and a half discs of rehearsal and outtake material from the various Davis–Evans collaborations, and much of it is from the *Miles Ahead* sessions. There are glimpses of Evans's mild-mannered but insistent directing of the ensemble: he never loses his cool, but he keeps on until things sound just the way he wants them. Davis had played his own part in conceiving the results, working with Evans on the scores in advance of the studio dates, but it was clearly Evans who was taking overall responsibility for the results. No wonder Davis remarked that 'Gil has a way of voicing chords and using notes like nobody else'.

Avakian, though, was producing the date, and he was also recording the music in an early form of stereo, which in 1957 was just coming into use, although as usual it was only classical music which was recorded in this medium at first. (The long-playing format was introduced primarily for the purposes of issuing classical records in a more digestible form, so that connoisseurs could work through a Beethoven symphony without having to get up and turn a record over every few minutes. The idea of using it to make long-playing jazz and popular records was at first highly unorthodox.) Phil Schaap, who oversaw the reissue of the complete Davis–Evans recordings in 2000, notes that only a three-track tape machine was used, which caused a problem when it came to creating finished pieces using overdubs. When Davis was obliged to overdub a part, 'the edited takes in mono were in one channel, Miles overdubbing was in the second and a combined mono mix was simultaneously created on the third. Doing it that way meant, in 1957, that the album – or at least the four songs using overdubs – would have to come out in mono.'

Ever since, the album has had a somewhat chequered time of it as far as availability is concerned, since its reissue in the 1980s emerged with a series of outtakes substituted for the master versions. This was because the overdubbed master versions couldn't be released in anything resembling true stereo at the time. Columbia eventually solved the problem with a digital remix, although not before Avakian had, in 1993, restored the mono version to the catalogue

– with a few tiny changes to a couple of tracks. (As the producer wryly suggests in his notes to the 'complete' edition, 'If you want to drive yourself crazy, compare the original LP to the two CD versions in these places. All three are slightly different from each other.')

The significant point is that Davis was entirely prepared to enter into overdubbing in order to get a superior result. In the end, Columbia actually booked a further session on 22 August where Davis, alone in the 30th Street Studio, overdubbed a few final parts on to the otherwise finished tracks. Part of the mass of rehearsal and outtakes material (which is mostly interesting to hear once – it's hard to imagine anyone putting these discs on again for pleasure) includes his overdubbed solo on 'Miles Ahead', by itself, much as the trumpeter would have heard it, with the music barely audible at the back of the mix – an eerie eavesdropping on a musician at work.

The saxophonist Art Pepper described the results better than anybody: 'Gil's understanding of Miles was perfect.' Evans's achievement was to create a setting which suited his soloist so shrewdly that it became almost an extension of Davis himself. It was wasteless writing, almost frugal in its choice of gestures, yet one which in its way teemed with incident: one can listen to these scores over and over and still find surprising details, even after many careful hearings. Max Harrison's description of the music as 'light imprisoned in a bright mineral cave, its refinement such that at times the music flickers deliciously between existence and non-existence' is a wonderful metaphor, although not everyone agreed: Whitney Balliet found the music encouraged Davis to be 'moony, saccharine and ... downright dirge-like'. Some of the later Davis–Evans collaborations do slip in that direction, but *Miles Ahead* is surely too fresh and, in its spare way, urgent to fall into those traps.

The musicians on the date were many of the best New York studio professionals. Danny Bank remembered Evans as 'great by example. He didn't open his mouth too much but he kept stressing his points until everybody knew what he was talking about.' Some of the other players on the date groused a little at the exhausting routine of rehearsal and multiple takes, but there seemed to be a consensus that the sessions were producing something exceptional. Davis himself, who professed little liking for most of the things he had done on record thus far, declared his appreciation. It must have been a personal triumph for Avakian, who had gone out on a limb with an artist whom his accountants most likely thought to be a long way from a sure thing. In the event, on its release the record began selling quickly.

The intial sleeve photograph depicted an elegant white woman in a chic hat, on board a yacht, with a small, smiling child to her left. It was an image which seemed to have nothing to do with anything on the record, but it was typical of the way instrumental albums were being packaged by the American industry at that time. The whole concept of record-cover art was still in its

infancy, and the various sleeves which had been used to house Davis's albums thus far make up a very motley bunch. Only rarely does his own image figure at all, a common situation for black musicians at this point: even hit-makers such as Nat Cole were regularly denied a place on their own front covers. Davis complained to Avakian, who concurred that more suitable artwork could be made, but pointed out that the sleeves were all manufactured and it would take weeks of delay if there were any changes now. So the first 100,000 copies went into record stores with the original artwork: thereafter a new design, which featured Davis in a playing pose, replaced the old one.

Ordinarily, it would take a very long time to sell so many copies of a single jazz record, if that many were sold at all. Five thousand copies of any jazz LP in the new twelve-inch format was a good result. But Davis was a coming artist for Columbia, and very much on the up: a promotions department could never have been gifted a more marketable jazz musician. He was a bandleader whom other musicians looked up to; a recognized individualist on the instrument which was still seen as the most symbolic in jazz music; a dapper, sharp-dressed, handsome young man; a controversial and outspoken figure who resisted archetypes, yet had a magnetism which drew in audiences rather than driving them away. Every time Davis complained that he didn't want to play showbiz games, didn't feel he had to be a cheerleader or a clown for his audiences, it beckoned more people to him. His taciturn approach only invited more attention. And there was the matter of his first name: Miles, which seemed to suffice for all occasions. Nobody ever referred to him as 'Davis'. As much as he cut himself adrift from the crowd, it seemed everyone enjoyed the easy familiarity of first-name terms. It turned up in his album and tune titles; and this very record declared that Miles was ahead.

Columbia had picked 'Blues For Pablo' and 'The Maids Of Cadiz' off the album as the two sides of a single release, but it was the album which sold, and helped to boost the label's standing as a leader among those companies producing jazz for a record-buying audience – and this was an audience ready to be flattered for their fine taste. *Miles Ahead* may have had a unique cast to it, but other records showcasing a brass player with an orchestra had already been made: Dizzy Gillespie had recorded some sessions with string charts by Johnny Richards, and – although he wasn't specifically identified on the album covers – Bobby Hackett, a player whom Davis himself especially admired, was the lead instrumental voice on what was a hugely successful sequence of mood-music albums under the nominal leadership of Jackie Gleason (most of them were packaged with come-hither sirens on the front cover, a move which might have inspired the original artwork for *Miles Ahead*). Davis and Evans, though, were making art music. If there was any point of comparison among long-playing record artists, it wasn't with a jazz musician at all, but with Frank Sinatra, who was then well into his sequence of immortal vocal recitals made for Capitol Records. Under arrangers such as Billy May, Axel Stordahl and Gordon Jenkins, Sinatra fashioned a long, literate sequence of interpretations which seemed to bridge popular taste and fine art. With *Miles Ahead*, Davis appeared to be working in the same realm.

Once the sessions had been completed, Davis went back to the business of a working life with his quintet. There was no prospect of creating the arrangements of *Miles Ahead* outside the recording studios. Instead, the quintet was playing again, although in its current incarnation – with Sonny Rollins once again the tenor saxophonist, and Red Garland, Paul Chambers and Art Taylor in the rhythm section – it made no studio records. An engagement at Café Bohemia in July resulted in three broadcasts, one of which has been issued on an unauthorized CD [6]. 'Bye Bye Blackbird' and 'It Never Entered My Mind' display a band overloaded with talent but one that worked together with a degree of unease. The problem remained that Rollins, whose Prestige albums had started to create a real stir, was only biding his time in Davis's group until he would go out on his own; and he duly left in September. During the summer months, meanwhile, Thelonious Monk's quartet with John Coltrane had been playing a long residency at the Five Spot Café in Cooper Square. Monk would continue to play there, on and off, until 1959, but it was the band with Coltrane that was causing excitement, and Davis himself went down to hear them on a number of occasions.

Replacing Rollins was always going to be difficult, and in the end Davis made the surprise choice of the Belgian saxophonist Bobby Jaspar. He had been one of the favourite sons of the Paris club scene and in 1955 married the singer Blossom Dearie and moved with her to New York. Davis had heard him play with a J. J. Johnson group, and liked his style, which had a certain feline grace to it: European musicians were still routinely considered second-class citizens by the American jazz establishment, but Davis had been to Paris and was untroubled by such slights. If anything, it might have encouraged him to hire Jaspar. The leader had also fired Red Garland, which had led to Art Taylor's angry departure as well. Philly Joe Jones returned to the drum role, and Tommy Flanagan took over at the piano. The group didn't last long, but one gig at Birdland in October has survived in the form of some thirteen minutes of music on [5]. The sound is poor but the music on 'All Of Me' is good enough to make one regret that there is so little by this edition of the band. Davis plays a long, rather indecisive solo and is followed by a lithe and inventive Jaspar and a springy, creative solo by Flanagan, whose ability to be a useful witness at several key points in jazz history (he would play piano on Coltrane's *Giant Steps* session two years hence) is sometimes forgotten. A much briefer version of 'Four' sounds hurried in comparison and fades out early, although the surviving trumpet solo is exciting.

This line-up, though, didn't last long. Davis had his eye on another saxophonist: Julian 'Cannonball' Adderley, an alto player from Florida who had made a sensational New York debut some two years earlier. Adderley had been working in the city with his own group, which also featured his brother Nat, who played cornet, but had been offered a job with Dizzy Gillespie. Davis began to pester him to join his quintet instead. Eventually, as October came to an end, Adderley agreed, and the quintet then went out on a package tour, 'Jazz For Moderns', which also featured bands led by Gerry Mulligan, George Shearing and Chico Hamilton. Nothing by this edition of the band was recorded, though, and Davis abruptly broke the group up again following a final concert at Carnegie Hall on 22 November, since he had a booking to return to Europe as a guest soloist.

Back in his old haunt of Paris, Miles found himself playing in a band which mixed some old friends (René Urtreger, the bassist Pierre Michelot, Kenny Clarke) with a young saxophonist named Barney Wilen. Two tracks from a set played at the Olympia Theatre on 30 November and a more or less complete set from Amsterdam on 8 December were captured from the tour (on *Legendary Performance in New York 1959* [9] and *The Complete Amsterdam Concert* [10], respectively). Davis sounds in good spirits, as he had been on his previous visit to France. There is little of the tension or plangency present in his American recordings of the same period: it is a sketch of a jazz musician on holiday. Wilen, who often comes on like a more charged-up version of Dexter Gordon, was a good if then rather raw saxophonist. He is clearly playing second fiddle to the guest star, but wants to make his own mark too. Wilen later remembered that on one of the early dates on the tour, Davis went up to him during a number and said, in one of his stage whispers, 'Barney, why do you keep playing those terrible notes?' But there was a happy atmosphere in the group, and the music from the Amsterdam concert, with Clarke pushing the group in a jovial good humour, is very enjoyable. Davis plays a lovely, almost lilting treatment of 'What's New' which sets aside the pain inherent in the song's lyric, and though he is clearly coasting at times on some of the faster numbers, he rises to some of the more taxing pieces, taking an elegant course through 'Well, You Needn't'. One other live souvenir from the European sojourn exists, a television broadcast made in Stuttgart on 18 December [5]. There is a brief, plaintive 'Yesterdays' with a trio led by the pianist Horst Jankowski, a 'Round Midnight' done with Erwin Lehn's Orchestra in a fairly brash arrangement which Davis unexpectedly pierces with some intense phrasing, and an almost high-stepping swing arrangement of 'Walkin'', which again Davis rises to, graciously adopting a manner which was hardly his forte.

The surprise achievement of the tour, though, was the trumpeter's work on a film soundtrack. The director Louis Malle had completed a thriller, *Ascenseur pour l'échafaud* (*Lift To The Scaffold*), and was interested in having a jazz soundtrack to go with it. Malle was a Miles fan and it seemed like a perfect opportunity for all parties. Had he been seeking the sort of composed music which was the norm for even jazz-oriented soundtracks of the period, Davis would surely have refused the project: but Malle wanted the music to be as improvised as possible, to work in a kind of alternative world to the action on the screen, instead of simply preparing descriptive cues for what was happening. Davis was unsure and responded that he had never tried to play for films before, but after a screening of the movie he assented, and quickly put together a series of ideas.

In the event, Davis and the rest of the quintet put together the music in one day. There was no single theme to act as a motif for the music. As it exists in the soundtrack album of the same name [11], the music consists of ten episodes – given their often abstract feel, one hesitates to even describe them as numbers – with titles such as 'Julien dans l'ascenseur' and 'Sur l'autoroute'. Wilen is only on three tracks; one piece is a bass solo by Michelot, and another is a bass/drums duet. The album runs for barely twenty-five minutes and only eighteen minutes of music were featured in the film itself (which also uses a fragment of the 1954 Prestige version of 'Blue 'N' Boogie'). Away from the movie, as with so many soundtrack albums of whatever origin, the music does feel isolated and fragmentary. But there are some wonderful pasages, such as the dialogue between Davis and Wilen on 'Au bar du Petit Bac', and these are finished in such a way as to belie the amount of improvisation which had gone into them: every piece was more or less worked up on the spot, with Davis having only the slightest of preset ideas to hand before the music was recorded. In the film itself, the music seems absolutely essential, even as it refuses to follow familiar ideas about scoring and its function: typical Miles Davis.

The Other Records

1 *Rare Unissued Broadcasts* (Yadeon 502)
2 *Collectors' Items* (prestige/OJC)
3 *Music For Brass/Birth Of The Third Stream* (Columbia)
4 *Rare Live* (Century)
5 *Miscellaneous Davis* (Jazz Unlimited)
6 *Rarities From Private Collections* (Golden Age Of Jazz)
7 *The Miles Davis Quintet At Peacock Alley* (Soulard)
8 *Miles Davis & Gil Evans: The Complete Columbia Studio Recordings* (Columbia)
9 *Legendary Performance In New York 1959* (So What) NB: despite the title, this does include the 1957 Paris tracks!
10 *The Complete Amsterdam Concert* (Celluloid)
11 *Ascenseur pour l'échafaud* (Fontana)

Scales And Tones

1957–8

Davis returned home to the US five days before Christmas, and the quintet was quickly reconvened. Miles had a fondness for the holiday season, and he liked to be in or near his home town at that time of year, so the group had an engagement in Chicago in late December. Before any further recording was done, though, the line-up changed again: John Coltrane returned to the fold.

There was something inevitable about it. Davis had been quietly observing Coltrane's progress in the Thelonious Monk group, and was well aware of the advances Trane had been making while engaged in the rigours of Monk's difficult music. His tone had hardened further, his phrasing had become more pointed and controlled, even as his solos grew longer and more extravagant with notes. It was a strange period for Coltrane. He had struggled to be appreciated in Monk's band: compared with the pianist's characteristically elliptical, Chinese-puzzle logic, he could sound clumsily overpowering, and many complained that his playing had a chaotic and incomprehensible bent, even as audiences flocked to hear what was clearly a powerful and unique jazz ensemble. On top of that, there was the fact of his continuing drinking and narcotics addiction. But something happened to him in 1957 that helped him deal with the worst of his addictions, and when he made *A Love Supreme* in 1964, he characterized the experience as 'a spiritual awakening which was to lead me to a richer, fuller, more productive life'. It has usually been explained as Coltrane simply going home to his mother's house and getting rid of his habit by the cold-turkey method which had supposedly released Davis from the same ordeal. Whatever the truth of it, Coltrane was in much better shape when he concluded his final week with Monk's group at the end of 1957. (Ironically, Monk himself was absent from the band. His substitute was none other than Red Garland.)

Davis called Coltrane and insisted that he return, and Coltrane agreed. It was New Year's Day, 1958, and the start of an extraordinarily busy year for Davis's group. During 1958 they played seventeen club residencies of a week or more, in addition to various single concerts. Davis was featured in a January edition of *Time* magazine, the sort of thing which was accorded only to a handful of jazz players (Brubeck and Ellington were other such honorees, although Davis typically saw the other side of such acclaim, usually wondering aloud why it hadn't happened earlier or if there was a racial subtext). From being a man who had been scuffling to meet his narcotics bill only a few years earlier, he was now one of the best-paid musicians in the music. Columbia's royalty cheques were buying fine clothes and fast cars. Where Davis had once been an evasive, nocturnal shadow on the Detroit scene, in New York people liked to glimpse him in clubs, and watch him watching others. He was becoming iconic in a way that earlier jazz leaders had never approached. His diffidence towards a showbiz attitude, his tightlipped demeanour, easy elegance and cool awareness of his milieu fascinated a young audience. In 1958, rock'n'roll was sweeping past jazz in catching the imagination of a teenage crowd that might once have moved towards jazz. Davis appealed to a somewhat older, more affluent, more discriminating audience, and there were still plenty of them. But he couldn't change the way the jazz business worked, at least not overnight. His sextet may have been the warmest act in the music, but it was still spending most of its time playing long residencies in what were mainly small clubs. The college circuit, which Dave Brubeck worked to great success, was not opening up to him.

Milestones

COLUMBIA

Two Bass Hit; Billy Boy; Straight, No Chaser; Milestones.
Miles Davis (*t*); Julian 'Cannonball' Adderley (*as*); John Coltrane (*ts*);
Red Garland (*p*); Paul Chambers (*b*); Philly Joe Jones (*d*). 4/2/58.

Sid's Ahead; Little Melonae; Dr Jackle
As above. 4/3/58.

For a long time it was thought that the sessions for *Milestones* took place in April, and thus after Adderley's Blue Note album which featured Davis as a sideman and is discussed below. In fact, the album was completed in two sessions in February and March. It was an eagerly awaited record, the first evidence of the band that everyone was talking about. Yet it was a curiously retrogressive project in some ways. The music chosen for the record suggests that, with the exception of the title track, Davis was stuck for new material. Four of the six pieces on the original album ('Little Melonae' remained unissued until the complete Columbia edition of the CD era) are blues. 'Two Bass Hit' (John Lewis), 'Straight, No Chaser' (Monk) and 'Dr Jackle' (Jackie McLean) were old pieces in Davis's repertoire. 'Billy Boy' was another steal from Ahmad Jamal's repertory, and 'Sid's Ahead' was a reworking of 'Weirdo' (itself a derivation of 'Walkin'') from one of the Blue Note dates of 1954. Only 'Milestones', a title which Davis had already used on a John Lewis piece in 1947, was new, and it was little more than a simple eight-bar melody constructed in an AABBA form.

Yet the playing and improvising by the group are close to overwhelming. The ensembles have a power which arrives with an electrifying impact: the quintet that made the Prestige sessions has become supercharged. There is a new assertiveness, a focus which the old band – even though the only change is the inclusion of Adderley – never quite caught hold of. Columbia's engineer, Harold Chapman, secured a bigger and more vibrant sound than the quintet had previously enjoyed, but the tightness and fluency of the band are what make the difference. Of the veterans in the group, Coltrane and Chambers have made clear progress, and Jones plays to his imperturbable high standards. Only Garland seems to be any kind of weak link, and that is in effect hidden: aside from 'Billy Boy', which is set up as a feature for the rhythm section, the only track he plays a solo on is 'Straight, No Chaser'.

Garland's eclipse isn't an indication of a decline in his powers. He simply doesn't fit with the way Davis's music was moving. In the old quintet, Garland's lightness and upbeat feeling were a necessary part of the complex equation of that group's music. In the sextet, which was altogether more purposeful and attuned, the need for his style of playing all but disappeared. Suddenly, his input has an almost trivial feel to it, which 'Billy Boy' seems to symbolize: it is not so much an agreeable change of pace and feel as an irritating distraction to the onward course of the rest of the music on the record. Garland must have realized that he was again being sidelined, and there was a contretemps between him and Davis during the March date which resulted in the pianist stalking out of the studio before 'Sid's Ahead' had been put down. As a result, Davis himself had to play the piano part on that piece.

The three sextet tracks recorded at the February session see the group's capabilities unfolding like a blossoming flower. 'Two Bass Hit' conceives John Lewis's theme with an almost dapper deliberation. The three horns create a montage of interlocking motifs and the unisons are rich but not overripe. Adderley plays the first solo, Coltrane the second, and Davis absents himself from any improvising. 'Straight, No Chaser', Monk's unforgettable blues, is played with an almost monumental mastery in both its theme and the ensuing solos. One thing less often remarked about this group is the timbre created by Davis, Adderley and Coltrane when playing together – an opulent blending of metal and reeds which can create shivers of pleasure by itself. 'Straight, No Chaser' is a tune often played in a lolling, half-humorous way, but both the master and the alternate take which survives are notable for their severe accuracy – this isn't a blues played for laughs. The dissonant harmony of the horns on the second statement of the theme gives it an extra, sardonic bite, which restores the piquancy of Monk's original idea. Adderley again is the first soloist and he rushes out of the blocks. His solo on the master is a headlong piece of invention, phrases effortlessly run in double- and triple-metre, the bluesy lilt in his tone not so much souring as putting a razor edge on his sound. Davis follows him in a complete contrast. This is Miles in one of his dancing moods, still holing the solo with numerous rests but swinging with a serene inventiveness. He starts his improvisation (on both the master and the alternate take) with a phrase picked straight off the end of Adderley's outburst, but thereafter the two solos follow a similar mood and a very different variety of phrases. Coltrane enters and more or less blitzes his surroundings. This is a blues he must already have improvised on scores of times during his stint with Monk's group, and he hammers through eight choruses that have him ransacking the chords for every note he can fit into the frame, the almost frantic arpeggios punctuated by longer notes that seem to halt his progress momentarily before it careers off again. Ira Gitler christened Coltrane's approach in this period 'sheets of sound', and the two solos he essays on these takes exemplify that dictum.

Garland, in his one solo of the date, inevitably cools things off, but Chambers and Jones close up around him and the rhythm team have a glorious moment in the sun. Philly Joe's all but patented rimshot-on-four, the 'Philly lick', seems to swing everything up a notch, and Garland closes his solo with a device which is an ingenious piece of scholarship in action: he paraphrases, in block chords, the trumpet solo which Davis played on the 1945 'Now's The Time' with Charlie Parker. On the first take, he sounds unsure of how it went, but on the master he has it about right.

This paves the way for 'Milestones' itself. The simplicity of the piece, from a structural viewpoint, contributes to its fascination. Instead of creating a theme around a chord sequence, Davis used two scales. The opening sixteen-bar section suggests the F major scale in the Dorian mode, but the second section, also sixteen bars, is settled on the scale of C major, which is the Aeolian mode. The recapitulation lasts for eight bars and goes back to F major. The music works from a harmonically drifting feel, see-sawing between the two different scales, the first more assertive, the second almost wistfully inquiring. Here, as a departure, the three horns harmonize with much more delicacy than on the other pieces. The principal theme is blipped out with a staccato feel, but the B section melody is counterpointed between trumpet and saxophones with haunting grace. Solos from each of the horns, Davis again sandwiched between Adderley and Coltrane, are beautifully done, although an alternate take shows that by the time of the master they had ironed out some vagaries which the earlier version reveals. Throughout, Jones and Chambers maintain a superbly swinging pulse, the bassist roving all over his instrument as the take approaches its fade-out. In a clever sleight-of-hand, Chambers also plays a significant role on the B section of the theme: he misses the first beat of each bar, sounding pedal notes on the remaining three beats, and then slips back into walking mode for the closing A section. The effect is to suggest that the music slows down, whereas the pulse actually remains the same.

It is a famous piece of music – infernally catchy, and hard to dismiss from the mind once heard – but its suggestion of a way forward for Davis and, arguably, the rest of jazz is palpable. This was far from the first time a jazz group had tried making music with a new set of principles potentially displacing the tyranny of chords: the difference was, this was one of the leading bands in the music doing it. It isn't a flawless track: Davis almost delivers a clinker on the final exposition of the theme, and it's perhaps surprising that they didn't have another try at it. But the point had been made. In an oft-quoted interview with Nat Hentoff, Davis explained why he liked the form: 'When you play this way, you can go on forever. You don't have to worry about changes and you can do more with the line. When you're based on chords, you know at the end of thirty-two bars that the chords have run out and there's nothing to do but repeat what you've just done – with variations.' What Miles suggested was a way of approaching the old dependence on chords in a strikingly fresh way: 'Fewer chords but infinite possibilities as to what to do with them.' Hence the difficulty with this edition of the sextet was, again, Garland, whose more traditional approach was entirely dependent on chords, a not entirely unreasonable position for a piano player. The final piece recorded on that day was Garland's feature, 'Billy Boy', which was an Ahmad Jamal steal whose ubiquity eventually came to exasperate its originator: 'Everybody did it, and I didn't get paid for it.' Based on a familiar American folk song, it is skilfully handled by the pianist, and again Chambers and Jones rise to the occasion and lock into a delightfully swinging groove, even if one listens in impatience for the return of the horns.

The second session got off to an inauspicious start when the quarrel between Davis and Garland – supposedly over the pianist becoming sick of Davis telling him just what to play – left the band without its regular pianist. On 'Sid's Ahead', the horns harmonize the theme with no keyboard support, and when Coltrane starts his solo, Davis shifts over to the piano and plays the sparse, ominous accompaniment to the saxophonist himself. It lends a strangely disenfranchised quality to the music, as if the players are performing in a stoic obligation, even though a key component is missing. Davis then plays seven choruses of trumpet which offer his starkest improvising of the record. He doesn't make any attempt to brighten the atmosphere: there's a nocturnal chill in the playing, and even Jones and Chambers play some of their least springy parts. Davis's penchant for mewling at certain notes, achieved through a pursing of his embouchure, might have flirted with self-parody, but this is intense playing. Adderley finds it more difficult to find something useful to say in his solo, although, as elsewhere on the date, the sheer strength of his sound is a pleasure. He is followed by Chambers, who delivers what must have been one of the longest bass solos yet played on a jazz album, with Davis again playing tolling chords at the piano. The horns return to spell out the skeletal theme.

The remaining piece on the original album is Jackie McLean's 'Dr Jackle' (persistently referred to on LP and CD as 'Dr Jekyll'), a boppish blues which goes off at a dangerously fast tempo. Garland was still at the piano at this point and his edgily prodding accompaniments seem to fire up the soloists even more. Davis plays an appropriately fast solo which proves that, although slower tempos suited him better, he could still handle an authentic bebop charge. But the real exhilaration in the track comes in the chorus trading which goes on between Coltrane and Adderley, two hungry men eating up blues changes. One other piece was recorded at the date but not issued on the original album, another McLean composition, 'Little Melonae', which Davis had previously recorded at one of his Prestige dates. This time both Garland and Adderley are absent. There is a somewhat desultory statement of the theme, and on the bridge Davis throws in a sly reference to Gerry Mulligan's 'Walkin' Shoes'. Over the steady stroll of bass and drums, there are gleaming trumpet and tenor solos. There was already enough on the album, and this piece is perhaps more throwaway in feel than the others, but even a cast-off by this band is wonderful to hear.

While Garland's argument with Davis suggests a band of less than agreeable disposition, it's their collective strength as both soloists and group players that makes *Milestones* the masterpiece it is. As backward-looking as most of the material on the record is, the music feels absolutely of its moment: even setting aside the implications of 'Milestones' itself (on the original album release, first pressings of the LP went out with the track labelled as 'Miles'), it sounds very different to whatever the other leading small bands of the day were creating.

Scales And Tones 1957–8

Art Blakey's Jazz Messengers and the Horace Silver group still played a driven variation on the classic bebop form, now usually called hard-bop, which mixed gospel, blues and bebop strains in a music which was nearly all muscle. Dave Brubeck's group was a musicianly vehicle for its leader's extravagant investigations into musical form. Whatever band Sonny Rollins happened to be leading was a mere backdrop for his own mercurial improvising. The drummer Max Roach had been drifting between various line-ups since the death of his trumpeter, Clifford Brown, in a car accident two years earlier. Gerry Mulligan was still leading a pianoless quartet, although the star-crossed Chet Baker had long since departed, and Art Farmer now took the trumpet role. If any one group set out a challenge to Davis's eminence, it was the Modern Jazz Quartet: John Lewis had, after all, been a regular collaborator with Davis earlier on. But the quiet, velvet textures of that group conceived an entirely different climate to that of the Davis sextet.

Miles had reason to be proud of his band. Having a front line that could boast Adderley and Coltrane as your sidemen was advertisement enough for the leader's pole position. Adderley, in particular, brought a brilliant new component to Davis's music. The sensation which the saxophonist created on his arrival in New York in 1955 – he sat in with an Oscar Pettiford group at the Café Bohemia and was, a few hours later, the talk of the town – had subsided into complaints that he was little more than a particularly adept Bird copyist, and perhaps it hadn't helped that thus far most of his appearances on record had been on relatively ordinary sessions for Savoy and Emarcy. But Cannonball – the nickname derived from a childish variation on 'cannibal', which was bestowed upon him as a boy because of his prodigious appetite – was a much more remarkable player than that. Actually, not much of his playing really recalls Parker, beyond the velocity of his delivery: he plays more continuously than Parker ever did, his legato phrasing achieved with little apparent effort, his tone indecently fat and voluptuous. He has a formidable sense of timing: there always seems to be a space in the music for him to execute some piece of daredevilry and come up without a stagger, a large man's natural grace. There wasn't much bluesiness in the Davis quintet, and the leader liked the lick of down-home spirituality which Adderley's sound seemed to represent. Notions of soulfulness were starting to make their way into jazz, primarily through Horace Silver's style of writing, which brought the word 'funky' into the jazz vocabulary, and, as shrewd as ever, Davis could point to his alto player as the man who brought some soul into his Olympian outfit.

Besides this, great alto players were actually not exactly thick on the ground at this point. Sonny Stitt spent as much time on tenor as he did on alto; Lou Donaldson and Phil Woods were hardcore boppers; Jackie McLean was unreliable and an ill fit for any Davis band; Paul Desmond, Art Pepper and Lee Konitz were much cooler archetypes. If there was going to be an alto player in the Davis band, it had to be Cannonball. A few days after the second *Milestones* session, Davis underlined his appreciation of Adderley's work by appearing on a date for Blue Note, *Somethin' Else* [1], which would be the altoist's only leadership date for the label (he had previously appeared on a Louis Smith Blue Note session under the pseudonym 'Buckshot La Fonque').

It has regularly been assumed, given Davis's prominence on the record, that this was really a Miles date in disguise, but Chris Sheridan had it confirmed by Nat Adderley that this was indeed Cannonball's gig: Alfred Lion of Blue Note wanted the trumpeter on the date, since he felt that by himself Adderley was not necessarily a significant draw for record buyers. In the event, the music is outstanding and each player shines in perhaps equal measure. With the rhythm section of Hank Jones, Sam Jones and Art Blakey, this is a more outwardly relaxed and less intense date than those under Davis's name, even though the improvising has some impassioned points to make almost throughout. The long treatment of 'Autumn Leaves', which Davis claimed credit for, features the trumpeter on the theme statement before an expressive solo by the nominal leader. Davis and Hank Jones, as always a model accompanist, sketch out a concluding meditation on the tune which rather leaves Adderley in the shadows, but he reasserts himself on a jaunty 'Love For Sale', and on the blues of the title track he outplays the trumpeter altogether. Nat Adderley's 'One For Daddy-O' is another blues, and after the simple theme statement the altoist peels off a jubilant phrase which lets him steam into another shapely solo. Davis is parsimonious with his notes in comparison, but he does much better here than he did on 'Somethin' Else'. 'Dancing In The Dark' is a ballad feature for the saxophonist, and is despatched with the romantic flourish which one might associate with Johnny Hodges: Chris Sheridan has suggested that the playing here is so fine that Davis preferred Adderley to sit out ballads in his own band because the competition was too fierce. It is certainly difficult to square Cannonball's reputation as a mere purveyor of blues licks with this gorgeous treatment. One other track remained unissued until the 1980s, and was then christened 'Alison's Uncle' (Nat's daughter Alison was born on the day of the date): in fact, it has since been identified as a Hank Jones theme called 'Bangoon'. While Davis acts as a looming presence on the record, the sunnier outlook of Adderley's music is the feeling one takes away from the disc as a whole.

On 17 May, a radio broadcast caught the group at the Café Bohemia, although Adderley disappointingly wasn't present. A new figure, however, was: these airshots mark the first appearance of Bill Evans with the Miles Davis group. Davis had replaced Red Garland with Evans some five weeks earlier, and outwardly it was an extraordinary move for the leader to make. Evans was virtually unknown at the time. He had recorded one album for the independent label Riverside, a mostly trio set called (in the somewhat pompous manner of jazz marketing at that time) *New Jazz Conceptions*, which had at least showcased an interesting writer – his charming ballad in three, 'Waltz For Debby', was introduced at this date – and a capable if unassuming stylist. Evans had a lot of training behind him: he had been through years of classical study and had worked in dance bands and obscure gigs. The Riverside album brought him some exposure, and he also recorded with Charles Mingus and George Russell, the latter especially providing him with two superb features in 'Concerto For Billy The Kid' and 'All About Rosie'.

Davis liked Evans's style, because it suggested a way for the keyboard to enter into the more free-flowing manner which had been suggested by 'Milestones'. Evans's whole style was, in some senses, suggestive. He found a method of playing which voiced harmonies in ways which let melodies flow with greater freedom, softening the edges on chord sequences so that a soloist had more options. But probably even more important was his deep knowledge of music, which he freely imparted to the inquisitive Davis. They spent hours doing little other than talking about music, especially classical and modern composers, and Evans introduced his leader to Ravel, Khachaturian and others. Davis had heard much of this before, but Evans in all likelihood showed him how to soak up what he needed from each of the composers.

It was a strange alliance, since, for one thing, Evans was a white musician, in what was the leading black jazz group. (Davis, who was consumed by the effects of racism for most of his life, was never beyond making remarks about 'white opinions' and the like, yet if he wanted a white player in his band, he went and got him.) Like Davis, who was perhaps a fundamentally shy man who learned to front that crippling weakness with coldness and aggression, Evans had a taciturn bent. His posture at the piano – hands almost flat on the keys, back bent, his face pointed down over the instrument – was telling body language. The music recorded at the Café Bohemia, released on *Live In New York* [2] includes an unremarkable 'Four', and rather more interesting versions of 'Bye Bye Blackbird' and 'Walkin''. Evans solos on both pieces and sounds entirely different to Garland, playing open-spaced lines with, at times, scarcely a chord struck among them. Davis has the mute in tight on 'Bye Bye Blackbird' and both here and in the open solo on 'Walkin'' he uses repeated short phrases (quoting from 'Blues In The Closet' at one point in the latter) to get from one end of the solo to the next. Coltrane is his customary strong self.

An interesting snapshot, but a mere prelude to the next studio session, which was scheduled for 26 May. This time there was another change in the line-up, and it was the long-standing but undependable Philly Joe who was obliged to leave. Jones had continued to cause problems because of his persistent drug habit, in a band which had otherwise moved towards a more cleaned-up attitude (Adderley was never a drug user). In his place, Davis hired the 29-year-old Jimmy Cobb, who had previously worked with Adderley in the saxophonist's own band. Cobb wasn't an original the way Philly Joe was, but he was keen to please his boss, and in the event he fitted right in.

The new band cut four exceptional titles at their first session. Yet they were already very different in character to the music set down at the *Milestones* sessions. The first three pieces were all given a mid-tempo reading, and the impression was that Davis wanted to avoid the more combative approach of the previous dates. (Cannonball Adderley suggested that the leader felt that Cobb wasn't as thrilling as Philly Joe could be at fast tempos, and Evans didn't sound as good on the more swinging pieces; so the decision was a pragmatic one.) 'On Green Dolphin Street', the Bronisław Kaper film theme which was yet another piece appropriated from Ahmad Jamal's book, is given a momentous treatment. Chambers, as he did on 'Milestones', plays a key role, switching between an eight-bar vamp and a straightforward eight bars of walking bass. Davis almost croons the melody with the Harmon mute firmly in place, and he is followed by the, as usual, more mercurial Adderley and Coltrane. Evans, making what was effectively his debut on this track, seems to leaf through Kaper's chord sequence, sifting his voicings in such a way as to proffer the theme as a kind of hip mood music. There is scarcely a false step in the whole performance, brooding but repudiating any sentimentality. 'Fran-Dance', which was dedicated to Davis's latest love, the dancer Frances Taylor, is actually based on an unworthy novelty hit, 'Put Your Little Foot Right Out', although this barely seems credible given the ravishingly tender approach which Davis confers on the melody. As before, the saxophonists and Evans then have their say, although here even Adderley and Coltrane seem quietened. 'Stella By Starlight' had already had some currency as a ballad late in the bebop era, but here Davis slows it almost to a crawl. He is eventually picked up by Coltrane, who manages to intensify the music without rupturing it. Compared to the two previous tracks, this seems like a self-conscious set-piece, a hint at the way some of Davis's music would turn in on itself.

Chambers and Cobb requested something they could work up some kind of groove on, so Davis closed out the session with a fast treatment of 'Love For Sale', which never made it to a record release until the 1970s. Compared to the version on *Somethin' Else*, this one goes on and on, running for nearly twelve minutes, but the solos are again full of invention and the chipper rhythms of Chambers and Cobb keep the music light on its feet. Columbia used the first three tracks to fill out an album which otherwise consisted of the *Ascenseur pour l'échafaud* music, calling the whole thing *Jazz Track*, but *'58 Miles* [3] brings them together in one place.

Davis was about to begin a very busy summer of work as a leader, but on 25 June he was performing in what turned out to be one of his final sideman roles, on a session of music arranged by the French composer and conductor Michel Legrand, who had been imported by Columbia a year earlier as one of their leading players in what was then a burgeoning wave of easy-listening records. Sparked by the huge sales success of long-players by the likes of Mantovani and Frankie Carle, the big labels found they had a ready market for music which dozed peacefully in the background to everyday activities, and they even began releasing albums which were deliberately tailored to dining, cleaning or whatever. Legrand's albums weren't quite that calculating, but their various programmes of tunes associated with European capitals had a continental appeal which tickled an audience of armchair travellers. The young arranger was himself, though, something of a jazz fan, and he persuaded Columbia to sponsor an album where he led an all-star orchestra through a notably surprising sequence of charts, on material as disparate as Fats Waller's 'Jitterbug Waltz', Louis Armstrong's 'Wild Man Blues' and John Lewis's 'Django'.

Davis – as well as Coltrane, Bill Evans and Paul Chambers – performs on those three pieces and a version of 'Round Midnight'.

Twenty-six years old when he made this record, Legrand was a very different musician to the sort of hacks who were making hay in America's easy-listening boom. As Max Harrison suggests in a sleevenote to one edition of *Legrand Jazz* [4], 'Every one of Legrand's scores embodies an exact understanding of the character and structure of each theme, of its potential for development in terms of orchestral writing and improvisation, of the styles of the soloists he would employ and of how they would relate to the scored material: everything acts together.' Thus Davis is crafted into the treatment of 'Jitterbug Waltz' with rare skill, his playing – on a piece which seems almost diametrically opposite to the kind of jazz he was then performing – sensitive and fully involved. On 'Django', he decorates around John Lewis's theme – played by vibes, guitar and harp – before becoming the principal soloist on a gently reflective treatment. 'Wild Man Blues', which features dissonant vibes and is unrecognizable next to Armstrong's famous original from 1927, has a brief, softly spoken Davis solo on open horn. 'Round Midnight' trades the starkness of Davis's other versions for a treatment where he is 'surrounded with unpredictable gestures which are different each time' (Harrison). The fascinating point of comparison in all this music is with the contemporaneous settings which Gil Evans had devised for the trumpeter to play on. Legrand had been through years of study as a precocious youth, and knew his trade inside out; Evans was an instinctive musician with very little in the way of technical resources. Somehow these very different men both came up with original and striking settings for one of the leading soloists in jazz (besides Davis, Legrand's record also featured Phil Woods, Herbie Mann, Ben Webster and Art

Farmer). In the end, Legrand's record was a one-off: he has done occasional jazz work since, but nothing on a similar scale, and has occupied himself mainly with soundtrack and more conventional orchestral work. Yet this ear-opening and consistently absorbing record deserves to be far more widely known than it is.

On 3 July, Davis was headlining at the Newport Jazz Festival. Three years on from the appearance which seemed to place him on top of the mountain, he was now in the midst of his most intense creative period. Festival sets, though, weren't the place to showcase radical departures, and what the trumpeter offered was a typical Miles Davis set (caught on *Live At Newport 1958* [5]) – although he was part of a longer programme which was meant to be in homage to Duke Ellington, the leader merely played his own repertoire. 'Ah-Leu-Cha' goes off at a preposterously fast pace, even though – as occasionally heard elsewhere – Miles's own solo suggests that his predilection for slower tempos didn't preclude him from being master of a quick one. Coltrane bulldozes through his solo, in full command of the horn, and Adderley picks him up in his most swinging mode. The audience must have felt they were being lashed round the ears. Thereafter the set relaxes into more familiar tempos, for 'Straight, No Chaser', 'Fran-Dance', 'Two Bass Hit', 'Bye Bye Blackbird' and a closing 'The Theme'. If anyone suffers in the mix, it's Evans, who is often even quieter than the bass. This set has not been well received down the years – a *Down Beat* live reviewer found little to do other than complain, and even groused that Coltrane was becoming a bad influence on Adderley, and subsequent coverage of the live album has been at best mixed – but as rough as the music in some ways is, it underscores how the Davis sextet could be almost unbearably exciting in person. Coltrane is the dominant soloist – he plays a furious solo on 'Two Bass Hit' and a marathon one on 'Bye Bye Blackbird', in both cases eating up the space which would have otherwise gone to Adderley – and careful listening to his playing shows how commanding he then was: it might have sonded inchoate next to the ruthlessly precise Davis, but it is often awesome saxophone oratory. Jimmy Cobb plays so well that Jones isn't really missed, and though he often scarcely sounds right in this company, Evans calmly stays true to himself.

One important event had occurred at Miles's record label. George Avakian had departed Columbia to begin working for Warner Brothers. In his place came Calvin Lampley, a rare example of a black executive at a major company. Lampley had trained as a classical pianist and was keen to make his mark in his new capacity. What could Columbia do with Davis which would be a plausible follow-up to *Miles Ahead*, a landmark sales success for the jazz division? Lampley's idea was actually uninventive. George Gershwin's opera *Porgy And Bess* had been enjoying a great deal of attention in both the jazz and the popular field. Verve had just released an album adaptation which starred the voices of Louis Armstrong and Ella Fitzgerald, a major film version was in production, and the small independent label Bethlehem had already recorded its own jazz version of the work, with Mel Tormé and many of its artists in featured parts. For Lampley to suggest to Davis that he and Gil Evans create their own version of *Porgy And Bess* seems almost akin to jumping on a bandwagon, and Davis was, indeed, cool on the idea at first.

Soon enough, though, he agreed to pursue the suggestion. His current muse, Frances Taylor, had been appearing in a stage version of the opera. George Gershwin was a white Jewish New Yorker whose experience of the people depicted in *Porgy And Bess* was negligible, but Gershwin's songwriting had long been a fruitful resource for jazz improvisers and, as source material went, Gershwin was more than plausible. Besides, the idea of doing an opera must have appealed to a musician whose playing sometimes aspired to the singing of arias.

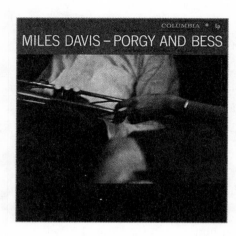

Porgy And Bess

COLUMBIA

My Man's Gone Now; Gone; Gone, Gone, Gone.
Miles Davis (*t, flhn*); Ernie Royal, Johnny Coles, Bernie Glow, Louis Mucci (*t*); Joe Bennett,
Frank Rehak, Jimmy Cleveland (*tb*); Dick Hixon (*btb*); Willie Ruff, Julius Watkins,
Gunther Schuller (*frhn*); Bill Barber (*tba*); Cannonball Adderley (*as*); Phil Bodner,
Romeo Penque (*f*); Danny Bank (*bcl*); Paul Chambers (*b*); Philly Joe Jones (*d*);
Gil Evans (*arr, cond*). 22/7/58.

**Here Come De Honey Man; Bess, You Is My Woman Now;
It Ain't Necessarily So; Fisherman, Strawberry And Devil Crab.**
As above except Jimmy Cobb (*d*) replaces Jones. 29/7/58.

Prayer (Oh Doctor Jesus); Bess, Oh Where's My Bess; Buzzard Song.
As above except Jerome Richardson (*f*) replaces Bodner. 4/8/58.

**Summertime; There's A Boat That's Leaving Soon For New York;
I Loves You, Porgy.**
As above. 14/8/58.

Where *Milestones* had been a record of disparate pieces with a form imposed on them, *Porgy And Bess* is a ready-made entire work which is gently and comprehensively dispersed. Gershwin's opera had by now become a commonplace item to American audiences, and many of the melodies would have been as familiar to listeners as any Tin Pan Alley standard. Evans, though, often used Gershwin's music as a mere starting point for his own elaborations. He ignored entirely one of the most famous parts of the score, 'I Got Plenty Of Nuttin'', and used only the skeletons of 'My Man's Gone Now' and 'Bess, You Is My Woman Now'. 'Gone', which immediately precedes 'Gone Gone Gone' on the record, is a variation on Gershwin's gospel melody, conceived primarily as a drum feature for Philly Joe Jones. 'Fisherman, Strawberry And Devil Crab' is a melange of a number of motifs in the original. If Columbia or anyone else expected some kind of literal translation of Gershwin's original, they were disappointed.

That said, the results didn't sit uncomfortably with the prevailing mood music of the time. Compared to *Miles Ahead*, there is much less rhythmical variety in the different pieces, and a lot of the scoring is played at a dirge-like tempo. This does prevail upon Davis to be more of a soliloquist than previously, and he responds with playing which has an eloquent self-regard: though balanced, at times precariously, between maudlin introspection and a more clear-eyed lyricism, he makes such pieces as 'My Man's Gone Now' and 'Bess, You Is My Woman Now' into vehicles where his playing amounts to poetry of the highest order. Aside from 'Gone', the most renowned track is Evans's delicate tranformation of 'Summertime'. Although this song has become tired by now through an overabundance of interpretations by singers and instrumentalists alike, Evans makes one listen with fresh ears: the sonorous counter-melody which he gently drapes against Davis's keening delivery of the tune is a simple but perfect touch, and here, for once, the tempo has just enough swing in it to lift it out of the processional feel of much of the record.

The preponderance of very slow speeds helps make *Porgy And Bess* more of a piece than *Miles Ahead*, but at times it does feel too slow, and fine as Davis is on 'Bess, Oh Where's My Bess' and 'My Man's Gone Now', these pieces seem too long. The opening crackle of 'Buzzard Song', the irresistible pulse of 'Gone' and the quirky finale of 'There's A Boat That's Leaving Soon For New York' are exceptions which stand out more readily because of their solemn surroundings.

'There's A Boat', in particular (which drops in a quote from 'Gone' along the way) is akin to a shattering of mood after the five pieces which preceded it on side two of the original LP. Evans continues to display a rare variety of resource in his orchestrations, having the woodwind players use alto flutes as well as their more conventional instruments, and going as far as having Ernie Royal as lead trumpet on some pieces and Louis Mucci handling that role on others, where the arranger felt there might be a useful difference. 'Prayer (Oh Doctor Jesus)' is a particularly beautiful example of scoring, where Davis engages in a kind of call-and-response with an ensemble that is subject to continuous shading of tone and emphasis. If there is a significant advance on *Miles Ahead*, it might be that Evans is concerned to make every dynamic contrast count, the volume of the orchestra dying down to a whisper at some points, and up to dramatic tutti in parts of 'There's A Boat'.

Davis switched between flugelhorn and trumpet across the four sessions. The original sleevenote writer Charles Edward Smith opined that he played flugelhorn for all the open parts and a trumpet for the muted passages, but some of the open playing, on 'Gone, Gone, Gone' for instance, is surely done on trumpet. Either way, he gets a consistent richness of tone from both horns, and Columbia's engineers caught him impeccably. More unfortunately, what they also often caught – even in the master versions of the tracks – were mistakes and inaccuracies by some of the other musicians. As ever, Evans had enlisted the best players New York studios could offer – many were holdovers from the *Miles Ahead* sessions – but even they were taxed by his scores, and even across four sessions some of the pieces were imperfectly played. The most notorious example is 'Gone', on which there are clearly audible wrong entrances on the master. An earlier take, number four, is included on Columbia's latest CD edition: Philly Joe reputedly preferred his playing on this one, and it is hard to disagree with him, but the ensemble playing is even worse. Evans and Davis may have been the masters of their idiom, but this was still budgeted as a jazz album, and they couldn't take for ever to get it right. There was also the question of Evans's abilities as a conductor: the musicians liked his easygoing style, but noticed how vague he could be on points where a trained man might have been precise.

Nevertheless, the record stands as a monument not only to Davis and Evans but also to the other players on it: Bill Barber, whose tuba melody on 'Buzzard Song' is as sonorous as anything Davis himself might have contributed; Ernie Royal, the 'tune detective', whose impeccable lead work points the ensemble with superb clarity; and Philly Joe Jones, whose swansong this was with Davis, threading his way through the orchestral parts of 'Gone' with a genuine jazz-man's flourish. All those involved should have been proud of the results.

Davis was certainly pleased, and he liked the way the music this time chimed in with what he was doing with the sextet. On 'It Ain't Necessarily So', Evans has the french horns punch out a figure behind the trumpet solo which sounds very like the melody of 'Milestones'. In the 1958 interview with Nat Hentoff which was one of his few detailed discussions of his work at that point, Davis pointed out that 'When Gil wrote the arrangement of "I Loves You Porgy", he only wrote a scale for me to play. No chords. And that other passage with just two chords gives you a lot more freedom and space to hear things . . . all chords, after all, are relatve to scales and certain chords make certain scales. I wrote a tune recently that's more a scale than a line. And I was going to write a ballad for Coltrane that's just two chords.'

As it turned out, nobody would have to wait too long to hear the further results of this work.

The Other Records

1 **Cannonball Adderley, *Somethin' Else*** (Blue Note)
2 ***Live In New York*** (Jazz Door)
3 ***'58 Miles*** (Columbia)
4 **Michel Legrand, *Legrand Jazz*** (Columbia/Philips)
5 ***Live At Newport 1958*** (Columbia)

So What?

1958–9

On 9 September 1958, the sextet was obliged to play at what amounted to a promotional concert for Columbia's jazz division. With artists such as Davis and Brubeck helping to dominate jazz record sales, and with Duke Ellington (who had returned to the label after a period away), Billie Holiday and Jimmy Rushing on board, Columbia may not have had the hardcore credibility of such a leading independent as Blue Note, but they were selling many more records. The label decided to celebrate their position at the head of the market with a gala concert at New York's Plaza Hotel, featuring Ellington, Holiday and Rushing as well as the Davis band. While there seems to have been no imperative to get a record out of the event, the sextet's set was recorded anyway, and was eventually released for the first time in 1973 as *Jazz At The Plaza Vol. 1* [1]. Jimmy Cobb recalled: 'I remember having to play Sam Woodyard's drums [Woodyard was Ellington's drummer], which were set up in his configuration. Miles and the rest of the band were set up, it seemed, a long way away from me, like on the other side of the room.' The inauspicious circumstances seemed to extend to the recording, which starts with Davis so close up in the mix that his first notes are shocking, and then finds him some way from the microphones on both 'If I Were A Bell' and 'Oleo'.

The music, though, makes up a brimming and exciting forty minutes. 'If I

Were A Bell', a recall from the quintet's Prestige sessions, leaves Adderley out and restores the black and white contrast between Davis and Coltrane, the leader exacting and incisive with the Harmon mute, the saxophonist tumultuous and overcrowding in the way he imparts his solo. 'Oleo' is rendered as little more than a bebop sprint, though one created by masters: Adderley comes in with a quote from 'Secret Love' and from there blows with exuberant abandon. 'My Funny Valentine' is shared between Davis and Evans as a ballad feature, before Chambers plays a long solo somewhat tarnished by the indifferent sound quality. 'Straight, No Chaser' closes proceedings: Adderley impetuously comes in before the other horns, Davis is finally in front of a microphone, and the four principals each play a strong solo. Evans by now sounds as if the quicker tempos which the group could handle were becoming more congenial to him, and his brisk solo cleverly paves the way for the sudden return of Monk's melody.

A few other broadcast souvenirs have survived featuring the sextet in this period. On 9 August, *Bandstand USA* aired the sextet from Washington's Spotlite Lounge (*Four-Play* [2]), with the full band featured on 'Walkin'' and 'All Of You' (which for some reason is regularly listed as 'All Of Me' on many unauthorized releases which feature a version of that song – this is a quite different tune), and Adderley sitting out on 'Round Midnight'. Less than twenty minutes of music in average sound, and while the band sounds fine enough, only a Davis fanatic will need to hear it. The group were back at the same venue in November, and another airshot dated to 1 November includes versions of 'Sid's Ahead', 'Bye Bye Blackbird' and 'Straight, No Chaser'. This time the band had undergone another change: Bill Evans had departed, and Red Garland had returned to the piano bench. Exactly why Evans decided to leave at this point is unclear, but it probably stems from a number of pressures building up on him. Taking the piano role in the most high-profile band in the music wasn't going to be easy for anyone; for Evans, it was doubly difficult: he hadn't been through the road-warrior experience of some of his fellow players (and was also a white man in an otherwise black group, an unusual situation at that time and one which brought its share of strange looks and stage whispers), and who was sensitive enough to find the regimen of touring and playing several sets a night mentally and physically draining. He was also a heroin addict, which didn't help. At the end of October, after eight months, he gave notice and went to stay and recuperate at his brother's home, in Baton Rouge.

Garland's return – or, at least, Evans's departure – might have stalled the progression of Davis's music. But the truth was that while performing the regular ritual of the nightclub residency, Davis seemed uninterested in trying to secure the sort of breakthroughs he was achieving in studio work. Every set was based on the same handful of originals and favoured standards, as the surviving live recordings suggest. Davis disliked rehearsals (Adderley could remember only five taking place in the entire two years he was with the sextet), and his own apparent reluctance to write material discouraged the inclusion of anything fresh in the band's book. Coltrane and Adderley were pursuing their own careers on record – at the beginning of 1959, after several prolific years with Prestige, Coltrane signed a new deal with Atlantic, and Adderley was making records for Emarcy and Riverside – and either felt that their own input wasn't required or preferred to save it for their own projects.

The November music at the Spotlite Lounge, released on *Miles Davis All Stars* [3], suggests not so much a creative impasse as a group treading some water. Perhaps it didn't matter to the band members so much. Coltrane's questing approach to improvisation meant that almost anything would do as a starting point (an approach which was mirrored in his solo work in the 1960s, when a small group of originals came in for relentless and repeated scrutiny). Adderley, an entertainer as much as a music-for-music's-sake man, was happy to give what the people wanted, which would have been selections from the group's records. Davis, reflecting his now customary mix of offhandedness and intensity, played to a high standard while seemingly careless about what was actually in the setlist. Nevertheless, 'Sid's Ahead' and 'Bye Bye Blackbird' are both performed with surprising relish, perhaps in part owing to Red Garland's return: he gets an extended solo on each, and the diffidence of Evans is entirely transformed into a punchy and gregarious style, very much Red back on home turf. The following 'Straight, No Chaser' might be even better, but unfortunately it fades after an excellent trumpet solo: the broadcast had run its course.

The Davis sextet was still busy in the New Year. They were booked at Birdland for two weeks, from 1 to 14 January, and from there played the Sutherland Hotel Lounge, Chicago (21 January–1 February), Civic Opera House, Chicago (14 February), and Apollo Theater, New York (13–19 March), and eventually were back at Birdland, New York (16–29 April). *Bandstand USA* offered listeners another chance to hear them from the New York club on 3 January (also released on [2]), the programme opening with a long version of 'Bags' Groove' (misidentified on some releases as 'Walkin''). Davis sounds, for once, rather bored with Milt Jackson's blues, and plays a solo with some figures repeated almost to distraction. Coltrane marches serenely through some typical choruses, and Adderley, invincible in this setting, peels off an incendiary solo: at some points Garland lays out, as he often did with Coltrane, but even so Cannonball's delivery, for all its abundance of notes, is nothing like Coltrane's. The pianist then plays his own merry variations on the setting. 'All Of You' features only Davis and Coltrane before the broadcasters again had to fade out the music ('Bags' Groove' ran for a marathon fourteen minutes).

In the meantime, though, both Adderley and Coltrane had been off leading their own groups when the sextet wasn't working (on one night, at Birdland, their respective bands shared the same bill). Adderley had been keen to go out on his own but Davis had been hanging on to his alto man by giving him extra responsibilities, effectively as road manager for the group. Coltrane, who had been with Davis for over three years, was now widely perceived as one of the leading solo voices in the music and felt he ought to be his own man. Davis found a way of getting round that problem, temporarily, by having his attorney, Harold Lovett, assist Coltrane in setting up the new deal with Atlantic, sorting out his publishing rights, and then using Miles's booking agent, Jack Whittemore, to find him gigs with his own working group. It seemed inevitable that the days of both Adderley and Coltrane were numbered as remaining members of the sextet, but this would have to do for now.

The year 1959 would prove to be something of a landmark period for jazz, on and off record. As the various trails emerging out of the bebop era began to diverge, Davis found himself in an awkward position. While the sextet remained one of the most sought-after groups in the music – Davis had set increasingly stringent demands for engagements, asking for the highest fees and the best conditions, and turning down gigs which he didn't care for, all of which served to heighten interest and increase the demand for his playing – there were other rumblings in jazz which were creating at least as much interest among the music's hardcore followers. The Texan saxophonist Ornette Coleman had made a couple of records for the West Coast label Contemporary, which showcased a music that went a step further than the modal hints of 'Milestones': when Coleman came to New York in 1959 and began making records for Atlantic, it unveiled a quartet sound which proposed an abandonment of either chords or modes, and based improvisations around freely formed melodic resources. Cecil Taylor, the mercurial young pianist who had been at work on the New York scene since the early 1950s, had thus far attracted very little attention, but his few appearances on record had already suggested that his music would be every bit as radical as Coleman's. Sonny Rollins was about to absent himself from the scene altogether, dissatisfied with aspects of his own playing and the groups he worked with, but John Coltrane was ready to step into Rollins's shoes as the leading tenor saxophonist and his first record for Atlantic, *Giant Steps*, would focus attention on his own testing of the limits of post-bop improvisation.

There were other signs of individuality within a mainstream which was otherwise packed with hard-bop footsoldiers. George Russell, though at this point mainly involved in teaching, was about to form a regular small group for recording and occasional performing, which would embody some of the ideas he had been investigating over the previous decade or so. A cadre of young players, including the saxophonist Eric Dolphy and the trumpeter Booker Little, were starting to push beyond the parameters of chord-based playing, even in otherwise conventional surroundings. The reed player Jimmy Giuffre had a band with the guitarist Jim Hall which suggested a folksy variation on the so-called chamber jazz of the West Coast and would ultimately lead him to his own kind of free playing. The eccentric Chicagoan bandleader Sun Ra led an 'Arkestra', which released albums on its own label, Saturn, and played concerts that had the appeal of a night at the circus.

Much of this activity was conducted away from the glare of the New York scene, and Davis was perhaps too occupied with his own musical direction to pay much mind to what musicians such as Coleman were up to. But if he aspired to being the one who set the pace in jazz developments – a matter of simple human vanity, which was hardly disguised by Miles's outwardly indifferent demeanour – his current band was doing little other than marking time. Wynton Kelly came into the group in February, as the replacement for the interim Red Garland: though still young (twenty-eight years old), he had worked professionally since he was in his middle teens, and had thus far had little high-profile work. Kelly was a typically swinging hard-bop stylist, but he also had something of the thoughtful gentility of Bill Evans about him, and he was particularly able at accompanying soloists in such a way that they felt that they were getting maximum support.

Kelly was set to make his first record date with the band on 2 March, back in Columbia's 30th Street Studio. As usual, Davis hadn't given any of the members of the sextet much information about what they were going to play, but it was going to be all new material, no standards, no makeweight dependence on simple bebop lines. Kelly arrived in good time at the studios, but the first thing he saw dismayed him: Bill Evans was there, too.

Kind Of Blue

COLUMNBIA

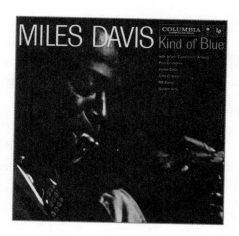

Freddie Freeloader.

Miles Davis (*t*); Cannonball Adderley (*as*); John Coltrane (*ts*);
Wynton Kelly (*p*); Paul Chambers (*b*); Jimmy Cobb (*d*). 2/3/59.

So What; Blue In Green.

As above except Bill Evans (*p*) replaces Kelly. Same date.

Flamenco Sketches; All Blues.

As above. 22/4/59.

Evans and Davis had, in fact, been planning the entire date between them. Evans had by this time returned to New York and begun working as the leader of his own trio. Davis approached him about appearing on the sextet's next record, and in the days leading up to the first session the two musicians discussed ideas at Davis's house. Davis had in his mind the music that the group with Evans had been playing on pieces such as 'On Green Dolphin Street' and 'Fran-Dance', though perhaps taken a stage further in its release from obvious chordal progressions. One piece that Evans had recorded for his album *Everybody Digs Bill Evans* (made for Riverside the previous December) was a theme called 'Peace Piece', a gentle meditation which was itself derived from a lick in Leonard Bernstein's song 'Some Other Time'. Drifting between tone centres, gently circling around a motif, it hinted at timelessness, a patient linear motion, going forward in waves rather than stepping up a vertical course.

The origin of the five *Kind Of Blue* compositions has always been open to discussion. Davis claimed them all for himself, only reluctantly acceding that Evans had had much to do with them, something which rankled with the pianist in later years. As Evans told it, 'Blue In Green' was entirely his, he had at least as much input into 'Flamenco Sketches' as Davis, and the three other pieces were more or less germinated by Miles, although there was most likely discussion over each of them as they preplanned the date. It isn't hard to sympathize with Evans's hurt. Quite aside from any artistic credit, the publishing royalties which Davis and his estate must have received over the years are astronomical, given the record's continued success over the best part of five decades.

The first piece recorded, though, was 'Freddie Freeloader', which Davis wanted Wynton Kelly to play on rather than Evans. Named for a sad-sack hanger-on, who used to be a barkeeper in Philadelphia and later ran errands for Davis, it's a twelve-bar B-flat blues of the sort which had been a staple part of Davis's repertoire for a long time. The theme is simplicity itself, a series of two-note motifs that fall softly on Kelly's almost clanging piano part. Having run through it twice, the horns make way for the piano solo, which unfolds with Wynton Kelly's decisive rhythmic bounce, mixing single-note lines with block chords and purveying a decidedly unblueslike bonhomie. Davis picks him up and works through six choruses. It is a clever mix of dynamics, plangent notes followed by soft, dying-away phrases, rests, a moment of jauntiness followed by a crestfallen blue note. At the start of the fifth chorus he seems to be setting out on another solo altogether, seeming to turn the sound inward, but he then works through a climactic though not overcooked last chorus, which leads the way for Coltrane's booming entry. It seems so loud, after Davis, that it might have been absurd, but Trane tempers it with a thoroughgoing sonority that holds on to every note. Some of the old effusion has been drained off: as many notes as he plays, they are more considered in terms of the rhythmic progress of the solo. Adderley, who follows, is the master of rhythmic flexibility, and he executes some typically rambunctious turns and spins. It leads to a final chorus which is as down-home as he ever got with the sextet. Throughout all these solos, the comping of Wynton Kelly is quite delightful and it continues through the brief space allotted to Paul Chambers. Kelly's uncanny ear for knowing which chord to feed next is part of it, but there's also the spontaneity of his choices, damping some chords, snapping off others. The horns return for a simple recapitulation of the theme. This was take four, and the only finished take: they didn't play it again.

Thereafter, Evans took over at the piano. How the material might have sounded had Kelly remained at the keyboard is anybody's guess, but Evans was, after all, one of the principal architects of the date. They moved on to 'So What', which actually opens the completed album. It is far and away the most famous piece on the record – the most famous piece of music Miles Davis was ever involved with. Structurally, there is nothing very radical about the piece. The track opens deceptively, with Evans seemingly noodling through a few chords, as if warming up at the piano, with Chambers behind him. They play a unison figure before a couple more piano phrases, a bass arpeggio; then Chambers suddenly picks up the melody line which introduces the tune proper. The eight-note figure is answered by a two-note tag, an 'amen' sound, played at first by the piano alone; then on the second eight bars Evans is joined by the horns. The bridge repeats the trick, but this time it is played up a semitone, landing on the D flat major scale; then on the final eight bars they revert to the tonality (a C major scale) they began with. That is basically all 'So What' is concerned with. It broods on for a little over nine minutes, taking in solos from each of the horns as well as Evans before going back to the original theme. So we have a thirty-two-bar AABA format – an invincible part of standard songwriting – which obliges the musicians to fashion statements from a field which is constructed out of two simple scales.

The mystery of the piece is its air of elusive, almost secretive possibility.

One feels that the solos could go anywhere, could follow any path, could drift on without stopping, and not feel 'wrong'. It is a defining piece of jazz, if one identifies that music as something played by intuition and living on its instincts. For once, there seems to be no contrast in the solos played by Davis, Coltrane and Adderley: they move seamlessly together, as if each man were playing his part in a predetermined plan. Evans's accompaniments are handsomely shaded, although one has to strain to follow him: the ear is drawn irresistibly to the horns and what they are saying. On his own solo, which features some surprisingly dissonant voicings that he plays on the bridge, the horns riff behind him. In the end, the music drifts back towards Chambers and his ostinato melody, Jimmy Cobb ticking impassively at his ride cymbal, Evans playing the so-what tag, and the entire piece fading away into silence. In the studio, preserved on the master tape but not on the record, Cannonball Adderley broke everyone up by suddenly crooning the first line of 'With A Song In My Heart'.

Who actually wrote 'So What'? As with everything else on the record, Davis claimed credit for it, but the mysterious hand of Gil Evans may have played a part: several of those involved, including Jimmy Cobb, Gil's widow Anita and Teo Macero, have all suggested that Evans was the one who wrote the little prelude which prefaces the melody, and as Cobb remarks, 'Man, it *sounds* like Gil's stuff.'

The last piece recorded that day was 'Blue In Green'. Bill Evans subsequently traced its origins to an idea tossed his way by Davis, the trumpeter saying to him one day, 'What would you do with that?' as he showed him the musical symbols for G minor and A augmented. The results, supposedly, were 'Blue In Green', a piece which Evans had already hinted at, as Bob Blumenthal points out in his essay for the latest Columbia edition of the session, in a version of 'Alone Together' which he had recorded as a sideman on a Chet Baker date a few weeks earlier. Here, the tempo is funereal. Evans, in his own notes used on the original album jacket, describes it merely as 'a ten-measure circular form', but it isn't as simple as that. Although the piece initially sounds like something which is going in cycles around those two chord shapes, there seem to be the bones of three separate themes, the first stated by Davis (on muted trumpet), the second by Evans and the third, briefly, by Coltrane. Evans and Davis then recapitulate their earlier expositions. The improvising, even more so than on 'So What', has an inevitability about it which is eerily complete, perhaps in part owing to the simplicity of the framework. Studio chatter before the take suggests that Coltrane wasn't going to play on this piece, but was invited by Davis to play his part, more or less at the last minute. Either way, the three soloists – superbly guided by Chambers, whose adroit lines are the map to the treasure – make something remarkable out of Evans's sketch. Whether one hears the results as wistful, melancholic or nostalgic, or none of those things, the music surely has an ageless beauty to it.

The intention was to set down one more track on that day, but despite the fact that the three finished pieces were each the only completed take that needed to be made, there was no time left to do more. So the group reassembled on 22 April to complete the album. 'Flamenco Sketches' was the other piece that Bill Evans had basically worked up in consultation with Davis. The opening chords are an immediate recall of the piano solo 'Peace Piece', and the pianist later remembered that 'I thought that maybe, instead of doing one ostinato, we could move through three or four or five levels that would relate to each other and make a cycle, and he agreed and we worked at it at the piano until we arrived at the five levels we used.' Evans then wrote out the scales for each of the musicians: a photograph of Adderley's music stand clearly shows the sketch the pianist had given him. In the album notes, he stated that the five scales are 'each to be played as long as the soloist wishes until he has completed the series'. The group recorded a first take in its entirety – it is the only surviving complete alternate from the two sessions – but engineer, Fred Plaut, felt that the sound wasn't up to standard and requested that they continue. After a further four breakdowns, another successful take was completed.

Again the music unfolds to a drifting, contemplative pulse (Jimmy Cobb might have been wondering if he was ever going to be asked to swing again).

The solos – a muted Davis, Coltrane, Adderley, Evans – pursue an airy, spacious feel, almost an alfresco setting, as if the differing modes suggested a traveller's musing. The producer, Irving Townsend, noted it down in his session log as 'Spanish', not knowing what the title might be. Certainly the various modes hint at an exoticism which is a long way from the metropolitan feel of American jazz. The four soloists make what they can of these open-ended parameters, and even the cheerful Adderley touches on a plaintiveness which is very different to his usual blues terminology.

Finally, 'All Blues'. Going back to the blues, which had also started the first date, might have settled everyone down after the difficult 'Flamenco Sketches', but this is just as demanding a piece to play. The time is ostensibly 3/4, but it can also be counted in 6/8, which in some ways suits the material better. Chambers plays an ostinato riff throughout the piece, which runs out to a little over eleven and a half minutes. The saxophones harmonize on a three-note figure which can be sourced back to 'Milestones', and Davis states the melody on muted horn. Evans plays a trill over Chambers's introduction of his riff. After each horn soloist, he vamps on the bass riff himself for a few bars, a palate-cleaning exercise which opens the way for the next man. Davis has time to take out his mute for his opening solo, and it's one of the most dynamically varied he plays on the record, spearing, almost harsh notes mixed with phrases that come out at not much more than a mumble. Adderley seems a little below par, in a situation which would have suited him ideally, and he is outshone by Coltrane, who glides – if monuments can glide – through his allotted time. The introductory music is then brought back before Davis seems about to embark on another solo, this time with the ensemble passage as a backdrop: but there is an abrupt fade.

There was enough for a finished album here.

Kind Of Blue was the title Davis bestowed upon his record – it was a name of his choice, which was itself a surprise, since hitherto Miles had been entirely careless about naming either compositions or albums – and it was released on 19 August 1959. Columbia must have known they were on to a winner, and one which would build on the fine sales success of both *Miles Ahead* and *Porgy And Bess*. The album received consistently favourable reviews and the label spent a lot of marketing money – for a jazz album, a huge amount – advertising their product. By the end of the year it had sold handsomely. But the *Kind Of Blue* legacy had barely begun to be formed.

For Davis, as with virtually all of his records, it was not much more than another stop in the studios. While he appeared to save his most creative and groundbreaking work for the little time he spent making records, the paradox was that he then seemed to forget about them very quickly. Of the five originals on the record, only 'So What' and 'All Blues' were used as part of his regular live set. As boldly as those pieces were performed on the many occasions that Davis returned to them, nothing ever recaptured the translucent feel which the sextet secured in Columbia's studios.

Kind Of Blue has since sprouted into the stuff of legend. It is the most admired and feted jazz record of the LP era. Countless copies reside in households that otherwise cannot boast even a single other jazz record. Its ubiquitous presence extends to shopping malls and restaurants, everywhere where someone has made a decision to offer some background music which is a little more hip than the average slice of easy listening. Its durability seems invincible, embraced by the first generation of Miles fans who bought it more than forty-five years ago, and passed down through every subsequent tribe of Western music-buyers, all attracted by a mystique and elegance which is, like the sound of the music, ageless.

Many attempts have been made to analyse the reasons for the music's lasting appeal. Perhaps the easiest way to explain it is to suggest the many things which *Kind Of Blue* is not: it is not troubling, not abrasive, not much like the other jazz of its period, and not very difficult to assimilate. It can create an aura of tranquillity and rest. The tempos aren't too fast and they do not disturb. Next to even the other records by the sextet, the music is unruffled and placid. If it sounds good drifting through the haze of a summer's day, it is also a perfect after-midnight record. Nobody dares to say a disrespectful word about *Kind Of Blue*.

Whether it is really the best of Miles Davis is, at this point, unimportant. *Milestones* is a better jazz record – more swinging, more powerful, a superior showcase for the sextet as a working ensemble. That music and the tracks which made up half of *Jazz Track* (which was actually released after *Kind Of Blue*) offer the most complete portrait of the band. *Miles Ahead* is a stronger vehicle for Davis as a soloist, and is uniquely arranged. But *Kind Of Blue* will always be the signature Miles Davis record. It works as an album, not as a gathering of tracks. It epitomizes Davis as Svengali, elegantly mysterious, not quite one thing – almost, nearly, kind of.

One incredible aspect of the record was Columbia's cavalier approach to detail. The sleeve, which featured a characteristically moody shot of Miles in performance, listed band members as Julian Adderly, Wyn Kelly and James Cobb. The titles of 'All Blues' and 'Flamenco Sketches' were reversed on both the label and the album jacket, and for years some fans thought that was the correct titling. Most extraordinary of all was that half the record was released at the wrong speed, and it remained that way right into the CD era. The music had been taped simultaneously on two different machines, one of which was running slightly slow, and it was the tapes made on that console which were used for side one of the original LP. It wasn't until a remastering engineer noticed the difference when comparing tapes – in 1997! – that anyone realized that for nearly forty years listeners had been hearing half the record a quarter-tone sharp.

As an influence, it fed slowly into the jazz mainstream – it wasn't even a quiet revolution. The music didn't suddenly go over to modal playing overnight, and there were plenty of other insurrectionary moves afoot, with Coleman and Coltrane about to make their mark (Coleman made his New York debut at the Five Spot in November 1959). In 1959, *Kind Of Blue* served mainly to affirm Davis as a one of a kind leader and pre-eminent soloist. This was bolstered by another media event, which took place during the period between the *Kind Of Blue* sessions: a one-off television special for CBS, part of a series on the arts then being made by the producer Robert Herridge (who was also responsible for the famous *Sound Of Jazz* broadcast, from two years earlier). Davis didn't want to be on the programme at first, but fortunately he relented, and the telecast consists of the group (minus Adderley, who was suffering one of his frequent migraine attacks) playing 'So What' and an orchestra directed by Gil Evans doing three pieces from *Miles Ahead*, 'The Duke', 'Blues For Pablo' and 'New Rhumba', all released on *Legendary Performance in New York 1959* [4]. 'So What' was set up mostly as a feature for Miles, and ends with his signature gesture of walking off camera while Paul Chambers plays the finale of the tune. It is a few precious minutes of one of the great jazz ensembles playing together. The segment with Evans finds the orchestra – which includes several of the musicians who worked on the studio recordings – playing in a more rumbustious style than the music of the album. This, too, counts as an invaluable survival, one of the only times the music was ever performed outside the studio.

The sextet worked through the summer and into the autumn, but the personnel fluctuated. Both Adderley and Coltrane hankered after leading their own bands, but Davis was paying excellent money, and Coltrane in particular was still nervous about becoming a full-time leader. For a brief period in the summer Jimmy Heath took on Coltrane's role, but during a stint at Birdland in August, Miles's restless tenorman was back in the group. On one especially muggy evening, 25 August, the group made a radio broadcast from the New York club, and a surviving 'So What' [4] suggests that the group was in fine fettle. Late in the evening, Davis escorted a young white woman up the steps of the club, hailed a taxi for her, and then stood outside the club for a moment to have a cigarette. The sidewalk was busy, and a patrolman asked people not to loiter and crowd the street. When he told Davis to do the same, the trumpeter mildly told him that he worked at the club, and was just getting some air. From there it seems to have turned into a confrontation, and it ended with Davis being beaten and arrested by a group of officers. A photograph exists of Davis arriving at the station house: his head has a tousled bandage on it, his jacket and shirt look soaked in blood. It would be shocking enough in a southern town, but for a celebrity figure in New York, it seems staggering, even for an era when civil rights issues were only beginning to gather momentum. (The best response anywhere in the press was a courageous headline in, of all places, the British music paper *Melody Maker*: it ran the photo under the headline 'This Is What They Did To Miles'.)

The event wasn't even a nine-day wonder in the city: although Davis's cabaret card was revoked for a time, which prevented him from playing in New York, the charges were soon enough dropped and a suit Davis brought against the city faded away. He had been in gaol before – Irene had had him arrested for evading his parental responsibilities some years earlier – and he seemed outwardly unfazed by the incident. But if it added to the legend of Miles, it did so in a troubling way. Some suggested that this already unforthcoming and defensive man became even darker in his outlook. Twenty-five years after the event, he titled one of his records *You're Under Arrest*, the words the policeman had said to him that night. At Birdland, Coltrane and the others played the final set without him.

The Other Records

1 *Jazz At The Plaza Vol. 1* (Columbia)
2 *Four-Play* (Jazz Music Yesterday)
3 *Miles Davis All Stars* (Jazz Band)
4 *Legendary Performance In New York 1959* (So What)

So What? 1958–9

I'm Going Out
To Hear Miles

1959–62

Davis spent the rest of 1959 with his working situation in a state of flux. The legal difficulties connected with the arrest were one problem. Another was the personnel of the sextet. Cannonball Adderley finally left at the end of September: Davis offered him the formidable sum of a guaranteed $20,000 a year to stay, but the altoist was set on going out on his own, and enlisted his brother Nat as his fellow front-line musician. In fact, Nat had been deputizing for Miles while the sextet finished its stint at Birdland in August. 'I played just over a week and, at the end, Miles telephoned. In that raspy voice of his, he asked,"How much you want me to pay you?" I told him I don't charge because I was happy to do that. But Miles insisted: "How much money should I pay you?" I said $100 a day, because it was a great band and a thrill to be out there. There was a pause and he said, "You ain't worth that," and hung up. I never did get paid.'

Davis had taken to missing a lot of sets. He would frequently play no more than the first number in a club set and then disappear. There were some grumbles in the press, as there were about other aspects of his stage demeanour, such as refusing to announce song titles, or strolling offstage when another musician was soloing, but these tended to add to the accumulating mystique of Miles. Coltrane was still there, but his recording sessions for

Atlantic consumed much of his creative thinking and he, too, missed some sets: in New York, George Coleman, who would later join Davis full-time, deputized on occasion.

As far as records were concerned, there was another project in hand. In the modern era, it seems scarcely credible that a musician who had, in a twelve-month period, already recorded the music of *Milestones*, *Porgy And Bess* and *Kind Of Blue*, would be looking to start on another major project before the year was out. But Davis and Gil Evans had come up with an idea for another collaboration. Spanish music and Spanish culture in general had attracted Davis's attention. He went to see a company of Spanish dancers, at Frances's behest, and then went out and bought a stack of flamenco records. He and Evans looked through Spanish musical scores, and while in California he had heard a record of Joaquin Rodrigo's *Concierto de Aranjuez for guitar and orchestra*, a piece which started to haunt him.

The piece became the central part of *Sketches Of Spain* [1], the third and most ambitious of the Davis–Evans alliances. Again, Evans assembled an extravagant orchestra (four trumpets apart from Miles, two trombones, two flutes, plus tuba, oboe, bassoon, bass clarinet, harp, bass, drums and percussion). The scoring of the Rodrigo piece lasted, in its recorded form, a little over sixteen minutes, and took up most of the first side of the LP, but there were four other pieces: a brief arrangement of a de Falla melody, 'Will O' The Wisp', and three pieces – 'Solea', 'Saeta' and 'The Pan Piper' – which were credited as originals by Evans. Actually, they were not: as Gil admitted to the author in 1983, 'Those numbers credited to me are traditional tunes. You don't get royalties on public domain numbers.'

It was a very difficult task for everyone involved. Evans, even more than he had been on the two earlier records, was finicky to the point of driving the engineer, Fred Plaut, to distraction. Every part of the score had to be just so. Teo Macero, a saxophonist and musical theoretician who had recently joined Columbia as part of their jazz team, was entrusted with overseeing the production, and he soon realized that studio time for the project was going to be substantial, even in comparison to the previous Davis–Evans albums. Although the album's master takes were completed on four studio days, there were in the end seventeen sessions of rehearsal and recording. Evans had set his musicians challenges which taxed the very best of them. The lead trumpeter, Ernie Royal, grumbled that 'These look like flute parts we're playing', and Davis, who had a bout of the flu around the time of

the earliest sessions, didn't even play at all at first. By the end of it, he seemed all but sick of the music: 'I was drained of all emotion and I didn't want to hear that music after I got through playing all that hard shit. Gil said, "Let's go listen to the tapes." I said, "*You* go listen to the tapes."'

Davis and Evans put their all into the project, and *Sketches Of Spain* does sound like a record where its creators were trying too hard. However some might complain about the legitimacy of jazz musicians tackling establishment music from Europe, there is nothing any more sacrosanct about Rodrigo than there is about Jerome Kern or George Gershwin, and the luminous music of *Porgy And Bess* has just as much gravitas as the Spaniard's guitar concerto. But Evans effected a thoroughgoing transformation of Gershwin's material; with Rodrigo's music, he sounds effortful and oddly lacking in grace. Perhaps the most problematic part of the 'Concierto' is its awkward construction: rather than flowing into a convincing whole, the various episodes feel pinned together, as if Evans were medleying Rodrigo's music with bits and pieces of his own. What had happened to the beautiful interlinking that he had secured so gracefully with the *Miles Ahead* music? In place of that, there are wilfully strange sonorities arising out of the various sections. The dynamics of the score seem to jolt from passage to passage (one can sympathize with Fred Plaut's head-shaking), and while Rodrigo's lovely central melody does seem to work as a binding agent, there is no real development out of it.

If Evans and Davis felt they were securing a genuine truce between an American improviser's approach and the Spanish roots of the composer's inspiration, they failed: the music scarcely ever feels Spanish at all, couched in far more American-metropolitan terms than that. A particular problem is the assimilation of Davis's rhythm section into the music: Chambers and Cobb are seldom as easeful as they were on the Gershwin project, and the percussion parts (played by Elvin Jones and Jose Manguel) never seem authentic. Yet the smaller pieces do work rather better. 'Will O' The Wisp' is stiffly orchestrated and feels overmuscled, but 'The Pan Piper', with Davis playing tight muted decorations over a continuous ripple of flutes and an overlaid brass motif, is agreeably exotic. 'Saeta' starts as a march performed by the orchestra, but this dies away to a long, humming chord played by the woodwind, over which Davis pitches a starkly organized flugelhorn solo, the usual fatness of the instrument's tone here traded for a squeezed, almost parched sound. When the march returns, as if bookending a dream, the effect is strangely bittersweet. 'Solea', which closes the record, has some of Evans's best work: he creates a flamenco-styled setting which shifts behind Davis for a dozen minutes or so. Because Davis is so high in the mix, the orchestra sometimes feels recessed, but here the rhythmic elements and the parts played by the drummers are much more effective. Davis, though, sounds tightened up by the task of being the concerto soloist. He preens on some notes, strangles others, and sounds as if he's struggling to get through it. No wonder he felt exhausted at the end of it.

The record was eventually finished on 11 March 1960. At that point, Davis had had enough of making records for a while, and he had been booked by Norman Granz to undertake an extensive tour of Europe, the first date scheduled for Paris on 21 March (released on record as *Paris Jazz Concert* [2]). Besides Kelly, Chambers and Cobb, Coltrane made the trip with the quintet. As usual, Trane had been fretting over his sideman role, convincing himself and almost everyone he talked to that he should be out leading his own group, yet he scarcely played like a man bored with the music or uncomfortable with his lot. At the Paris Olympia, an enthusiastic crowd greeted the band, and Davis called

'All Of You' as the first number. Light on his feet, the leader must have beguiled the audience with his opening solo, but then they were witness to Coltrane at his most unshakeable and relentless. Chorus after chorus went by, and after several climaxes had seemingly already passed, Coltrane began hitting what sound like harmonics, extraordinary saxophone sounds, as if he had said every last thing on the horn and was beginning to dismantle it altogether. There were what might have been either jeers or cheers from the crowd at this point, but there was a decent enough ovation as he finally stood down. In the end, 'All Of You' ran for an exhaustive seventeen minutes. Much of the rest of the set – 'So What', 'On Green Dolphin Street', 'Walkin'', 'Bye Bye Blackbird', 'Round Midnight' and 'Oleo' – follows a similar path, although Davis's own solos got progressively more heated and asymmetrical as the night went on. The crowd responded with a mix of approbation and, perhaps, bafflement.

It was the first of twenty-two dates, taking in France, Norway, Denmark, West Germany, Italy, Austria, Switzerland and Holland, although besides the Paris show, recordings from only three of the remaining gigs have survived. The two sets recorded in Stockholm (*Live In Stockholm 1960* [3]) on 22 March offer some of the best evidence of the quintet's last hurrah, in decent sound and at length. Playing on the now classic modal form of 'So What', in the later set, Davis starts with some degree of circumspection but is soon enough close to altogether losing sight of the shoreline of the tune. On 'Walkin'', a tune which by now Miles had almost played to exhaustion, Kelly lays out for long stretches of the trumpet solo, freeing up Davis to play as daringly as he wishes. On 'So What', Coltrane seems to be toying with the melodic motif of 'Willow Weep For Me' before unleashing a tumbling improvisation. On 'Walkin'' he paces himself cleverly until the last few choruses, where he almost roars out one convolution after another. The playing of the two lead voices would be close to exhausting for listeners if it weren't for Kelly, Chambers and Cobb. Wynton Kelly's ability to come up with a long drink of water after the wood alcohol of Coltrane is miraculous on number after number, and he does it without greatly depres-surizing the music or taking any turn towards the trivial. Chambers and Cobb make little obvious attempt to change tack from soloist to soloist, instead focusing on making the entire performance swing. This comes out clearly in the set from Scheveningen (*Live in Holland* [4]), made almost at the end of the tour on 9 April (the Copenhagen set caught on *Copenhagen 1960* [5] is fore-shortened and currently very difficult to find). In solos such as those on 'So What' and 'On Green Dolphin Street', Coltrane turns the taps on full from the start, as if limbering up for a leadership career which, he now knew, was only a matter of days away. But all of this music is exhilarating as a final extended exposure for one of the great creative partnerships in the music.

As soon as they returned home, Coltrane gave in his notice, and this time he meant it, opening with his own band for an extended stay at the Jazz Gallery in May. As long as Davis had had to prepare for this departure, he still seemed unsure what to do, though with hindsight that hardly seems surprising: within a few months he had lost two of the most imposing soloists in the music. His first step was to hire Jimmy Heath, who had filled in for Coltrane on occasion during the previous summer; but Heath was on parole after serving a term for narcotics offences, and couldn't travel far from his home town of Philadelphia. Eventually, Davis settled on Sonny Stitt, who in a sense combined Adderley and Coltrane since he handled alto and tenor with equal facility.

Stitt was an almost perverse choice for Davis. The veteran bebopper had set-tled his career into a pattern which he would continue with right up until his death in 1982: travelling constantly, working as a solo with local groups, making records as a leader whenever the opportunity arose. He was the epitome of the road jazzman. Perhaps Davis felt that he needed a reliable professional who would simply turn up and play the music, whatever was put in front of him. He had shown interest in another young musician, Wayne Shorter, who had recently joined Art Blakey's Jazz Messengers, but Shorter felt that he wanted to stay with Blakey for now. So Stitt came into the fold in June, playing his first gig with Davis at the Los Angeles Jazz Festival, and from there working in San Francisco, Chicago and New York.

Norman Granz had booked Davis into another European tour in September and October, and this time he was playing mainly in England, his first appearances there. As it turned out, he got a surprisingly prickly welcome from the tabloid press, who had seemingly been forewarned that an unpleasant, anti-white musician was about to invade their stages. But the English fans were in the main delighted at getting the chance to see Miles, even if he did turn his back to them while on stage. There might have been more disappointment if he *hadn't* played up the image. He certainly got a warm ovation at Manchester's Free Trade Hall on 27 September, the only recording from this leg of the tour which exists (*Free Trade Hall Vols. 1 & 2* [6]). The music has lost much of the urgency which attended the quintet with Coltrane. Instead, there is the kind of no-frills fire which Stitt was a master of. His solos don't disappoint in their skill and inventiveness, and on 'All Of You', for instance, he flirts with whistling high notes that might have surprised Charlie Parker. But he always thinks in bebop paragraphs: one chorus stands apart from another, and the sort of headlong momentum which Coltrane would routinely impose on an entire solo, necessitating its length, is entirely absent. Virtuoso that he was, Stitt could comfortably deliver just as many choruses, but they are deprived of his predecessor's questing intensity.

At Manchester, Stitt played mostly alto. Davis himself showed few signs of throttling back: on the long version of 'All Blues' he plays one of his harshest, least accommodating solos, his tone acidulous and hectoring, ending on low notes which rasp out of the bell of the horn. In Paris, the Olympia audience, many of whom probably saw the quintet with Coltrane some months earlier [2], apprehensively expected more fireworks. On the basis of the opening 'Walkin'', they seemed more likely to come from Davis than Stitt: he tears through a solo where his tone sounds bitter and frayed. Stitt, playing tenor on this tune, is almost chastened in comparison. Yet that gives way to a stealthy treatment of 'Autumn Leaves'. Davis extracts a bittersweet solo from the chords, the mute pinching off the bloom on the notes, and Stitt, back on alto this time, mooches elegantly through a tune he had probably played many times away from this group. The two sets (recorded with rather less fidelity than the Coltrane concert from March) unfold in this way, never quite predictable, even when the material chosen has started to take on a same-old same-old quality. Even if Stitt was no real match for Coltrane, the music is still intense and absorbing. Perhaps the Stockholm concert recorded on the final date of the tour, 13 October (and also issued on [3]), offers the best of this band's music, in superior sound. The version of 'All Blues' is quieter and more reposeful than it was in Paris, while 'If I Were A Bell' is bright and energetic.

After the tour ended and Davis returned to the US, though, Sonny Stitt departed the band in December and went back to his old way of working: there would never be any studio recordings of the quintet with Stitt in the line-up. As usual, Davis was playing in Chicago around the Christmas season, and he had to hurry to find a replacement. He settled on Hank Mobley, another tenor saxophonist. Mobley was a hip and interesting choice for the group. He grew up in Philadelphia and had made a name for himself on the scene there, working in Art Blakey's Jazz Messengers for some time and becoming a prolific artist on Blue Note, as both a leader and a sideman. Mobley used what he called a 'round sound', without the hard edges of Coltrane or Rollins, and dependent on a foggy and lightly vocalized tone. Rhythmically, he sounded unemphatic, but the lack of plangency in his tone disguised a clever and very inventive way of particularizing his solos: often he would work against the beat, or use unusual phrase lengths or shapes. Mobley is one of those jazz musicians that the hardcore audience especially admire and seek out: never likely to break away from the stalwart clientele that follows the music through its fashionable ups and downs, he remains a much admired figure, long after his death, even though he is all but unknown to most of the owners of *Kind Of Blue*.

In the Davis group, he addressed the material with his usual punctilious and thoughtfully earnest manner. In March 1961, Davis went back into the studios to make a new small-group record, his first since *Kind Of Blue*. The music on *Someday My Prince Will Come* [7] is an intriguing mixture of what might almost be called past, present and future Miles. There are a pair of unsettling originals, a perky waltz, two sweet old ballads and a fingersnapping blues. The quintet with Mobley plays on most of the tunes, but John Coltrane was enlisted by Davis almost as a guest star on two tracks, and Philly Joe Jones sits in on 'Blues No. 2', an extra number which wasn't included at the time of the original release. Most of the music sounds to have a sunnier disposition than might have been anticipated. The title piece casts the Disney tune (originally from *Snow White*) in a skipping 3/4, which Davis and Chambers introduce on a vamp before the tune eventually moves off. It is the quintet at its most lyrical, and Mobley, although he does sound hesitant in his solo, offers a quiet departure from what his predecessors were doing. Coltrane's solo is in comparison very grand, and has usually been held up as a crushing riposte to Mobley, but even he sounds comparatively lyrical. 'Old Folks', which follows next, is a strange choice for Davis, a maudlin old ballad, although here Mobley's softly spoken improvisation is truly lovely. 'Pfrancing' is the blues, sprung around a catchy call-and-

response melody line, leading to solos by everybody except Cobb. Wynton Kelly, perhaps inevitably, is very good here. In some ways, Kelly is the star of the whole record: his usual chipper sense of well-being enlivens all of his solos, his accompaniments are deft even for him, and on the next track, the decidedly moody 'Drad-Dog' (named in reverse homage to the CBS president, Goddard Lieberson), he underscores how he could play in the Bill Evans style when he wanted to. This themeless episode does sound like something which might have been part of a longer piece, something that Teo Macero, by now Miles's regular producer and someone entirely unafraid to use studio editing to get a better result, might have pulled together.

'Teo' is the most dramatic track. It follows the form of 'Flamenco Sketches', down to having something of a Spanish tinge, with Cobb's bouncy stickwork even suggesting a Latin lilt to the rhythm, which is basically in three. Davis plays a piercing open solo before Coltrane starts out on a marathon improvisation which builds into some of his most roiling figures: both are working over scales which they can modulate when they see fit. Davis returns to deliver another solo that acts as a bittersweet coda to the piece, the final occasion when he and Coltrane recorded together. At nine and a half minutes, it is both intense and somehow low-key. But it was not quite the end of the original record: Davis plays a dead-slow version of 'I Thought About You' on muted horn, with Mobley inserting just a short solo of his own: it sounds like a plaintive throwback to some of the ballads on the Prestige dates. 'Blues No. 2', a blues on a head arrangement, offers a brief reminder of Philly Joe's ability to kick and lift any Miles Davis group he played in.

On the cover was a particularly handsome photograph of Frances Davis. Frances and Miles had now been formally married for some time, and they lived in a large house (a converted church) which stretched over five levels, and where Davis's children also stayed (Irene had long since moved away from the city). Davis's stock as a celebrity and a media personality as well as a jazz musician had continued to grow, as had his personal fortune: he was probably making more money from jazz record sales than any of his contemporaries, with the possible exception of Dave Brubeck, whose star had perhaps waned a little since the late 1950s. As far as Columbia were concerned, he was a guaranteed source of income. Album sales of rock'n'roll records had yet to make a significant impact – it was still seen as very much a teenage, singles-based music – and Davis could lay title to a business stature on a par with that of many leading American entertainers. So it was somewhat to his label's displeasure that Davis hadn't shown much inclination of late to make records, at least not at the prodigious rate which was expected in those days. The label's solution was to make some live recordings, the first official Miles Davis in-concert albums: even the 1958 Newport set had been recorded more or less by chance. It all happened at a San Francisco club called the Blackhawk.

In Person
Friday Night
At The
Blackhawk

COLUMBIA

Oleo; No Blues; Bye Bye (Theme); All Of You;
Neo; I Thought About You; Bye Bye Blackbird; Walkin';
Love, I've Found You; If I Were A Bell; Fran-Dance;
On Green Dolphin Street; The Theme.
Miles Davis (*t*); Hank Mobley (*ts*); Wynton Kelly (*p*); Paul Chambers (*b*);
Jimmy Cobb (*d*). 21/4/61.

Ralph Gleason's original notes for the pair of single LPs which Columbia first released offered a smart and revealing portrait of both Miles Davis and the Blackhawk itself, and fortunately Columbia have kept them in the current CD editions of the music, which, with no fewer than thirteen tracks more than any previous issue, are now a substantial portrait of what Davis and his group were doing in 1961. It is not entirely representative: Miles's habit of not bothering to play on sets which he didn't feel like performing isn't captured, since he made sure he was playing whenever the tapes were rolling. His solos are also a substantial part of every tune: he wasn't going to be far from the listener's attention on his own record. But in other respects, the albums feel like a truthful and vivid realization of the quintet's music, set down across a total of seven separate sets, three from Friday and four from Saturday.

In Person Saturday Night At The Blackhawk

COLUMBIA

If I Were A Bell; So What; No Blues; On Green Dolphin Street; Walkin'; Round Midnight; Well, You Needn't; The Theme; Autumn Leaves; Neo; Two Bass Hit; Bye Bye (Theme); Love, I've Found You; I Thought About You; Someday My Prince Will Come; Softly As In A Morning Sunrise.

As previous. 22/4/61.

The 'truth' of this music has often been hard to figure out, if the LP editions are anything to go by. What sounded like jitters in the pulse of the music in its earliest incarnation was most likely down to editing between different versions of the same song. Jimmy Cobb told Ian Carr that 'They'd take the same tunes and Miles would find solos he liked better on one version than another, and if it was close enough he'd just splice. They spliced that album to pieces.' Although on the latest CDs Columbia are, for once, notably quiet about the state of the original tapes and what needed to be done to them, the music does seem to be restored to its correct length and pacing. The first set on Friday even starts with a spectacular clinker by Davis in the opening to 'Oleo', which he quickly puts right in a fierce ensuing solo. The engineers were clearly getting a balance with the initial tune, since Jimmy Cobb's ride cymbal seems overpoweringly loud and all but buries Hank Mobley. By the time of the following 'No Blues', things seem to be on a more even pitch.

'No Blues' – actually an uninspired retitling of 'Pfrancing' – is one of the highlights of Friday (the Saturday version fades after mere seconds, suggesting a tape had run out). After the many 'unauthorized' live dates from various European sojourns and occasional American broadcasts, it's agreeable to hear the inner workings of one of the leader's groups in something approaching a professional and well-mixed sound. By modern standards the Blackhawk recordings are still relatively poor. In one way, this is a little surprising: Columbia could surely have afforded the best possible location facilities, yet the sound isn't as good as that on, say, Bill Evans's celebrated Village Vanguard recordings of the same period, which were made with no more than a single tape deck and two microphones set up near the stage. But what does come across is the packed intimacy and close-knit atmosphere which has always made jazz gigs in small clubs stand out for their queer mix of intensity, relaxation and a communal empathy, between artists and audience each sophisticated enough to create a mutual appreciation. Davis was already chafing against the limitations of playing in clubs, and disliked noisy patrons and working for owners who sometimes had a plantation mentality. But the Blackhawk was a rather different venue. Eddie Henderson, a trumpeter who had a family connection with Davis (Henderson's father was a doctor who often treated Miles), recalled that 'people from the black community of San Francisco, the real hipsters, would come out to see Miles. It was the thing to do to say, "I'm going out to hear Miles."'

The rest of Friday's music is pitched much as a typical Davis album. The second set opens with a long and somewhat diffuse 'All Of You': for once, using the muted horn doesn't seem to be working for Davis on this tune, and much of his main solo is made up of disconnected remarks which don't go anywhere much. Mobley is similarly dispersed, possibly in consequence: unsurprisingly, it is usually Davis whose inspiration or otherwise dictates how a performance will turn out. The following 'Neo' is much more vibrant, even though Mobley sounds far less confident than Coltrane did on the studio version. 'I Thought About You' is almost a straight retelling of the studio track made a few weeks earlier, and by the time of 'Bye Bye Blackbird', decorated with a beautifully agile Kelly solo, the band seem settled into a jaunty mid-tempo groove. But Davis then kicks off 'Walkin'' at a very fast pace, and takes a spitfire course through his solo, which runs out of steam a bit before he's finished. The reliable Mobley likes the tempo and serenely skims through his choruses. In the end, he also comes up dry, and the solo peters out before Kelly takes over. To call anyone inexhaustibly inventive is patently absurd, but it does seem close to inconceivable that Kelly will run out of ideas, even on the blues. Admittedly his solo is about half the length of theirs, but in comparison to Davis and Mobley, the pianist sounds as fresh at the close of it as he does at the start. He then finishes the set with the brief coda of 'Love, I've Found You'.

The third set wraps up most of Davis's current repertoire: long treatments of 'If I Were A Bell' and 'On Green Dolphin Street' sandwiching a more concise 'Fran-Dance'. This time the muted solo on 'If I Were A Bell' is smartly sustained and involves a delicious bit of dialogue between trumpet and piano along the way. 'Fran-Dance' has little of the distilled eloquence of the studio original and Mobley sounds bland. But 'On Green Dolphin Street', gracefully set up by Kelly's Garneresque intro, is a swinging closer, although Miles has perhaps started to play this solo from memory, ending with the steady rip up to a high note (he does much the same on Saturday). He doesn't take the mute out for the entire set.

Strong as the Friday music is, it's shaded by the Saturday discs, which stretch across no fewer than four sets. 'If I Were A Bell' opens the first and it's a measured and lyrical statement from the leader that directs the way. 'So What' is taken at a formidable clip, a *lot* faster than the studio original, which dissolves all its mystery but replaces it with an urgent and exciting impetus that stands it up as a fine blowing vehicle. 'On Green Dolphin Street' starts the second set with a treatment which is much the same as the previous evening's, but from there it leads into a terrific 'Walkin''. Given the countless times Davis

136

must have already played this tune, over many years, his creative inspiration here is genuinely remarkable, pushing the blues tonalities out as far as they'll go, mixing almost babbling short-note lines with bullseye high figures, lolling back on Kelly's chords at some moments, driving ahead of them at others, closing his main solo with three uncomfortably piercing long notes before unexpectedly switching to a final passage where he trades fours with Jimmy Cobb. The unenviable job of following this is left to Hank Mobley, who placidly makes his own feast out of the blues changes. Kelly's most boppish solo of the night maintains the heat of the music, and though an arco solo by Paul Chambers inevitably cools things off a little, the final flourish by the band caps a thrilling performance. Which, oddly enough, seems to get somewhat muted applause.

The rest of the evening offers repeat visits to 'Neo' and 'I Thought About You', but otherwise features a variety of other Davis staples. 'Round Midnight' was another tune that was ossifying a little as a Miles set-piece, but he does play it beautifully, gently dismantling the melody and lingering on long, favourite notes. 'Well, You Needn't' is taken at an aggressively fast pace which both horns steam through. Mobley's solo has a slightly chaotic edge to it – for him, at least – which may account for its being edited out of the original LP, one of several tracks which were altered in this way. By the time of the final set (released for the first time in the latest CD edition), Davis would most likely have left the stand to the rest of the band in normal circumstances, but he plays through 'I Thought About You', 'Someday My Prince Will Come' and 'Softly As In A Morning Sunrise' with no suspicion that he'd had enough.

In the end, Columbia mustered close to four hours of music out of their recording time, although barely half of that ever appeared on LP. Davis spoke not a word which can be heard on the tapes. The audiences sound keen, perhaps respectful, but not noticeably overwhelming in their approval. It was, as Eddie Henderson suggests, a neighbourhood gig by a band that was swinging on familiar turf: 'The difference between the band with Coltrane and Adderley and the Blackhawk band was that the band with Mobley, Kelly, PC and Cobb was more in touch with the people. The audience could recognize the tunes. And it swung. You could see people's heads moving.'

In some ways, this was the last Miles Davis group that could suggest that intimacy. Henderson goes as far as suggesting that 'Eventually, the community lost touch with his music and Miles lost touch with the community.' That hints at a nostalgia for a time when jazz was the preferred music of black neighbourhoods, long before soul and hip hop displaced it, and perhaps it was inappropriate to oblige Davis to maintain such a closeness. But the band that played that engagement at the Blackhawk certainly took its place in a long line of groups that came out of bebop, and that still conversed freely in a language that, as much as he personalized it, Davis spoke along with everybody else. Brian Morton has suggested that these sets propose Davis as a passionate exponent of a great vernacular art form, and for all his aloofness and isolating maturity, Miles wasn't simply talking to himself.

The two discs offer what is some of the most pleasurable Miles Davis music of its decade. Unburdened of the need to play the great artist of the Evans collaborations, or the shrewd innovator of *Kind Of Blue*, Davis simply gets on with the job and gives his best. They are idealized versions of what the band probably sounded like: Miles is playing for the microphones, at length and front and centre.

The Blackhawk may have been just another stop in a busy working life, but Davis's next engagement was much more high profile. On 19 May, he played a major concert at Carnegie Hall which, in the end, was a significant and conspicuous triumph for him, despite several circumstances suggesting that the results could have been damaging. The idea was to mix pieces by the quintet with some of the Evans orchestrations, played by a full ensemble and with Gil himself conducting. A packed audience in one of New York's most prestigious venues attested to Davis's standing. But things nearly went badly wrong. Both

Evans and, perhaps surprisingly, Miles himself were uneasy and nervous (even the normally temperance-minded Gil was sipping whiskey before the show). The major sponsor of the show was the African Research Foundation, who wanted the event as a fundraiser for their activities supporting medical workers. Yet Max Roach and some other activists had got wind of the event early on, and Roach had told Davis bluntly that he shouldn't be supporting a body which they suspected of being little more than a disguise for colonialist activities. The trumpeter had ignored his old sideman, but at the concert itself, a few numbers into the first half, Roach and two others appeared at the front of the auditorium, holding up banners protesting against the event. A stunned Davis stopped the music and left the stage. There was still most of the Evans music (including all of the Rodrigo 'Concierto') left to perform, but Miles didn't want to go on. Eventually, he was persuaded, though it soured relations between him and Roach ever after.

Little of this drama comes across on the record with any clarity. This was in part because, at the last minute, Davis had capriciously vetoed Columbia's idea of documenting the concert, claiming that he had already recorded much of the material recently enough. A fuming Teo Macero nevertheless managed to set up a couple of hidden microphones and secretly taped the music on a cheap portable system. Thus what should have been a classic jazz live album exists only in semi-bootleg sound on *At Carnegie Hall* [8]. The later parts of the programme certainly have a virulent intensity, on the trumpeter's part in particular: it's hard to find playing of such raw-nerved playing as that of Davis on 'Teo' and 'Walkin'' anywhere else in his discography, even though much of the music is marred by distortion in the sound: one can only sympathize with Macero's frustration in trying to get a decent document of the event. The 'Concierto' is played in a more decisive and less mannered way by the soloist, 'So What' comes over with tremendous spirit (complete with the introduction freshly scored by Evans for the orchestra) and there is the only record of a new piece by Gil, an arrangement of 'Spring Is Here', which Davis plays with great feeling. Always, though, one is disappointed by the sound, which is perhaps the poorest of any record in the Davis Columbia catalogue.

The company put out the record anyway. In the meantime, they wanted more of the Gil and Miles partnership. But Davis had other problems, as much to do with his health as anything else. He had begun to be severely troubled by what turned out to be sickle-cell anaemia: regardless of the punishments Davis had subjected his body to through drug abuse (and he was still a heavy cocaine user), this is actually an inherited disease, which causes the gradual blockage of blood vessels, often leading to severe and painful inflammation of the joints. A night's performance was becoming a physical trial, and though he refused to admit how much pain he was in, he spent less and less time on the bandstand. The kind of set heard on the Blackhawk records was becoming a memory.

'Miles can only perform when he *is* and *knows* he is ready to give some-thing of himself. When he has nothing new to say, he would rather not play for

audiences or record in the studio – and he doesn't. Miles makes a record in the studio only after long periods of thought and preparation.' Thus ran some of the gaseous sleevenotes to what would prove to be the final Davis–Evans collaboration, *Quiet Nights* [9]. Coming after the Olympian standards of their previous works, it seemed like a crash-ing disappointment when it was eventually released in 1964: three sessions between July and November 1962 yielded only six brief pieces running a whisker over twenty minutes, which amounted to barely half an album. The first date was recorded just as Stan Getz's *Jazz Samba* was riding high in the charts, ushering in a craze for the light-Latin sound of the bossa nova, and perhaps it was unsurprising that Davis and Evans should have their own take on that music with 'Corcovado' and 'Aos Pes Da Cruz'. This is, by its very nature, indolent music, but the partnership's version of it sounds more exhausted than laid-back. The completed version of 'Corcovado' was so short that Teo Macero had to splice an alternate take of 'Aos Pes Da Cruz' on to the end to get it up to a decent length (and even then it ends with what must have sounded like an inexplicable fade). 'Song #1' is as sketchy as its title suggests, long on atmosphere – admittedly, Evans did atmosphere better than almost anyone else at that point – and thin on musical substance, as pretty as some of the textures are. The rather rare Rodgers and Hart song 'Wait Till You See Her' worked out somewhat better: Evans blows his clouds of sound over and around the chord sequence, and Davis plays a poignant lead line over the patter of congas. Here and there one almost feels the whiff of exotic lounge music à la Martin Denny, but it is gracefully done. The two final pieces were recorded on 6 November. 'Song #2' is another half-finished piece: a single extended phrase intoned by the orchestra, Davis playing a variation on it, the pulse falling away altogether and a brief coda handled by the harp. 'Once Upon A Summertime', a heart-sore ballad which suited Davis perfectly, is given a processional reading, the trumpeter content to do little more than embellish the descending melody while the ensemble lowers in the background. If one can appreciate what is really manufactured bathos, it's beautifully made, and Evans constructed one of his most elongated endings to the score.

But that was all that came out of the sessions. Teo Macero was faced with an expensive studio bill and twenty-odd minutes of sometimes unexceptional music. In the end, he filled out the LP with a small-group track from a session Davis recorded the following year and stuck it out. Evans was displeased; Davis was furious, and barely spoke to Macero for a long time afterwards.

There were, though, a few other tracks that were made during the course of the inauspicious *Quiet Nights* sessions, arising out of an improbable alliance with Bob Dorough, a singer and songwriter whom Miles had got to know while working in Los Angeles. Columbia had had the audacity to ask Davis to contribute a track to an album of Christmas songs, and the trumpeter had thought of getting Dorough to write something suitably choleric to act as a kind of anti-Yuletide message. In the end, a sextet played the music to Dorough's 'Blue Christmas' and another song, 'Nothing Like You', at a session on 21 August. The band included such unfamiliar Davis sidemen as the trombonist Frank Rehak (who had actually played on the sessions for *Porgy And Bess* and *Miles Ahead*), percussionist Willie Bobo and saxophonist Wayne Shorter, then on loan from Art Blakey's band. 'Blue Christmas' itself is a sardonic rebuke to the season of goodwill, although not an especially eloquent one, and the track has ever since only turned up on sundry Davis compilations (such as *Blue Christmas* [10]). The other song, 'Nothing Like You', was eventually released as part of the much later *Sorcerer* album. Gil Evans arranged both tunes and they scarcely caused a ripple. Two days later, Davis went back into the studio with the same band and recorded an instrumental version of what was probably Dorough's great hit, 'Devil May Care'. That was the end of the singer's brief association with Miles Davis.

As 1962 drew to a close, Davis found himself in poor shape from any professional point of view. Aside from his health worries, he had notably failed to capitalize on the kind of profile he had secured with the Carnegie Hall concert of eighteen months earlier. The recent project with Evans had been all but stillborn. Then came a double blow: first Hank Mobley left the quintet, and then the rhythm section quit too: under the name of the Wynton Kelly Trio, they decided to go out and work for themselves, rather than rely on a leader whose outlook on live performance seemed cynical and indifferent. As on several previous occasions, the departure of his sidemen appeared to take Davis by surprise. He had had the group booked into a number of engagements at the start of 1963, and suddenly he had no band.

It was an astonishingly muddled position for the man who was still widely perceived as the leader of American modern jazz. Ornette Coleman's arrival in 1959 had provoked a small earthquake of excitement, but after several significant albums for Atlantic he had left the label and had enjoyed little recent impact. Thelonious Monk had settled into a regime of regular work with a stable quartet featuring the tenor saxophonist Charlie Rouse, and had all but stopped composing any new music. Max Roach and Art Blakey led bands which tended to speak their own kind of mainstream, and appealed to nobody outside the core jazz audience. The real terrors of free jazz – men such as Albert Ayler and Pharoah Sanders – had yet to make an appearance. Sonny Rollins was only just emerging from a period of seclusion. Bill Evans, whose trio with Scott LaFaro and Paul Motian had enthralled many in the jazz audience, had been devastated by LaFaro's death in a car accident and was only beginning to work his way back. Gerry Mulligan was fronting a big Concert Jazz Band, but couldn't find enough work for it. Only Davis's former sideman John Coltrane was leading a group and playing a repertoire which seriously challenged Miles as the premier small-group leader. Miles was still the man. Except he had no band. Club owners began suits against him over his failure to fulfil their gigs. He needed a whole new line-up, and quickly.

The Other Records

1   *Sketches Of Spain* (Columbia)
2   *Paris Jazz Concert* (Trema)
3   *Live In Stockholm 1960* (Dragon)
4   *Live In Holland* (Century)
5   *Copenhagen 1960* (Royal Jazz)
6   *Free Trade Hall Vols. 1 & 2* (Magnetic)
7   *Someday My Prince Will Come* (Columbia)
8   *At Carnegie Hall* (Columbia)
9   *Quiet Nights* (Columbia)
10 *Blue Christmas* (Columbia)

All The Rockets Taking Off

1963–6

At least Davis had a new saxophonist, a young white alto player named Frank Strozier, who had been part of the Memphis scene in the early 1950s before departing for first Chicago and then New York. It's unclear who recommended whom, but somehow Strozier became part of a Davis group with fellow Memphis players Harold Mabern (piano) and George Coleman (tenor sax). On bass, another new name came in: Ron Carter, originally from Detroit, then playing in New York with Art Farmer's quartet with Jim Hall. Carter had already worked with Cannonball Adderley and others, and he had a formidable background as far as music education was concerned: his first aspiration was to play classical cello, but he discovered early on that being a black cellist didn't open a lot of doors in the classical music establishment. He already had many years of study behind him before he began working on the New York scene. Davis heard a distinctive player: Carter could solo or accompany with the same unflinching strength, and his harmonic knowledge was profound enough for him to be able to devise ways to elaborate on whatever music was being played without losing his way or letting his timekeeping role suffer. The band was all but complete, but Davis needed a drummer, and for the West Coast engagements he had coming up he hired one of the stalwarts of the Los Angeles scene, Frank Butler; the group was all set for a residency at the Blackhawk.

While in California, Davis decided to make a record with the group, but for some reason he dropped Strozier and brought in the English pianist Victor Feldman, who had by this time been a California resident for several years, to make the date in place of Mabern. The sessions went well enough, although in the end only half of the tracks ended up on what became the record of the group, *Seven Steps To Heaven* [1]. The keepers were all slowish ballads, and curious choices at that: instead of anything more modish, Davis picked

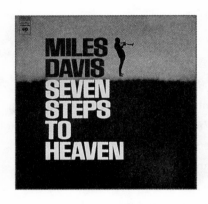

the ancient W. C. Handy tune 'Basin Street Blues', the wistful valentine 'I Fall In Love Too Easily', and the almost mordant 'Baby Won't You Please Come Home', a saloon singer's favourite of the sort Frank Sinatra sometimes used, although Miles reputedly took up the idea after hearing Shirley Horn, one of his favourite vocalists, do the song in a club at one of her customary dead-slow tempos. The results suggest one of the interesting what-ifs which are scattered through the Davis discography. 'Basin Street Blues' runs for more than ten minutes, 'Baby' for almost eight and a half, and 'I Fall' for nearly seven minutes. Though each starts out at a crawl, Butler gradually swings them into a more easygoing tempo, and Davis, the Harmon mute unmoving, doodles magisterially through the melodies. Carter's backing, sounding no more than subtly assertive after years of the more plangent Paul Chambers, is smoothly inventive at every turn. But it's Feldman's scintillating playing which often takes the ear. Victor Feldman was something of a prodigy in his native England, and when he went to America in 1955 he never lacked for work and eventually became a fixture on the Los Angeles session scene. On every tune, he finds interesting chords to settle behind the trumpet lines, filling in an unexpected space without seeming garrulous and tinkering with broken counter-melodies that support Davis with superb ideas. His solos, which have the aerated bounce that served him so well in the Cannonball Adderley band, follow the same level of invention. Even the grouchy Davis, who was at times exasperated by Frank Butler's playing on the date, liked Feldman enough to invite him to continue with the band; but the pianist was too busy and said no.

Butler's skittering beat on the fast pieces recorded on the session may have been why Davis decided to re-record those titles back in New York. The Los Angeles version of one of them, 'So Near, So Far', has survived and is included on the current CD edition. The tune, co-written by the English drummer Tony Crombie, is worked out around a central melodic motif which sounds a little like the rhythm one might use in saying its title, and in rehearsal Butler couldn't seem to figure out how the beat was spread through the theme. The California version swings in its own rather bright way, but one can hear why Davis was dissatisfied with the way it turned out. The other piece recorded at these sessions, 'Summer Night', was a quartet feature for Davis and the rhythm section which was eventually used as the fill-up track on *Quiet Nights*. The by now rather studied melancholia that Davis works up here is usefully leavened by Feldman's sensitive but unsentimental playing. He would have made a fascinating long-term addition to the Davis group.

Back in New York, though, another pianist was about to get the call from the trumpeter. Jimmy Cobb had also been filling in on drums during the later part of the scheduled tour by the sextet, but once back East, Davis dropped Cobb, Strozier and Mabern (neither of whom, in the end, ever recorded with Miles) and again rebuilt the band, though Coleman and Carter remained. He was soon enough alerted to the presence of Tony Williams, then working in a Jackie McLean group. On 14 May, Williams was playing drums in the group which re-recorded the fast numbers the touring band had previously cut in California. On the New York version of 'So Near, So Far', the difference between Williams and Frank Butler is startling. He seems to be constantly playing fast, yet the pulse is kept light and evenly shaded. He plays double-time tattoos on the cymbals while answering them with rimshots, rapped-off remarks on the head of the snare, or a brief, flickering rejoinder on the tom. The only thing he seems to be scarcely using at all is the bass drum (Davis later claimed that he 'made' Williams incorporate that part of the kit into his technique). He hardly plays a straight four-beat time at all, the wellspring of jazz rhythm: instead, the beat is implied, while he constructs new rhythms which overlie it. This wasn't the moving-in-waves free drumming that players such as Sunny Murray were investigating at the same time, but it was the most free-thinking kind of metrical playing that jazz drumming had thus far produced.

What was extraordinary was that Tony Williams was still only seventeen. Once the drummer had joined Davis's band, Ron Carter was made his guardian: in some states, Williams was still too young to even be allowed into certain clubs alone, which meant that he had to be accompanied by Carter. He had the fresh vivacity of youth and saw himself as a student of Davis's music, learning all the trumpeter's famous solos on record, breathing in the music until he knew it so well that his responses were instinctual and seamless. When one considers some of the drummers who had worked for Davis in the past, Williams must have seemed almost like a youthful puritan, uninterested in stimulants and obsessed only with music. He was also young enough to like a lot of the sort of music that people his age were listening to – soul and rock'n'roll, music many of Davis's generation had previously dismissed as virtually beneath them.

On 'Seven Steps To Heaven', a piece co-credited to Davis and Victor Feldman, the group play a theme that sounds like yet another variation on the 'Milestones' motif, and coming after 'Basin Street Blues' on the original album running order, the effect is startling: everything feels fresh, trim, upbeat. The piece unfolds briskly and confidently, even though this band had scarcely played together thus far. There are solos given to everyone except Ron Carter, and even Tony Williams has a brief solo passage, which sounds oddly familiar: eventually, realization dawns that what it sounds like is a Miles Davis solo played on kit drums and cymbals. If there is a slight weak link, it's the piano: on what would have been Vic Feldman's vehicle, the newcomer, Herbie Hancock, played a rather vague and misty solo.

Hancock had been working with a variety of New York hard-bop groups.

In his home town of Chicago he had been a brilliant young pianist, playing Mozart with the Chicago Symphony at the age of eleven, and subsequently working in local jazz groups. He had been in Donald Byrd's band since 1961, and had already been given the chance to do his own date for Blue Note, *Takin' Off*, which featured a composition that would remain one of his enduring greatest hits, 'Watermelon Man', a tune that was covered soon enough by everyone from Woody Herman to Albert King. Davis knew of Hancock and had heard him play, without offering the slightest indication that he was interested in hiring him. Nevertheless, one day in May 1963 Herbie took a call from Miles inviting him over to the Davis household, where the band – with Carter, Coleman and Williams – rehearsed for two or three days on the group's repertoire. Davis listened and eventually played a little, but otherwise kept out of it. The payoff was the record date, which was Miles's way of telling everyone they were in the new band.

'Joshua', the final piece recorded that day, was another Feldman tune, based around what sounds like an inversion of the 'So What' vamp. It completed an album that emerged a while before *Quiet Nights*, the release of which infuriated Davis so much that he all but broke off relations with Teo Macero and refused to do any more studio recording for some eighteen months. Instead, the band were documented on gigs, although that was actually not much of a problem: Davis was so energized by his new line-up that he set up as many dates as he could. Broadcasters and bootleggers also started to record the band. At a club called the Jazz Villa, in St Louis, some thirty minutes of music comprising 'All Blues', 'I Thought About You' and 'Seven Steps To Heaven' were taken down (*Live In St Louis And Paris 1963* [2]). Though the sound quality is only average, dominated by Williams's drums, the music has the anticipatory thrill of a team of relay athletes beginning to stretch their muscles and find out how they work together. 'All Blues' gets a terrific motor from the drums, with Coleman launched into a climactic piece of overblowing which, given his usual impeccable control, hints at how much Williams was invigorating the group. Davis sounds a little sour on his ballad feature 'I Thought About You', but there is a compensating passage where Hancock and Carter trade solos and fashion an atmosphere of steadily evolving camaraderie. 'Seven Steps' comes in at maximum velocity after what appears to be a missing introduction, and works through a fierce round of solos.

This is a taster for the recordings that would come out of a summer swing through the burgeoning festival circuit by the Davis quintet. On 25 July, they were in Paris, and on the next three days they were at the Antibes Festival, and recordings from all four performances exist. The Paris set [2] offers only an extended 'Stella By Starlight', at a moribund tempo, and a quickfire 'So What', but the sound is so poor that the music is barely listenable. The

Antibes material, in both the unauthorized set of 26 July, *Côte Blues* [3] and Columbia's marathon *Miles Davis In Europe* [4], which even in its original LP form ran for over an hour, is much clearer. The opening 'So What' on [3] goes off at a similar velocity to the Paris version of the night before, and Davis reprises some of his ideas, suggesting that he was working through ways to deal with this veteran part of his set at its new fierce tempo. Thereafter the tunes follow a similar format: Davis counts off a fast intro, he takes the first solo, and is then customarily folowed by Coleman and then Hancock. Mostly, the saxophonist and pianist get much more space to improvise than the leader chooses to take. On the first night, 'Stella By Starlight' goes at an amiable pace, which Hancock especially thrives on, his solo drifting from busy lines into extravagantly spaced, impressionist chords. 'Seven Steps To Heaven' bustles along, although the rhythm section cleverly halve the tempo at some points as a kind of breathing device, and it leads straight into a furiously fast 'No Blues', which gives Williams some solo space between Davis and Coleman. The saxophonist tends to run cycles of notes when he gets to a climactic moment and it can sound like pattern-playing, but technician that he is, he still finds a way out of it that sounds uncontrived.

On the second night, the material covers much of the rest of the Davis repertoire, including 'Autumn Leaves' – long and steady, with Coleman double-timing much of his solo; 'Milestones' – nuttily fast, with Williams's cymbals a blur and Davis, the bell of his horn engulfing the microphone, stingingly assertive; 'I Thought About You' – Coleman absent, and Davis pealing out luscious, severe open-horn phrases; 'Joshua' – back to maximum velocity, and Miles seeming to lose his way after a spectacular start to his solo, which he then rights again; 'All Of You' – a performance with superbly vivid solos by Davis and Coleman, yet directed largely by Carter, playing his ripest harmonic undertow, and Williams, who is brilliant behind each soloist, especially Coleman; 'Walkin'' – again fast and very long, with Davis falling back on a trademark lick where he moves up to a note that he then shakes like a fist, before Williams plays a riveting solo; and a final 'Bye Bye Blackbird' – Miles reducing the theme almost to Morse code before tossing around some quotes, Coleman and Hancock sailing through their solos, and an extended tag ending which is deliciously stretched out – before they work through a surprising six minutes of the perennial set-closer 'Bye Bye' (alias 'The Theme'). This was a band that didn't seem to want to stop playing.

On the final night, 'If I Were A Bell' and 'So What' were recorded via an ORTF broadcast and are also included on [3]. The standard is played at much the same tempo that Davis came to prefer, brisk but not overwhelmingly fast, and the trumpet solo is in a familiar shape to the ones he regularly played on this tune. Coleman's solo, while made up of passages which by themselves aren't especially striking, is typical of his quietly inventive approach to a long moment in the spotlight. He plays, in particular, a carefully paced phrase on one chorus which he then revisits, on a different chord, on the next. 'So What' is set at a slower tempo to the version from the first night, and is an altogether more expansive and thoughtful treatment, more in the mood of the original, even if Tony Williams still plays with his trademark urgency.

If Davis's repertoire had changed little, though, the way it was played by this group had at a stroke altered the shape and feel of Miles's music. Every piece was stretched out to a greater length: Coltrane used to take what people considered marathon solos, but now Coleman and Hancock were routinely going on at the same length, Carter and Williams sometimes soloed as well, and even Davis himself, often parsimonious with his own playing, had begun to take longer improvisations. Williams's ease at any tempo was making the music faster, more driving, more open to rhythmical complexity. Carter's unassuming virtuosity made him a less obvious presence than Chambers, but a more versatile and sophisticated contributor to the band. And Hancock, after his cautious start, was rapidly coming into his own. After pianists such as Garland, Evans and Kelly, Miles now had a player who could work in a style that could approximate any of his predecessors, yet which had its own ingenuities and daring. His solos were hard to predict before they began: on a fast tune he might play a kind of cool bebop, right-hand lines unfurling at a terrific pace, gentrified by a touch so even and calm – the legacy, perhaps, of his classical grounding – that he made every tone in the sequence ring with the same clarity. At ballad tempos, he could be elusive, even mysterious. But he might also collaborate with Carter and Williams in tactics which unsettled obvious musical routes: they were already working up novel ideas amongst themselves, trying switches of tempo or changes of emphasis, anything to break up the simple ching-chinga-ching of the post-bop rhythm section.

Davis and Coleman weren't much privy to these discussions. Davis liked a band that was trying new things anyway. For Coleman, it was rather different. Of all the Davis sidemen of the 1960s, he is arguably the least recognized, the most overlooked in terms of the quality of his input. Coleman wasn't any kind of revolutionary: his big, hearty sound had some of the gravitas of the swing masters as well as the more severe style of the Coltrane–Rollins generation. Arriving in the line-up after the lighter, more maverick Hank Mobley, he might have been thought by Davis followers to represent a switch back to the more muscular approach of Coltrane in particular. But George wasn't much of a

152

pathfinder. He had enough technique and innate drive to match anything that Coltrane could put out, but he had little of that musician's taste for the grand quest. On the music that has survived by this edition of the group, his playing is a rock-solid line to earth which perhaps stabilized the band at a time when its other members were looking for epiphanies of one sort or another.

In September, Davis and Gil Evans were asked to write and perform some music for a new play which was soon to open in San Francisco, *Time Of The Barracudas*. The partnership worked on the music for two weeks and recorded some thirteen minutes of it in Columbia's Hollywood studios on 9–10 October. The play was a flop and the music was scarcely heard, emerging only many years later as part of Columbia's unabridged Davis–Evans edition, *The Complete Columbia Studio Recordings* [5]. It consists of some twenty cues for the purposes of the play, stitched together with Evans's customary finesse, and as slight as it might be, a footnote to the famous collaboration, the playing is very beguiling, especially on the theme which would later re-emerge as one of Gil's favourite stock pieces, 'Hotel Me'. Davis plays with care and attention, and the musicianship of Carter and Williams, handling the rhythm work for the first time on a Davis–Evans recording, is gripping.

As 1964 came around, the quintet had run up plenty of road work and were a settled and impressive unit as well as a meeting of five strong individuals. But the music on *My Funny Valentine* [6] and *'Four' And More* [7], stands as the final official statement by this edition of the band. Both discs emanate from a single concert held at New York's Philharmonic Hall on 12 February 1964; they have also been combined as a two-disc set under the title *The Complete Concert*, but have latterly been restored to their original form in the latest CD incarnation.

Davis was about to turn thirty-eight years old – still a young man, even in jazz terms, and arguably at the peak of his powers as an instrumentalist at least. Although jazz was soon to begin wilting in the face of a boom in pop music – a development which the first American tour by the Liverpudlian group the Beatles was about to ignite – Davis, a cultured, cutting-edge black, found himself well placed to act as a sort of silent spokesman on issues he had previously summed up or commented on via a withering remark. It was a humid time in American society. Voter registration drives were being held in Mississippi and Louisiana, southern states which had held out against modern notions of equality and emancipation as a matter of course for decades. The NAACP (National Association for the Advancement of Colored People) was holding a series of events to raise funds to assist in the drives, and in one of them the Miles Davis quintet was performing at Philharmonic Hall.

The band were unhappy before they even took the stage. They hadn't played together for some weeks. Backstage, Davis calmly told the group it was a benefit and they wouldn't be paid. Ron Carter, for one, was furious: 'After a few moments of silence, I began to pack up my bass. I said I thought it was unfair that after being off for two or three weeks, he expected us to play for free at the first job back. So he asked how much we wanted.' In the end, Davis agreed to pay the band, and the ensemble moodily walked out on stage to a packed house. The CD package photographs show a dapper line-up of hand-somely dressed men in tuxedos and clean white shirts. If this was a protest concert, it was conducted with stringent decorum.

After the first half, the group walked off feeling even more dejected. Herbie Hancock remembered that 'the acoustics were very weird in that place. I think ours was the first jazz concert that had been performed there. The acoustics were so bad for us on stage, when I played a chord I couldn't hear anyone until the chord died down. So I played very cautiously.' Yet the music on the two live records which resulted is outstanding: heated, inspired, the fast tempos faster than a Davis band had ever played before, the slow tunes almost agonizingly felt and naked. Columbia decided to follow a bizarre course by programming one album of ballads and one of fast pieces, which resulted in one visit to the sepulchre being balanced by a speedfreak's delight. Taken together, as they should be, the music remains compelling.

Even if not always beguiling or even convincing, Davis's three choruses which open 'My Funny Valentine' are painfully dramatic. He works out a

154

tender, chilly variation on the opening measures of the melody and from there steps off into what sounds like a personal darkness, throwing out some of his most anguished-sounding cadences, hitting strange high notes and dying-away phrases that are fascinating but hardly beautiful. The sumptuous tone he had developed in the later part of the 1950s, and which is so effective in his Evans collaborations, has been traded for a more metallic, pinched feel which has at this point become his favourite. In comparison, Coleman's solo that follows has nothing of the same impact, even if its much more songful timbre is quietly effective, particularly on his last chorus. 'All Of You' pursues a more standard interpretation but is stretched out to almost fifteen minutes, while 'Stella By Starlight' returns to the more chastening mood of 'My Funny Valentine'. Davis often claimed to be playing music for music's sake, but these performances suggest more of a dramatic approach than a purely musical one. 'Stella' does, though, inspire a moving lamentation by the leader, again softened in its aftermath by Coleman's more conventional solo. 'I Thought About You' is a superb coda to the rest. Davis plays a crawling opening chorus which manhandles the melody as Williams impatiently tries to kick the group into time, only for the rhythm to fall away again, until Miles eventually accedes to the drummer picking up the pace. Coleman strolls in after the trumpeter abruptly drifts off some way into the first eight bars of the next chorus, and Hancock follows with a solo where he seems to play every phrase with absolute decision. Davis returns for a final tilt at the melody, which he sourly uproots. There is very little that is conventionally pretty on the record.

The 'fast' music of *'Four' And More* is close to relentless. 'So What' goes off at a furious pace, which scarcely lets up throughout the record, and 'Walkin'', which follows, sounds like it's even faster. It seems like a senseless piece of programming for Columbia to have sequenced the two records in this way, but it certainly makes for a thumping, in-the-face experience as far as the listener is concerned. Given the difficulties the group were having with the on-stage sound, it's all the more remarkable that the music is delivered at such a high level: Hancock, Carter and Williams play with an exultant confidence and

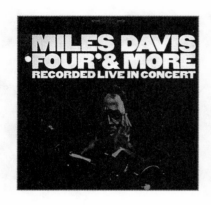

bravura. If there is a slight hint of weakness in the group on the quick numbers, it's in Davis's playing, ironically enough. In some of his solos he falls back on the same devices – trills, an arpeggiated rip to a splattery high note – in such a way that he seems careless about which tune he's playing or which way he's going with it. In comparison, this is George Coleman's moment. The variety he brought to the slow pieces at the concert is carried through to his improvising on the fast tunes, mixing long and short phrases, imposing his buffed, handsome tone on each line. Compare the angry buzz of Davis on 'Four' with Coleman's smoothly agile solo, surprisingly subtle in its dynamics.

Altogether quite some document. But it was the last of Coleman with Davis. He remembered: 'I gained a lot from being in the band. It was one of those situations where I used to be careful about harmonics, but then I began to get more adventurous, take some chances. One of the things that was really positive for me was I got the chance to stretch out.' But there was another side to 'fronting' the band. Though the surviving concert recordings suggest that Davis was leading by example, there were many other nights when his ailments were too painful for him to be standing and playing for long periods, and other times when, as often before, he simply lost interest in playing the full quota of club sets. Coleman had begun to dislike Miles's penchant for stardom, which didn't leave out the other band members so much as leave his own presence and playing unreliable. So he gave in his notice.

Davis had had an unhappy year thus far. His mother had died at the end of February. He and Frances were going through a stormy period in their relationship, when his jealousy and short temper could result in beatings and Frances at times fearing for her life. His physical condition was outwardly strong – he was, after all, still in his thirties, and he maintained a lightweight's trim physique – but the pain brought on by his condition was something he numbed with champagne and cocaine. Coleman's departure was, as usual, something he seemed unfazed by yet unprepared for. He still had Wayne Shorter on his mind, who had played on the session with Bob Dorough, but Shorter remained reluctant to leave Art Blakey, and Tony Williams was petitioning for the induction of Sam Rivers, a little-known saxophonist who had first built a reputation in Boston. At forty-four, Rivers would have been considerably older than anyone else in the band, but Williams liked his independent style, which had some of the free thinking which was starting to become a hot dialect in the New York jazz of that period. At the time, Rivers was working with – of all people – the blues guitarist T-Bone Walker, but with no other player even in the starting blocks and with another series of club dates already booked and almost upon him, Davis went with his drummer's pleading.

The sole surviving recording of this band was taken down at a concert in Tokyo, on 14 July (*Miles in Tokyo* [8]), before a tumultuously enthusiastic audience. Though the material is yet another parading of 'If I Were A Bell', 'My Funny Valentine', 'So What', 'Walkin'' and 'All Of You', this is another distinctive set. After the almost fuming energy of the Philharmonic Hall concert, this one is a good deal calmer and more restrained. Davis plays more thoughtfully and with the passionate intensity he had displayed in New York cut back to a less forbidding level. 'My Funny Valentine' offers one of his loveliest interpretations of the song, although it gathers a frosty severity as it goes on, and Rivers's solo is gently persuasive, leading to Hancock playing a soliloquy at the piano. The pianist contributes one of his most exploratory solos on 'So What', climaxing with him tunnelling through the lower sonorities on the keyboard, inspiring Williams to create an answering 'knock' on the tom, before the rhythm section wind up to bring back the horns – a dazzling example of their spontaneous empathy. 'Walkin'' finds Davis slipping back into the routine he'd worked up on this number, but is starred for Williams at his most powerful – his solo

sequence stops the show before he calmly returns to the beat and sets up Rivers. The saxophonist ought to be the main point of interest in this only recorded evidence of him with Davis, but as well as he plays, he does tend to sound like a fish if not out of water, at least in the wrong pool. The bop-blues of 'Walkin'' finds him refusing to play a single bebop phrase, his tone grey and lean, a bluesy grunt underpinning figures that sound harsh and peeled raw.Still, as his work on 'My Funny Valentine' suggests, he wasn't exactly playing free jazz, a movement which he has always been a conservative presence in.

Rivers didn't stay long in the band, although this was in part because he already had other commitments back home and wanted to fulfil these rather than remain in the quintet. It is hard to agree with Tony Williams's judgement that 'he changed the sound of the band before Wayne arrived' – the sound of the band was changing anyway, simply through the ever-increasing adventure which, in particular, Williams himself was introducing to the group's musical approach. Listening to these performances suggests that what Davis needed most wasn't an 'outside' player, but someone who could bring fresh material to the stand.

Which is what Wayne Shorter did, soon enough. Having pestered Shorter for months – in his own oblique way – Davis got his wish when the saxophonist was finally persuaded, as much by Herbie Hancock and Tony Williams as anyone else, to join the quintet. At thirty, Shorter was a young man already laden with playing experience. He had grown up in Newark, New Jersey, and had long been considered by friends and contemporaries as an amiable outsider, the youth who painted 'Mr Weird' on his saxophone case while still in high school. Fascinated by the sciences – especially astronomy – as much as by music, he first secured some prominence in a Maynard Ferguson small group, before his engagement by Art Blakey in 1959. Shorter had done long periods of practice with John Coltrane, who regarded him with an almost fatherly pride, and his early records – a few as a leader for the small Vee Jay label, and numerous dates with Blakey – suggested a Coltrane acolyte whose playing mixed the grand style of running the chords with a more oblique, unpredictable shaping of solos into periods of aggression, apprehension and repose. He could drop a flatulent honk into an otherwise gently prescribed passage, switch from boppish phrases to a funky, dancing delivery, and move from a loud flourish to an undecided silence. It was hard to think of another player who sounded quite like Wayne, even as he sounded like he had learned from many other players.

It was that individuality which in all likelihood appealed most to Davis, after years of fine but less maverick players such as Hank Mobley, George Coleman and Sam Rivers. He must also have heard the queer bag of compositions which Shorter had contributed to the Blakey book, including the likes of 'El Toro', 'Sleeping Dancer Sleep On', 'Lester Left Town' and 'Sincerely Diana'. Perhaps more than anything else, Davis needed Shorter as a new, strong composer.

To start with, though, Shorter was simply pitched into the standard regime of touring, with the same set the Davis quintet had now been playing for several years. A TV broadcast, in very cloudy sound, has preserved a version of 'No Blues' from 10 September, but the first real evidence of the new band comes in a number of recordings from the European tour which got under way a few weeks later. Columbia released a set recorded in Berlin on 25 September (*Miles In Berlin*) [9]. The sound is only monaural and isn't a great deal better than one of the unofficial tapes which captured the band at various points during its existence, but the music grips. Shorter's presence adds a dynamic and already authoritative ingredient to the personality mix. His solo on 'So What', taken at its now familiar headlong tempo, is riddled with strange turnings, holes, byways, asymmetrical shapes and darkly tinted tones: in its layerings and ambiguities, it exemplifies the complexity Shorter would begin bringing to Davis's music. If anything, this spurs Hancock – abetted by Carter and Williams – to take extra chances in his solo which follows. 'Stella By Starlight' is set up by one of Hancock's most thoughtful intros, and is then steeped by Davis in his particular stark melancholy, although the impact is a little spoiled by distortion in the sound. Shorter comes next with a solo that echoes Coltrane at some points, but otherwise takes – like Davis – a spare melodic journey through the ballad's structure, culminating in an almost straight reading of the final measures of the tune (which elicits great applause). The way is then left clear for Hancock to improvise a sequence that might as well have come out of Debussy. The quintet at its best, which renders the closing 'Walkin'' as something of an anti-climax.

The Paris date, *Paris, France* [10], though poorly recorded, is at least worth hearing. 'Stella By Starlight' follows a similar pattern, if a less decisive one, and 'Autumn Leaves' features some fine interplay between Davis and Williams, although the fidelity is at times so constricted that it's hard to hear what's going on. The German concert from Sindelfingen on 8 October (*Live In Sindelfingen 1964* [11]) is an improvement technically. 'Milestones' starts with a trumpet solo made up of startling, staccato bursts of sound mixed with long, irregularly placed rests. Shorter then picks up the initiative with an extraordinary note that sounds like some ancient field holler, which signals the rhythm section to fall into silence, before the group abruptly storm back into tempo. The saxophonist then toys with the main theme in a bleary, almost inebriated manner and Hancock plays a terse and attacking solo. This then turns into a jam on the regular 'No Blues', which climaxes with Hancock playing what is a surprising precursor of the kind of funk solos he would be habitually running through on his own records some years hence. In all, this lasts for seventeen minutes. 'All Of You' is an intricate meander, where the rhythm section play for stealth rather than propulsion. 'Joshua' is a focused, driving performance

160

throughout. On 'Autumn Leaves', Davis almost dances through his solo, complemented by the rhythm players doing some telepathic work behind him, and Shorter's brawny continuation is a gusting relief of tension. 'Oleo' is crisp and mercurial. 'Walkin'', from the same evening, is on *Seven Steps To Heaven* [12], an unauthorized release different to the Columbia album of the same name, though this follows much the same path as Davis was wont to pursue on this tune. Measure for measure, this music is at least the equal of the official Berlin release.

After their return to the US, Davis at last prepared for another studio recording, the first since *Seven Steps To Heaven*. The sessions for *E.S.P.* [13], recorded in January 1965, were produced by Irving Townsend in Los Angeles – Teo Macero was presumably still *persona non grata* – and featured seven new pieces. 'Agitation' is credited to Davis alone, and he also took a composer credit on 'E.S.P.' (though it sounds like a classic example of Shorter's writing), 'Iris' (ditto) and 'Eighty-One', which is otherwise a Carter composition. After the bustle and intensity of the concert recordings, this one emerges as an almost tentative beginning to the group's progress. Most of the pieces have a rather quiet, reined-in feel, appropriate perhaps for an entirely new set of written music. David and Shorter improvise with much of their expected daring, but there are no spectacular shouts or explosions from either musician. This is in keeping with a set of pieces that depend on simple melodic motifs, or sometimes hardly any melody at all. Carter's 'Eighty-One' relies on a bass riff that recurs through the track, but the horns roam freely. 'Agitation', the one piece which made it into Davis's regular concert set, starts with a thoughtful drum solo from Tony Williams, then has its nibbling melody parsed by Davis on muted trumpet, before the other players ruminate over pedal tones from Carter and

Miles Davis/E.S.P.

a stop-start rhythmical feel. 'Mood' befits its title: it seems all but shapeless, spun out of a four-note see-saw. Shorter's 'Iris' is one of his typically elusive melodies, the kind of mournful ballad form he would investigate extensively on his Blue Note records of the 1960s, and both he and Davis place beautifully cadenced solos on top of it. Hancock's 'Little One' seems like one of the pianist's introspective rambles, yet shifts gracefully into waltz-time for its solos. The most urgently delivered piece is 'E.S.P.' itself. Over Carter's fast walk, the soloists play strong improvisations that nevertheless knit with the air of apprehension the theme seems to generate, played as a unison by trumpet and saxophone with Shorter adopting a nervous high register.

Simply as a term, 'E.S.P.' sounded like it might be a manifesto for the way the group was intending to perform, as some kind of act of telepathy rather than a project run to strict musical rules, although it is more likely that Shorter chose the name out of his cosmological interests. Either way, the feel of the record, muted as it is, was a dramatic break from any previous Davis studio album. There were no standards and, with the modest exception of 'Eighty-One', little that had anything to do with the blues. Davis had spoken caustically of many of the free-jazz adventurers who were, by this time, in full flow in New York's musical environment, yet in its use of space, pulse, melody and abstraction, this was where the music of *E.S.P.* was heading, although it was couched in calmer and less openly dramatic form. The group, though, was still in the early stages of finding its collective feet. But the album didn't presage any burst of new activity because Davis's physical condition worsened significantly in the first months of 1965. The problems with his hip had become so intense that he was scarcely able to walk, and he had a bone graft operation in April which left him in a wheelchair and with one of his legs in a cast. He managed to break this leg again in August, and then returned to hospital to have an artificial hip joint inserted. It wasn't until November that he was able to contemplate regular work again.

The Complete Live At The Plugged Nickel

COLUMBIA

**If I Were A Bell; Stella By Starlight; Walkin';
I Fall In Love Too Easily; The Theme; My Funny Valentine; Four;
When I Fall In Love; Agitation; Round Midnight; Milestones;
The Theme; All Of You; Oleo; I Fall In Love Too Easily; No Blues;
I Thought About You; The Theme.**

Miles Davis (*t*); Wayne Shorter (*ts*); Herbie Hancock (*p*);
Ron Carter (*b*); Tony Williams (*d*). 22/12/65.

**If I Were A Bell; Stella By Starlight; Walkin'; I Fall In Love Too
Easily; The Theme; All Of You; Agitation; My Funny Valentine;
On Green Dolphin Street; So What; The Theme; When I Fall In Love;
Milestones; Autumn Leaves; I Fall In Love Too Easily; No Blues;
The Theme; Stella By Starlight; All Blues; Yesterdays; The Theme.**

As above. 23/12/65.

Chicago's Plugged Nickel, on North Wells Street, remained the favourite haunt of Davis in that city, and as usual he had himself booked into that part of the country during the Christmas season. The club played host to the Davis group for some two weeks. It was a popular and, as jazz clubs go, successful place: it did good business for much of the 1960s, even during periods when the music wasn't much of a commercial draw, and only closed later in the following decade. Davis told Teo Macero that it would be an appropriate time to record the quintet, and Columbia duly set up equipment to take down a couple of nights' worth of music, but at the last minute – just as he had done at Carnegie Hall four years earlier – the trumpeter changed his mind. Macero, by now fed up with Davis's capricious attitude, was ready to have all the expenses charged against the artist's royalties, but in the end Davis relented and the recording went ahead. As a result, Columbia's engineers took down all the music played on the nights of 22 and 23 December, seven sets in total. It is probably the most comprehensive account of a jazz group at work, at length, to have been documented thus far in the busy story of making jazz records. Ron Carter suggested that it gives the listener the chance 'to hear all the train wrecks, and all the rockets take off, too'.

Davis had been grumbling about the problems of working in clubs for a long time. His difficulty remained that there was, at this point, no real alternative if the band was going to get regular and repeated work. The college and concert circuit was lucrative enough, but it hadn't opened up consistently to jazz groups and there weren't enough gigs to keep the band in business. As princely as the quintet was, it still had to perform in the system that club work demanded, which meant multiple sets per night and obeisance to club owners and audiences that Davis himself seemed to regard – in a remark he once made to Max Gordon, proprietor of New York's Village Vanguard – as 'a plantation'. Thus the Columbia engineers were able to record a huge amount of music across the two evenings – it was no more than two typical nights' work. Most of it the label sat on for literally decades. A single record was released in Japan in 1976, and a more expanded edition was issued in America in 1982 (and even then several of the tracks were given some hamfisted editing). In the end, a full eight CDs' worth of music was issued as a complete edition in 1995, thirty years after it had been created.

No other musical art form asks quite as much of its performing artists as jazz, in its unadorned club setting. Davis and the rest of the quintet were booked into the Plugged Nickel between 21 December 1965 and 2 January 1966. They were off on 24–25 December for the Christmas holiday, had a further day off on the 28th, but otherwise played the period as a continuous booking. The band without Davis also did a matinee show on Sundays. And straight after the Plugged Nickel residency, they were performing again in New York, working at the Village Vanguard for much of January and the first week of February.

As exhaustive as the Plugged Nickel set appears to be, this was just two nights out of ten, where the musicians were expected to play a physically and mentally demanding music in front of a modest audience, who may or may not have been paying attention, who might have heckled or otherwise behaved in a disrespectful way, and who may have been more interested in their drinks or their dates than what was being created for their listening pleasure. Applause could be scattered or muted. The work would have started early in the evening and ended in the small hours of the morning. This was a long time for tired hands to wield drumsticks and fatigued lips to blow into mouthpieces. Although Williams and Hancock were still young and relatively fresh faces on the club circuit, Carter, Shorter and Davis himself were veterans of this working environment who had few illusions about its capacity to belittle and demean the finest efforts of singular artists.

Which makes the sustained creativity displayed across the eight CDs of the Plugged Nickel music all the more astonishing for its intensity, grace, passion and, perhaps most exceptional of all, its consistent high spirits engendered by the level of group interplay. Some of the later sessions begin to droop, as the night has worn on and tiredness of one sort or another takes its toll, but there is always something going on which takes the ear. Club gigs, as every follower of the music knows, are a mixture of artisanship and occasional flashes of inspiration. Whatever repertoire is under musical discussion by the players, much of it is made up of practised routine, a falling back on patterns that are recognizable as safety nets, and tried formulae which the players know will fill up space – because there is always a lot of space to fill, if the job entails hours of playing music. Davis and his group were still playing variations on the set-list which had now been in place for many years – 'Walkin'' was a tune that Davis had been playing nightly for something like ten years. A record had been completed of new material, but only 'Agitation' was deemed suitable by the leader to be an addition to the live set. One could be forgiven for expecting the quintet to merely take care of business during the residency.

Instead, the five musicians constantly change, evolve and shift the parameters of their music. The only way to really introduce a dramatic change into a repertoire which had been so thoroughly investigated by several editions of the Davis quintet was to begin to break down its structures altogether, to move towards a position where it scarcely mattered where one tune ended and another began, to disperse the received wisdom about a tune – how it was 'meant' to sound, what sort of climate of feeling it was supposed to exist in – and use it as a starting point for some much more individual and one-of-a-kind performance. What if, for instance, 'My Funny Valentine', by now a premier example of the popular ballad as a vehicle for jazz lyricism, could be shorn of its moony sentimentality and recast as something much more intense and profound? This was a tune Davis had been closely associated with via his comparatively sedate (if classic) Prestige version, and admirers probably looked forward to his variations on that approach. Even the bleak, stricken poignancy of the Philharmonic Hall version, which gave the title to the album of music from that concert, was a recognizable development of his other treatments of the tune.

The 'My Funny Valentine' played at the Plugged Nickel – second set, first night – is nothing like any of those. Hancock plays a breath-holding introduction. Davis starts it so slowly that the rest between his first and second phrases starts to sound as if it will go on for ever. He then crawls through a solo which refers teasingly to the melody at just a few spots. The rhythm section bring the tempo in, but Davis still leaves as many rests as placed notes, and although the music eventually falls into a familiar shape, the trumpeter introduces a mocking, ugly edge into his tone which threatens to make a gargoyle out of Richard Rodgers's melody. Hancock chords serenely in the background, and finds his own dialogue with Williams, the two men securing a rocking counterpoint to Davis at one point while Carter acts as the line to earth, walking imperturbably. A full eight minutes have gone by before Davis eventually decides – seemingly abruptly – that he's said enough, and Shorter steps up. He abstracts a few phrases out of the melody before building a solo which patterns a different melodic circuit out of the tune that, ingeniously, eventually leads back to the original melody, which earns him some warm applause. Carter then plays half a chorus of his own, faintly goaded by Williams's brushwork, and Davis returns (with a mis-hit lemon) and settles the melody back down again. Before anyone has realized it's over, 'My Funny Valentine' is gone and the quintet have shifted into 'Four'.

The following night, Davis called the tune once more, again on the second set. This is a more easygoing treatment, drifting comfortably into tempo in the first chorus, and though Davis throws some slurring, argumentative edges into his solo, it follows a more straightforward path until the forcing, harshly coloured phrases which wind it up. Wayne Shorter refers to both the original melody and to Duke Ellington's 'In A Sentimental Mood' in his opening chorus, before shifting between what seem like two solos, a commentary on the original tune and a wilder investigation of some scale patterns. This time Hancock moves up to take the next solo, which is in his customary thoughtful manner, and even though Williams tries to unsettle the placid momentum, the pianist paves the way unerringly for the trumpet's return to resolve the tune.

What the doubtless many other versions of the song which were played over the Plugged Nickel residency were like, one can only guess at. On the evidence of the continuous variation which all the material over these two nights was subjected to, it was more of the same – nothing ever really in the same vein twice. Previously, Davis groups had settled for the rewards of small alterations of detail and nuance when approaching the familiar cargo of material. Without surrendering that refinement, this band was pushing on into whole new areas of music. Their confidence was at a peak: there didn't seem anything they couldn't try, or make work for them. Wayne Shorter later remembered that 'When we came off, we couldn't say nothing to each other. We were lethargic in a princely way. It was like, "let's not touch this". You were in the royalty of the moment, and such royalty need never be tampered with.'

Not that everything works, or is properly resolved or realized. The compelling matter is how much they try, how many ideas are tossed out, half-worked, some parts left unexploited, some pushed too far, but everything heated and uplifted by the daring and the executive skill. The five members of the group all emerge as individuals, with different sets of strengths and vulnerabilities – it seems churlish to describe them as 'weaknesses' – which intertwine to form the most remarkable collective jazz could have known at this point. In comparison, such groups as John Coltrane's quartet or Charles Mingus's ensemble seem top-heavy with the influence of their reigning maestro. Davis was unflinchingly the leader, yet he let each of the other men have so much leeway that the band was in effect a particularly vivid kind of cooperative.

Wayne Shorter especially emerges in this set as an improviser of uncanny mastery. Years of playing had given him an exceptionally appealing saxophone tone, tenacious and muscular yet able to touch on a lovely sonority too, and that helped make ideas which might have sounded outlandish coming from other horn players instead emerge with an authority and a buttonholing immediacy that convince you that, well, maybe it wasn't such a strange idea after all. Herbie Hancock is, along with Ron Carter, the quiet, underscoring strength in the group. Where previous Davis pianists had been skilful compers and adroit feeds, always ready to give the soloist a helping hand, Hancock goes his own way, all but standing apart from whoever's out front, yet remaining a binding and sympathetic presence. Where everyone else bar the bassist plays loud, Hancock is soft and insinuating – which, again, doesn't mean that his ideas are any less surprising and original. A bass player could hardly expect to match the other players in this group in terms of standing out, and Ron Carter knew that this wasn't his task. What he does is exert control. At moments when the other four could be anywhere but the centre of the music, Carter is there as the integrating force. He carries the beat when everyone else ignores it, or sounds a tone centre when the others have drifted far from it. Basses were still not recorded too well on jazz records, but his loamy, pliable tone keeps coming out of the dark.

Tony Williams continues to push back the barrier on how daring a drummer could be in a group that wasn't quite a free-jazz band. He is less respectful and more challenging than he was on the group's earlier records. Of all the members of the quintet, he is the one who sometimes suggests a musician who is trying too hard (he was, it should be remembered, still only nineteen) – occasionally his changes of pace and emphasis and his denial of the 'old' functions of the jazz drummer fail the music. But that should be set against the many inspirational things he tries, even if they don't always come off. It never appears to bother Davis, who seems to thrive off Williams more than any other member of the group. Still, it should be remembered, working his way back from a long lay-off, Miles isn't always playing at his best across these two nights: sometimes his tone has gone too sour, the deliberately disfigured sound on ballads more perverse than creative, and there are moments when one feels that the group is almost too good for him – Shorter can sound more at home than the leader does. But one always feels that, even when he's silent or merely preparing an entry, Davis is overseeing his men with his baleful authority, and it wouldn't be the same without him. One wonders what one of the quartet matinees sounded like.

The most appropriate way to hear this music is to play the CDs end-to-end – or at least, the Friday discs in one stint, and the Saturday ones in another.

That gives some approximation of how the group had to sustain itself during a long night's work. As it goes on, the music becomes more dishevelled – the final set on Saturday in particular presents a band at times ready to fall asleep on the stand, yet still rousing its collective strength to distil a thoroughly engaging set out of fatigue and nerve ends – and a more graphic portrayal of an ensemble mixing high art and dutiful contractual commitment. Friday's third set includes an amiably swinging 'All Of You'; an 'Oleo' which Tony Williams pushes to its speed limit – Hancock, seemingly numbed, sits out altogether on the trumpet solo; 'I Fall In Love Too Easily', something of a newcomer to the Davis book, and a skilful but drooping reading compared to one the band had played in its first set; 'No Blues', which runs on past the seventeen-minute mark, where Davis seems to be in an audible scrap with Williams, and the rhythm section mutates the groove over and over again across the course of the piece; 'I Thought About You', commenced by Davis in his pinchiest tone, traversing a complex terrain that moves in and out of ballad tempo, and where, towards the end, Davis returns for a single phrase, lays out, listens to several audience members telling him to 'Play it, Miles!', does nothing for a long time, and finally consents to wrap it up; and a final and almost abstract (or distracted) version of 'The Theme', stretched out to eight minutes. They may have been tired, but it sounds like the music didn't want to let them go.

170

The soundmix of *Live At The Plugged Nickel* remains imperfect. Herbie Hancock is too far down in the mix throughout, and in consequence many of his felicities are dulled. Williams, inevitably, is often too high, and Davis is so upfront that some of the acidity in his tone sounds overdone at times. If anything, all this adds to the feel of being present at the occasion: nobody ever gets to hear a perfect mix in a club anyway.

Davis didn't get to complete his residency at the Village Vanguard. He was forced back into hospital on 31 January 1966, this time with a liver ailment, and after being discharged spent the next three months doing little other than sitting round the house and going for walks. His relationship with Columbia wasn't in the best of health, either. Although the Plugged Nickel concerts had represented a bounty for the company, nothing from them would be released for more than ten years. There was still a lingering feeling at the company that another collaboration with Gil Evans should be pursued, mainly because their previous albums had been such a sales success, and in fact Davis had already received an advance for such a record. But no music had so far been forthcoming.

Instead, Davis eventually went back on the road with the quintet. Ron Carter had become a hot property on the New York session scene – like the rest of Davis's group, he hadn't been idle during the trumpeter's enforced long absence of the previous year, and had quickly built up a lucrative career as a sessionman – and disliked going out for extended stays away from the East Coast, so while out West in May and June Davis sometimes had to call on Richard Davis or Gary Peacock as bassist subs. A single concert, in Portland, Oregon, exists as a recording (*No (More) Blues* [14]). On 'Stella By Starlight', Davis plays a long solo that starts with starkly spaced notes and moves into overdrive above a veritable firestorm from Williams, and 'Agitation' is another tempest. But the sound is very shabby, and on his only documented appearance with the trumpeter's quintet, Richard Davis is virtually inaudible most of the time. On 4 July, the group appeared at the by now long-established Newport Jazz Festival, but this time the group's music had little impact beyond the day itself. Nevertheless, as a unit the quintet continued to grow in confidence and ability, and its next studio record opened up the possibility of breaking further new ground.

The Other Records

1 *Seven Steps To Heaven* (Columbia)
2 *Live In St Louis And Paris 1963* (Golden Age Of Jazz)
3 *Côte Blues* (Jazz Music Yesterday)
4 *Miles Davis In Europe* (Columbia)
5 *Miles Davis & Gil Evans: The Complete Columbia Studio Recordings* (Columbia)
6 *My Funny Valentine* (Columbia)
7 *'Four' And More* (Columbia)
8 *Miles In Tokyo* (Columbia)
9 *Miles In Berlin* (Columbia)
10 *Paris, France* (Moon)
11 *Live In Sindelfingen 1964* (Golden Age Of Jazz)
12 *Seven Steps To Heaven* (Jazz Door)
13 *E.S.P.* (Columbia)
14 *No (More) Blues* (Jazz Door)

A Fine Madness

1966–7

The next Davis record eventually emerged under the name *Miles Smiles* [1], with a threadbare cover design of a beaming Davis boxed in under the title. Any listener searching for logic or consistency in the quintet's development would have been surprised by the compositions chosen. There were three new originals by Shorter and one by Davis, but there were also two tunes contributed by a pair of saxophonists: Eddie Harris's catchy 'Freedom Jazz Dance' and a piece by Jimmy Heath, 'Gingerbread Boy', which would become a staple number called on by groups looking for a useful bebop theme to jam on.

The record did, though, cohere into a whole which makes it one of the most satisfying documents by this edition of the quintet. For one thing, Davis sounds in much better heart than he did during the Plugged Nickel sessions. His sound is rounder and more groomed, and his phrasing has returned to its old decisiveness. Shorter's playing remained at his customary high level, each of his solos following unpredictable paths without suggesting anything that intentionally jars with his surroundings – a very different approach to the sort of deliberately combative freedoms some of the free-jazz musicians were then putting forward. But the most striking characteristic of the disc is the further developments going on in the rhythm section. Herbie Hancock plays less and less as a member of the ensemble and more as a soloist. On long sequences of the music, he lays out altogether, because there isn't much for him to do: with the bare modalities on show in the writing and the lack of preset harmonic directions, the piano has lost its role as the feed to the soloists. On theme statements such as that on 'Dolores', Wayne Shorter's edgy melody which the two horns harmonize across a series of sections of varying length, Hancock isn't even there. Below, one hears the regularly astonishing ferment that Carter and Williams are cooking up between them.

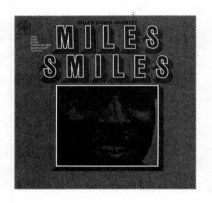

The bassist and drummer had already set down performances that suggested new ways for the rhythm section to operate in a post-bop jazz small group. On *Miles Smiles* they inch a little further forward. The only piece taken at anything resembling a ballad tempo, 'Circle', is the most conventional from a rhythmical point of view, and is of interest mostly for the lyrical improvising of Davis and Shorter. Everything else makes manifest the further adventures of Carter and Williams. The bassist realizes that Williams is purposely getting further away from the drummer's expected timekeeping role, and he compensates by anchoring the ensemble even more tightly, though not rigidly. This comes across best, perhaps, in 'Footprints', one of Shorter's three originals and one of the most enduring of all his many compositions. Following the yearning melody statement carried by trumpet and tenor – and there is a brilliant bit of business on the final measures, where Williams suddenly rushes the beat and Carter plays in a fast four himself, a pattern they return to on the same bars of each succeeding chorus – the drummer strays all over the place in accompanying the soloists, carrying much of the pulse on his cymbals, retarding and then quickening the time again, using the drums for dramatic interpolations and cross-pattern playing, or lighting a sudden firework on his crash cymbal as a solo reaches a particularly demonstrative point. Throughout a tempestuous performance, Carter hangs on to a 6/4 riff which keeps the music smartly focused.

The two compositions credited to hands other than those in the quintet conclude the record, and offer some of the most striking music. 'Freedom Jazz Dance' had been something of a hit on a record which had come out the previous year, by Eddie Harris, a Chicagoan saxophonist. (Harris was no stranger to that kind of success, having enjoyed a million-selling hit some years earlier with his version of the theme from the movie *Exodus*. He was a canny and talented musician, and his move towards his own kind of fusion later in the decade was in its way a maverick parallel to the course Davis would follow.) Harris's theme, a clever blues motif cast in a call-and-response style, is made to seem anything but down-home in the quintet's treatment. Filled out by Hancock's doomy, tolling chords, Carter's stockpiling of busy riffs and Williams basing his contribution on a continuous though uneven roll on the snare, it's a tautly blazing rendition. On the record, it moves into 'Gingerbread Boy', an even more power-packed performance. Williams here stokes his cymbals up to something close to incandescence, the listening Carter reverts to his skilful fast walk, and Davis in particular turns in his most biting solo of the date. With Hancock again laying out for most of the performance, this doesn't sound much like the Miles Davis quintet. Instead, it dawns soon enough that it resembles the Ornette Coleman quartet of 'Ramblin''. As he does on several of the tracks on the record, Davis begins talking to Teo Macero in the control room before the last note has even died away. The last sound on the record is Miles calling, 'Teo...Teo...Teo...' At least they were talking again.

Recorded over two days in October 1966, *Miles Smiles* presaged a period when Davis would be much more active in the studios. In January 1967, he took the surprise step of adding a second saxophonist to the group, the tenor player Joe Henderson, who remained with the band until April, during which time the group toured extensively in one of the jazz package shows that were then still popular in America, the World Series Of Jazz. Frustratingly, nothing by this edition of the band seems to have survived as either an unofficial or an authorized recording. Then there was a stint on the West Coast, again without Ron Carter, and Davis used either Albert Stinson or Buster Williams as a deputy bassist. Williams actually took part in a recording date during this period, when, on 9 May, Davis took the quintet into Columbia's Los Angeles studio and set down a number of titles, none of which he eventually approved of. The only issued survivor, 'Limbo', eventually turned up on a sampler of previously unheard tracks, *Directions* [2], which emerged in 1981 (presumably other music still exists in Columbia's archives and will be released at some point). Another one of Shorter's elusive, faintly melancholy melodies, it has a more expansive feel than the version that would eventually turn up on *Sorcerer*, and Williams fits right in. This time, Hancock is fully involved, playing almost in the front line throughout.

Davis went straight back into the studio on his return to New York, where he recorded the tracks which were eventually gathered into the album *Sorcerer* [3]. The title track was a Herbie Hancock tune named in honour of his bandleader, and most of the other tunes were penned by Wayne Shorter, although there is

also one by Tony Williams, 'Pee Wee', which for some reason Davis doesn't even play on. It was rounded out by the incongruous inclusion of the leftover track from the date with Bob Dorough from several years earlier, 'Nothing Like You': presumably Teo Macero was looking for a fill-up, and he remembered that track.

The record suggests something of how giants can be vulnerable too. The compositions are strong and provocative, the playing has skill and heat, the interaction pretends to the high level that was now commonplace for the quintet: yet somehow the results seem flat compared to most of their other studio recordings. With the record lacking a single standout of the order of 'Footprints', the listener waits for peak moments which never arrive. 'Vonetta' is a characteristic Shorter ballad, phrased in his best lyric style with his usual dash of obliqueness, and it's handsomely explored by Davis and Shorter, yet Williams's contribution – which consists mainly of a series of quiet though martial snare rolls – seems oddly inappropriate, a rare example of the quintet's use of contrast within the ensemble for once sounding wrong. 'Prince Of Darkness' is a kind of ballad, too, though it shifts through several situations: for Davis's solo, which has some of his best playing on the record, the music remains in the medium-up mode, but behind Shorter and Hancock, who plays with a beautifully spare eloquence, Carter and Williams try different things. 'Pee Wee', the tune which Davis sits out, sounds like Williams copying Shorter: these sorts of pastel moods, where weak melodies are bolstered by an at least interesting underlying harmony (something Herbie Hancock was always very good at pointing up), have become familiar as ballad settings in acoustic jazz in the past three decades. 'Masqualero' is meant to possess a Spanish tinge, but listeners will struggle to hear it in a piece that has an uncountable tempo and tends to resolve around a piano lick which Hancock tinkers with as the soloists play. 'The Sorcerer' itself has the novelty of trumpet and saxophone in a solo dialogue that has the feel of an extended chase chorus, each man playing eight bars before the other takes over. Hancock remains silent at the keyboard during this passage, which is otherwise a rarity on the record: his extended absences as on *Miles Smiles* seem to have been abandoned for the moment.

On the cover of the record was a photograph, in profile, of the actress Cicely Tyson, whom Miles had known and quietly courted for a number of years. His marriage to Frances, celebrated by her appearance on the covers of both *Someday My Prince Will Come* and *E.S.P.*, had ended with her departure from their New York home (they were finally divorced early in 1968). But Davis made no specific commitment to Tyson. In the meantime, he was still plagued by his health problems, his arthritic joints continuing to cause him much pain. He talked fruitlessly with Gil Evans about further collaboration work – at one point, a rumour went round that they were finally going to have a working big band together – but it came to nothing. The quintet remained his principal focus. For all its magnitude, despite all the staggering ideas and results it had created during its existence thus far across scores of performances, there was still relatively little by the band which the Miles Davis follower could hear – three studio recordings were all that were available at that time. Yet the group was pushing on towards its apogee.

Nefertiti

COLUMBIA

Nefertiti; Fall; Hand Jive; Madness; Riot; Pinocchio.
Miles Davis (*t*); Wayne Shorter (*ts*); Herbie Hancock (*p*); Ron Carter (*b*); Tony Williams (*d*). 7–23/6/67.

*N*efertiti is probably the least known of all of Davis's great records. Prepared and recorded just prior to the period which would produce the more epochal *In A Silent Way*, it was the last great statement by the acoustic quintet, a band whose intense levels of creativity must have seemed, at times, impossible to sustain. The free flow of ideas which nurtured the group through its period of existence ought to have drained most musicians, and in later years it was indeed suggested (in a famous piece by the *New York Times* writer Peter Keepnews) that the creativity of the band was so overwhelming that its constituent members took the path of jazz-rock as a kind of cop-out, the simplicities of that music absolving them from the demands this situation had placed on them. Recorded over three studio sessions, the music seems to be a kind of summing-up of where the quintet had been and a hint of where Davis would go next, in its gentle, timeless moments.

These occur mostly in the three Wayne Shorter compositions (Davis, again, took no compositional credit on the record). On Tony Williams's 'Hand Jive', the quintet is in its familiar up-tempo mould. The theme is dispensed with swiftly and then there are solos in turn by Davis, Shorter – both with only bass and drums in support – and Hancock, the whole performance powered by Williams at his most impetuous: often it is as if the group are relentlessly accelerating down a gradient where only Carter, often clinging on via pedal points, has some idea where the brakes are. Hancock's following 'Madness' has some of the same feel of the drummer rushing the beat, although this piece is distinguished by an especially fine solo by Davis, steadily shifting towards a high-note climax which then falls away into a kind of crestfallen silence as he winds down from it. Shorter then takes over and Hancock seems undecided whether to accompany him or not, pecking out a few chords before leaving the stage to the saxophonist. The music all but comes to a stop as Hancock then begins a section where he has some dialogue with Carter, then tempts bass and drums into giving him a springboard to move back into tempo. This is a beautifully clean, pointed performance by all hands, the notes deftly chosen and unpredictably placed, and when the horns briefly state the theme a final time over a curious discordant vamp, the seemingly inappropriate title takes on an eerie relevance. Is this what a fine madness sounds like?

Hancock's 'Riot' follows – he also recorded this in a longer and more diffuse version on his *Speak Like A Child* album for Blue Note, but here it is despatched in a whisker over three minutes. Over a beat from Williams that resembles a fast shuffle, Shorter and Davis play brief solos which are this time thickened and embellished by a densely chorded counterpoint from Hancock, who then embarks on his own improvisation before being interrupted by the horns restating the theme. One might expect this to have a curt, unfinished feel, but the track seems to exist for as long as it needs to.

Good as those three pieces are, Shorter's three compositions lift the album on to a higher level altogether. It was supposedly Davis's idea for the melody of 'Nefertiti' itself to be played over and over by the horns, with no consequent improvising by trumpet and tenor: instead, the major variations come from the playing of piano, bass and drums. The mournfully lovely theme is repeated again and again, across almost eight minutes, and even as Hancock, Carter and Williams ebb and flow in their responses, so do Davis and Shorter soften or increase their volume, at one point Shorter falling a beat behind his leader so the theme sounds contrapuntal. A penultimate interlude leaves the music to piano, bass and drums, before the horns return for a final reprise and leave the very last word to Williams, who raps out two parting strokes on the snare. An extraordinary piece of music.

'Fall' is, if anything, an even more attractive melody, ascending to a tag which trumpet and tenor keep returning to. At first Davis improvises around the line while Shorter holds it, and then, after Hancock's charming solo, their roles are reversed (and Davis has inserted the Harmon mute). Carter eventually becomes the lead improvising voice as the horns gently reiterate the melody a few final times and Williams scuttles his brushes towards silence. Finally comes 'Pinocchio', a more straightforward swinger, the wriggling melody used as a framing device for the horn solos. In his outing, Shorter then gets into a position where he is effectively trading bars with the drummer. The track ends too quickly, after barely five minutes, when it feels as if the players could easily have sustained a much longer performance.

Nefertiti apotheosizes a number of things about the quintet. Tony Williams never had a better studio sound on his records with Miles than he gets here: the cymbals have an extra degree of shimmer, he is upfront without drowning out the others, and the sound of his drums has a tunefulness which isn't as clear on their other records. Wayne Shorter plays with unerring invention and displays one of the most compelling tenor sounds of the time, dark but not grainy, elegant but never lacking in muscle or assertiveness. His writing had already reached a formidable level, and his input here only underlined what a remarkable period he was moving through as a composer (something his Blue Note albums also demonstrated). Davis himself played at least as well as he did on any of the quintet's records, his sound restored to its proper radiance.

Most of all, the record speaks with a seriousness and purpose which was particularly rare in its time. Having all but abandoned the older repertoire – though Miles and his men continued to play some of the warhorses in their live set – in the new material the group didn't bother to approximate the simple emotional appeal of tunes such as 'Bye Bye Blackbird' or 'My Funny Valentine'. As lyrical as a composer such as Shorter could be, lyricism was beside the point. Some musicians were dismayed at the quintet's sequence of records and complained that they sounded too samey, too much from the same cloth: what Davis sought was a consistency of tone, a movement away from peaks and troughs and obvious light and shade, just as he had shifted his live set towards playing continuous music rather than performing one tune and breaking for the next. For all its variety of tempo and thematic material, *Nefertiti* does emerge as a single entity, a work of movements.

It was a mixed time in the jazz mainstream. Cannonball Adderley's group remained one of the most popular, with its emphasis on communicating with its audience, Cannonball's genial on-stage presence setting the tone, and the music blending the upbeat feel of funk and soul with a more literate core of jazz improvisation. On the black club circuit, organ combos continued to be very popular, led by men such as Jack McDuff, Jimmy Smith, Johnny Hammond and Don Patterson: their bluesy, down-home style sounded perfect on what came to be called the chitlin circuit, a clubland where audiences expected a dose of hot, funky entertainment from their musician entertainers. At the high-art end of the music, musicians such as Albert Ayler, Archie Shepp and Pharoah Sanders played a fierce, free style that seemed to chime with the mood of unrest that was abroad in a changing American society.

Nefertiti came from neither direction. It summed up all of the orthodoxies as well as the apparent contradictions in Davis's position. Although still roundly settled in the interactive small-group situation that Davis had favoured for many years, it had unshackled so many of the restrictions which that setting normally imposed that it was close to a free ensemble. Although brimming with creative energy, *Nefertiti* often chose to express this with quiet and restraint. While each of the members of the band was accomplished to the point of being among the leading virtuosos on his instrument, it wasn't their individuality that emerged, but the sound of the group as a unit. When looking back on those years, Miles's sidemen later reminisced how a wrong turning could be righted, how there sometimes seemed to be nothing 'correct' to play, how sounds and feelings rather than chords and melodies had begun to shape the decision-making in the music. *Nefertiti* chronicles some of that

adventuring with the added polish of high studio craft and, perhaps, Teo Macero's skilful focusing of the group. It is the quintet at its most finished.

For that reason, it might also be the last Davis record to find significant favour among the audience which liked the 'old' Miles best. Before the year was out, the trumpeter had begun to move towards a position that was a decisive break with the jazz tradition which, for all his chafing against it, he was at this point still personifying.

Three other pieces were recorded during the same period as the *Nefertiti* sessions, but only saw the light of day in 1976, when they were released as half of the patchwork release *Water Babies* [4]. All three were Wayne Shorter compositions, and the saxophonist clearly didn't wish to see them consigned to oblivion, since he revived all of them for his 1969 Blue Note album *Super Nova*. 'Water Babies' itself was recorded at the same session as 'Nefertiti' and is a wistful theme which has the feel of a waltz, without quite falling into that metre. Hancock lays out a recurring cycle of chords which Davis and then Shorter decorate. 'Capricorn' works from an even barer setting, the theme cursorily spelt out by the horns before the solos, and with Hancock not playing until his lightly fingered solo the mood has gone back to the music of *Miles Smiles*. Davis seems to have little to say on this piece, for once noodling rather aimlessly around Carter's propulsive line, and the major statement comes from the composer. The most interesting of the three, though, is 'Sweet Pea', possibly named for Billy Strayhorn, Duke Ellington's composing partner, who had died a few weeks earlier. The piece has a spare, doomy feel, accentuated by Williams here playing mainly on his snare in a series of broken martial figures that hark back to some of the parade music of *Sketches Of Spain*. This is a piece which is strikingly different to anything else on *Nefertiti*, and it would have made a more than worthwhile addition to that record: but at almost nine minutes in length, it was too long to find a place there.

Davis and the quintet toured Europe in the autumn of 1967, and again a few recordings have survived. The only easily accessible one comes from a concert in Paris on 6 November (*No Blues* [5]). The music draws on a mix of the very old – 'Round Midnight', 'On Green Dolphin Street', 'I Fall In Love Too Easily' and even the now ancient 'Walkin'' – and the new, including 'Masqualero' and 'Riot'. Mostly, though, the quintet seems content to continue investigating familiar terrain and extracting the last ounces of juice out of even these pieces. 'Round Midnight' commences with Davis in his lonely balladeer mode before the music is comprehensively exploded by Tony Williams and Wayne Shorter plays a solo which is thick with upwardly curling phrases. From there the set expands and contracts around its chosen material like a beating heart. 'No Blues' has a drum solo and a storming dialogue between Shorter and Williams. 'Masqualero' has what sounds like Hancock reaching into the piano's innards to pluck some koto-like counterpoint. 'I Fall In Love Too Easily' departs so completely from its moorings that Hancock's quiet reprise of the chord sequence towards the end is shocking. The sense that the musicians could almost be playing on anything, that it scarcely matters which thematic fragment they might be starting from, displays how far Davis was prepared to go in evading predetermined routes. 'Walkin'', which has its theme hurried out of earshot within seconds, has long since lost any meaning with regard to its origins. Yet the playing throughout the concert is thoroughly absorbing, Davis himself playing with great commitment, and though Carter suffers as usual in the live soundmix, it is well worth finding.

It was an altogether remarkable tour, one of the last jazz touring extravaganzas of its time: the promoter, George Wein, had billed it as the Newport Jazz Festival in Europe, and besides the Davis quintet there were such established stars as Thelonious Monk, Sarah Vaughan and a Newport All Stars group, as well as young bands led by Archie Shepp and Gary Burton. When Davis played at London's Hammersmith Odeon, he was on the same bill as Archie Shepp's quintet, and Londoners have never forgotten the incendiary mix of Shepp's fuming free jazz and Davis's equally intense though much less confrontational music.

But on his return to the US in November, Davis found himself at another crossroads. Long used to being a pacesetter and a man whose every note had been followed, he was now, at forty-one, an ageing veteran whose stock was wobbling. Jazz had gone into an almost catastrophic decline as a commercial music. The club circuit which had once sustained the music across America had felt a cold wind as rock and soul music began to draw audiences – especially young audiences – away from jazz and towards less demanding, more approachable sounds. The Summer Of Love of 1967 found very little space for jazz: it was a time when rock groups and soul singers were annexing a significant part of the entertainment dollar. After the so-called British Invasion spearheaded by the Beatles in the early 1960s, American bands had followed their example, and groups such as the Byrds, Love and the Grateful Dead had stockpiled huge audiences for which a balmy Californian summer – crystallized in Scott McKenzie's one-off hit 'San Francisco' – acted as the perfect climate. The Beatles themselves had moved swiftly on from being a smart beat group to an experimental, albums-oriented band, whose *Sgt Pepper's Lonely Hearts Club Band* astonished their audience. The Beach Boys, once a harmless surfing group, created their own album-length masterpiece in *Pet Sounds*.

A Fine Madness 1966–7

Bob Dylan had shifted from coffee-house troubadour to a scathingly eloquent if maverick spokesman for a generation. Davis had created some of his earlier masterpieces at a time when singers such as Fabian and Bobby Vee rode high in the charts, but he faced much sterner competition from musicians who were much more than the vanilla pop stars of before.

This was all white music. But the black neighbourhood audiences which had once thrived on hard-bop had also left jazz for soul music, either the lighter 'Sound Of Young America' of Motown, or the more intense performers such as Wilson Pickett and Otis Redding. And there was one black musician whose eminence must have frightened Davis more than any other: Jimi Hendrix, the brilliant guitar virtuoso, whose appeal bridged both the black and white audiences, and whose instrumental skills were analogous to Davis's own. Two kings in neighbouring countries. Miles had to figure out how to stake his own place in that new realm.

The Other Records

1 *Miles Smiles* (Columbia)
2 *Directions* (Columbia)
3 *Sorcerer* (Columbia)
4 *Water Babies* (Columbia)
5 *No Blues* (Jazz Music Yesterday)

A Portion Of The Music Inadvertently Gets Repeated

1967–9

Davis had never been much involved in the making of popular music. His difficulty at the moment was that even his kind of jazz wasn't very popular. *Nefertiti* was close to a record of art music. As refined as his work had become, the audience which had followed him with records such as *Porgy And Bess* and *Kind Of Blue* had been comprehensively dispersed by his subsequent progress. His records were selling some 40,000 copies each, still handsome numbers for a jazz record, but a distinct decline on what was once expected of a Miles Davis album. Columbia knew they had an important artist in Davis, and were concerned to make the most of him: the long-suffering Macero remained optimistic that there could still be some productive alliance between Miles and Gil Evans, and the general manager of Columbia, Clive Davis, thought that he was the kind of musician whose catalogue and eminence were ultimately worth a great deal to the company, even if his current records weren't paying their way. But Davis made life difficult for both himself and Columbia. He constantly asked for more advances, sometimes spending hours on the phone with Clive Davis or one of his lieutenants. In the meantime, Teo Macero waited to see what he wanted to record next.

A European tour at the end of 1967, as part of the Newport Jazz Festival in Europe, had suggested little change in Davis's priorities. The set remained tied to such familiar pieces as 'I Fall In Love Too Easily', 'On Green Dolphin Street' and 'Agitation'. The brief extracts from the Karlsruhe concert heard on *Bitches Brew Live* [1], though they are in very poor sound, have all the plangency and focus which the band could turn on and off almost at will, something heard at greater length (and in superior sound) on the Paris concert (*No Blues* [2]). The fierce rate of change which would become a norm of the rock era was nothing like as prevalent in jazz, and seeing and hearing this unrepeatable group was certainly enough to appease most audiences, even if the more loyal among them must have been listening to Davis playing 'Walkin'' for more years than they could remember.

Back home, from this point Davis became a more frequent visitor to the recording studio, using it as much as a rehearsal room as anything else. On 4 December, the quintet assembled in Columbia's New York location with a new recruit, a young studio guitarist named Joe Beck, who had been busy as both an instrumentalist and an arranger on the city's session scene (he probably knew Ron Carter from that work). The result was 'Circle In The Round', a piece that was, by Davis's previous standards, an absolute marathon: the version which was eventually issued on the compilation record of that name [3] runs for some twenty-six minutes, and a further version on the Columbia *Complete Studio Recordings of the Miles Davis Quintet 1965–1968* [4] recordings, supposedly prepared by Macero in 1969, adds a further seven minutes, mostly at the beginning. Although it's unclear how much tape splicing was involved and how much of the music was actually assembled from multiple takes – possibly as many as thirty-five of them, although it's hard to see how all that work could have been completed in a single day – both versions are a vivid premonition of where Davis would eventually take his music.

The sound of the group is already very different. Herbie Hancock plays celeste rather than piano, and this effectively shifts him to a halfway-house between the acoustic instrument and the tinkling shimmer of the electric keyboard, which Davis would oblige him to use next. Tony Williams takes up a role that combines traps drummer and percussionist: much of the time he is playing a continuous rattle on both drums and cymbals, only occasionally reverting to the punctuating manner he had become more accustomed to. Meanwhile, Joe Beck plays a non-stop drone based around a repeating figure that is sustained for almost the entire piece. Carter shadows the guitarist's part, although he emerges to take a solo at one point. Davis takes no fewer than five solo passages for himself, while Shorter plays a more circumspect role. The horns use the recurring melody in 12/8 as the lynchpin of the performance. The feel of something cycling on endlessly had been a familiar motif in Davis's work, but only in theory: for the most part, performances had never lasted that long, on or off record. Here was one which, in one version, broke the half-hour barrier. But it lacks the relentlessness of Davis's later experiments with long form, and there are too many water-treading sequences. Seemingly dissatisfied, Davis didn't authorize its release until the 1970s.

Miles did, though, continue to use Joe Beck, even though he later claimed that Beck was the reason the track didn't work out (a harsh judgement on a musician who was clearly doing as he was told throughout: all he has to do is play the guitar drone). There was a final 1967 date a few days after Christmas, and several sessions in January and February of 1968 that resulted in finished work which was, nevertheless, deemed not right for release. 'Water On The Pond' [4] came out of the 28 December session. This was Hancock's debut on the new electric piano – a Fender Rhodes – which Davis had acquired for him. The leader had had the idea after hearing Joe Zawinul play an electric piano with Cannonball Adderley's band, a device that had seemed to make Adderley's music funkier as well as more obviously electric in feel. Hancock was arguably right to trust his instincts: the lovely touch and pastoral feel he has almost routinely mustered in his all-acoustic music has never really translated to the electric setting. But Herbie soon liked what he could do with the keyboard. He didn't feel drowned out by Tony Williams any longer, and there was something dense and thickening about the piano's sound which allowed him to assert himself more strongly in the quintet.

On 'Water On The Pond', it still has a tinny sound. The track itself is a light-weight piece, with a faint Latin feel, with Beck and Carter doubling each other's lines. In January, they recorded an even less substantial piece, simply called 'Fun' [4], which had the swing player Bucky Pizzarelli in to replace Beck on guitar. Davis only plays on the brief theme statement, which has a feel vaguely reminiscent of one of Sonny Rollins's calypsos, and then disappears and leaves the rest to Shorter. For all its inconsequentiality, this is a track where one can hear the band starting to move towards the weightier feel, with more bottom, which Davis was apparently after. As he later put it to Art Taylor: 'If you can hear a bass line, then any note in the sound that you play can be heard, because you have the bottom. We change the bass line quite a bit on all the songs we play. So I figured that if I wrote a bass line, we could vary it so that it would have a sound a little larger than a five-piece group. By using the electric piano and having Herbie play the bass line and the chords with the guitar, and Ron also playing with him in the same register, I thought it would sound good.' It was about as conservative a move towards rock as could be imagined, with the guitar used almost exclusively as a textural instrument, but it was the start of something.

The next guitarist he tried was George Benson, who played on 'Paraphernalia' (on *Miles In The Sky* [5]) at a date on 16 January, and 'Sanctuary' [3] and 'Side Car II' [3] on 15 February. Benson was not the first musician to be bemused by Davis's studio tactics. They played for what seemed like hours without recording anything. Tony Williams kept telling him what he should be playing, while Miles himself said almost nothing. In the event, Benson fitted into 'Side Car II' rather well, playing counterpoint to horns and piano, and fitting into a space somewhere between rhythm and solo instrument. He does rather less well in Wayne Shorter's 'Sanctuary', a slow melody which sounds like one of Wayne's bouncier tunes retarded and fragmented to emphasize its melancholy. Benson is stuck with comping a commentary on the solos and he sounds mystified next to the experienced Hancock. Nevertheless, Davis still asked the guitarist to join his band, which George declined after some soul-searching.

A Portion Of The Music Inadvertently Gets Repeated 1967–9

One of the great jazz superstars of the next decade, Benson had other music to play.

'Side Car I', the first take of the piece, certainly sounds less finished without him, and another piece recorded at the January date, 'Teo's Bag' (alias 'The Collector'), is not much more than a frenetic piece of blowing, Davis uncorking a solo which works around runs through different scales while Williams plays with a sort of pent-up fury behind him (the piece in the end finishes rather abruptly, with what sounds like a tape splice just after Hancock's solo). None of this music was deemed ready for any sort of release; but 'Paraphernalia' was put out anyway. It was eventually released as one of the four tracks on [5], which had a by-numbers pop-art cover suggestive of something vaguely psychedelic. The remaining three pieces on the disc were recorded by the quintet over three days in May.

Miles In The Sky is the first album to suggest that the old quintet is on the way out. 'Stuff', which leads off the record, is seventeen minutes of thinly attired jamming on a basic rock vamp. Hancock, again on electric piano, plays mild variations on the same riff all the way through, Williams plays a straightforward rock beat for much of the time – here and there he starts to slip back into his old polyrhythmical jazz groove, but one can almost see Davis casting a baleful glance in his direction as he does – and even the magisterial Ron Carter plays electric bass. Davis and Shorter dialogue on little melodic motifs but eventually both take long solos. The trumpeter sounds in snapping spirits, whereas Shorter seems to find himself wrangling with a beat whose stiffness he can't

penetrate. The music offers up the strange impression of a snake shedding its skin: a prodigiously talented band suddenly shifting gear to play simple matters without betraying themselves. Ironically, perhaps, the one who sounds most at ease is Herbie Hancock: he's doing nothing more than trotting out bluesy little snippets, and is bemused at how easy it all is.

The rest of the record continues the portrayal of a group in awkward transition. 'Paraphernalia' is an intriguing piece. The melody is cast in a minor mode which would have a rather depressing feel if it weren't for Williams's superbly crisp and springy playing, zinging the hi-hat almost throughout, interpolating snare shots which in context sound like bursts of gunfire, and using a climactic roll at certain points. Hancock is back on acoustic piano and Benson, in what was at the time the only issued evidence of his work with the group, plays a capable enough solo. Playing the tracks in their issued order suggests a group going backwards, because the next one was Tony Williams's tune 'Black Comedy', which reverts to the classic quintet sound of *Miles Smiles* and *Nefertiti*, Davis and Shorter spinning solos off a tremendous rhythmical onslaught from Williams, while Hancock and Carter anchor the tune around a recurring pedal point.

The final 'Country Son', though, seems to vacillate between periods. There is a varying rhythmical background, the soloists playing over first a funky time, then a rollicking 4/4, then a brooding ballad feel. Hancock picks up his solo in the meditative mode, after Shorter, and seems to be heading for one of his soliloquies, but then the funky feel takes over and he decorates that pulse rather amiably. Davis plays the final solo, which gradually builds to one of Tony Williams's most explosive climaxes, and then recedes again, ending in the ballad feel. It's an inscrutable piece of music, continually changing mood and destabilizing itself.

Miles In The Sky is no sudden departure from Davis's jazz aesthetic, let alone any kind of betrayal of it. One could have surmised that he might just as easily have returned to an all-acoustic format thereafter. But he must have enjoyed enough of the likes of 'Stuff' to have decided that was the line he would take further. Columbia, meanwhile, was still gamely trying to get him to complete another project with Gil Evans. Prior to the *Miles In The Sky* sessions, Davis and Evans had indeed been back in the studio together, on 16 February, when they had a number of tries at a piece eventually titled 'Falling Water' (on *Miles Davis & Gil Evans: The Complete Columbia Studio Recordings* [6]). Davis wasn't the only one to be taking some exploratory steps towards the new world of rock: Gil Evans, too, had found aspects of that milieu of more than passing interest, and he had taken a particular shine to the music of Jimi Hendrix, whom he admired as both a performer and a composer. For this date, Evans assembled a band of two guitars plus mandolin, electric piano, a section of low brass, woodwind, harp and percussion. There is little enough to go on in terms of what a full-scale project would have amounted to, four completed takes of a single four-minute piece, but it does present a possible fusion of the old Miles-and-Gil with something more self-consciously contemporary: the guitars and piano create a rippling cloud of arpeggios through which Davis blows clarion lines and the brass and woodwind glower in response. The last two takes on [6] suggest that the music was, as so often before, drifting magically into place. But it was the final time Miles and Gil would ever record together.

One of the mysteries of the Davis discography is the way his work with Evans petered out into nothing. It wasn't as if their relationship had in any way soured. Evans had had a hand in some of the music played at the various studio sessions of early 1968, and he would also be involved in Davis's next small-group record. Evans probably spent more time in Miles's company than any other figure outside Davis's own family, and Gil's apartment was sometimes used as a bolt-hole both for Frances and for Miles himself, if he was having one of his clandestine affairs. For all their differences of temperament and personality, they were very close. Yet they never managed to even begin recording another album together. Right up until Gil's death, in 1988, there were still whispers of some grand epic in the works. Teo Macero managed to winkle out of Miles in 1968 that they were interested in doing music from (of all things) both *Doctor Doolittle* and *Camelot*. There was often word of a grand transmogrification of Puccini's opera, *Tosca*. In 1983, Evans spoke of a three-way project with himself, Davis and George Russell. It all came to nothing. It might have been down to the costs of doing such a project (particularly after the price of both Davis and

Evans gradually went up, in the 1970s and 1980s); or it could have been due to the laissez-faire way both men conducted much of their professional lives. In that respect, 'Falling Water' was a last, tantalizing glimpse of what might have been. Around the same time, they played a concert together which featured the quintet and an orchestra under Evans's direction, as they had at Carnegie Hall seven years earlier. They played a set which included staples from different parts of Davis's career, including 'Round Midnight', 'Agitation' and 'Nefertiti', as well as new Evans orchestrations, including one of Aretha Franklin's soul hit 'You Make Me Feel Like A Natural Woman'. Yet if it was ever recorded, the tapes have long since been lost.

There was another aborted record date, too, on 25 January, when a pair of Herbie Hancock tunes, 'I Have A Dream' and what would become one of his greatest hits, 'Speak Like A Child', were attempted but never finished by the quintet plus Joe Beck (rehearsal extracts can be heard on [4]). For his next studio album, though, Davis assembled the quintet for what would turn out to be the final time. *Filles de Kilimanjaro* [7] was really divided in two:

three tracks cut in June were bookended by a pair which were set down in September. The June music was the final showing by the quintet. Hancock is back on Fender Rhodes, Carter is playing electric bass – a situation he had begun to be uncomfortable with – and Williams is again the barometer who seems to swing between jazz and rock and back again. 'Tout de suite' begins in a ballad mood but then shifts abruptly into a kind of free time, Williams ticking relentlessly at his cymbal while Carter and Hancock snipe humorously at each other in a dialogue which is then decorated by Davis and Shorter in turn. It is a vivid final instance of the quintet's empathy and spontaneous ingenuity: nobody gets in anyone else's way, the time seems impossible to count yet entirely logical, everything is busy yet uncluttered. There is a moment of queer nostalgia as Hancock's solo winds down, and the rhythm section voice, just for a bar or two, 'All Blues'. Then Davis and Shorter return to restate the piece's almost shapeless melody.

'Petits machins', alias 'Little Stuff', is germinated from what could almost be a riff out of Miles's 52nd Street days, but that motif is quickly obliterated as the solos unfold over a noisy backdrop from Williams, stuttering rolls, hissing top cymbals and miniaturized climaxes compressed into a typically super-abundant piece of drumming. Carter, as he does on much of the music on this record, tends to work from after-beats, latching on to riffs or pedal points and rather quietly voicing them from the bottom of the mix. Davis's desire to get more bottom in the group wasn't really working here, but it still made for compelling listening. And then it suddenly stops. 'Filles de Kilimanjaro' itself builds on a long, wistful melody, the rhythm opening out from a 5/4 shuffle over a vamping bass into a more disjunctive feel, which the rock-steady Carter resolves in a recurring, descending phrase. This time, Williams also restrains himself and sticks with a steady, rockish pattern. The dialogue tends to be between Hancock, whose electric piano is high and resonant in the mix, and the horn soloists. Strangely, though, the melody which nurtures the piece at the start isn't revisited at the end: instead, Davis and Hancock alternate phrases in what amounts to an extended coda.

Three completed tracks weren't enough for a record, but Davis was about to embark on a long summer of work, and there was no time to fit in another session. It was the last time Ron Carter played on a Miles Davis record. Fatigued by the travel and dissatisfied with the way the electric bass seemed to be Davis's only current requirement, Carter had had enough. Miroslav Vitous took over for an engagement at New York's Village Gate, and Carter played only one further festival date with the band, in August. His full-time replacement was, though, a complete surprise. Davis had been in London, where he had gone to hear Bill Evans play at Ronnie Scott's club, and in the support group, led by the pianist Pat Smythe, a young, skinny, bearded Englishman named Dave Holland was playing bass. Davis liked him enough to offer him a job, and the unknown

Holland had to fly to New York on a Thursday in time to take over the bass role the next night.

He wasn't the only new member of the band when the sessions for *Filles de Kilimanjaro* were completed. Herbie Hancock had fallen ill while away on his honeymoon, and had had to miss some dates in August. Miles took on a pianist named Chick Corea, who had been working with hard-bop leaders such as Blue Mitchell and Harold Land, as well as handling a stint in Stan Getz's quartet. In the event, he fitted in so well that Davis decided to stick with him, and Hancock, who had by now leadership aspirations of his own, having still been making records for Blue Note on a regular basis, departed altogether. Herbie had been finding the quintet hard going of late. In an interview he gave around that time, he came up with a nice metaphor for the direction the music had gone: it was 'like trying to make conversation never using any words you ever used before'. Next to the simple stuff on Hancock's own records, it was a tough ask.

'Frelon brun' was the first of the two tracks the new-look quintet recorded in September. Based mainly on a four-note bass riff which the piano sometimes echoes, this was a step on from the funky punch of 'Stuff'. But a more considerable piece was 'Mademoiselle Mabry'. Corea and Holland play the key role here, since they work from an eighteen-bar structure which is entirely composed, and is repeated over and over, decorated by Davis and Shorter in turn. A curious mix of funk and poignancy infests the feel of the piece, which Williams creates his own elliptical commentary on.

The record has a much more composed feel than *Miles In The Sky*, and it should be no surprise to learn that Gil Evans had a great deal of input into the record. Exactly how much isn't clear – Davis, as usual, took sole credit for all the compositions, and the retiring Gil would later only make a mild admission that he had had some involvement. In hindsight, almost everything on the disc has traces of his touch: the ensemble voicings, the sifting of written parts and free space, the ghostly quality to some of the moods. As far as newcomers Holland and Corea were concerned, though, Davis ran the group and the sessions like some kind of Svengali, a magician. There never seemed to be any specific instruction from their leader. New 'compositions' would arrive as a few symbols or a few chords on a piece of manuscript: 'Try this, there.' A track as through-composed as 'Mademoiselle Mabry' was a rarity indeed (and suggests in particular that it was Evans who had taken the trouble to notate it).

The mademoiselle of that title was Betty Mabry, a young singer and woman on the scene, whom Miles had quickly grown infatuated with, leaving Cicely Tyson for once out in the cold. Although Betty was almost twenty years Miles's junior, they were married that September. Her face is the one on the front of *Filles de Kilimanjaro*, which also has the legend 'Directions In Music By Miles Davis', a rather curt rejoinder to anyone who might have suggested that the likes of Teo Macero had anything much to do with the way the trumpeter's albums were turning out. Betty and Miles didn't enjoy a lengthy marriage – a little over a year was as long as their stormy relationship lasted – but her youth and interest in the latest music helped push Davis a little further in the direction of the rock scene.

That impetus wasn't easy to spot if one went by his live work. Anyone who attended one of the gigs by the Davis quintet that autumn wouldn't have been particularly surprised by anything they did: Holland was playing acoustic bass, and only Corea was using an electric keyboard. (He kept trying to use the acoustic piano if there was a good one on the premises. Davis would always stop him by saying something along the lines of 'The piano is over, Chick.') Dave Holland, who was still just settling into a role he had been thrown as if walking into a whirlwind, was amazed to find that the revered Miles Davis wasn't that big an attraction, even on the club circuit they were playing, at venues such as the Plugged Nickel, the Both/And Club in San Francisco and Shelly's Manne-Hole in Los Angeles. Sometimes there would be no more than thirty or forty people in the audience.

Davis was experiencing the same as everyone else in American jazz. The audience had departed in such large numbers that the music felt as if it belonged to another time. His own progress had been logical enough for anyone who had followed him over the past ten years, but he had been systematically unpinning the things which listeners had recognized as particular to his work. The spine-tingling moments that had stood out on major records such as *Milestones* were no longer as easy to find: by clouding melodic lines, eliminating chorus lengths, subdividing beats and diffusing obvious swing, Davis had lost many of his listeners. He had become difficult. Anyone who had loved the fragile, wounded poignancy of Miles in ballad mode was as likely to be dismayed as fascinated by the likes of [5]. As Davis had always said, what he did was play music, fulfil a musician's role, not entertain. But paying customers were no longer so eager to listen.

A year earlier, his longtime sideman John Coltrane had died, of complications relating to liver disease, a legacy of his earlier addictions. Coltrane had, unlike Davis, embraced many aspects of free jazz: his records had become dark and full of tumult. As with Davis, he hadn't given up on his old material – he was still playing his favourite ballad 'Naima' at his final concerts – but the formulas of bebop and its aftermath had lost any relevance to him. Coltrane had become a paradigm of the existential soloist, his concerts going on for hours, each performance a search or a journey without end. Yet this had struck a chord with many audiences: unlike Davis, always looking inward, Coltrane's mix of spiritual ecstasy and truth-seeking turbulence seemed to chime with a sense of unrest that was abroad and palpable in many Western societies.

And there was one jazz group whose music did appear to speak to the kind of audiences that otherwise bathed themselves in the sound of Jimi Hendrix and Jefferson Airplane. The music of the Charles Lloyd group had made it on to the same festival stages as the great rock heavyweights of the time. Lloyd was not an especially remarkable saxophonist, but records such as *Forest Flower* (1966) had a beatific quality which the West Coast rock community easily recognized, and in the pianist Keith Jarrett and drummer Jack DeJohnette, Lloyd had two exceptional young talents who were also great showmen. Davis must have been jealous when Lloyd's band played one of the headline spots at the 1966 Monterey Rock Festival.

If he was going to extricate himself from a music which seemed to be ossifying by the minute, Miles Davis had to make a much more determined move away from acoustic, straight-ahead jazz. It wasn't paying his bills, and Miles was no longer 'the man'. So he jumped.

In A Silent Way

COLUMBIA

Shhh/Peaceful; In A Silent Way/It's About That Time.
Miles Davis (*t*); Wayne Shorter (*ts*); Josef Zawinul (*p, org*); Herbie Hancock, Chick Corea (*p*); John McLaughlin (*g*); Dave Holland (*b*); Tony Williams (*d*).
2/69.

Four other recording sessions took place prior to those which resulted in this album, and each sowed seeds of what would turn out to be *In A Silent Way*. On 11 November 1968, the new quintet plus Herbie Hancock (who, though no longer an official band member, was nevertheless invited to take part in many of Davis's record dates) recorded two long pieces, Wayne Shorter's 'Two Faced' and Davis's own 'Dual Mr Anthony Tillmon Williams Process'. 'Two Faced', in its final form – constructed by Teo Macero in 1976, when the piece was belatedly issued on *Water Babies* [8] – runs for just over eighteen minutes. It is an eerie piece of music, static, floating, leaving the listener waiting for something to happen which never arrives, even though the track is full of incident. Davis and Shorter introduce it with a kind of subdued fanfare, before the main melody, stated by bass and piano in unison, sets up the tone of the piece. The melodic material is throughout so far down in the mix that it heightens the mysterious nature of the music. Fragmented further by rippling tremolos in the pianos, who intersect softly and with feline grace, the music alternates between that first melodic subject and a second, set up by a bass vamp. Davis, Shorter and the two pianists each has his varied turn as soloist, and all the way through – and this in a piece which was edited together by Macero from numerous takes and stops and starts – the remarkable Tony Williams constructs a drum part which binds together each of the disparate sections. Even when played loud, 'Two Faced' seems most distinctive for its resolute quietness.

'Dual Mr Anthony Tillmon Williams Process' is an altogether more shape-less piece. There is no proper melody, not much form other than a recurring bass motif (echoed in one of the pianists' left hands), and a stop-start rhythm which the drummer (real name Anthony Tillmon Williams) clearly relishes, after his almost minimalist role on the other piece. Funky in a dry, soulless way, taking a boogaloo beat and razoring it up, the horn improvisations sound like the stop-time solos of old-fashioned hot jazz.

Next, on 25 November, the same band plus Josef Zawinul assembled to record another single piece. Cannonball Adderley's pianist had long been observed by Davis – when he wrote the hit 'Mercy Mercy Mercy' for Adderley's band, Davis most likely thought a lot more of him – and the Viennese expatriate was inevitably very interested in what Davis was doing, too. The first piece recorded was 'Splash', which Zawinul doesn't play on. Made up of six-bar sections in 5/4, with a bar in 6/4 used as a breather, this is another piece with a bluesy feel, a stop-go impetus, and a vague sense of disassociation, since the bass and the pianos between them make up a cloudy, even murky bottom

202

end to the music. Williams this time thrashes his way through much of the piece in his best full-on style. 'Splashdown', which was left unissued until the release of the so-called *Complete In A Silent Way* [9] sessions in 2001, does include Zawinul, here playing organ, although he does little more than sound a few reedy chords near the beginning. The rest of it is another almost funky, stop-go piece with rhythmic patterns in the keyboards and bass standing in for real melodic material. Tony Williams again plays superbly inventive fills and punctuations to accent every section.

At the next date, on 27 November, Zawinul was considerably more than a bystander. Both 'Ascent' and the two versions of 'Directions' set down on that day were credited to him as composer. 'Ascent' is a meandering sequence of harmonic patterns with little or no rhythmic interest: everything centres around the wash of electric keyboards (two electric pianos and organ, with some embellishment via either some sort of electronic attachment or perhaps some modification of the amplifiers through which they were being played – Corea remembered that he liked to mess around with that kind of thing during this period). Davis enters two-thirds of the way through, with a declamatory if rather pretentious-sounding insistence. This follows what was actually Wayne Shorter's recorded debut on the soprano saxophone. If it has the stately, processional feel of some of the old music with Gil Evans, there is something ponderous and effortful about this track, which has little of the limpid beauty that Zawinul and Shorter would later secure in their music together in Weather Report. It also feels poorly recorded, the bulbous sound of the electric keyboards crudely mixed with the trumpet and drums.

'Directions' was a more grooving piece, and it must have appealed to Davis immediately: he began using it as the opening number in his live sets, even though this version of it wasn't released for many years. After the initial theme statement, Davis takes off on a solo which is driven furiously by the drummer – who was not Tony Williams. Jack DeJohnette, formerly of Charles Lloyd's group, had been seconded by Davis, since Williams was now intent on forming his own group. DeJohnette was and remains a drummer of enormous skill and power: here he plays an outwardly simple, ferociously driving beat, which anyone who liked rock could instantly identify with, but he accents all of the beats in a 4/4 pulse so cleverly that the same ears could hardly tell that they have actually been listening to a jazz drummer. No rock drummer could use their reflexes in quite this way. Again, Miles had found the right man for what he wanted to do: DeJohnette couldn't rival Williams's creative genius, but as an executant, he was flawless.

Both versions of 'Directions' are basically two steps ahead of where Miles was. If the music of *In A Silent Way* would be evanescent and enigmatic, 'Directions' looked directly forward to his next phase, where rock and jazz improvisation were dramatically fused. Davis plays two trumpet solos which are almost shockingly forceful on the two versions, and the tune itself was written in B natural, an uncomfortable key for horn players but a good one for guitarists. Again, though, neither track saw the light of day until the 1980s. What Davis's audience would have made of 'Directions', had it been released around the time of its recording, is anybody's guess.

In February 1969, Davis again assembled his quintet, plus Hancock and Zawinul, in Columbia's New York studio. Tony Williams was on the point of starting his new band, a trio called Lifetime, with the organist Larry Young and the English guitarist John McLaughlin, who had just arrived in New York. But Miles wanted Tony on his date, and when he met McLaughlin, he suggested that he come along too. So it was an octet which was assembled on the morning of 2 February.

The two pieces they recorded that day more or less announced the revolution. Each lasted an entire side of a single LP. There were three electric keyboards – two Fender Rhodes pianos and an organ – trumpet, soprano sax, electric guitar, bass and drums. When the record was released, in the summer of 1969, audiences had only just got used to the sound of [7]. But this was a considerable step on from even that record. The idea of side-long tracks wasn't especially outrageous to any rock audience. The Grateful Dead, on their double live album *Live Dead*, had included a track called 'Dark Star' which lasted for well over twenty minutes. The jazz audience was more circumspect. What Davis did, though, was sweeten the pill. The music has a gentle, almost amiable mood about it. Tony Williams plays a simple shuffle beat on his cymbals almost throughout 'Shhh/Peaceful' (some listeners might even be reminded of the drum part on Isaac Hayes's 'Shaft'). John McLaughlin, not yet the speedfreak picker of the Lifetime and Mahavishnu Orchestra records, plays melodious, ringing lines. Davis uses an open horn and stays in his warm middle register. The keyboards tend to percolate somewhere between the bottom and the middle of the mix. The music is as charming as it is inventive. One might almost hear it as a jazz record to softly convert a rock listener to the music's most beguiling mood.

The most extraordinary thing about the record wasn't readily apparent to most listeners. Teo Macero, working in consultation with Davis (though to what extent is never really clear), created the master takes on the record via a great deal of creative editing. This was most apparent on the second side of the LP, which comprises 'In A Silent Way/It's About That Time'. In an astonishing move, Macero used 'In A Silent Way' itself twice – it starts the second side, moves into 'It's About That Time' and then, in its identical form, is heard again. Although the album runs for almost forty minutes, thanks to this and other instances of Teo's creative editing, it basically uses only thirty-three minutes of music.

At the session, Davis typically gave the most minimal instructions to his musicians. He gave Chick Corea a chart with a few chords and symbols and never said another word to him. Joe Zawinul's lovely tune, which was used as the title for the album, was later recorded by its composer on his own *Zawinul* album, and restored to its full complexity. Davis eliminated some of the chords, and then told John McLaughlin to play the melody on a single chord. Dave Holland later remembered that there wasn't even a sense of it being a record date, more like a series of unstructured rehearsals. Yet all the while, Teo Macero had the tapes spinning in the control room.

'Shhh/Peaceful' – hardly a title which suggested anything to cause a disturbance – started with a melodic form of sorts, via yet another bass doubled by Chick Corea's left hand, a device that had already been used several times on the preceding sessions. But on the issued master Macero eliminated the opening section and just used the various improvisations which the group had recorded. What he then went on to do was to splice Miles's opening solo back into the music at around the thirteen-minute mark, which implied that was the melody. A shapeless series of improvisations, with only the bass vamp as a reference point, was given form and coherence entirely by the editing. Keyboard phrases, some of them drawn from rehearsal sections, were used as other markers during the piece. Wayne Shorter's soprano solo, which starts at just past the nine-minute mark, is the very centre of the piece. Some of the edit points sound glaringly obvious, even to untutored ears, but as a pioneering example of what would become the way Davis would make his records, it was a remarkable feat by Macero to construct the two sides of the record in such a flowing, unforced way.

Zawinul didn't especially care for the way Davis 'edited' his theme 'In A Silent Way' (although he was shrewd enough to ensure that he received sole composer credit and retained the copyright). John McLaughlin's statement of the melody, over an arco drone from the bass and the sound of single, dotting notes from one of the pianos, leads to a soprano/trumpet unison which walks slowly through the empty spaces of the tune. Abruptly, as the last note dies away, 'It's About That Time' comes pumping in, over an insistent rimshot/hi-hat beat, which is just as suddenly dispersed as a recurring three-bar motif of six chords are played by the pianos and McLaughlin takes his solo. Then a bass riff emerges to displace the keyboard part. The backing keeps shifting between the keyboards and the bass riff, creating a sense of something timeless but not quite static, and Shorter – notably subdued – and Davis play their solos. It was, again, a triumph of creative editing by Macero. Then, 'In A Silent Way' itself makes its second appearance.

Not everyone was impressed. The veteran jazz critic Martin Williams suggested that because of incompetence in the studio 'a portion of the music inadvertently gets repeated at one point'. He was entitled to some sense of outrage – jazz was not noted for including the same music twice over on the same record – but it underlined that the notion of a studio edit and mixdown had yet to be perceived as any part of the creative process in making jazz records. In fact, creative use of the studio had been important to jazz record business since the beginning of the LP era. Even a fundamentalist label such as Blue Note, the prime source of hard-bop records in the 1950s and 1960s, would often use master takes spliced from different performances. Alfred Lion, their producer, always liked the cleanest possible delivery of the theme, and if it meant applying that to another take with hotter solos, he went ahead and did it. But Macero and Davis were going several stages further, constructing entire pieces out of fragments which, in their own right, hardly counted as finished performances. It was already a significant part of the making of rock records, and at the high-art end of things, movements such as *musique concrète* embraced the procedure as their *raison d'être*. For it to be accepted in the live medium of jazz, where producers were often seen more as meddlers than useful presences, it would take a lot of getting used to.

Not everything from these sessions was either used or even very worthwhile. When Columbia got round to issuing their complete edition in 2001, they also included two tracks which had been finished at a session two days later, on 20 February. This time Tony Williams was absent, and his place was taken by Joe Chambers, one of the more adventurous drummers on the New York jazz scene, but a man clearly struggling with his duties. 'The Ghetto Walk' rambles on for almost twenty-seven minutes and is a mostly dreary and uninvolving piece which suggests the fine line that Davis and Macero were walking between powerful music and mere noodling. Chambers knew he wasn't really playing the right kind of groove – 'The drums were still in that swing thing. They were not tuned correctly for the big fat funk beats that this music implied' – and his drumming tends to drag the ensemble along, too jazzy by half. Again, the music is grown from a bass line rather than a melody, but as assembled by Macero the piece lacks any sense of unity or progressive development. A much briefer piece, 'Early Minor', was another Joe Zawinul composition, which had already been debuted on a Nat Adderley album. This again has a gloomy and half-cooked feel, but it does come to life in its closing minutes with one of Davis's most haunting solos, cast in his best ballad tone.

Columbia's dredging of its archives for every scrap of Davis material – a process which has more or less dominated their jazz reissue programme of the past ten years – hasn't been especially kind to the music of the *In A Silent Way* sessions. The three-disc *Complete In A Silent Way Sessions* [9], which is padded out with some of the tracks from *Filles de Kilimanjaro*, includes an alternative edit of 'Shhh/Peaceful' which only shows how astute Macero's work was on the original. While the producer has had to take any amount of criticism, over many years, concerning his cutting and pasting of Davis's music, his constructions have stood the test of time better than many would have predicted. One only has to listen to the useless remix of 'In A Silent Way', by one DJ Cam, on *Panthalassa: The Remixes* [10], to realize how well Macero understood what Davis wanted.

*I*n A Silent Way was released in August 1969. By this time, the Davis quintet – with Shorter, Corea, Holland and DeJohnette as the regular line-up – had at last been breaking in a new set. The group was busy on its usual circuit – the Plugged Nickel, the Village Gate, the Blue Coronet Club in Brooklyn – and while there was still an occasional old piece in the programme, the group were also playing pieces – 'Sanctuary', 'Miles Runs The Voodoo Down' – which their audiences had thus far not had the chance to hear on record. In the case of the latter, it hadn't even been recorded yet.

Their look was changing, too. In place of the impeccably suited ensemble which Davis had run throughout the 1960s, now they were dressed in the looser, more colourful fashions of the day. Ever the dandy, Miles began to affect huge sunglasses, kaftans, silk shirts and baggy pants. It was a much better fit for the way he was now working on record, too: for his next studio sessions, which also took place that August, the last tenets of jazz formality were finally swept aside.

The Other Records

1 *Bitches Brew Live* (Golden Age Of Jazz)
2 *No Blues* (Jazz Music Yesterday)
3 *Circle In The Round* (Columbia)
4 *Complete Studio Recordings Of The Miles Davis Quintet 1965–1968* (Columbia)
5 *Miles In The Sky* (Columbia)
6 *Miles Davis & Gil Evans: The Complete Columbia Studio Recordings* (Columbia)
7 *Filles de Kilimanjaro* (Columbia)
8 *Water Babies* (Columbia)
9 *The Complete In A Silent Way Sessions* (Columbia)
10 *Panthalassa: The Remixes* (Columbia)

He Didn't
Erase Anything

1969–70

The sales figures for *In A Silent Way* were good, if not as startling as Macero in particular had hoped. The album actually made a dent in *Billboard*'s chart on its week of release (number 134, not quite with a bullet), and its momentum was decent enough: the new FM radio stations, which had developed as a consequence of the interest in album-orientated rock, were playing it. Many listeners who could pretend that they had been hip to Davis all along could now stack his records alongside the album-rock giants without it seeming jarringly out of place. The dreamy, open-ended grooves of *In A Silent Way* functioned as drug music, too. Still, in the end the album only sold in the region of 90,000 units, a major advance on where Davis had been but not the breakthrough Macero and Clive Davis had hoped for.

The quintet's live work was hazily documented by a few bootleggers: sets from New York's Central Park (*Miles Runs The Voodoo Down At Central Park* [1]) and Rutgers University (*Odds 'N' Ends* 1969–73 [2]) were taken down from somewhere in the audience, but the surviving sound is so poor that it's hard to judge what the band were really doing. Not much superior is the set which Columbia itself eventually released from the Juan-les-Pins Festival in July (*1969 Miles – Festiva De Juan Pins* [3]): another noisy and ineffective soundmix sabotages this one, although the best passages have a wildness and intensity which suggest that the music, while still bridging jazz and rock and sounding at times as if the band weren't even half-way across the divide yet, was stumbling across some remarkable things. Music from the second night of that festival was also retained in Chick Corea's tape collection, and features in a very small dose on *Music Forever & Beyond* [4].

This edition of the quintet was recorded only parsimoniously, whether officially or via illicit microphones. Corea is remembered only peripherally as a Davis keyboard player: Hancock, Zawinul and even Keith Jarrett are often held in higher esteem. Yet his best work with Davis amounts to much of his best playing anywhere: he was one of the few jazz pianists to attempt to impose a genuinely personal aesthetic on the Fender Rhodes, and though his later adventures on synthesizers in the 1970s and after would be by comparison bombastic and annoying, in the exciting times of that first period with Davis, he was always ready to surprise. Dave Holland's bass work was a studious mix of functionality and personal enterprise: when holding down groove patterns on the electric instrument he quietly got on with the job and was very effective at it, but he still soloed mostly on the acoustic bass, where his skill and rapid thinking took precedence. Jack DeJohnette didn't try to compete

He Didn't Erase Anything 1969–70

with Tony Williams: instead of his predecessor's ceaseless recomposition of rhythms and structures, he simply played the beat, with as much flair and intensity as he could muster.

The odd man out was, increasingly, Wayne Shorter. By now the longest-serving veteran of the group, he had brought nothing really new to the book for some time, and his playing, while still marked by his maverick invention, no longer had the impact and incisiveness of his work of a few years earlier. In the studio, as Davis's groups began to grow larger and more unwieldy, there was less space for Wayne to make his mark, and he began to seem like a mere contributor rather than the creative powerhouse he had been around the time of *Nefertiti*.

Yet the group was clearly still a remarkable outfit when it was on and happening. The European visit which was to close out Miles's touring year, in October and November 1969, suggests in its unofficial recordings that the quintet was getting much closer to an effective rapprochement between its various directions. The concerts in Rome (spread between *Bitches Brew Live* [5] and *Miles Davis* [6]), Copenhagen (*Another 1969 – Miles Vol. 2* [7]) and Stockholm (*Another 1969 – Miles Vol. 3* [8]) battle through often indifferent soundmixes to show how Davis could still blend the likes of 'I Fall In Love Too Easily' (now used mainly as a cooling-off interlude, and a duet between Davis and Corea) with 'Spanish Key' and even 'Bitches Brew' itself, then still unheard by the audiences. In place of the dynamic variety of the Carter–Williams–Hancock band, this one fed off a more linear, sometimes relentless beat, stuttering and skipping rather than swelling and contracting. Shorter's solos on the Rome 'Bitches Brew'/'Miles Runs the Voodoo Down' found him still full of ideas, though sometimes shadowboxing in his own, tense space. As it turned out, these recordings were almost all that would exist of the quintet as a working band. Columbia planned to make a live album at New York and Philadelphia dates that August, but the idea fell apart, and instead Davis went into the studios in New York on 19 August. Three days later, he had hours and hours of music in the can. Then the work started.

Bitches Brew

COLUMBIA

Pharaoh's Dance; Bitches Brew; Spanish Key;
John McLaughlin; Miles Runs The Voodoo Down; Sanctuary.
Miles Davis (*t*); Wayne Shorter (*ss*); Bennie Maupin (*bcl*);
Chick Corea, Larry Young, Joe Zawinul (*p*); John McLaughlin (*g*);
Dave Holland, Harvey Brooks (*b*); Jack DeJohnette, Lenny White,
Don Alias (*d*); Jim Riley (*perc*). 8/69.

U nlike Davis's other groundbreaking records, *Bitches Brew* is almost as famous for the circumstances of its creation as for the music itself. While there is little enough to demystify about the circumstances of records such as *Miles Ahead* and *Kind Of Blue*, which were completed in the straightforward manner of most jazz record dates, *Bitches Brew* was fashioned under conditions which amounted to a kind of serene chaos. Thirteen players were involved across the three days of recording – almost enough for a big band – and the involvement of such sounds as Bennie Maupin's bass clarinet lent an outlook which was entirely different to the way Davis's small-group records had been made in the past. It was music that relied on texture, groove, weight. The old jazz logic of head–solos–head is entirely abandoned. The ensembles ebb and flow, or sometimes just stand still, thickening around

He Didn't Erase Anything 1969–70

a single point. The pieces are long, without climaxes or obvious points of excitement.

Davis had prepared for the recording dates in much the same way as he had for many others, but with just a fraction more attention to detail. Musicians were effectively told to be ready to turn up at the appointed time, without knowing much about what they were going to do, yet there had been some rehearsals at Miles's house, which newcomers such as Lenny White had been involved in. White was a young drummer, still only nineteen, who had previously been working in Jackie McLean's group which Miles had already lifted players from in the past. Bennie Maupin had been working with Horace Silver and was a regular playing partner of Jack DeJohnette's. Harvey Brooks was a staff producer at CBS who also played bass, and who had worked on a session with Miles's wife Betty. Don Alias was a friend of Tony Williams, who suggested him for the date. Jim Riley was a friend of Alias's who pestered him to be allowed to come to the date, and Davis suggested he pick up something to shake on a couple of pieces. Thus, the make-up of the group had its usual laissez-faire quality. What Davis thought was that, with the new way of working, involving if necessary a vast amount of post-production work, anything could be fixed later.

On a session which started at ten in the morning, the musicians were laid out like a small orchestra, DeJohnette, White and the rest of the percussionists on one side, the others facing them in a semi-circle, with Davis situated in the middle on what amounted to a conductor's podium. From there, he pointed, gestured and otherwise directed what he wanted. Matters had started badly, with, as Teo Macero remembered it, a furious argument between himself and Davis over some matter to do with Teo's secretary. If anything, it spurred the leader on to his prickliest and most inventive form. But the sessions, in the end, felt more transient and shapeless than epochal. Chick Corea recalled that the four- and six-hour sessions had the air more of rehearsal periods than of distilled, red-light recordings.

When they had been in the studio for three days, there were something like nine hours of music on tape and available for editing. As Bob Belden, who worked on many of the Davis reissue packages of recent times, put it, 'If anything sucked that he recorded, Miles would have had Teo erase it. With *Bitches Brew*, he didn't erase anything.' What Macero and his engineers constructed out of this mass of material was five long tracks, ranging from a little under eleven minutes for 'Sanctuary' to exactly twenty-seven minutes for 'Bitches Brew' itself, plus the brief 'John McLaughlin', which followed 'Spanish Key' and closed out side three of the original double-album set.

Joe Zawinul's 'Pharaoh's Dance' opened the record. The group rehearsed and recorded part of it on the first day, and finished it on the third. Although the piece is actually a typical slice of Zawinul – a few simple melodic ideas given strength and finesse through their deployment across several sections – on the record it sounds like it could have been written by anybody. What you hear is a thick churn of rhythm, heavily amplified instruments – both acoustic and electric – laid over one another until the music seems, at times, impenetrable. The track is actually a brilliant piece of post-production by Macero: Bob Belden's notes to the *Complete Bitches Brew Sessions* [9] detail nineteen specific edits in the track, which also uses echo and reverb chambers, and tape loops to create riffs or licks, particularly from the keyboards (the point around eight minutes into the track, which mixes loops and reverbed trumpet, shows how much detail Macero was applying, even on a piece of music that was outwardly ragged and without structure). After fifteen minutes of hectic activity, the piece seems about to die away, but then the rhythm players settle into a simpler groove and Davis, thrust right to the front of the mix, improvises deft little patterns in an extended coda.

'Bitches Brew' itself starts with one of Davis's favourite bass keyboard patterns, over which he throws some wailing phrases, themselves coloured by echo effects. After a pause, this rubato section gives way to another bass riff played by Harvey Brooks (one can just hear Davis snapping his fingers to cue the bassist in), counterpointed by the bass clarinet. Via use of loops, this is employed as a fundamental root in the mix, the drummers flailing over the top, McLaughlin chewing off bits of riffs, and Davis playing phrases which often emerge at half-tempo. The music quietens and then builds up again as the trumpeter plays what sounds like a riff figure that he seems to turn inside out and back again. Wayne Shorter gets a brief turn out front but just as rapidly steps back again. Eventually, the first section is recapitulated, before the groove sequence is reasserted. At around the twenty-minute mark, 'Bitches Brew' runs out of steam. The final seven minutes run through a noodling sequence for the pianos before the opening section is brought back for a final time. Macero had again imposed a logic on what had been a lot of music through creative editing, but the track is simply too long.

Length for its own sake does seem to have been one of the special traits of *Bitches Brew*. Some of the decisions made in putting the tracks together suggest that part of the album's statement was the idea of a music without end, or at least without the familiar beginning, middle and climax created by regular performance practice. 'Spanish Key' had already been played extensively by the quintet in its live work, and here it exists as what is more or less a single and only modestly edited take. It starts with one of the drummers leading off an unappetizing rock beat, which sounds like it could be the work of any bar band, but it swiftly gathers a dense momentum as the other players join in. The bass clef sonorities are heightened by a clever mixing of bass clarinet and the pianists' left hands and Davis plays the main melodic motif, a simple run ending on a long held note. Wayne Shorter's soprano solo is perhaps his best moment on the record, and Davis plays some typically pithy things. More than any other track on the set, though, 'Spanish Key' was let down by the soundmix. As creatively as Macero approached the task of editing and mixing Davis's music, his engineers were still finding their way in using microphones and recording consoles to set down what was a tremendously loud band, even without their amplifiers. The bottom end of 'Spanish Key' is so muddy that it is often virtually impossible to figure out what's on the floor of the original mix. In one way, that hardly matters: it heightens some of the mystery of the record, and embodies some of the drifting between genres which Davis was trying to imply. But the overall punch was weakened. Just as nearly everything Jimi Hendrix recorded was dimmed, if only a little, by the inadequate recording technologies of his time, so was Davis's first electric phase softened, at just the moment when it should have bitten. (The remastered edition completed for [9] is much cleaner, restoring the top end which Dolby noise reduction had muffled, and with a much superior separation of the instruments. Yet there is a notable loss of immediacy, ironically enough, in the trumpet sound.)

'John McLaughlin', the brief piece that follows 'Spanish Key', was actually a fragment of 'Bitches Brew' which Macero isolated as a showcase for the guitarist, who plays the central role. So to side four, which starts with 'Miles Runs The Voodoo Down', a title imposed on the piece by somebody else and which Davis reportedly disliked, though he never saw fit to change it. Although this had already been played live by the quintet, in the studio it turned out rather differently: after a few tries which didn't feel right, Don Alias, who had been doing percussion thus far on the date, spoke up and suggested a different drum groove, something he had played for New Orleans bands. He ended up playing at the kit and directing a kind of second-line feel into the music, which, with the overlaid polyrhythms, has a bow-legged funkiness about it. Davis emerges towards the end of the piece and plays a strangely contrasting solo, mixing his buzziest low notes with shrill, spattering lines that dance around the top of the stave. Around him, keyboard clusters ring eerily. The track tapers off into silence.

The final piece, Wayne Shorter's 'Sanctuary', had already been recorded at one of the rejected August sessions. It opens in the vein of 'I Fall In Love Too Easily', as a duet between Corea and Davis, and the melody is then played in unison by Davis and Shorter while the rhythm section begins scuffling around them. Davis works his way through this process of exposition twice, although again it's hard to see why, other than for the purposes of filling up space. As a piece of music, though, it is the one extended bout of lyricism on the record, and is perhaps Wayne Shorter's farewell gift to the group he had worked with for so long.

Every musician who played on the record appears to have been interviewed about it at some time or another. Their accounts all lead in the same direction: the music was often germinated by other hands, but it was Davis who fashioned and persuaded and compelled the shape and direction of the sound, by trial and error, working through an idea, suggesting rather than commanding, and giving the other players their collective heads. There were chords he wanted to hear, to get something started, but after that, it didn't matter what they played as long as it worked. And even if it didn't work, there was always some sweetening that Teo could do, or there was some other section they could drop in. The latter point was largely obscured from the other musicians: none of them were privy to the mixing process, and when Joe Zawinul first heard a finished *Bitches Brew*, he didn't even recognize the music. The impression the players had was of this seigneurial figure, speaking hardly at all, directing with a sweep of his arm, making magic. Small wonder that the idea of Miles the mystic, Miles the shaman who conjured unprecedented results out of almost nothing, was enhanced further by the circumstances of *Bitches Brew*.

As with Ornette Coleman's early music, the sounds on this record have long since lost their capacity to shock. Old-school jazz reviewers were often disturbed or even appalled by what they heard, though Davis didn't care much about that. There were suggestions that he had sold out to commerce, that he was pandering pathetically to a youth market he couldn't be a part of, that the electronics and studio fiddling were covering up a paucity of inspiration. Whatever else *Bitches Brew* was, it was scarcely a sell-out, and the music was about as pop-oriented as John Cage or Elliot Carter: side-long tracks steeped in percussive noise (Clark Terry thought it sounded like a jungle-movie soundtrack), leading players who often said very little, ensembles that were steeped in murk – yes, there was a guitar player on there, but often he was barely audible.

As a statement by the leading jazz personality of his day, it was a tremendous act of provocation. At a time when jazz was starting to retrench, the furthest limits of free expression having already been breached by the likes of Albert Ayler, its older tradition was beginning to reassert itself: Duke Ellington and Louis Armstrong were being recognized as honoured elders, and although the bottom had dropped out of the hard-bop market, the idea of jazz as a repertoire music, which would gain further ground in the 1980s, was starting to be formulated. Davis, who had hitherto expressed at least an interest in what his jazz contemporaries were doing, separated himself from virtually all of them at a single stroke.

Yet the world of *Bitches Brew*, as bewildering as it sounded to some, still held logical links with Miles's creative past. It was still a record filled with jazz improvisation: there may have been post-production trickery applied to some of the notes he made, but Davis was still playing a trumpet out of which came his signature sound. There was nothing on the record which was even close to what Davis himself perceived as the noise-making of the free avant garde. A musical rationale underpinned every decision both in the playing and in Macero's studio surgery. It was a set of performances by an ensemble, an improvising collective, which worked in a way that could hark back to the old polyphony of the New Orleans bands that had got the music under way, seventy years earlier. The fact that the leader of the group played what was more or less the same instrument as that used by the first 'King' of New Orleans, Buddy Bolden, only underlined how far things had come, and how much they stayed the same.

Bolden's eyes might have widened if he had had the chance to see the sleeve which *Bitches Brew* came housed in. Designed by Mati Klarwein, an artist who had already done album covers for Jimi Hendrix, the front cover features an elaborate painting which shows two black women embracing as they gaze out at a thunderstorm swirling over a cobalt sea. When the cover is opened, two more women are seen against a glistening night sky. A pink face looks out in profile on one side, a Nubian one stares impassively out on the other. The heady colours and mysterious images hint at some strange pan-cultural mix which suggests that the music, if such it represents, belongs nowhere, yet has a black heritage fuelling its existence. The title, *Bitches Brew*, might be suggestive in a different way, using as it does Davis's favourite generic term for women, even though he later claimed that it was something taken off a restaurant menu. It was certainly a rather shocking title for a respectable label such as Columbia, and a respected artist such as Miles Davis.

Miles himself is sometimes conspicuous in his absence from the record. Ian Carr suggests that he 'dominates proceedings throughout' and that he plays a lot of trumpet, but compared with many of his 1960s records he is actually spread thinly on a record which is necessarily dominated mainly by drums and keyboards. What happens is that every entrance he makes has an intense drama about it: only on 'Sanctuary', where he and Shorter play through a more or less conventional quintet piece, does he assume a more familiar role. On the other long pieces, he comes and departs with a sometimes shattering inten- sity, Macero always making sure that he is right in the listener's face. While this might make listeners hungry for more, it also left many of the passages without him sounding slack.

There was more than enough in the can for what was needed for *Bitches Brew*, but Davis went ahead and completed five more sessions between November 1969 and early February 1970, most of which was left unreleased until it was all included on [9]. It was a hectic and somewhat anxious period for him in personal terms. Betty had been present at the *Bitches Brew* sessions and he seemed to look to her for approval of the music, but the two of them soon began fighting and the marriage was over practically before it had begun. Davis then took up with another, equally young, woman, Marguerite Eskridge, who eventually bore him his youngest son, Erin. Eskridge had a native American background and seems to have been a pacific influence on Davis, even helping him change his diet to vegetables and water and getting him to give up smoking. This didn't, though, do much to stop his drug habits: he continued to snort cocaine, and Eskridge later claimed that his drug problem brought about their parting.

A bizarre incident befell them both on the evening of 9 October 1969. Davis had driven Eskridge home and they were in his car together outside her building when another vehicle drove past. Someone fired five bullets into their car. Davis suffered a slight graze from one of them, and after hospital treatment, they were promptly arrested on a charge of possession of marijuana, some of which had been found in the car (the charge was later dropped). Miles had been worried by gangster threats. Mobsters still had a hold on many of the clubs he played in, and he wasn't the amenable type. But it could as easily have been related to a drug situation. Over the years, that kind of difficulty has cost several jazz musicians their lives.

In the midst of all this, recording continued. On 19 November, the band reassembled with some new faces: a teenaged white saxophonist, Steve Grossman; Herbie Hancock and Ron Carter; a sitar player, Khalil Balakrishna, and a tamboura and tabla exponent, Bihari Sharma; another very young drummer, Billy Cobham, who replaced both Lenny White and Jack DeJohnette; and the Brazilian percussionist Airto Moreira. Regular faces Holland and Shorter were absent, and so was Joe Zawinul, who hadn't been too enamoured of the *Bitches Brew* sessions. Introducing the Indian instruments lent a surprising new texture to the ensemble. The rasp of the tambour and ring of the sitar were by now almost familiar sounds to Western ears, since the hippie trail had long since made the appropriate pilgrimage east, the Beatles had done their Indian bit, and Ravi Shankar had acclimatized the ears of thousands to the disciplines of Eastern classical music, even if it was more often used as a soundtrack to a dope-smoking session. An album had even been issued in Britain under the title *Curried Jazz*. Davis, though, used the players on what amounted to a funk track in 'Great Expectations' ([9] and *Big Fun* [10]). A simple melody played by the horns was set off against a thundering bass riff in 7/4, and when the instruments all lock into it, the effect is sheer exhilaration. There is very little variation across its fourteen or so minutes, the 'improvising' focusing mainly on the percussive variations, but as a clotted musical tumult it's strangely compelling. Another key difference is that McLaughlin, unlike on the earlier sessions, here uses a wah-wah pedal effect on his guitar parts, which makes the music seem rockier and his own playing more varied. On [10] it was immediately followed by Joe Zawinul's 'Orange Lady', although that was left uncredited on the record and buyers assumed that they were hearing a second section to 'Great Expectations'. Zawinul's agreeable melody would receive his own treatment on the debut album by Weather Report some months hence: here it stands as a beatific meditation which has an unfolding inevitability about it, the tambour in particular sounding some lovely textural notes.

Two other pieces cut that day were set aside until Columbia released their complete *Bitches Brew* edition [9]. 'Yaphet' sounds like a samba rhythm overlaid with whatever came into the players' heads. Again, the use of tabla and tamboura lends an improbable linking of musical traditions, but the whole piece is formless if amiable enough. The most annoying element – here and on the other music recorded that day – is Airto's use of the cuica, the Brazilian instrument which approximates a sort of tepid moaning sound. 'Corrado' starts with an amusing souvenir of the Miles-and-Teo relationship (or marriage). Teo asks, ' Is this gonna be part two, or . . .', only to be cut off by Miles snapping, 'It's part nine – what difference does it make, motherfucker?' To which the patient Macero mutters, 'All right, all right, here we go, stand by, it's part . . . something.' As it turns out, it's little more than a lumbering jam based around three chords. Maupin's bass clarinet, so effective as a textural device, here sounds enfeebled as a solo voice, and Miles plays a long semi-solo over a deafening Cobham racket before McLaughlin steps up. Thirteen minutes drag by, and one senses how much nonsense this band could create to go with their masterworks.

Nine days later, the ensemble was assembled again. This time Larry Young rejoined Corea and Hancock, DeJohnette was included as well as Cobham, and Dave Holland replaced Ron Carter. This wasn't a very productive session, three tracks only seeing the light of day on [9], and another turning up, peculiarly enough, as an edited take on the A-side of a single, which was released even before *Bitches Brew* went into the record stores. Nor was the music auspicious. 'Trevere' sounds like the start of something much longer and more focused, but merely stops after six minutes: as Bob Belden dryly puts it, 'Some perform-ances and compositions were not defined and not considered "releasable" (until the sessions became "legendary")'. 'The Big Green Serpent' is three minutes of mood music. Two completed takes, if such they were, of 'The Little Blue Frog' feature what is little more than a jam in the key of G, one settling into a groove that goes on for twelve minutes, another more moody and fragmented. For the single, Columbia used the last three minutes or so of the final section of the second take, and any Davis fans who bought it must have been baffled by the cryptic extract: Davis doesn't even play on the first half of it. Throughout the date, the exasperating sound of Airto and his cuica keeps filtering through.

Davis must have liked it. In December, he added the percussionist to his working quintet, which still involved Wayne Shorter, even though he hadn't been present on the recent record dates. But Shorter did rejoin the group which cut three further sessions over an eleven-day period between 27 January and 6 February 1970. At the first, the band numbered Davis, Shorter, Maupin, Zawinul, Corea, McLaughlin, Holland, Balakrishna, Cobham, DeJohnette and Moreira. 'Lonely Fire', credited to Davis as composer, consists of a single melodic motif which Davis repeats consistently over a rhythm that never settles into a real beat. Shorter then takes over and plays the same motif. Eventually, Holland finds a bass riff and the music settles into a groove, with sundry solos from horns and keyboards. After twenty-one minutes, and a return to the opening section, it peters out. This was eventually released as one of the four sides of [10], some four years after it had been made. 'Guinnevere' didn't make it to an album until the mixed bag of outtakes which made up *Circle In The Round* [11]. Based on a David Crosby song, the music drifts around the central melody but subsides into some aimless playing over a plodding beat, somewhat in the manner of the rock grooves which Davis would investigate later in the 1970s but without the punch and accelerated power. On both this and the previous session, Balakrishna had contributed little of consequence, and the Eastern tinge which the Indian instruments had applied earlier may have lost some of its appeal, since he didn't play on the next date.

The next day, the same group minus Balakrishna cut a Wayne Shorter tune, 'Feio', and a Joe Zawinul piece, 'Double Image'. 'Feio' is an odd study in contrasts: Holland repeats a three-note figure over and over, the horns harmonize on the mournful melody, McLaughlin throws in jagged shards of heftily distorted phrasing, the keyboards tattle to themselves, and the drums play a series of swelling snare rolls cut off by sudden cymbal shots. Davis's horn is treated with echo and what sounds like a little electronic dappling. Balanced between a dirge and some hyperactive rushing, it works surprisingly well, in part because it doesn't ramble on like the two pieces set down the previous day: 'Feio' runs just under twelve minutes in length.

'Double Image' settles into a groove while the horns create a lugubrious harmony on the melody. Holland's supple lines give the music lift, since it is otherwise grounded in a dull rock beat from the drums, plus some nattering from Moreira's bits of percussion. It hardly gets itself above a trudge, and unsurprisingly they had another go at it the following day, this time led off by McLaughlin in his rockiest clothes. The drums play stuttering figures that never quite resolve into the beat of the previous version, and Holland this time keeps coming back to a single note that nails the floor of the tune. This is the Davis band getting close to playing their own sour kind of rock'n'roll, and it eventually turned up as part of *Live–Evil* [12].

A further take of 'Double Image' was cut at the final date on 6 February along with Joe Zawinul's 'Recollections'. Although the composer's penchant for folkish melodies was often obscured by the settings they found themselves in, here the gentle meander which the group use to negotiate the music has a sweetness and unforced elegance which is wholly beguiling. The sound is lighter – Maupin wasn't present, and DeJohnette is the only traps drummer, Cobham credited only with playing triangle – and the deftly variegated keyboards, using ring modulators, echoplex and wah-wah devices, seem to snicker and scurry around the stately horn lines. This return to an approach resembling the stillness and meditation of 'In A Silent Way' might have seemed a backward step: it remained unreleased until [9] – as did the two and a quarter minutes of 'Take It Or Leave It', actually a fillet from Zawinul's original model for 'In A Silent Way', and a pretty melody which seems to emerge in pulseless waves.

A few weeks later, on the weekend of 6 and 7 March, Davis played at Bill Graham's New York rock venue the Fillmore East, where he was the opening act on a bill which also included two leading white rock groups, the Steve Miller Blues Band and Neil Young and Crazy Horse. It was a watershed moment both for Miles and for Clive Davis, the Columbia boss. Clive had pestered Miles for months to play at somewhere such as the Fillmore East. A furious Davis had been so incensed at the idea the first time around that he even threatened to leave Columbia altogether. For a time, there was a rumour that he wanted to sign to Berry Gordy's Motown, the black pop label which had enjoyed fabulous success in the 1960s. Later, another rumour suggested that he changed his mind because he found out that the label was largely funded on 'white money'. In any case, Davis could hardly afford to leave Columbia. His usual pattern of asking for advances on a regular basis, whether records were forthcoming or not, had left him hopelessly in hock to his label in financial terms. Clive Davis still felt that Miles was a valuable, prestige artist for Columbia, but even he had begun to feel that he would never recoup all the money that the company had already paid to Davis. And now, with Miles going electric, surely this was the perfect moment to focus him squarely on the young, album-rock audience who were quickly becoming the dominant force in the marketplace.

Davis's initial raging subsided quickly enough. After all, wasn't this just the opportunity he wanted to get away from the club circuit that he had come to detest? The Fillmore was typical of the kind of large-scale venues that had begun to appear all over America. As big as aircraft hangars, with acoustics to match, the new rock venues were quickly displacing the dance halls which had once been filled with couples dancing to the big bands of the swing era and after. Jazz groups didn't play in these places: the intimacy which small-group hard-bop thrived on was impossible to manufacture in these huge arenas. You needed amplifiers and a lot of noise. This was just what the Davis sextet was now delivering.

But Miles was still suspicious of rock promoters such as Bill Graham, and he couldn't see how audiences of young, white hippies would respond kindly to his music. He had a point: next to the simple offerings of Steve Miller and Neil Young, one a white bluesman and the other an electrified folkie, Davis was creating music that demanded a lot of his audience. Yet the band 'rocked', in a way that a Davis group never had before, and even if they weren't sure what was going on, the audience could respond to the sheer power and volume which Miles and his men were putting out.

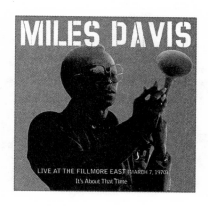

The show of 7 March, finally released for the first time on *It's About That Time* [13], thirty-one years after it was recorded, says much about the shock and adrenalin rush which Davis was creating with the band (the previous night's music has also been made available on *More Live At Filmore East* [14], but the poor sound is a deterrent to much enjoy-ment). The music goes by like a whirlwind. Chick Corea once opined that the music recorded at the *Bitches Brew* sessions was actually a rather tame version of what the working band was getting up to in live performance, and listening to these two sets – which, despite their 'official' status, suffer a little from only average fidelity, the engineers perhaps caught unawares by the volume of the group – one can hear what he means. DeJohnette's beat is furious, never as virtuosic as Tony Williams but concentrated and straight-ahead as Williams never was. Corea's piano parts are thrilling and full of unprecedented sounds and shapes: changing and colouring his Fender Rhodes tone with effects of every kind, creating grazing dissonances and superheated distortions as he went forward, he must have made heads turn by himself. Holland's electric bass was still working to a jazz dialect – even when he was playing simple patterns, he rarely sounded funky the way some of his successors would, the habitually clean and nimble execution adding a melodic strand to the group mix. Wayne Shorter was playing his last gigs with the band that weekend, yet he betrays little sign that he was anything less than wholly committed to the music. His soprano playing on the first 'Spanish Key' is astonishingly hot and powerful, his tenor playing on his own 'Masqualero' – almost reinvented for the electric band, with every step in the melody crashingly articulated – coolly magisterial.

Most of all, Davis sounds utterly invigorated. The spare delivery of *Bitches Brew* is displaced by a breathtaking intensity, long lines squalling up to screaming high notes which he scarcely went near during the Plugged Nickel sets of five years earlier. In spite of whatever amplification or embellishment was being used, it still sounds like a supercharged new edition of the old Miles, the familiar human sound embedded in his delivery.

Extraordinary things were created almost at will by the group, such as the babbling development of the first version of 'It's About That Time', a slug of collective improvisation which drew cheers from a probably mystified audience. Somehow it segues into a sliver of Davis's old set-closer 'The Theme', which the few Davis fans who were possibly in the audience that night surely didn't recognize. It might have been his way of saying that the past was over.

The following month, Columbia at last released *Bitches Brew*. The record was difficult and abstruse, but somehow it began clicking with the right buyers, and it went on to sell more than 400,000 units, dwarfing any of his previous records and at last reaching the sort of tally which Macero and Clive Davis had been hoping for all along. A gold record was earned and there was a Grammy Award too. After decades of winning plaques from the jazz publication *Down Beat*, Davis was finally breaking into wider circles. It was the start of some five years of drainingly intense activity.

The Other Records

1 *Miles Runs The Voodoo Down At Central Park* (Electric Blue)
2 *Odds 'N' Ends 1969–73* (Electric Blue)
3 *1969 Miles – Festiva De Juan Pins* (Sony)
4 *Music Forever & Beyond: The Selected Works Of Chick Corea 1964–1996* (Stretch)
5 *Bitches Brew Live* (Golden Age Of Jazz)
6 *Miles Davis* (Jazz Door)
7 *Another 1969 – Miles Vol. 2* (Stardust)
8 *Another 1969 – Miles Vol. 3* (Stardust)
9 *The Complete Bitches Brew Sessions* (Columbia)
10 *Big Fun* (Columbia)
11 *Circle In The Round* (Columbia)
12 *Live–Evil* (Columbia)
13 *Live At The Fillmore East (March 7, 1970): It's About That Time* (Columbia)
14 *More Live At Fillmore East* (So What)

Dark, Dark

1970–75

As it turned out, the 1970s would probably be the bleakest decade of Davis's life. In the early part of it, though, he was concerned mainly to work and record music and otherwise establish himself with a new audience which was remote from the admirers he had built up over many years. Jazz had become a dirty word to him, one which spoke of exploitation and the plantation mentality that he had come to despise in his business. As he looked around, he saw more reason than ever to align himself with black currents in popular music that looked and sounded far more relevant to contemporary American life than anything jazz had to offer. Jimi Hendrix was by now a veteran of his milieu, but still a vitally relevant figure, and an instrumental virtuoso who was a plausible counterpart to Davis himself. Another veteran, James Brown, was making the hardest and funkiest music of his career. A newer figure, Sly Stone, had emerged and was creating music which was a dramatic bridge between black pop and a darker, more radical music. Davis was most likely in two minds about the way the wind was blowing: pleased that black musicians were gaining ground and credibility, but concerned that he might not be a part of it too unless he acclimatized himself quickly.

The Fillmore East gigs were a learning experience on both sides. Davis had probably baffled a large part of his audience, and in return they scarcely registered his performance. He was angry that Bill Graham had paid him only a fraction of his usual fee for a major gig. But it was time well spent. After the release of *Bitches Brew* a few weeks later, Davis was quickly moving towards the right circles. Clive Davis, with the hubris which attends the pronouncements of most record industry leaders, was already claiming credit for the upswing in Miles's fortunes, but he was entitled to do so: a less sympathetic label chief would have stopped bankrolling the trumpeter's projects a long time before, and it was Clive who had persuaded his errant genius that the time had come to play for the 'right' people.

It seemed that Davis might almost be agreeing with him. After years of ignoring record company politics, Miles began going to conventions and dinners. He also began talking to the press, having largely avoided all but a handful of relatively trusted writers for most of his career. As the sales began to roll in for *Bitches Brew* – 100,000 within a few months – he softened, after a fashion.

There was still plenty to be done in the studios. Even before the first Fillmore concerts, Davis had been setting down more tracks, and it was a cycle that would take him through to the end of the year. On 18 February, a band consisting of Davis, Maupin, Corea, McLaughlin, Holland, DeJohnette and a second guitarist, Sonny Sharrock, recorded some music which would later turn up as part of *Jack Johnson* [1]. This was subsequently remade as 'Willie Nelson' on 27 February by a quintet of Davis, Steve Grossman, McLaughlin, Holland and DeJohnette. The remake is little more than a groove piece, set off by a simple bass rock-riff, with Grossman, Davis and McLaughlin – who sounds the most able by far in the context – all soloing. By itself, nothing much, but it was grist to Macero's mill, and when they came to make [1], it was there in the bank. One other piece was also set down on 27 February, and eventually came out as part of *The Complete Jack Johnson Sessions* [2]: 'Johnny Bratton', a slow, treacly jam which starts with an impassioned solo by Steve Grossman and has a tart, ineffective one by Davis.

On 3 March, the band produced the elephantine 'Go Ahead John', eventually released as one side of *Big Fun* [3]. The same quintet was involved and interested listeners will have to plough through forty-five minutes of five different takes included on [2], which were boiled down to a mere twenty-eight and a half minutes for the issued version. Over a bluesy sort of riff structure played by McLaughlin, his tone tightened to its maximum by the fuzz/wah-wah combination, he duets with Davis while Holland executes what sounds like a neanderthal rumble. Macero constructed this marathon and juiced it up by looping Davis at some points and overdubbing him on his own solos, as well as giving McLaughlin's guitar an even more unearthly quality by shifting him around the stereo spectrum, something he also does with DeJohnette's drums. Teo does, in point of fact, use this – and another device, instant playback, which was a kind of long-interval tape-delay – with the heady abandon which characterized technicians trying out new technologies for the first time. It's all far too long, but the sequence where Miles seems to be duetting with himself does have a lonely beauty about it. McLaughlin also got a piece more or less to himself, 'Archie Moore' [2], where he works with only bass and drums, playing a funereal blues that gets thoroughly nasty as it goes forward. A nice reminder that McLaughlin came from the land of Jeff Beck, and it would have made John a good B-side at the time.

Wayne Shorter and Bennie Maupin replaced Grossman on 17 March, for the session which produced two takes of 'Duran' [2], one of which previously came out as part of *Directions* [4]. A faster groove tune, anchored by Holland's snapping riff, this has McLaughlin anticipating the sort of waving and soaring he would make a speciality of in the Mahavishnu Orchestra. On the long version, the group roars to an almost transcendent climax, Shorter's soprano clambering over Maupin's doleful sound while the guitarist fires off jubilant chords. For once, Davis feels like something of a bystander on this piece. Three days later, it was Davis, Grossman, McLaughlin, Holland and Lenny White together for a single track, 'Sugar Ray' [2], one of the strangest of the pieces recorded in this period. Over a stop-go bass riff which McLaughlin hangs choppy little phrases on, Davis plays a straining melody and White tries to burst out of the rhythmic box. Ineffective as a stand-alone theme and of little value for intercutting, small wonder that this remained unheard for more than three decades.

Next came the sessions for [1]. Davis had been approached by a producer, Bill Cayton, who was making a documentary about the life of the famous black boxing heavyweight from the early part of the century. His interest piqued, Miles went deeply into the facts of Johnson's life and even ended up writing his own sleevenotes for the album when it was eventually released. There seems little doubt that he saw Johnson's various travails as a mirror for his own: a prominent black figure who had two white wives, was frowned on by white society but loved fast cars and the best champagne, and was exploited all the same by moneyed white interests. In the meantime, the sextet was in a state of flux, as suggested by the various different line-ups which had been accompanying Miles in the recent studio dates. Wayne Shorter had finally departed, to begin working with Joe Zawinul in their new venture, Weather Report. Chick Corea and Dave Holland were also itching to start their own group, but for the time being they remained: however, Miles already had his eye on a new bassist. Michael Henderson was barely of legal age – his photo in the *Complete Bitches Brew* edition makes him look like he's hardly out of school – yet he had already been playing with Stevie Wonder, and Davis had heard him and liked what he heard. He offered to bring the bemused Henderson – who didn't have much idea who Miles Davis was – to New York, and a day later the young man was playing bass on the first of the *Jack Johnson* sessions.

Henderson is in some ways the key contributor to the record. Where Holland would have chosen a more obviously jazz-inflected feel, Henderson had never played any jazz, only soul and funk, and he probably couldn't have played a line like Dave Holland or Ron Carter if he'd tried. Instead, he played vamps and

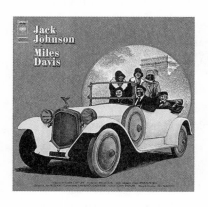

on-the-one grooves that sounded immortal, as if they could simply loop on and on – not a robotic sound, just even, unfussy, almost neutral in its potency. Henderson was cut more from the cloth that made the great Motown bassist James Jamerson, than in the tradition of Ray Brown and Paul Chambers.

Davis also wanted Buddy Miles, Jimi Hendrix's drummer, on the date, but in the end made do with Billy Cobham, who remembered the session as mildly chaotic in the by now accepted Miles Davis fashion. The group were cooling their heels in the studio while Miles and Teo conferred in the control room. McLaughlin, already bored with waiting, began trying some figures on his guitar strings. The displeased Davis called for quiet. But the guitarist carried on, Henderson and Cobham joined in, and before they knew it a jam was under way, which Davis then walked into. The result was 'Right Off' (a typically dry Davis title, cocking a snook at the black argot of 'Right on!'), although the idea that the side-long, twenty-seven-minute epic was some piece of spontaneous magic is soon enough laid to rest by actually listening to it. After some ten minutes of the band grooving along, Macero spliced in a piece of ambient playing, which sounds like Davis blowing over a ring modulator, before the groove returns. A different backdrop emerges around the eighteen-minute mark, which is worked up from a Sly Stone riff, and this lasts for a couple of minutes before the original beat is reinstated. The band then thrash on until the end. One completely unexpected moment arrives when Herbie Hancock suddenly starts playing, on a cheap Farfisa organ. Hancock had simply been on his way home with a bag of groceries and had looked in at the studio, only for Miles to second him into the band and have him see what he could do on an instrument he hadn't even seen before. The queer, roller-rink sound he gets out of the keyboard for a few passages is one of the strangest incidents on the record.

'Right Off' is often lauded as one of the classic Davis performances of the period, but careful listening (rather than surrendering to the admittedly seductive groove) suggests that it is no better and probably rather worse than many of the studio tracks which Macero compiled. It might be the funkiest piece a

Davis band had put down thus far, but its sheer length and lack of enduring steam take a lot of the impact out of it: one feels relieved when it's done. Davis's entrance on the track has been celebrated in musical analysis because he sets right a potential foul-up: McLaughlin was modulating to a different tonality, Henderson hadn't noticed, and Davis started his solo on a note that would work in either of the two keys. But his playing, for all its intensity, seems disjointed and often inappropriately forced. Whatever else he had gained in the way his music had turned, some of the long-form elegance of his acoustic days has been traded for thinking in sharp sentences rather than finely turned paragraphs. It might be right for what he was doing, but one could understand the dismay of many long-term Miles admirers.

'Yesternow' took up all of side two, and was an amalgam of parts of 'Willie Nelson', a brief fragment of 'Shhh/Peaceful' and new material based around a soul riff played by Henderson while McLaughlin lightly strokes chords, some sustained, others bitten off. More considered, better played, with space and dynamics given full creative rein, this is a superior track, and it ends with the ghostly finale of a brief orchestral passage, over which the muted Miles intones some final phrases and the actor Brock Peters recites an epitaph for Jack Johnson.

The record wasn't released until February 1971, but Davis was mightily pleased with it, and even took the remarkable step of giving Teo Macero a nod in his sleevenotes: 'But dig the guitar and bass – They are "far-in" – and so is the producer Teo Macero. He did it again!' It was overdue praise, since Macero had been piecing together hours of Davis's music into workable forms. Years later, when Columbia began releasing their 'complete' editions of the various periods of Davis's career, the fragmentary nature of the trumpeter's way of working was fully manifest, as was Macero's skill in creating listenable results. The piecemeal nature of [2] in particular, which exposes many of the nerve ends in the sessions in ways which perhaps only musicologists can really enjoy, is evidence enough, and though Macero has kept his own counsel with regard to Columbia's milking of all this material, one doubts if he has been pleased with the way the bones have been comprehensively picked over.

The sextet, with Steve Grossman now a regular replacement for Wayne Shorter, was recorded by Columbia on the second evening of a four-night stint at the Fillmore West in San Francisco, on 10 April. *Black Beauty* [5] was for many years available only as a double-LP set in Japan. As a record of the small group in performance, it's not far short of the impact of *It's About That Time*. Grossman may not be the equal of Shorter, but his piping solos have the charge of an awesome virtuosity behind them. Grossman had been an exceptional prodigy: according to Dave Liebman, Steve's brother, who had been a teacher at Berklee, 'just got a hold of Steve and said, "You do this. You're not coming out of that basement until you do this" ... by the time Steve was eleven or twelve, he

could play like Bird.' Grossman had all the modern saxophone masters down pat, and the flair and energy of his playing have their own kind of excitement, even if he doesn't have the maverick imagination of a Shorter. Holland and DeJohnette are still carving enormous rhythmic circles out of modest materials, and Davis himself sounds in acerbic, driven form. But the most exciting element is again the work of Chick Corea. Overdriving his effects units to the limit, making his piano resemble everything from an overamplified guitar to a crumbling gothic organ, what ought to sound like the most dated thing on the stage is actually the most fascinating. A few older pieces are still clinging on in the set, such as the 'I Fall In Love Too Easily'/'Sanctuary' segue, but otherwise it is all the newer material which runs through the programme.

Davis couldn't have wanted a better keyboard player than Corea at this point, but he seemed undecided about how many players he needed, and in May he brought in another one: Keith Jarrett. One of the stars of the Charles

Lloyd band, Jarrett had been making records of his own for a couple of years and, like his fellow players, was at first doubtful about using electric keyboards. But he wanted so much to work with Davis that he overcame this antipathy easily enough. On 19 May, the band consisting of Davis, Grossman, Jarrett, Hancock, McLaughlin, Henderson, Cobham and Moreira, plus a second bassist in the shape of the sessionman Gene Perla, worked on two tracks. 'Honky Tonk' was intended as 'roadhouse' music by Davis, and mixes stop-start funk with a cornball rock'n'roll riff that McLaughlin must have been laughing at even as he played it. Edited down to six minutes, this piece was used as a filler track on *Get Up With It* [6] four years later, although [2] includes two longer takes of it. The complete edition also released a piece called 'Ali', made on the same day, for the first time, in the form of two completed takes. For some reason, Gene Perla

plays the twisty bass part rather than Henderson, and Jarrett thumps away at a Rhodes that is so distorted that the notes are at times barely identifiable. Davis plays his trumpet through an octave pedal which alters his sound, too, so the entire piece has the air of an overheated power station. In a typically curious juxtaposition, Miles chooses to play rather gently and gracefully on both takes.

Two days later, the band had slimmed down to a quintet, with Davis, Jarrett, McLaughlin, DeJohnette and Moreira working through an entirely different kind of piece. 'Konda' sounds much more like Jarrett's natural territory, a pastorale of sorts on which he plays an attractive introduction (and on a more natural-sounding piano). From there, in a piece which was supposedly recorded in five separate sections, the music, with no bass and only retiring work from both DeJohnette and Moreira, drifts along in the manner of a thinly spread tone poem, which eventually dissolves into electronic burbling and finally breaks into tempo around the eleven-minute mark. If anything, it resembles the sort of mood music which Weather Report would make a much better fist of in their early records. An edited version came out as part of [4], but the complete track is on [2].

This kind of sound-painting continued on the next three sessions. 'Nem

Um Talvez' (Not Even A Maybe) was a piece by the Brazilian instrumentalist and composer Hermeto Pascoal, whom Miles had invited to take part in the sessions of 27 May and 3–4 June. A dreary, droning piece mainly for trumpet and keyboards, whatever life it might have had is all but stifled by the passionless recording. Four versions (numbered up to take 19!) are included on [2], and one is used on *Live–Evil* [7], along with the other two pieces which Pascoal also contributed. But 'Selim' and 'Little Church' sound like the same piece as 'Nem Um Talvez', slightly redecorated by having Pascoal sing wordlessly along with the trumpet, for which Miles attached a wah-wah pedal for the first time. Besides these, there was a throwaway up-tempo piece called 'Little High People', two takes of which are both marred by Moreira contributing some of his silliest noisemaking (at one point it sounds like he's blowing a kazoo). Percussionists were often the clowns in jazz-rock bands, and Airto seems to have started the trend.

The one substantial thing to come out of these dates – which proved to be Davis's final studio sessions for almost two years – was a roiling, themeless, two-part jam called 'The Mask', by a band made up of Davis, Grossman, McLaughlin, Holland (playing acoustic bass), DeJohnette and Moreira, with three keyboard players: Chick Corea on a Rhodes with a ring modulator, Keith Jarrett on a second Rhodes with a wah-wah attachment, and Herbie Hancock playing organ. The first part is an eight-minute maelstrom, which Davis doesn't play on, and which is basically a battle between the rhythm section and however many of the keyboard players are involved. A lot of it might not be much more than noise, but it's an exhilarating noise, and it's rather amusing to find Keith Jarrett, whose latter-day saintly sensibility would have scorned such nonsense, being involved. The second part is a slowly creeping groove where Holland walks up and down the scale and the other musicians gather like clouds. It rumbles on past the fifteen-minute mark and is capped by Davis's patented 'Teo, play some of that.' They obviously didn't like it that much, since it went unissued until the release of [2].

Since the *Bitches Brew* sessions themselves, Davis had taken a group into the studios on sixteen occasions between November 1969 and June 1970. Teo Macero must have stockpiled hour upon hour of tapes, with countless takes and fragments adding up to an unfeasible sprawl of music. In his early days of making records, Davis had acquired a reputation of wanting to get the job done quickly, and a dislike of having to do multiple takes of the same piece. He had completely gone back on that philosophy. Now he would rather keep working at something until the feel was absolutely right. But what *was* right?

Some of the same thing went on with his live recordings, which Macero also had to mastermind. Later that June, the Davis band played four consecutive nights back at the Fillmore East in New York, and Columbia recorded every night. Macero trimmed and stitched the music until it fitted on four sides of a double LP, *Miles Davis At Filmore* [8], each side titled 'Wednesday Miles', 'Thursday Miles' and so forth. None of the individual tunes were otherwise

identified; instead, Macero made each side a medley of some of Miles's recent greatest hits. So 'Saturday Miles', for instance, consists of 'It's About That Time', 'I Fall In Love Too Easily', 'Sanctuary', 'Bitches Brew', 'Willie Nelson' and 'The Theme'. The band included Grossman, Holland, DeJohnette and Moreira, but at its centre was the stormy partnership of Chick Corea and Keith Jarrett. Where Corea had been a one-man arsenal on the earlier live sets, when Jarrett also threw his weight behind the electronic effects the music was even more aggressively busy, as the two players' fingers roamed over the keyboards and the effects units.

It wasn't, though, anarchic. The audience might have been puzzled about what was being played and where the material was coming from, but Davis seems in full command of what was happening. Although it's not always easy to tell, given the tight way in which Macero edited the tapes, Miles had developed a system of cues whereby the musicians knew when he wanted a new piece to come up: all he had to do was play a bar or two of the melody. A set full of unfamiliar music, with no titles mentioned and no apparent starting or stopping, would whirl past the ears of the audience, and they might imagine that the whole thing had been a near-improvisation. Instead, Davis controlled every switch.

The Fillmore set has often been disregarded over the years, but it has many absorbing passages, and while one wonders how it would have sounded without Macero's terse editing, his approach has the probable merit of thinning stretches where the group merely filled space. The problem for Davis seems to have been how to make sure he was consistently heard. His answer is usually to blow as loudly as possible and in the upper stretches of his horn, which in one sense is no answer at all: for a player whose entire technique had been founded on making the most of his middle range and blowing without undue force, he is going back on most of his jazz principles. Yet it's still a musician improvising trumpet parts in the way he always has done. Sometimes he can sound close to desperation, shrieking out a note off the top of the stave to make sure he is cutting through the surrounding barrage, and can come dangerously near to hamming his lines. At other points, as in the bracingly intense reading of 'It's About That Time' which closes Thursday's set, he makes it work. As much as he controls the music, he sounds like the one who is most vulnerable: while his young band relish every over-the-top flourish, Davis is the one who is having to unlearn things in order to flourish himself.

Corea and Jarrett certainly take their opportunities to go crazy. The zip and zap of the opening to the Saturday set is sheer sonic mayhem, and terrific fun as much as anything else. There are spoilers, too: Moreira's presence is often superfluous, at worst distracting and trivial. Grossman appears to get very little space, in part because he was playing a lot of tenor, and Davis only wanted to hear soprano and apparently ordered Teo to cut those solos. But it was a band chasing down numerous avenues, some of them inevitably revealing themselves to be blind alleys, and there is so much to listen to as they do so that one hardly begrudges the weak spots.

In August, the saxophonist Gary Bartz took over Steve Grossman's role. Bartz was a good deal older – just coming up to his thirtieth birthday – and a veteran of several hard-bop situations, having been a sideman with Art Blakey, Max Roach and others, and with a couple of albums of his own for Milestone already under his belt. Where Grossman was something of an adept mimic, Bartz had his own thing going on, which was marked by a very big sound – though he played alto and soprano, he was almost in the Sonny Rollins lineage of grand, invincible saxophone improvisers. He went with the rest of the Davis group to the Isle Of Wight Rock Festival that same month, a sort of British version of the Woodstock event of two years earlier, where parts of Davis's set were scissored by Teo into two chunks which eventually turned up on a pair of Columbia compilations from the event, now available as *Message To Love* [9]. Miles had them titled as 'Call It Anythin'', although again it was a medley of his recent material. The players remembered the event mostly for its size, with anything up to 400,000 people in attendance. The surviving music seems to push the rhythm section ever further forward, and a shade closer to funk.

It was also the last recording to feature Dave Holland and Chick Corea, since both departed to form their own group, Circle. Holland in particular wanted to try more open-ended kinds of improvisation: his little masterpiece for the ECM label, *Conference Of The Birds*, recorded two years later, hints at some of the ways he saw his music moving towards a blend of free and structured playing. But Davis's band wasn't offering that kind of opportunity. The interesting thing was that both Corea and Holland felt that the group was still working, deep down, to the old disciplines of jazz: that themes and solos and their accompaniment still dictated much of the content, even as things were churning up around them.

Davis might have felt the same thing. But he was disinclined to do too much about it yet. It was, after all, still one very impressive band. Michael Henderson came in full-time as Holland's replacement, and Jarrett continued to play the electric keyboards by himself. For the most part, this edition of the band was scarcely recorded officially by Columbia: another set from the Fillmore West, from 17 October, is preserved on *What I Say? Vol. 2* [10]. The band tear into 'Directions', which eventually peters out into a slow-starting 'Honky Tonk', which then brews back up into 'What I Say'. Davis plays fierce open horn and some almost quacking lines with the wah-wah attachment, and Bartz snarls through a solo on 'Honky Tonk' which must be as free as any saxophonist ever played with Davis. 'What I Say', a new piece, evolves from a tick-tock rhythmic riff that various band members overlay while Davis plays a bubbling high-register blast. As scruffy as the recording quality is, the feel of how intense and loud this band was does sink in.

Gary Bartz, who had been used to working in front of the racket of Art Blakey and Max Roach, felt that it was as loud as any rock band he'd ever heard. It was a period when ear-trashing amplification systems were begin-ning to dominate live rock shows. Legendarily loud groups such as the Who and Black Sabbath played at painful volume levels, and it was a trend which Davis fell into line with. In December, the band played four nights at a

club in Washington DC, the Cellar Door, and Columbia recorded all the music. Out of it came [7], although Teo Macero used only material from the final night's music – when John McLaughlin had been invited to join in as a sort of guest star. Columbia have for some time been promising to release mate-rial from the previous three evenings and it was released as this book went to press. Macero turned the Saturday music into four LP sides with his customary editing

panache, although there are some of his strangest choices of splicing, such as when he cuts off the fierce groove which had been built on the opening 'Sivad' (alias 'Directions'), inserts a few seconds of the studio version of 'Honky Tonk', and then sticks on the live treatment of the same piece (this was all long before the original 'Honky Tonk' would see the light of day). He also uses the desultory studio pieces with Hermeto Pascoal, discussed above, as side-closers or openers.

Keith Jarrett felt that the Saturday music was unrepresentative, since McLaughlin's presence held back some of their usual more freely engaged playing, and next to the wild abandon of the playing on [10], one can see what he means: a lot of [7] does sound much tamer. But it does set out, in decent sound, the kind of momentum the group could generate. 'What I Say' exalts Michael Henderson's skill at latching on to a one-chord riff and calmly pumping it for twenty-one minutes. DeJohnette sounds like he might be growing tired of backbeats in this situation – something which eventually led to him leaving the following year – but gamely plays with all the necessary muscle. If Bartz doesn't sound as exciting as he did at Fillmore West, he is partly overshadowed by McLaughlin, who plays sensational music on 'What I Say' and 'Inamorata'. The two long pieces, respectively titled 'Funky Tonk' and 'Inamorata', are both actually medleys created by Macero: the first blends 'Directions', 'Inamorata' and 'Funky Tonk', the second reprises 'Inamorata/Funky Tonk' and then moves through 'Sanctuary' and 'It's About That Time'. When [7] was released in November 1971, Davis fans would have been surprised most at hearing the leader spending so much time in his highest register – he claimed that area of the horn had never suited his older music, but the electric medium all but demanded it – and with the wah-wah attachment on the trumpet. Some jazz listeners might even have been reminded of the muted playing of Bubber Miley with Duke Ellington, five decades earlier: Miles gave up on much of his individuality of tone with the wah-wah device, but he was smart enough to give it speech-like cadences too. His work on the opening minutes of 'Funky Tonk' is a vivid picture of what he was coming up with. Keith Jarrett gets a solo feature in the middle of 'Funky Tonk' and 'Inamorata' comes to a curious end: Conrad Roberts, in tones that suggest a mix of Superfly and Paul Robeson, intones a brief poem which seems to equate music with masculinity, and after this the music swells back up with a much rougher and more violent-sounding mix – actually, an oddly effective way to end the track.

It was the end of an incredibly prolific year of work, in the studio and on the stage. It had been less than two years since he recorded *In A Silent Way*, but in that time Davis had shifted the axis of his music into another orbit altogether – without giving up on being Miles, still *Down Beat*'s pollwinner and still working in any jazz club for which he accepted a booking. He had already outlasted Jimi Hendrix: the genius of rock guitar had died in London that September, after choking to death following a barbiturates overdose, and the album project which the two giants had proposed, circling around each other like a pair of wary heavyweights, never came to pass. It was left to old faithful Gil Evans to make an album made up of Hendrix compositions, in 1974: Davis never played anything by him.

Jazz-rock was gaining ground. Besides Davis, there were American bands such as Tony Williams's Lifetime and the newly formed Weather Report, with Joe Zawinul and Wayne Shorter; and for some time Herbie Hancock had been leading groups which mixed jazz with funk and maybe a little rock. All these were bands led by ex-Davis sidemen. But in England there was Soft Machine and Ian Carr's Nucleus, and elsewhere in Europe there were bands that hadn't been slow to mix jazz improvisation with rock feel, or the other way round. Some groups came at it from the other direction, too: Frank Zappa's Mothers Of Invention had a line-up which used saxophones and other horns and attacked Zappa's fiendishly constructed music with a very different approach to the *lumpen* rock aesthetic.

None of this was giving Davis much pleasure: when bands such as John McLaughlin's Mahavishnu Orchestra began outselling him and winning over rock audiences more easily than he did, he raged. Opening for rock acts at stadium shows was something he became used to in this period, but he was Miles Davis: who were these white motherfuckers? In 1971, the personnel of the band began to shift again, and became blacker: DeJohnette left in August, Moreira moved over to Chick Corea's new band, and Leon 'Ndugu' Chancler and the percussionists Don Alias and James 'Mtume' Foreman came in for the European tour which ended the year. Ndugu and Mtume were young men who brought another slug of soul music to the band: more in tune with Sly And The Family Stone than the literature of hard-bop. Chancler in particular was a step away from Jack DeJohnette, and Mtume displaced Moreira's incessant tinkering and fiddling with a more basic rumble of percussive noise from congas and hand drums. It bothered Keith Jarrett, who had begun to separate himself from the rest of the group, and it certainly thickened the bottom end, which shifted even further from any semblance of swing rhythms. Surviving recordings from the European tour, of which *Miles Davis + Keith Jarrett Live* [11], recorded in Milan on 21 October, and *What I Say? Vol. 1* [12], from a concert in Vienna on 5 November, are typical, suggest a band being pulled primarily in one direction, by the rock-like Henderson, towards a music that wasn't slick enough to be funk, was too improvisationally complex to be rock, yet had left virtually every one of its jazz procedures at the door. As usual, the unofficial recordings are often muddy and not up to par, but enough of the music comes through for the listener to discern the band's power.

One change was that Jarrett was playing much more conventionally at this point. Although he is often described as the most 'out' player in the group, chafing at the more conventional tendencies of the rhythm section, the splintery electronics and experimental wildness which marked his playing while Corea was also in the band have been largely wiped away. The sane and thoughtful solo on 'Spanish Key' from [11] is characteristic of the way he was moving, and one can hear him applying much of the harmonic vocabulary which he would celebrate fully in his early (acoustic) recordings for ECM. Bartz remains a major improviser even if his tone seems to have rarely been effectively caught by microphones. And Davis spindles his sound with ever more recourse to the wah-wah, or blasts his way to the forefront.

It had been a mixed year for Davis. Marguerite Eskridge's son with him, Erin, was born on 29 April, but Marguerite was tired of Davis's return to regular drug use and left their home in New York. There were battles with the IRS over taxes, and his health was starting to worsen again, with a gallstone causing him pain and new worries over his arthritic hip. Miles fretted that his music had

Dark, Dark 1970–75

become too esoteric at a time when black audiences felt connected to Sly Stone, James Brown and Marvin Gaye. A remark later attributed to Jack Bruce seems particularly pertinent: 'Miles wants to be Jimi Hendrix, but he can't work it out on trumpet.' How could Miles Davis compete with the soul musicians who dominated the black music charts?

His answer was to enlist the help of another British musician, Paul Buckmaster, whom he had met in London while on the 1971 tour. Buckmaster played cello and had a mixed background of classical and avant garde studies, and he had the idea of a project which might mirror some of the work of the German composer Karlheinz Stockhausen, using motivic cells as musical forms, thick textures of sound, a grand pulse around which other elements – as jarringly abstract or dissonant as anyone pleased – would whirl like planets. Yet it had to have the sort of feel which musicians such as Brown had as a given in their music. Was it possible to make a *bona fide* street music that also stood its ground as high art ?

On The Corner [13] was the result, even though it was certainly not what Buckmaster had in mind (he has even described it as his least favourite Miles Davis record). It was reviled in most quarters when it was given any media attention at all, and it sold poorly – if James Brown's audience were aware of its existence, they certainly didn't add it to their collections. Davis assembled a huge cast of musicians to play on the sessions, which were held in June and July 1972. Sixteen of them are listed in the latest CD edition, and there are probably others who aren't mentioned – Buckmaster himself, for one. Not only was there extensive editing and looping by Macero, there was multiple overdubbing, and musicians playing with little idea of what they might be contributing to. The saxophonist Dave Liebman was called in to the session at more or less the last moment, and Miles told him to just play – all Liebman could hear was the percussionists, and the faint tick of the keyboards, which were otherwise inaudible, being plugged straight into the mixing desk. Badal Roy, a tabla player, was told by Davis, 'You, start', and he simply improvised a line. Buckmaster had prepared charts for everyone, yet they were hardly even consulted. There were familiar Davis musicians such as John McLaughlin, Chick Corea – but not Keith Jarrett, who would never return – and Jack DeJohnette, and new names, including Al Foster, Carlos Garnett and Collin Walcott.

What they brewed up was a non-stop, thumping sound that did at times resemble the giant heartbeat that Buckmaster might have had in his plan, rooted in Henderson's little catalogue of riffs and the hissing hi-hat cymbal pulses which drove most of the pieces. Threaded through that were Roy's tabla parts, and over it were doomy-sounding organ, tinkling or thudding pianos, and bursts of saxophone, guitar or trumpet. Davis himself sounded absent for much of the way, but he plays a lot on the record too: the long wah-wah solo that overlays the opening section of 'Helen Butte' is very strong. The record starts with one marathon track and ends with another, and in between are the briefer 'Black Satin', which is heavily overdubbed and feels fatter and more focused than the other pieces, and 'One And One'. Nobody could complain about Davis giving his fans short measure: whereas most LPs ran for forty minutes or so, this one was fifty-five minutes long.

If the jazz press had been rough on recent Davis projects, it set new precedents for abuse of this one. The packaging, with its gaggle of cartoon blacks on the two sides of the cover, said nothing about who played on the record (a move which outraged many of the musicians who had taken part). Most of the musicians who played on it, if they commented at all, disliked it when they heard it. Columbia had little idea about marketing it to the kind of people Davis wanted to buy his records, and sales were modest. Davis fumed that nothing was being sent in the direction he wanted: how could he get his music across if his records weren't being sold in the right way, if he wasn't playing for the right audiences?

On The Corner is *sui generis*. Recent years have seen it wholly re-evaluated, to the point where many seem to consider it a lost masterpiece. It's more accurate to suggest that the record's neither as terrible as its many detractors claimed, nor as outstanding as its late admirers have insisted. Its dependence on rhythmical structures – at once loose and strictly patrolled – for its form would find numerous subsequent echoes in other musics, such as dub reggae, hip hop and drum'n'bass dance music. But that scarcely makes *On The Corner* a wellspring of any of these ideas, more an accident of history. Since the 'solo' instruments are for once not mixed to the fore, they tend to merge in with a backdrop that is really a foreground, creating an internal democracy which has the ear searching for peaks that aren't there. In fact, there are many creative stretches of improvisation, by Davis, McLaughlin and others, which seem to drift by almost unnoticed. At the time, detractors moaned that it was unendurably tedious, that nothing was really 'happening'. If anything, too much was happening – the complexity which Buckmaster had sought was there in abundance, but it was settled into a kind of wallpaper. The street-beat Davis had prized was there, too, but abstracted by the ingenuities of his other players and Teo's cutting and mixing. The only real melody in the set comes in 'Black Satin', which was actually released as a single at the time under the title 'The Molester'.

It was all calculated, measured. There was no natural 'feel'. 'I don't care who buys the records,' said Miles to Michael Watts of the British *Melody Maker*, 'as long as they get to the black people so I will be remembered when I die. I'm not playing for any white people, man.' He actually cared very much who bought the records.

It was the start of a bad period for him. Drugs, which shadowed him one way or the other for most of his adult life, were taking an ominous precedence in his day-to-day existence again. There were domestic incidents, a former tenant in Davis's building claiming that he had menaced her. In October, he crashed his car and broke both his ankles. Back at Columbia, Teo Macero was still sitting on piles of unreleased tapes, and probably wondering what to do with them all. The recent albums had secured nothing like the sales successes of *Bitches Brew*, which was starting to look like the peak of Davis's sales for the label.

One more track, 'Ife', came out of the *On The Corner* sessions, and was eventually released on the patchwork *Big Fun* [3]. Settled in a slightly more tepid groove, run off an endlessly repeated bass riff, this features, in addition to many of the *On The Corner* crew, Lonnie Smith on piano. Somebody contributes some burbling electronics at various points. Paul Buckmaster remembered writing little keyboard phrases to make up the melodic content of the piece, but melody hardly ever breaks through: as with most of what he contributed

to the *On The Corner* sessions, Buckmaster's ideas were either ignored, subsumed or so dispersed as to be unrecognizable. But it is a lighter, almost sunny piece overall, and in the final third of a track which runs for more than twenty-one minutes, the groove subsides altogether and Davis plays ballad lines over tolling chords on the organ.

The seemingly ad hoc way in which Davis had been gathering in players for these sessions ended with this track. Thereafter, he returned to his old concept, of using his working band, since in September he put together a fresh touring group. Carlos Garnett played saxophones, Cedric Lawson was on keyboards, and Henderson, Al Foster, Badal Roy and Mtume made up the rhythm section. But the most significant addition was Reggie Lucas: for the first time, Davis hired a guitar player as a member of his regular group. He had tried to persuade John McLaughlin to join him before, but McLaughlin smartly sensed that his own star was in the ascendant, and had turned him down. Lucas was young and virtually unknown.

The nucleus of the group minus Garnett but with Khalil Balakrishna on sitar, did a studio session on 6 September where they recorded 'Rated X', which eventually came out as part of [6]. It prefigured everything Davis would do over the next three years. He didn't play trumpet at all: he sat at a Yamaha organ and fingered droning, reedy chords that ran through the entire piece (and were mixed right at the front). Behind him, the band played a themeless jangle of sound on one chord, but they abruptly disappeared and reappeared at will, the engineers cutting them off and bringing them back while the organ buzzed on and on. Teo Macero remembered that the two elements hadn't even been designed to go together: the organ lines were actually part of something else. Utterly dark and disassociated, it is an amazing piece of music. If it doesn't sound like Miles Davis, it doesn't sound much like anybody else, either. Small wonder that Columbia executives refused to let Teo put it out at the time.

The new band were recorded for another double album at New York's Philharmonic Hall on 29 September [14], and the first piece played was 'Rated X' (though in a more linear performance, without the jump-cut edits which could be done in the studio). At this point, Davis's audience were at least accustomed to his new music: *On The Corner* was released around this time, and any who still harboured thoughts of his getting up to play 'My Funny Valentine' must have given up on it by now.

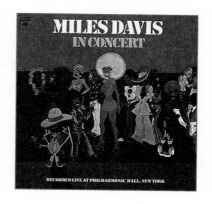

But the thick onslaught of the ensemble – with nine players, the largest working band Davis had run since the *Birth Of The Cool* group – must have been a formidable proposition. It certainly posed some problems for Columbia's engineers, whose sound on the resulting record is often muddy and unkind. The record has some very attractive moments, mostly in the form of solo passages fronted by Davis or Garnett, but these hark back to the older style of Davis band: the dense weave of instruments he had been seeking never seems apparent (much of the time, several of the players are barely audible). The sleeve of the disc has more atmosphere than much of the record. On the front cover (by the same artist, Corky McCoy, responsible for [13]), cartoon street people sport and parade for the observer (or voyeur).

The car accident in October left Davis in poor shape. One of his female friends, Jackie Battle, got his sister Dorothy to come to the house, which was in a state of domestic disrepair. He was hobbling around on crutches following the accident, but it didn't stop him from going and looking for drugs. He managed to get back in the studios in December, where he recorded a single piece, 'Billy Preston' [6], which sounded like it might have been another part of the [13] sessions: hissing cymbal beat, choppy bass riffs, knifing guitar chords, and Miles trawling lines across the top.

There was more trouble in February of the following year, when Davis and a woman were arrested outside his house for possession of a firearm and drugs, which were found nearby. The drugs charge was dropped, but Miles had to pay a fine over the gun and spent the night in jail. It was a strange period. Davis had plenty of time to sit around and brood about how his band would go. He brought in Dave Liebman as his saxophone player, who would stay well into 1974. Lonnie Smith joined for a time on piano, but was out by the summer, as were the Indian musicians. In April, he brought in another guitarist, Pete Cosey, a blues-band veteran from Chicago. Cosey was another seemingly unlikely choice for a Miles sideman: he had worked on many house sessions for the Chess label, liked peculiar sounds and unusual tunings, and didn't seem like either a rock or a jazz man.

In July 1973, the band toured Europe. Reviews were mixed, and many complained that Miles didn't seem to be playing all that much. But bootlegs of the tour scarcely support the theory. He is all over *Olympia, 11 juliet 1973* [15], often employing the wah-wah device, and leaving multitudinous rests and spaces in what would otherwise have been solos: now they were more like continuing commentaries on what the rest of the band were doing. It suited the way the ensemble sound was growing and evolving. Now the band was without any keyboard player, and with the guitarists often playing as rhythm instruments along with the bass and the percussionists, sometimes Davis wanted to be a rhythm player too: he drops in little motifs almost as a percussionist might. The one who carried the melodic tide was Dave Liebman: a Coltrane acolyte who knew his master's music probably better than any other American saxophonist. Liebman recognized that his task was to carry on in the lineage of Trane and Shorter, and his featured moments brim with notes, torrential in their delivery. When Cosey solos, he too is a blaze of sound, but different to Liebman: instead of the arpeggiated clusters of notes a saxophonist relies on, he has a full electronic palette to call on.

The Paris Olympia concert is only in average sound, but it is full of energy and light. A lot of the material seems unidentifiable. The straight man of the group is Al Foster, who went on to become one of Davis's few close musician friends, right up until the trumpeter's death. Foster's background was in hard-bop groups, a medium which he eventually went back to, but he could play in a style that followed the original lead of Jack DeJohnette but was more distilled, less thrashingly virtuosic. The other thing the band had begun doing was approximating the sudden halts which are used on 'Rated X': whoever is 'soloing' will suddenly find himself bathed in silence, only for the ensemble to crash in again within a few beats. And it isn't all tumult: some episodes emerge from only a light skittering of percussion, a stealthy fragment of groove.

Back in New York, Davis and the group – with an extra saxophonist, John Stubblefield – recorded 'Calypso Frelimo' [6] on 17 September. It is another marathon, at thirty-two minutes in duration, but not as long as was originally intended: Miles wanted to make a record that consisted of a single piece stretched across two sides of an LP. He plays organ throughout and probably overdubbed his wah-wah trumpet parts later. The piece is worked across three segments: a fast section with a lick of calypso melody over a sizzling undertow of percussion, which after ten minutes suddenly cuts out. Then, a long slow stretch sustained by a repeating bass riff and muezzin-like guitar chords sets up a trumpet solo which aches, even through the distortion effects Davis was using. Eventually the fast pace of the introductory section is reasserted, and steadily transmutes a Latin feel to a more aggressive funk workout. Dave Liebman felt that it was 'closest to what we sounded like live during my time with Miles'.

Later that autumn, the band returned to Europe for a second time. Just before they left, they played a gig at the Jazz Workshop in Boston, some of which is included on *Call It What It Is* [16]. 'Ife' ambles dreamily across thirty-four minutes, and two pieces which would eventually be called 'Prelude' and 'Zimbabwe' fill out the rest. Already the band have moved on a little. The dynamics have evened out somewhat, the pace is more consistent, with fewer shifting-down sequences that recede towards quiet. The *On the Corner* groove is back in the ascendant, with less detritus in the sound. Though that isn't always the case with surviving sets from the European sojourn, *Another Bitches Brew* [17], recorded in Belgrade, and *Palais des Sports 1973* [18], cut in Paris, two gigs a few days apart, mostly follow a similar pattern.

New York audiences would hear it again the following March, when the Davis band played at Carnegie Hall and Columbia's engineers were once again pressed into action. *Dark Magus* [19] became yet another double live album, although for many years it was available only in Japan. Though it is a record which many find special in the Davis lexicon, there are problems with it. Rough and turbulent, the music doesn't have the vividness of some of what this and the next Davis bands managed to secure, something Dave Liebman hinted at in his sleevenotes to the 1997 reissue. It was an odd occasion in that Davis threw two extra wild cards into the mix: the guitarist Dominique Gaumont, who had met Cosey while they were in Paris, and the saxophonist Azar Lawrence, a McCoy Tyner sideman who was effectively auditioning with the band. With three guitarists and two saxophonists, the band is back to being nine-strong. On the first disc, after nearly forty minutes of thunder, 'Wili, Part 2' takes the form of a ballad and features some exemplary playing from Liebman and Davis. The second disc is often soupy and marred by Gaumont's solos, which sound tiresomely unimaginative next to those of Cosey. In the passages dominated by the guitars, the transmogrification of a Miles Davis group from a jazz to a rock band is all but complete, except here it doesn't sound so good.

It was almost Dave Liebman's last hurrah with the band, but there was a final studio date in June. The month before, Davis had been touring in South America, his health wavering: he had a mild heart attack while in Brazil, and if that wasn't enough to sharpen his sense of mortality, he also learned of the death of Duke Ellington. 'He Loved Him Madly' [6], recorded on either 19 or 20 June, was Davis's threnody in memory of Duke, whose flowery, wry homage to his audiences – 'We would like you to know that we do love you *maadly*' – gifted the piece its title. For thirty-two minutes, the piece goes off like a procession in a cathedral, organ lines glowering at the bottom, guitar parts twanging dolefully above, Al Foster tapping out a military tattoo. There are a couple of strange edits before Liebman plays a haunted-sounding solo on alto flute and eventually Davis picks up his trumpet. Teo Macero used a new reverb unit which gave the group the sensation of sounding like it was in some great gothic tomb. Soft, spacey and as unearthly as anything Davis ever recorded, it is a luminous and unsettling piece.

Liebman had in fact already left the group, going on to form his own group, Lookout Farm. Many years later, he reflected on the Davis band of that time: 'That period was, like, chaotic, because he wouldn't let anybody do nothing but him. And you know, he didn't really know what he was doing. He wasn't enough of a musician, in a sense. He was great, but there were holes in his musicianship that did not allow him to really be able to tell you what goddamn chord to play, or the exact beat. Once Chick, Herbie and Keith were outta there, you had a bunch of rock'n'roll guys except for Al and myself. You really didn't have anybody that knew anything. What you had with us was almost like an *Ascension* vibe. It was polyphony like crazy, but not on purpose. It was because nobody knew what they were doing. But I think compared to the 80s it was much more raw and exploratory, and in a lot of ways a better feeling.'

Eventually Davis settled on the unlikely choice of Sonny Fortune as his new saxophonist. Fortune was another player from a straight jazz background – it was a little like Davis's choice in hiring Sonny Stitt back in 1960 – and at first he seemed like a poor fit for what was a very unjazzlike group. At a studio date on 7 October, Fortune played flute on two tunes that were eventually used to fill out the contents of [6]. 'Maiysha' was a lyrical piece which had the feel of a slow samba, although it is very messily played – the performance of that kind of music calls for an affected indolence, not sloppiness – and it eventually breaks into a rock beat with a mildly hair-raising solo over the top, probably by Gaumont. The other piece, 'Mtume', opens out from a threadbare guitar riff into an incoherent jumble of sounds, very heavy on the percussion, and not very interesting. Fortune was a negligible presence on the session, but he would play a much stronger role on the next recordings for Columbia – which turned out to be the last for a long time.

Agharta

COLUMBIA

Prelude; Maiysha; Interlude; Theme From Jack Johnson.
Miles Davis (*t, org*); Sonny Fortune (*ss, as, f*); Pete Cosey (*g, syn, perc*);
Reggie Lucas (*g*); Michael Henderson (*b*); Al Foster (*d*);
James 'Mtume' Foster (*perc*). 1/2/75.

Davis's physical condition was going from bad to worse. His hip was giving him terrible trouble: sometimes the joint would slip out of its socket, and with the legacy of the broken bones from the car accident of two years before, this made walking even a few steps painful and difficult. He had been taking morphine for some time as a palliative for the pain, which coupled with his drug and alcohol intake often had a dreadful effect on his general demeanour, weakness and vulnerability alternating with aggression and anger. His son Gregory, who had had his own problems with drugs, had taken to going out with him on the road, almost as a guardian for his father. Yet Davis continued working, and accepting every booking for the band. At the start of 1975, they were in Japan, and at Osaka they were engaged to play an afternoon and an evening show at the Festival Hall. Columbia recorded both shows, and released the first as *Agharta*, the second as *Pangaea* [20].

Agharta, though it didn't seem like it at the time, was a culmination of the way the music had been moving since *Bitches Brew*. Although the four sides were issued under the titles listed above, the material actually consisted of 'Tatu', 'Agharta Prelude', 'Maiysha', 'Right Off', the merest fragment of 'So What', 'Ife' and 'Wili'. It was recorded by Columbia's engineers with huge presence: it may not have the crystal clarity of some Davis records, but the sound has enormous vitality and body, even when losing some of its frequencies, and it came across with awesome power on a good stereo system of the day (collectors currently prize the original vinyl, since it actually sounds considerably better than Columbia's only CD edition to date).

The first side moves off from the 'Tatu' riff into a brief passage for Davis, before first Fortune and then Cosey fire off monumental solos, the one contrasting brilliantly with the other: where Fortune is all post-Coltrane chops and elegant fire, Cosey simply lays back and pushes his set-up to its sonic limit, scrawling out feedbacking and brutally distorted figures against the dome of the building. Both men play on over the rhythm section dropouts which were introduced on 'Rated X' and this only heightens the drama of the music. After Miles reinstates the theme of 'Agharta Prelude', Fortune returns on soprano in another dazzling cameo. Fortune may have been the most old-fashioned saxophonist Davis had engaged in years, but he seemed able to get the rest of the group to respond to him in ways which Liebman and Bartz only rarely had.

'Maiysha' then emerges blinking in the light, only to be torn asunder by another shredding solo from Cosey, until the melody is enigmatically restored by Fortune's flute. 'Right Off' is brought in under one of Cosey's passages, Henderson – who at once anchors and bounces the music at so many points during the concert – playing with impeccable invention. Davis then plays one of his best passages of the set. The mood at this point is one of almost light-hearted swing, and the bassist seems to have felt he could even try out a musical joke of his own, when he spends some time playing the familiar riff to 'So What' (which Davis had himself hinted at in some of his organ chords). The mix of 'Ife' and 'Wili' concludes the set, which includes more excellent

improvising from Cosey, Lucas and Fortune, although when Davis eventually plays his last trumpet passage, he sounds spent.

This sense of gloom, even exhaustion, has coloured many readings of what turned out to be Davis's final official recordings for several years. *Pangaea*, recorded that evening, reruns a slightly different group of pieces, but is definitely more weary: Davis is often conspicuous by his absence, and the general energy level feels much reduced, even though Fortune and Cosey still have dramatic moments to themselves. Yet the sweep and grandeur of *Agharta* has an almost epic timbre to it: it is a great band record, a set where even though Davis contributes only telling details, he still cues exceptional performances from his men. Whenever he had the chance, he would remind interviewers of how much his various sidemen had contributed to the quality of his projects (even if he might prefer to claim compositional and similar credits for himself): *Agharta* is a final – for the time being – vindication of how much his musicians gave to him.

The music on *Agharta* is, nevertheless, dark – but so was everything that Davis put his name on in the 1970s. He looked enviously at the huge listenership won by Sly Stone, Stevie Wonder, George Clinton – anybody who had the broad, black audience Davis coveted. Yet their music had threads of joy and simple exuberance which were completely alien to Davis's approach. In the past, Miles had drawn in listeners who loved his way with a ballad, his carefully brushed lyricism. Now he scorned the old ways: he wanted the new world that Hendrix and the others had conquered. The trouble was, he could only get there with music which was, in the eyes and ears of many, one-dimensional. He couldn't keep playing 'My Funny Valentine', but he had nothing 'beautiful' to replace it – only the stark, beautiful noise of *Bitches Brew* or *Jack Johnson* or *Agharta*.

His music had gained much in the way of complexity and density. Its lines of communication were rich, detailed, fascinating to anyone interested in a state of the art. But that was a small audience of connoisseurs – different in kind, but not in number, to the jazz hardcore who had followed and supported him for many years before. He was still on a major label, but it had indulged his recording whims for a long time, and now his producer had begun to compile albums from the Davis stockpile, records such as [3] and [6], which enraged Davis as much as they pleased him. *Agharta* came out early in 1976 ([19] and [20] were released only in Japan). By that time, Miles had stopped playing altogether.

The Other Records

1   *Jack Johnson* (Columbia)
2   *The Complete Jack Johnson Sessions* (Columbia)
3   *Big Fun* (Columbia)
4   *Directions* (Columbia)
5   *Black Beauty* (Columbia)
6   *Get Up With It* (Columbia)
7   *Live–Evil* (Columbia)
8   *Miles Davis At Fillmore* (Columbia)
9   *Message To Love: The Isle Of White Festival* (Castle)
10 *What I Say? Vol. 2* (Jazz Music Yesterday)
11 *Miles Davis + Keith Jarrett Live* (Golden Years Of Jazz)
12 *What I Say? Vol. 1* (Jazz Music Yesterday)
13 *On The Corner* (Columbia)
14 *In Concert: Live At Philharmonic Hall* (Columbia)
15 *Olympia, 11 juillet 1973* (Trema)
16 *Call It What It Is* (Jazz Music Yesterday)
17 *Another Bitches Brew* (Jazz Door)
18 *Palais des Sports, Paris 1973* (Jazz Masters)
19 *Dark Magus* (CBS/Sony)
20 *Pangaea* (Columbia)

Tais-Toi Some Of This!

1975–85

After the visit to Japan early in 1975, Davis returned to the US and carried on working. On some gigs, the band went out as a support act to Herbie Hancock, which must have been a humiliation for Davis. His former sideman had been enjoying much success with his band Headhunters, which mixed cheerful funk with jazz improvisation in a way which would have been mystifying to Miles. By the summer, Davis was becoming obliged to cancel gigs because of a further decline in his health, and by the end of the year a scheduled hip replacement operation was becoming a desperate necessity: but he then contracted pneumonia, which aggravated all his other health problems. There had been a few further studio sessions, but nothing had come out of them. Finally, the hip surgery took place right at the end of the year, and he began to recuperate, partly under the eye of Cicely Tyson, the one woman who maintained an occasional presence in his life.

Instead of starting a period of recovery, though, Davis almost fell into a tailspin. As he put it in his autobiography: 'I just took a lot of cocaine and fucked all the women I could get into my house.' He supplemented his intake of cocaine with prescription drugs, tranquillizers, beer, cognac, cigarettes and anything else that might appeal to him on a whim. The brownstone which had once been a showplace of interior design became dark and filthy. Television screens flickered for twenty-four hours a day, chattering to themselves in lieu of real human company. He scarcely went out for some two years. Musicians dropped by to see him – old friends such as Gil Evans, John McLaughlin, Jimmy Heath – but after a time, all but a handful of them stopped coming, because the experience was too depressing. Davis befriended a young man named Eric Nisenson, who harboured ambitions to cooperate on his autobiography, and for some time Miles treated Eric as his gofer, drug connection and general flunkey: Nisenson eventually got his wish to do a book, but it turned out to be a sad memoir, of his own writing, about this miserable period in Davis's life.

Davis still had money. Columbia was paying him what amounted to a salary, there were royalties off the old records, and Bruce Lundvall, the new head of the jazz division and a diehard Davis fan, couldn't abide the idea that the label was mistreating him in any way. Two compilations of outtakes from the stockpile, *Circle In The Round* (1979) and *Directions* (1981), at least kept his name before the public. Otherwise the word abroad was that Miles had 'retired'. There was a brief moment in 1978 when he worked on some music while staying with friends of the guitarist Larry Coryell, but nothing came of it.

The following year, a few hesitant steps were made to assist him to escape from what was turning into a half-life. George Butler, who had been appointed to a senior position at Columbia, began visiting Davis nearly every day, often doing no more than spending a few minutes chatting or just sitting with him. A new grand piano was bought in honour of Miles's 53rd birthday in May 1979. In July, Paul Buckmaster came to New York and attempts were made to set up a recording session, although each time it had to be aborted because there was some problem with Davis (he forgot to turn up, or he was injured in some absurd fracas in a drugstore). Nothing resulted from the initiative with Buckmaster, but once again Cicely Tyson intervened, and this time began taking a more proactive role in looking after the exasperating Davis.

Miles was bored and lonely, and there seemed to be little that could tempt him back into making music again. In the end, it was a family connection that did the trick. His nephew, Vincent Wilburn, was in a modest little band where he played the drums. He gave his uncle some tapes of their work, and it piqued Davis's interest sufficiently to get him to think about playing his horn, maybe setting up a record date for the group. George Butler probably couldn't believe it when Miles called and told him that he wanted to do something with this band of nobodies. But a date was set in April 1980 which would involve Vince's group, Miles and a saxophonist, Bill Evans (no relation to the piano player), who had been recommended by Dave Liebman. Teo Macero, still ready to run the board, prepared to take down whatever came out of the sessions. But little happened at first: Miles didn't even show up, or he didn't bring his horn, or he found he couldn't play it. By the middle of May, a number of tracks had finally been laid down, but it was a disappointing and wretchedly painstaking process. Teo had to use all his skill to piece Miles's solos together, so weakly and inconsistently did he play. The material was unexceptional, mostly either slow grooves or bouncy, pop-jazz songs.

Much had changed in Davis's long absence. Jazz-rock had been a bubble which had been deflated, even if it hadn't exactly burst. Groups such as Chick Corea's Return To Forever had taken the music towards athletics rather than art: speed of execution counted for more than content much of the time. The old keyboards, with their whistling sounds and strange analogue effects, had been supplanted by sleek polyphonic synthesizers, which had begun to develop a capacity to imitate any other instrument. Electronic drums and sequencers were also becoming a commonplace on all kinds of records, from pop to soul and dance. The kind of endless, churning music which the *Agharta* band had specialized in was out of favour. As studio technology continued to improve, rough edges were easily smoothed away: even mediocre players could be made to sound decent by a skilful producer.

Jazz itself had responded to these developments awkwardly and without any real sense of where to go next. There were players who all but took over Davis's old role as an instrumental balladeer, but with a smoother, more sentimental outlook. One such was a saxophonist, Grover Washington, whose records mixed his lightly appealing sound with backings derived more from the sweet end of soul music than anything resembling post-bop jazz. In 1980, Washington's *Winelight* album was a huge success. It was not much more than a step on from the sort of middle-of-the-road recordings which Wes Montgomery had been making in the late 1960s, or the lightweight fusion of Freddie Hubbard in the following decade.

Davis didn't seem sure of which way to go, and he wasn't going to get much help from his nephew's band, who were inexperienced and young and probably rather in awe of the old man. After weeks of work, Macero managed to pull together two tracks which were at least finished and in a fit state for release, the brief, almost disco-fied 'Shout' and a ballad that band member Randy Hall sang a dreamy vocal on, 'The Man With The Horn'. But Davis himself decided to abandon the project. Instead, he kept Evans on, added two guitarists, Barry Finnerty and Mike Stern, and recalled his old drummer, Al Foster. A

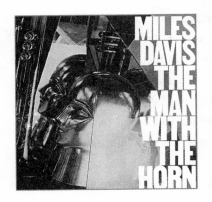

percussionist, Sammy Figueroa, was added, and completing the line-up was an electric bassist, Marcus Miller.

With Miles shakily at the helm, this group managed to complete the rest of what was eventually released as *The Man With The Horn* [1], the two earlier pieces supplemented with four other tracks, 'Fat Time', 'Back Seat Betty', 'Aida' and 'Ursula'. The patient Macero pieced together the takes: he had been used to sifting through hours of material from the old days, but this was an even more demanding task, trying to eliminate clinkers from Miles's playing, and making sense of a project which really had no vision to it at all. If Davis had customarily imposed some sense of order and an overall conception on everything he had previously done, this was entirely different: Macero's task was simply to get out a record that would indicate that Miles was on his feet and playing his horn.

Coming after *Agharta*, [1] seems like almost a debasement of Miles's music.

The title track was an embarrassing paean to the leader: considering Davis's state of health and competence, lyrics such as 'His music sets the pace/The master never has to race/Although he's much too fast/To ever lose' are almost comical. Hall's vocal was, though, appealing enough, and as a harmless novelty, with Miles gamely tootling in the background against the soothing cadences of the keyboards, it didn't cause any damage. In some ways, the other pieces were more disappointing. Davis had enlisted a good group: Foster was as reliable as ever, the slippery, adept Miller sounded like a great find, and Evans had strong chops in the tradition of Sonny Fortune and Gary Bartz. But the record seemed pointless. Long-time Davis fans didn't know whether to be simply pleased at the return of the master, or bemused that he was spending time playing such slight material.

'Fat Time', the track which leads off the record, is probably the best thing on it, the one piece where Mike Stern – whom Davis had heard at a Billy Cobham gig – takes the lead guitar duties. There are solos by Davis, Evans and Stern over a rocking beat supplied by Miller and Foster. Although only twenty-two, Marcus Miller had been a regular sessionman in New York studios for a couple of years, and was a skilful exponent of the kind of slapping technique which suggested a marriage of finger-plucking jazz bass and the plectrum twang of a rock approach. Although he only played comparatively briefly as a member of the Davis band, he introduced the style that all of Davis's bass players would thenceforth use.

All of [1] is, in the same way, a sketch for how Davis's work on record would go from here. Instead of the dense, endless rhythms of the 1970s, simpler rock and funk patterns would predominate. Guitar players would appropriate elements of rock playing – the huge power chords Finnerty uses to lead off 'Back Seat Betty', for instance – and saxophonists would take a decorative, subsidiary role, strangely isolated from the other players. Evans plays only soprano on the record, whereas he was known primarily as a tenor player. And there would be at least one attempt at a hit, that could be taken off the record and sold as a single, even a remix – another development which had been evolving in Davis's absence. Remixes were made of 'Shout', for a twelve-inch single. For Davis followers, the most encouraging thing about the record was the return of Davis's unalloyed (or so it seemed) trumpet sound. Though he began the sessions using the by now rather dated wah-wah pedal, he abandoned it early on and his playing is done with either the mute or the undoctored open horn.

Some of the new sidemen were surprised or dismayed that Teo appeared to offer little in the way of help or advice, the way producers usually would: he seemed more interested in getting the music down, and working on it later. But now Davis would himself begin to move away from that approach. At the moment, he was still barely in any shape to direct or conceptualize a record. His playing on 'Shout', which sounds like the sort of track Herb Alpert was then doing (and making a rather better job of), was, despite all of Macero's post-production, painfully inadequate.

Yet the record wasn't such a downer to listeners of the time, mainly because of its bright and powerful studio mix. Studios had moved on again in the six years since Davis's sabbatical began. Bass frequencies were fatter, more lubricious; drums had the wide-bodied kick that the new dance music of the time demanded. The music of [1] wanted for profundity, but it was plausible product. What Davis had to do next was rediscover his chops, and return to live performance.

It was slow going – the sessions in the end took a year to complete. But as soon as they were done, Davis prepared to go on the road. George Wein booked the trumpeter in to his annual New York festival in July 1981, and as a warm-up the group played a few nights at a club called Kix, in Boston, which Columbia recorded across all four nights. There was some preparation, several rehearsals at the Davis homestead which went off much in the usual manner – a bit of jamming, Miles making a handful of cryptic remarks, and everyone summarily expected to be fully conversant with the way it was all going to go – and then the young band nervously assembled with their veteran leader. The Kix recordings featured as part of *We Want Miles* [2], which came out the

268 |

following summer and was seen by many as the first real evidence that Davis had returned in a serious way. Besides these tracks – 'My Man's Gone Now', 'Fast Track' and 'Kix' – there was 'Back Seat Betty', from one of the shows at New York's Avery Fisher Hall, and two versions of 'Jean Pierre', from a series of concerts in Tokyo which took place in October.

This is the most vivid record of the sextet with Stern, Evans, Miller, Foster and a new percussionist, Mino Cinelu. The biggest surprise is the reappearance of 'My Man's Gone Now', from the *Porgy And Bess* project. Davis always claimed that he wouldn't go back to the old days, but for some reason this piece came out of the archives and, goosed up with a juicy bass vamp from Miller, it is explored for twenty minutes by the band, with Davis, Evans and Stern all doing some of their best playing on the record. Here and elsewhere on the set, Davis sounds both enlivened by the adrenalin of being back in live performance and surrounded by a proficient young band, and overwhelmed by the demands of playing trumpet in an exposed, open situation. He plays much more convincingly than he does on [1] (which first appeared during the tour, and immediately disappointed those who had witnessed the concerts), yet his own work and the overall feel of the group is unsettled and awkward. Davis is happy to cede large amounts of space to Stern, a decision which many in the audience regretted: eager to please his boss, Stern sounds overmuscled and at times dangerously close to a heavy-metal guy, as he did on the European tour of the following year. Evans is still stuck on the soprano saxophone on every track bar one, 'Kix', which has easily his best work of the album. It is a hybrid record, and once again Teo Macero had to work on music which he was grouchily dissatisfied with for much of the way: he felt that 'Jean Pierre', a childish but naggingly memorable tune that seems to have a French origin, was never satisfactorily recorded. The second version of 'Jean Pierre' was recorded at the Tokyo gig of 4 October, which can also be heard on the Japan-only release *Miles! Miles! Miles!* [3], which at least has the merit of focusing on the band as it stood at a single show.

The months during which the music was recorded were heady but exhausting for Davis. His comeback was greeted with an interest level which was fairly astonishing, given the antipathy towards much of his work of the middle 1970s. There were audience lines around the block at his appearances: there was a feeling abroad that a living legend had returned. But his health was wobbling again. A bout of pneumonia in the autumn laid him low, and then he was diagnosed as having diabetes. What mostly got him through was the support of Cicely Tyson, whom he finally married in November. Leonard Feather, who was a long-time friend of Davis and one of the few jazz commentators he trusted, looked back on this period as the most stable in Miles's life, because Tyson was such a rock to him. In January 1982, she went overseas on an acting assignment and Davis quickly fell back into his old ways, resorting to cocaine and cognac to get him through the lonely days. His road manager saw at once that his health was in a precipitous state, and had him put in hospital, where doctors gave him some blunt warnings about his physical well being. Then he had a stroke, and his right hand was paralysed. Cicely nursed him back to mobility, got him on to vegetables and Chinese herbs and acupuncture, and helped him slowly recover. Although many of the women in Davis's life subsequently talked of how he had 'empowered' them, despite the physical violence he visited on most of them, Tyson seems like the exception: she was strong to begin with, and her battles with Davis only made her stronger (she punched to the ground one woman whom she suspected of having a fling with her husband). But, in the end, Cicely was driven away too.

In April, Davis was still weak, but the band came to Europe, and unsuspecting audiences wondered what kind of Miles they would be seeing. At his London gig in April, there was unease at what seemed to be the oversized role offered to Mike Stern, and Davis often sounded frail, as well as looking it. But the old charisma had not deserted him. Some of the time he sat at a keyboard, and at one particularly pregnant moment he leaned forward and thoughtfully fingered a chord which sounded, at that moment, peculiarly magical. With hindsight, though, it is clear that the show was muted and despatched as quickly as possible. An audience used to staying out late was bemused to find itself going home at not much later than 9.15. The music photographer Peter Anderson, already obliged to try to take a photo from his seat in the stalls, arrived at a point when he thought the gig would just be warming up; in fact, it was coming to an end, and the author suggested to Anderson that he get busy as soon as possible. Peter managed to snap a handful of pictures: the last was of Miles waving goodbye from the stage.

Waving goodbye? This was surely not Miles Davis, the musician who turned his back on his audiences and never spoke, introduced tunes or even acknowledged the presence of an audience? Many were surprised at what seemed to be the new mellow Miles. He still didn't say anything, but there were smiles and waves and a generally softer approach: perhaps even he was taken aback at the interest in his return.

In summer, he began work on another new studio record. Teo Macero was still in charge as producer, but increasingly Davis himself wanted to try to utilize the procedures which studio technology had opened up: he was interested in click tracks (effectively a metronomic guide to assist players in holding on to a tempo on an unfinished track) and the wider sound spectrum that new synthesizers were offering. *Star People* [4] ended up being another mishmash of material and ideas. Davis teased his audience with glimmers of his old authority, and the sleevenotes which came with the record – by Leonard Feather, pitched mainly as a conversation with Miles in which the leader explained his concepts – all but suggest that this is a blues album. Davis's blues playing has often been held up as one of the great wellsprings of his art, but he always had a sidelong relationship with that imperative in black music: compared to those of a blues 'natural' such as Cannonball Adderley, his attempts at the idiom often sound studied or affected, and going back to the blues at this point felt like a vaguely desperate measure. Certainly his playing on the larruping blues groove of 'It Gets Better' sounds stilted.

'It Gets Better' was given a large assist by the uncredited Gil Evans, who yet again played a part in a Miles Davis record without receiving any acknowledgement or, presumably, payment. Evans worked up some of the material by transcribing solos from tapes of the band in performance. 'Star On Cicely' was extrapolated from a Mike Stern solo, and 'It Gets Better' came from a line the guitarist John Scofield had played at a jam at Davis's house the night before. Elsewhere, Evans suggested tempos and a few chords, and generally made constructive comments as the album fell into place. But it took a long time to finish. There were studio dates between August 1982 and May 1983, and two of the tracks, 'Come Get It' and 'Speak', were actually from tapes Davis had made of live gigs. 'Star People' itself lasted for almost twenty minutes and exemplified the album's mix of intentions. The introduction features a synthesizer flourish by Davis which he gave to Macero just before the producer was embarking on the final mix. It leads to what adds up to a series of blues solos, by a muted Davis, Stern, Davis, Evans, Davis again, and then a second synthesizer interlude. This is used as sealant to fix what sound like two separate performances: Stern then plays one of his noisiest solos before the trumpet briefly returns and the track comes to a flat stop. Foster is saddled with a very strange drum sound, where his cymbals have the quality of saucepan lids, and with a final nod to the old way of working, Miles calls 'Teo!' at the end, just like he used to.

This was a playing record: the structures are loose and act as framing devices for the solos. Davis sounds in good heart, his lip is stronger, but any comparison with his playing in his previous incarnations does find it wanting. Some of it, such as the feeble 'U 'n' I', is pure filler (as if the record needed it – it ran for nearly an hour, the equivalent of one and a half regular vinyl albums). 'Star People' itself is pointlessly long. At least it documents a band coalescing around their charismatic leader, although even here the album turns out to be catching the group in transition. Marcus Miller left half-way through (his replacement, Tom Barney, who didn't stay in the group long, plays only on 'Speak'), and John Scofield's induction took place during August. For some months, the band featured both Scofield and Stern.

John Scofield proved to be one of the most valuable of Davis's latter-day sidemen, and went on from there to be one of his most famous graduates. He had been playing around New York for several years, and Davis had first encountered him when he went to see Dave Liebman's band. Liebman recalled: 'He came to Seventh Avenue South and heard Sco with me. I said, "Good guitar player." He said, "I don't like him." I said, "No chords – just don't let him play chords." Sco was not a great voicer, he was a single-line player then.' Scofield was a very different stylist to Stern. He studied on the kind of jazz polytonality which players such as McCoy Tyner had investigated at length, and he combined that with a bluesy feel and a working knowledge of rock forms rather

than an obeisance to them. He preferred a cleaner, more open tone, although he knew the value of a little carefully controlled distortion, and he liked to use chromaticism in his solos. After he left Davis, he went on to become one of the major jazz musicians of his day: one of Miles's many protégés.

The album was notable for something else: its cover art, by Miles Davis. He had been drawing and sketching for some time (in his autobiography he claimed that he had always been partial to them, although other family members remembered it differently), and now they were becoming therapeutic for him. Thus far, the comeback albums had been given undistinguished cover art: [1] had a strange photograph of a metal mannequin's head leaning against a mirror; [2] used a small photo of Davis in performance surrounded by a sea of yellow, under the looming title. But this record featured figurines pencilled in a style over the next few years would become familiar in Davis's record designs: stiffly dancing stick people with exaggerated hips and posteriors and bulbous heads. The cover credit read 'All Drawings, Color Concepts and Basic Attitudes by Miles Davis'.

The Davis band toured widely for the rest of 1983, visiting Japan in May and Europe for two dates in October. He was getting back to his old regimen of almost constant touring, as if it were the only course of action open to him. But the band, like so many previous Davis groups, had its personal problems. Mike Stern was in difficulties over both drink and drugs, and his behaviour was sometimes problematical. Davis himself was not yet clear of cocaine use, and when this was coupled with his usual unpredictability, his sidemen – most of them still young and rather fearful of their boss – often quaked. Even so, on the evidence of one of the Japanese concerts, dated to 29 May and issued on *Atmosphere: Live In Tokyo* [5], it was an exciting band. The set is made up of such pieces as 'Jean Pierre', 'Star People' and 'It Gets Better', and the more prosaic studio versions are easily supplanted by the energy and flickering inspiration of the band, with Scofield and Stern proving oddly effective as an exercise in contrasts. Stern's habits, though, were getting the better of him, and Davis let him go a few weeks later.

That same month, June, work began on a further studio record. Another new band member had been inducted, Darryl 'The Munch' Jones, who took the Marcus Miller style on another notch: using a thumbpicking style, he played even harder and funkier commentaries on the music than Miller's. The other major difference was the absence of Teo Macero. There had been no particular spat between Davis and Macero: the trumpeter simply decided not to call Macero to become involved this time, and in the end that was the conclusion of their working relationship. The man who had steered Davis through countless studio occasions and had made sense of so many hours of playing was simply set aside. Teo realized that, like most of the women who had moved through Davis's life, he was just being dropped, and the marriage was over. Perhaps his way of working was becoming antiquated, in comparison to the way Davis saw his world shifting; now it was more about sifting and layering sounds, textures and soundstages, rather than the editing and recomposition which was how Macero had worked his magic.

Davis, though, still needed a producer of some sort. He could conceptualize and point out details, but he never tried to master the kind of technical craft a producer possesses, a mix of artistry and acumen, as well as the sort of distancing which allows an impartial judgement. Robert Irving, who had worked on the first sessions for [1], was drafted in to assist with keyboard parts, and in the end he got a credit as co-producer. Vince Wilburn was also involved, and he was eventually listed as associate producer. The truth was, as so often, Miles got bored with the detail of record-making, and was frequently absent from the sessions: perhaps he had begun to realize how much effort Macero had had to put in to make the old records presentable. Wilburn frequently had to play semi-finished tracks to Miles over the phone, waiting for approval or otherwise.

The seven tracks that make up *Decoy* [6] are pleasing but decentred, lacking any real reason to be gathered together: it feels like an album of strong outtakes, from some grander and more coherent project that was never realized. One piece, 'Robot 415', lasts a mere fifty-nine seconds, and another, 'Freaky Deaky' (reputedly named in honour of the comedian Richard Pryor), is nothing more than Davis fingering out synthesizer chords over a bubbling bass ostinato from Jones. Two other pieces, 'What It is' and 'That's What Happened', were edited from tapes of a set played at the Montreal Jazz Festival that July. Which leaves 'Decoy', a nebulous melody that is propped up by Irving's synthesizer orchestration, over a beat that mixes Al Foster's playing with a drum machine; 'Code M.D.', a riff-like melody that balances on two chords and is a feature mainly for Scofield and Irving's bank of effects, reeking of the early 1980s; and 'That's

Right', a blues paced out at a lethargic crawl. There is plenty of improvising, from Davis, Scofield and Branford Marsalis, a young saxophonist drafted in at more or less the last minute, on several of these tracks, which have real quality from moment to moment. Yet little seems to linger in the mind, except possibly the neon sound of Irving's keyboards. Nothing dates records faster than synthesizer sounds, which fall out of fashion very quickly, and like so much of Davis's music from this point onwards, the keyboards timelock the music. A further disappointment is the rhythmic element: drum machines drive more than one track, and the increasingly disgruntled Al Foster is asked to play almost anonymously.

The best playing on the record is on 'That's Right', and Davis sounds in better shape here than on anything he had set down since his return. But a simple slow blues was hardly the harbinger of great new things. Marsalis plays a handsome solo on this piece, too. He was the brother of the trumpeter Wynton, and played in Wynton's band: they had emerged at the beginning of the decade as mercurial young talents whose music was in a surprisingly conservative, acoustic, straight-ahead idiom. Two of four musician-brothers from New Orleans, Wynton and Branford had caused a stir as the front line of the veteran hard-bop band Art Blakey's Jazz Messengers, and Wynton in particular had taken on the mantle of spokesman for jazz as a great and living American art form. Naturally articulate, charming, sharp and personable, Marsalis was perfect fodder for the press, being many of the things Davis wasn't. When asked about Miles Davis, Wynton was unequivocal about his distinguished label-mate (both Wynton and Branford had been signed to Columbia in separate deals): he admired the Miles of the 1950s and 1960s, but 'Miles in the 1970s, that's not jazz'.

It was an irritation for Davis, and he started to think that Marsalis was getting more attention than he was from his long-time label sponsor.

You're Under Arrest

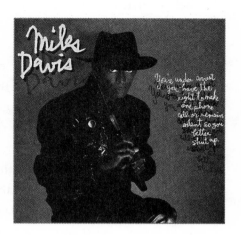

COLUMBIA

One Phone Call/Street Scenes; Human Nature; Intro: MD 1/ Something's On Your Mind/MD 2; Ms Morrisine; Katia Prelude; Katia; Time After Time; You're Under Arrest; Medley: Jean Pierre/You're Under Arrest/Then There Were None.

Miles Davis (*t, ky*, v); Bob Berg (*ss*); Robert Irving III (*ky*); John Scofield, John McLaughlin (*g*); Darryl Jones (*b*); Al Foster, Vince Wilburn Jr (*d*); Steve Thornton (*perc*); James Prindiville, Marek Olko, Sting (v). 1/84, 12/84–1/85.

Arguably, Davis's records since his return were all still in some kind of halfway house, between the old feel of loose, jamming structures, and a more anchored and song-based format. There was enough to at least please Davis admirers in most of the records, even though there were times when it felt like Miles was tossing his listeners a bone rather than creating anything coherent or lastingly worthwhile. *You're Under Arrest* finally imposed an order on what he was doing, even if it was the closest he would ever come to making a straightforward pop record, with its selection of covers, cameo appearances and precisely timed effects. At last, George Butler must have thought: a Miles Davis record with hooks.

The first session for the album took place in January 1984, but this yielded only a version of what would prove to be the enduring track on the record, 'Time After Time', and sessions drifted on through the rest of the year. In the interim, Davis had shed Bill Evans from his touring group and hired a new saxophonist, Bob Berg. Primarily a tenor player, Berg didn't even own a soprano at the time he joined the group, but that was the horn which Davis most wanted to hear, and Berg obligingly acquired and practised on one. Irving had also become a member of the full-time group. Much of *You're Under Arrest* was played on the road before it was recorded in its final state (another variation on recent procedure), and by the time they came to set it down, Davis and the group must have known much of the material well.

Yet the record feels more precisely in tune with the way records – pop records – were being made at that time than anything Miles had done thus far.

The tracks are cut to a manageable length, and emerge as plausible contenders for radio play. The material doesn't sound played in so much as groomed, tailored. Irving and Wilburn again did much of the production, even though Davis again gave himself a credit. They did an impressive job: in fact, the record's gestation was nothing like as smooth as it might have been.

Davis had actually begun sketching out the format for the record in 1983, straight after the *Decoy* sessions. The idea was to make an entire record of pop tunes. Gil Evans would take the chief arranger's role, and the results would be a 1980s equivalent of *Miles Ahead*. The group began making demos of perhaps dozens of songs. There was material by Tina Turner, Dionne Warwick, DeBarge, even the British pop songwriter Nik Kershaw. Turner's 'What's Love Got To Do With It', a classic hit of its time, was one which would surely have suited the sound that was eventually conferred on the final record. But none of this material actually made the cut in the end. Davis's illness prevented some of the sessions taking place, and though Gil Evans did do some arrangements, he was himself in demand, for tours and filmscore writing, and he didn't see any of the work through. By April 1984, Davis had had enough of trying to get Gil to play his part. They continued recording material, but just when it seemed the record was ready to be mixed, Miles changed his mind and abandoned almost everything that had already been done. A record which reputedly had a consistent ballad feel was entirely remodelled: although three of the pop covers remained, everything else was redone.

The finished record had a very different feel. Instead of *Miles Ahead*, the record is more like *The Times They Are A-Changing*. The title of the record is a sour reminder of Davis's many brushes with the law, and he turns it into dark comedy on 'One Phone Call/Street Scenes'. At the other end of the record, 'Then There Were None' dramatizes the end of the world. The record has a bustle and glitter which sites it very much in its time, but it has a tautness to it, too: Ronald Lorman and Tom Swift, credited as the recording and mix engineers, did an exemplary job, especially since George Butler pressurized them into delivering a final mix in a few days.

'One Phone Call/Street Scenes' starts with a vamp which goes back to 'Right Off' from *Jack Johnson*, and the second half plays around a figure from 'Speak' from [4]. Jones and Foster keep up a clean, tight groove which sustains the piece while little fragments of guitar and trumpet decorate the top. But the point of the piece is the dialogue which Davis came up with. The track starts with him sniffing violently, in imitation of a time-honoured narcotic procedure, muttering as synthesizers pretend to be police sirens, and then going 'Oh-Ohhh!' as a car screeches to a halt. Then a voice says, 'We gotcha! You have the right to make one phone call … we've been watching you, Davis, we know what you're doing … you got that girl in there … smokin' that marajaroney …'. The gag is that the 'police voice' is actually Miles himself, and he taunts his aggressors: 'What's that, cufflinks?' 'Handcuffs!' 'Handcuff some o' this down here …'. Eventually, Miles says, 'Call George!', just as his open trumpet comes in. At the end, three other voices take a role in the comedy: Steve Thornton gabbles something in Spanish, Marek Olko (a friend of Davis, who was a concert promoter) says a few lines in Polish, and Sting, who had come to the studio in company with Darryl Jones, whom he had been auditioning, barks out (in French), 'You have the right to remain silent, so *tais-toi!*' Davis responds with '*Tais-toi* some of this!', as the track fades. Not exactly luminous political art, but at least Davis got some of his own kind of gallows humour on to a record.

The other original pieces make up an interesting group. 'Ms Morrisine' is a piece of counterfeit reggae – the rhythm is bounced off a bass synthesizer line with electronic drum bursts interspersing it, and Davis plays the main melody line on an open horn which does sound remarkably like Herb Alpert. This leads directly into 'Katia Prelude' and 'Katia', both of which sit up as features for John McLaughlin's guitar, McLaughlin having been invited to come down and play by Davis (however premeditated a Miles Davis record might become, there always seemed to be room for some spontaneous manoeuvre). The circumstances of the track appear bizarre, considering the neat feel of most of the record: Davis and McLaughlin had walked into a studio and more or less just started playing, the engineers setting up the track on the board as they went along. While 'Katia' isn't much more than a jam, carried along on Jones's riff and underscored by long, long synthesizer chords, both McLaughlin and Davis play fiercely, and though some of the electronic stabs which fill up the surrounding space feel corny rather than dramatic, it's an arresting piece.

'You're Under Arrest' itself is another piece worked up from a John Scofield guitar improvisation. Played hard and fast, with Al Foster finally getting a chance to work on a groove, it skips along, with a little trumpet and tenor saxophone icing, before Scofield takes the final solo. Edited back from a longer duration into a tight six and a quarter minutes, this is the Berg–Scofield band doing its best work in the studio.

What the record is best remembered for, though, is its cover versions. Davis narrowed his choice down to three: 'Something's On Your Mind', originally a slow groove tune by the soul group D Train; 'Human Nature', one of the most lyrical pieces from Michael Jackson's hugely successful *Thriller* album; and 'Time After Time', a ballad by the singer-songwriter Cyndi Lauper. The settings for the songs are each carefully scored by Irving, simple guitar parts interleaved with pristine synthesizer arrangements: in the case of 'Human Nature', Quincy Jones's original production is assiduously followed. 'Something's On

Your Mind' is spiced up a little, the rather lugubrious feel of the original given zest by a slightly quicker tempo and crisper interplay, but 'Time After Time' replicates the mood of Lauper's somewhat bathetic original. As blueprints these are close to what would later come to be called smooth jazz, plain, faintly syncopated music which is designed for a radio format that lulls listeners into submission. The difference is the role Davis takes. No smooth-jazz virtuoso, a breed that makes a virtue out of playing instrumental lines in an entirely neutral style, could countenance the kind of personal element Davis puts into his playing here. He cracks notes, sounds as if he's reluctantly squeezing each melodic phrase out of the muted horn, and plays the role of a singer without becoming one: at any moment, one feels as if he may be about to burst into words. On both 'Time After Time' and 'Human Nature', he scarcely departs from the melody: like Ben Webster, he only has to impart a note or two to bring himself before the listener. This was the real return of the 'My Funny Valentine' Miles, and audiences loved it.

Davis didn't let either of those tunes go: he was still playing both of them at concerts only weeks before his death. 'Time After Time' was also released in an extended version on a twelve-inch single, and in performance it might go on for ten minutes or more. On *You're Under Arrest*, it precedes the title track, which then moves into the strangely poignant finale: after a brief fragment of 'Jean Pierre' and an even briefer reprise of 'You're Under Arrest', 'Then There Were None' forms a coda to the rest. Over a music-box melody by Irving which is a little reminiscent of Beethoven's *Für Elise*, electronic storms rage in imitation of a nuclear catastrophe and the plaintive sound of Davis's trumpet just breaks through. As it dies away, and a single keyboard note tolls like a funeral bell, Miles mutters, 'Ron, I meant for you to push the *other* button.'

On the front cover, an impassive Davis, bedecked in a sumptuous jacket, leather pants and a wide-brimmed hat, toted what was actually a toy machine pistol which the photographer, Anthony Barboza, had gone out and bought. There was also what Miles claimed was the real title of the album in full: *You're Under Arrest You Have The Right To Make One Phone Call, Or Remain Silent*

So You Better Shut Up. Instead of Marvin Gaye's *What's Going On* or Curtis Mayfield's *America Today*, Davis's political album was dry black comedy.

Not that Armageddon seemed to bother him much. When asked if he worried about the world coming to an end, he said, 'No! Only thing is, it might happen when you're somewhere you don't wanna be. Like, damn, why did it have to happen now, and not when I was swimming or somethin'?'

The Other Records

1 *The Man With The Horn* (Columbia)
2 *We Want Miles* (Columbia)
3 *Miles! Miles! Miles!* (Columbia, Japan)
4 *Star People* (Columbia)
5 *Atmosphere: Live In Tokyo* (Four Beat Sounds)
6 *Decoy* (Columbia)

White, Yellow, Orange, Red ...

1985–8

Davis was enjoying his new stardom, which was taking him far beyond his old jazz audience, even if he wasn't really selling records or concert tickets – at least, not the way the stars of the pop world he longed to be a part of were. His business affairs were a mess, but that never stopped him spending money or affecting the most extraordinary extravagance. He had had a decent manager, Mark Rothbaum, for some time, but in 1983 he had switched to being represented by Lester and Jerry Blank, a team which Cicely had recommended to him. The arrangement seems to have been an unhappy alliance, and soon enough Davis had to extricate himself from it, but it ended up costing him so much money that his beloved brownstone on 77th Street was sold to help get him out of debt. He then switched to new management, David Franklin, who would negotiate what turned out to be the biggest change in his renewed career.

In the meantime, he mixed playing, touring, spending, painting – and surviving numerous scares with his health. In 1984, he had another operation which resulted in a hip replacement and put him on crutches for some time. His diabetes was a constant irritation – he often liked to gorge on sweets and cakes, which regularly put him in a state of near-collapse – and his feet were in poor shape: when he played on stage, he often bent over, adopting a posture that almost folded him in half, which was less a pose than a concession to the difficulties of standing erect while holding a trumpet. At least his recreational drug intake had slackened off: since he was often full of prescription drugs anyway, perhaps more exotic stimulants had lost some of their appeal.

Painting began to interest him more and more, especially when he befriended a woman, Jo Gelbard, who lived in the same Fifth Avenue building that he now resided in. Gelbard was a painter and sculptor herself, and as they came to know each other and grew closer, she encouraged his work: 'He'd overpaint, way beyond what the composition called for – into the night and over into the next day, he just kept going, because he liked the texture of it, the colours.' If his music was sparse and full of space, his canvases were almost the opposite. His relationship with Cicely continued – Gelbard was the one Tyson had knocked down in the street, even though at the time she and Davis were not yet lovers – but their marriage was gradually coming apart.

Even so, Davis and Cicely were still a glamorous couple, dividing their time between the New York home and a house Cicely owned in a community of stars in Malibu. Miles was becoming feted in areas of the media which had previously seemed unaware of his existence. He had made a video for one of the tracks on *Decoy*, and filmed a commercial for Japanese television, which led to him doing another for Honda in America. In 1985, he turned up in an episode of the cop series *Miami Vice*, playing a pimp – a role which, as he wryly remarked at the time, he had once had some experience of.

Europe, the place which often honours jazz musicians otherwise neglected at home, had never forgotten him. In Denmark, he had been given the Léonie Sonning Music Award, an important prize usually offered to classical musicians. He seemed uninterested in the honour at first, and the Danish jazz composer Erik Moseholm tried to persuade him to come to the ceremony in December 1984, where the plan was to have Davis play a brief commissioned work, perhaps something by Gil Evans. Inevitably, nothing much came of that, but Miles did make the trip, and in Copenhagen the concert consisted of an extended orchestral work in honour of Miles, *Aura*, by a Danish trumpeter-composer, Palle Mikkelborg.

It was a great success. Although Davis was obliged to play only on 'Violet', the final segment of a work which lasted close to an hour, he seemed in good spirits, and didn't take much persuading to repeat the piece as an encore. John Scofield had come along as a second soloist, and began playing 'Jean-Pierre', and then Mikkelborg had the band play 'Time After Time', which Davis and Scofield happily blew on. It wasn't the first time that a European ensemble had surprised visiting Americans with their capabilities, and in the end Davis was on stage and performing for close to an hour.

A month later, Davis called Mikkelborg in the middle of the night and told him that he wanted to come over again and record the whole piece.

Aura

COLUMBIA

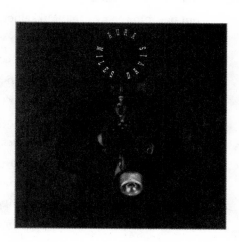

Intro; White; Yellow; Orange; Red; Green; Blue; Electric Red; Indigo; Violet.
Miles Davis (*t*); Palle Mikkelborg, Benny Rosenfeld, Palle Bolvig, Jens Winther,
Perry Knudsen, Idrees Sulieman (*t, flhn*); Vincent Nilsson, Jens Engel, Ture Larsen (*tb*);
Ole Kurt Jensen (*btb*); Axel Windfeld (*btb, tba*); Jesper Thilo, Per Carsten, Uffe Karskov,
Bent Jaedig, Flemming Madsen (*saxes*); Niels Eje (*ob, cor*); Thomas Clausen,
Ole Koch-Hansen, Kenneth Knudsen (*ky*); John McLaughlin, Bjarne Roupe (*g*);
Lillian Toernqvist (*hp*); Bo Stief, Niels-Henning Ørsted Pedersen (*b*); Lennart Gruvstedt (*d*);
Marilyn Mazur, Ethan Weisgaard (*perc*); Vince Wilburn (*elec d*), Eva Thaysen (*bv*). 1/85.

Twenty years after it was recorded, *Aura* is still among the least known of all of Davis's records. Its release delayed and largely unmarketed, its content oblique and baffling to the audience that wanted to hear 'Time After Time', it sits very strangely in the lexicon of later Davis albums. Yet it has probably the best playing he set down on any of his post-comeback studio recordings, and as far as originality and musical content go, the record stands alone.

The obvious reference to draw is to the Gil Evans collaborations, the trumpeter cast against a rich orchestral backdrop and performing a concerto-like role. But *Aura* doesn't sound like any of the Evans records, and Mikkelborg goes in a very different direction. Gil had often used electronics in his later music, but never in the way that Mikkelborg uses them here, and the Dane's musical procedures have little in common with Evans's instinctual, home-made language. None of this has stopped commentators hearing bits of Evans here and there in passages such as the horn lines of 'Yellow' or the later sections of 'Orange'. It would be better to hear the music as a sustained flight of homage by Mikkelborg to one of his great inspirations.

Palle Mikkelborg was forty-three when he composed *Aura*. He had been a professional trumpeter since 1960 and was a familiar presence on the Danish scene, a regular with the Danish Radiojazzgruppen, which he had led for some years, and a prolific leader of small groups. As a trumpeter, he was himself a Davis acolyte, with an even, undemonstrative tone and the kind of spacious phrasing which was Davis's bequest to a generation of European trumpeters. Having already done a lot of composing for film and television, he had plenty of experience under his belt, and *Aura* is authoritative and confident in its writing. Its foundation is in Davis's own name: Mikkelborg went through the alphabet, from A to Z, gave each letter a note in an ascending chromatic order, and then derived a theme using the notes given to M-I-L-E-S-D-A-V-I-S. The composition is basically grown from this ten-note motif. Mikkelborg tried talking to Davis about serialism and Messiaen, two sources of *Aura's* ingredients, but as usual Miles wasn't very interested in a background he felt remote from.

The performance the month before had been heavier with scored music: Mikkelborg found that Davis thought some of the more densely composed material wouldn't work, and he did his customary thinning and paring of sections which he didn't like. The cooperative Mikkelborg agreed and cut several sections, although it would have been fascinating to hear what had been lost. Still, what remains is exceptional, mixing banks of European harmony, dreamy pastorales, acidulous electronics, an overdubbed female voice that is turned into a choir, jarring electronic drums, the fizz of John McLaughlin's guitar, the eerie sound of old instruments such as the oboe and cor anglais, and Davis himself, recorded in a tight, close-up focus.

As a suite of interlocking pieces, the record doesn't make particular sense: it's more a sequence of moods, varying between darkness, brightness, tranquillity and aggression. Mikkelborg actually uses the orchestra only sparingly. Much of the time, there are soloists set against baleful synthesizer chords, thundering Simmons drums, or clacking rhythm players. It can often seem hardly like a big-band record at all. 'Intro' certainly doesn't set it up that way: a synthesizer drone gradually emerges, over which John McLaughlin – whom Miles had drafted in late on to play at the sessions – plays the 'Miles Davis' motif. The synthesizer part, which sounds very close to a passage from the German band Can's 'Quantum Physics', drifts on, before guitar and trumpet swap solos against a staccato rhythm played on keyboards and electronic drums. 'White', which follows, is pure Scandinavian brooding. Mikkelborg had prepared a tape, as the interval music at the concert, which consisted of a series of variations on the 'Miles' scale over which a synthesizer player added further improvisations. At one of the studio dates, Davis asked Mikkelborg if he could try playing over the tape, and in a darkened studio he did so. Most of Mikkelborg's horn players had already gone home, but the oboist Niels Eje was still there, and the composer quickly wrote out a part for him and suggested to the percussionist Marilyn Mazur that she add whatever she felt would work. Davis played two stealthy, feelingful solos with the mute in. Cast against the ancient dignity of the oboe and the pulsing permafrost of the electronics, the trumpeter should sound like a fish very much out of water, but his grave, sauntering lines work handsomely, tickled along with a few echo effects. If his older adventures with electronics suggested a humid jungle of noise, this one was more like a dance along a glacier. Davis had probably never heard the music of such ECM stalwarts as Terje Rypdal, much of whose work is quite close to this, and it would only be a brief dalliance in this style for him.

'Yellow' begins like a more structured continuation of the same mood, with harp, oboe and keyboard delicately plaiting the melodic line. The mood is sundered by a guitar riff, the stately entrance of stacked horns, martial drumbeats and a peal of keyboard sounds, which eventually take the piece out, the 'Miles' scale peering through, although Davis himself is absent. 'Orange' comes as a complete contrast, seemingly a simple backbeat over which McLaughlin solos, but Mikkelborg took pains to weave in barely perceptible references to some of the previous winners of the Sonning Award. Davis takes over from McLaughlin and plays a spattering muted solo, deftly riding on the beat, before playing a second solo on open horn, his lines all extrapolated from the trumpet's high register. The remastered CD issue of 2000 has much improved a track which sounded clouded in its first edition; but there is probably still too much going on, and some of McLaughlin's guitar ramblings could have usefully been cleaned off a track where Mikkelborg has himself already provided plenty of incident.

'Red' opens with a mesmerizing effect, trumpet phrases doctored with reverb until they dissolve down to a glistening morass, over which Davis continues playing while an ostinato guitar figure is entwined with a thumping bass riff. This eventually switches into a reprise of the rhythm section off 'Intro'. Over it all, Davis continues playing open horn. He had little time for Don Cherry's trumpet playing, but the many little, pirouetting figures he plays during this track offer a sometimes irresistible reminder of that other trumpet master. Davis went on to play a solo with the mute in, and since Mikkelborg liked both of them so much, they used both takes on the finished record – 'Electric Red' uses the muted version, but is cut back by some two minutes.

'Green' is one of the most effective movements. Over a synthesized backdrop, there are extended solos by Bo Stief on fretless electric bass and Niels-Henning Ørsted Pedersen on acoustic bass, the latter joined by Davis. Again, Mikkelborg uses the 'Miles' scale, a cor anglais, and the serenely beaut-iful sound of what appears to be a female choir, although actually it is the voice of Eva Thaysen in multiple overdub. Along with 'White', this pulseless, melan-choly mood painting is all but unique in the Davis discography. Mikkelborg intended it in homage to Gil Evans, even though it scarcely calls Evans's music to mind. 'Blue' follows: after an indeterminate opening, Davis plays freely placed phrases on the open horn over a juddering beat that is most of the way towards a reggae groove. In a strange mix of the pop feel of 'Ms Morrisine' from *You're Under Arrest* and more abstract material, which Mikkelborg has churning away somewhere near the back of the mix, the beat of 'Blue' even-tually shrivels and a muted Miles scatters phrases over a sequence where the brass players harmonize, leading to a music-box finale.

Davis doesn't play at all on 'Indigo', the most straight-ahead jazz theme on the record. Instead, the pianist Thomas Clausen plays a brilliant cameo, which even had Davis saying, 'The piano player was playing enough music.' But the finale, 'Violet', restores and celebrates the trumpet player's work. Mikkelborg worked up the piece from two chords, both derived from a text by Olivier Messiaen, and the music works as a kind of desolated blues, a blues stripped down to little more than a sensation spun out over synthesized drones. Davis and McLaughlin improvise solos over the top. As with the other tracks he appears on, McLaughlin's presence does imbalance the situation: he is too strong, and too weighty a counter for the more delicate Davis. Having a second lead soloist is something else which keeps this project at a remove from the great Evans collaborations.

Davis, though, does play some piercingly effective passages. Throughout a superbly recorded and mixed album – a tribute to the engineers Henrik Lund and Niels Erik Lund, the facilities at Copenhagen's Easy Sound Studio, and Mikkelborg's own sensitivity as producer – the trumpeter sounds like a more vivid presence than he does on any of his American records of the decade. Mikkelborg remembered that there were many clinkers and false steps in his playing which had to be edited out, but Davis had good reason to feel proud of the results: 'This music will be like nothing you ever heard.' He was right enough: it is certainly like nothing else in the Davis story on record. There are flaws in it, too: the most disappointing aspect is the recourse to using Simmons electronic drums to underscore the rhythms on several tracks, yet another sonic relic of its day. Davis had asked Vince Wilburn to add them to the tracks, but with hindsight it was a poor decision, especially when Mikkelborg handles all the other electronic elements so deftly.

In all, though, *Aura* was a remarkable record, which could also function as an appeasement: if long-time Davis fans were dismayed at the apparent flimsiness of some of the recent American records, this one reminded them of his ability to be an uncompromising artist. Yet Columbia didn't even give anyone the chance to hear it for four years. To Davis's displeasure, they didn't release it straight away, and in the circumstances which evolved later that year, the record abruptly lost all priority: because Davis had suddenly departed the label and shifted over to Warner Brothers.

Miles had raged at Columbia for years – since 1955, really, so for thirty years. He had seen out numerous changes of personnel at the label, had stayed with them during the entire period when Columbia shifted from being a middle-class, middle-of-the-road, rather homely place, where Johnny Mathis and original cast albums brought in the big money, to one of the power-house organizations in popular music, home of Bob Dylan, Bruce Springsteen and so many others. Columbia had always had a jazz representation which was small in number, but select: older players such as Dave Brubeck had long since gone, but they had Weather Report and Herbie Hancock, and with Miles Davis they could always boast they had the best man. George Butler, though, was also keen to develop Wynton and Branford Marsalis as superstars, and he had them recording classical albums for the label's Masterworks Division, as well as straight-ahead, acoustic jazz sessions.

Davis, an ailing man with often fragile chops, could hardly help but be intimidated by the presence of the smartest young trumpet virtuoso to emerge in many years, even if he would never admit to seeing it that way. In his autobiography, he claims to have had enough of Columbia when Butler called him and asked if he minded calling Wynton on his birthday, to send a greeting. That, and the situation over *Aura*, clearly rankled with him. But Davis had got over far worse spats with his label than that. The real reason for the switch was more likely money. In the way that major labels often do, Warners had been courting Davis for some time, both personally and through his representative, David Franklin. By the time Columbia got wind of the situation, it was already too late, and Davis had signed to Warners. It was a valuable deal: as a sign-on fee, the money Miles received was probably more than he had ever received in his professional life. But in other ways, it was a strange, short-term expedient.

For one thing, Franklin ceded significant ground over Davis's publishing rights, for both existing and future compositions. It is elementary in the art of record deal-making that publishing rights have huge financial importance: with the income streams from radio-play and cover versions, it is a fundamental which has to be carefully considered from all sides. Yet this didn't work out in Miles's favour. Had he stayed at Columbia, he might have ended up a much wealthier man. There were many years where the label paid for Davis as a prestige artist, and never looked likely to recoup their costs, but his catalogue had grown into something of vast proportions, and ancient records such as *Sketches Of Spain* and *Kind Of Blue* continued to sell well (and in the CD era, they would sell *incredibly* well). A fresh deal with Columbia, carefully negotiated, would have reinstated Davis with most of the cards in his favour, at a label which had always seen him through good times and bad. Instead, with the curious mix of acuity and offhandedness that characterized his attitude towards business, he ended up at a label which respected him, but never got too close. George Butler, who had visited Davis day after day during his darkest period, must have been disappointed.

Davis took some tentative steps with his new deal. He recorded a version of 'Maze', a piece inspired by the old-fashioned soul band of that name, which remained in his live set for a time, but was never released. Work then began on an album which would have finally tumbled Davis into the pop camp, with possibly very little going back. He began asking figures in the rock world – Bill Laswell, Steve Porcaro of the stadium-rock band Toto, George Duke – if they were interested in collaborating, but nothing got very far. Then Randy Hall, who had worked with Davis on the early sessions for *The Man With The Horn*, came back into the picture. Hall had become a successful producer, and Davis thought he might work the oracle on a record which would be a step further on from *You're Under Arrest*. Guest vocalists – Chaka Khan and Al Jarreau were two in the frame – would appear on some tracks, others would mix the funk and jazz feel which recent Davis groups had worked with. An album was completed, tentatively called *Rubberband*, and Randy Hall must have felt that he had at last got some compensation for the way his work on *The Man With The Horn* had largely been shunted to one side. But he reckoned without Tommy LiPuma.

An industry veteran, who had started out producing the likes of the Sandpipers in the 1960s, LiPuma undertook the George Butler role at Warners. He felt that Davis needed careful handling – on a personal level, and with regard to his product. During the many years at Columbia, the label had largely taken a laissez-faire approach to Davis's recording projects, leaving most of the decisions up to Miles and Teo Macero. LiPuma wasn't having any of that. He let the *Rubberband* sessions go ahead, and also, at Davis's insistence, put the trumpeter in touch with Prince, the dazzling young rock'n'soul virtuoso who was one of the biggest stars of that time: Miles himself compared him to a young Duke Ellington. One track came out of the collaboration, 'Can I Play With U?', by all accounts a typical Prince rock-funk song which Davis plays a modest instrumental role on. It would certainly have added further spice to the *Rubberband* project.

But LiPuma quietly buried the record. He didn't like Hall's work, and didn't care for the material; he also probably didn't care for the fact that he had had no involvement in the studio sessions. LiPuma wasn't really an old-fashioned record man. He was part producer, part corporate guy, ruthless about making records that would succeed: he had worked with dreary musicians such as Earl Klugh and Bob James, and made albums which worked on radio and with an audience that didn't really care much about jazz. He had the same thing in mind for Miles Davis.

The musician he thought would work as Miles's producer was another holdover from *The Man With The Horn*, Marcus Miller. The man who had brought a new toughness to the bassist's role in the Davis groups was also a skilled multi-instrumentalist: he knew all about the newest synthesizers, and had an equally skilled associate, the programmer Jason Miles. He also loved the bass clarinet, and liked to work it into as many tracks as possible. LiPuma had taken a call from Miller, who asked if Davis was looking for any material. Tommy suggested he work up some demos. Miller did as he was asked, and created what were close to finished tracks, where he played every instrument. He took them to Los Angeles, where LiPuma listened. He probably realized right away that this was just what he was looking for: a spotless, trouble-free Miles Davis record. He suggested to Miller that they begin at once. But, wondered Marcus, what about the band, the musicians? No, said Tommy: you play everything, just like you did on the demos. Then Miles plays over the top.

Tutu [1] was effectively a two-man record, made by Miller and Davis. There was one track George Duke had done, 'Backyard Ritual', which both Davis and LiPuma quite liked, and this was left largely undoctored. The rest was a sequence of lightly funky music, moodily underscored by synthesizer mel-odies and counter-melodies, over which Miles's trumpet doodles out lines. Miller had a very good ear for an instrumental hook, and tracks such as 'Tutu', 'Portia' and 'Splatch' catch the ear with a chord shift or a melodic fill. But it was music made by technocrats. Miller is a considerable musician, but when

allied with LiPuma, who liked records to be, above all else, clean, he came up with a sound which was chanceless and with nothing out of place. Compared to [1], *You're Under Arrest* sounds positively rough and ready. All Davis has to do is play lines that sound at least plausible as a decoration.

The track which probably exemplifies its approach is 'Perfect Way', a song by the 1980s pop group Scritti Politti. Davis liked the melody and the sound of the original so much that he wanted Miller to basically replicate it, which is what happens, and the track sounds like what it is: a piece of 1980s pop music. What seems shocking is that for the first time, there was really no live music-making involved in the record. LiPuma had imposed the way records were now being made, the 'correct' procedure, on even Miles Davis. There were no lightning inspirations in the studio, no sudden swerves of direction, nothing was worked up from some fragment of a sideman's solo: this was a military record.

It wasn't so much a capitulation to commerce as an admission that, for Davis, enough was enough. His publishing hardly belonged to him any more, so he didn't feel inclined to collar writing credits the way he once had. For most of his career, he had led bands full of brilliant sidemen, who could make extraordinary things happen in the prosaic surroundings of a recording studio; but his current band didn't have anyone like that in it, and besides, that wasn't how records were made any more. Most of all, Miles was tired. If he could get away with just playing his filigree parts, and leave the real work to others, and *still* get a record out of it which sold much better than many of his old ones well, that was fine. He could save the creative work for his live performances.

Tutu isn't a bad record, it's just a very tame, uneventful one. It sounds of its time – better than much else that was going on in 1986, but hardly a masterpiece. Some of the plaudits given to it by commentators then and since make the dispassionate observer wonder if they are listening to the same record. It is not remotely like anything which Gil Evans had a hand in, and not very much like anything else in the Davis discography, either: the first record which really has the feel that he is a guest on his own session, Marcus Miller's accomplice.

Randy Hall was philosophical about the way things had gone. He was invited to the album launch, still under the impression that at least some of the *Rubberband* music would be on there. But Randy heard nothing, and Miles eventually came over and apologised – it was just the way things were done now. Hall had been down this road before: 'The music industry is political and people will smile in your face at the same time they're stabbing you in the back.'

Meanwhile, the Davis touring band was still working. There was now a steady turnover in personnel. Irving had been joined by Adam Holzmann at the keyboards, and there was a succession of guitar players: Robben Ford, Dwayne McKnight, Hiram Bullock, Bobby Broom. Bob Berg stayed on through 1986, and was briefly replaced by the tempestuous tenor player Gary Thomas, who didn't like the gig much and quickly departed. In March 1987, the alto player Kenny Garrett joined, who would be the last in Davis's distinguished roster of saxophonists. Garrett was a versatile player: muscular, funky, with threads of Cannonball and Coltrane alike running through him. In May, the guitarist's role was finally settled on one Joe McCreary, usually called 'Foley', who was credited as playing 'lead bass', although it sounded like a guitar.

Davis was asked to write the score for a movie called *Siesta*, a Hollywood art-house picture with, as it turned out, very little going for it except a considerable cast of stars. He accepted, but then – perhaps a further indication of his energy levels – quickly turned the project over to Miller, who wrote the whole score in a couple of weeks. The soundtrack album [2] was a rather gloomy affair (although not as gloomy as the film, which was a box-office flop), and was set up as the ghost of *Sketches Of Spain*, brooding little arabesques played mostly on bass clarinet and keyboards, with Miles again employed in a decorative rather than an integrated role. It was quite well received at the time, but has been largely forgotten since, like most soundtrack records.

By the end of 1987, the Davis band had settled, and was still busy touring, in America, Europe and Japan. Davis wanted his live sets to be recorded and released, but Warners were wary of that, and in the end nothing was issued by them during his lifetime (the desultory *Live Around The World* [3], made up of live material from 1988 to 1990, didn't even emerge until 1996). His relationship with Cicely was disintegrating, and a White House dinner which the couple attended in honour of Ray Charles marked a low point in their affairs: Davis rebuked the efforts of a politician's wife at making conversation, cutting her off with a claim that he had changed music several times, and what had she done, other than be white? The spectre of racism never let him go. Eventually, he began to become violent towards Cicely and, just like Frances before her, she fled.

His relationship with jazz was as difficult as ever. By now, nobody expected that he would ever return to anything resembling his earlier style, and his constant belittling of jazz as an old, outdated music hardly endeared him to any diehard jazz fan: for years, he had groused that Columbia shouldn't even have been marketing him as a jazz artist. It continued to create friction between himself and Wynton Marsalis, a small war which had reached a sort of boiling point a year earlier, at the 1986 Vancouver Festival. As so often, both musicians were playing at the event, but this time Wynton walked on stage as the Davis band were playing, and seemed ready to sit in. Instead, Davis called a halt and wouldn't continue until Marsalis had departed. He duly did, but it conferred no honour on Miles: Wynton was, after all, doing no more than following a time-honoured jazz tradition, of settling a matter on the bandstand. Had the roles been reversed, the Marsalis group would doubtless have been much more accommodating, but Davis was no longer in any shape to enter into a cutting contest.

White, Yellow, Orange, Red ... 1985–88

Live material from the late 1980s suggests something of a surviving vitality in Davis's music. He continued to lead a succession of young bands, and while the players weren't inexperienced, they weren't set in their ways and had enough openness about them to move quickly in any direction their leader wanted. It was also much more of a directed band: whereas Davis had never bothered with rehearsals in the past, this time they were a regular occurrence, new ideas were tried, and sidemen were often given a quiet few words before showtime. It was as if Davis knew that playing music in person was all he had left, and he wasn't going to let carelessness screw it up.

Unofficial releases such as *From His Last Concert In Avignon* [4] and *Live Tutu* [5] are typical, in the way similar programmes can develop differently. Davis tends to reserve himself for the quieter passages, such as 'New Blues' [4], where he plays a delicate, knowing line, or the familiar set-piece of 'Human Nature' [5], which has developed into a speedier, amused kind of showcase for his reading of a trusted melody. 'Tutu' [5], which is airless in its studio incarnation, first sneakily then noisily comes to life, over a fourteen-minute stretch. By this time, Kei Akagi had replaced Robert Irving, but with Adam Holzmann still there, there was plenty of space and resources for often elaborate keyboard orchestrations. Sometimes a piece was hopelessly elongated, to the point where its origins seemed needlessly remote: the Plugged Nickel band had the genius to make that gripping, but this one wasn't in that class. Yet at other times the strange brew of personalities made up intriguing, unguessable performances. Besides the players already mentioned, there were figures such as the dour but very able tenor saxophonist Rick Margitza; the teenage organ wunderkind, Joey DeFrancesco; Marilyn Mazur, who had played on *Aura*, and joined for a time as percussionist, sometimes dancing with bells around her ankles; and the drummer Ricky Wellman, who had replaced Vince Wilburn some time previously, and who was a strong exponent of the Washington funk groove called go-go, which interested Miles for a time. There could be flat, overloud sequences (usually when Foley was taking one of his heavy-metal solos), when one wondered if Davis really had any grasp of nuance any longer, and then a sudden dynamic drop, where this stadium band might be reduced almost to a whisper. Such a transition comes in 'Tutu' on [5], where a guitar thrash is abruptly wiped away and Davis snickers in duet with the percussionist Munyungo Jackson.

Although it is stingily presented – eleven tracks from nine different concerts, hardly a bountiful offering from what must be many hours of recorded shows – [3] is at least a decent sampler of what this period of late, live Davis was like. Compiled by Adam Holzmann and Gordon Meltzer, the album in one way continues a familiar Davis tradition: the individual pieces are subject to heavy and sometimes intrusive editing. The brief 'Mr Pastorius', for instance, a threnody for the bassist by Marcus Miller, is pared back from an original nine minutes to three and a half, even though it stands as an effective feature for Davis's open horn. 'Amandla', a routine performance, at least captures one of the leader's latter-day acknowledgements: at the conclusion of a piece, he would often call the names of sidemen who had done a good job, and here he croaks out 'Foley – Adam – Rick – Benny.' 'Wrinkle', a leftover from the *Rubberband* sessions, gets a very fast funk interpretation, which doesn't suit Davis. 'Time After Time', from a 1989 show in Chicago, is played ruminatively on open horn at a gentle tempo, before he puts in the Harmon mute and plays the theme. There is a tiresome passage where Davis plays phrases and Foley mimics them back at him, but it is otherwise a sensitive performance. 'Hannibal', the closing track, makes an unexpected finale, since it is a track taken down at Davis's final appearance, at the Hollywood Bowl in August 1991. Weak as he must have been, the will to play seems to endure: he sounds much as he does elsewhere on the collection, a little fragile but otherwise the genuine Miles.

The cover photograph shows the strange figure who prowled the stages of these shows in his closing years. He had lost much of his hair, and striking though he still looked, with his dark eyes even more piercing when highlighted by his high forehead, vanity took over, and he began using a hair weave of dark curls. The immaculate suits had long gone – they were the preserve of Wynton Marsalis and his young-lion contemporaries now, and to Miles they looked ridiculous – and instead he swathed himself in Japanese designer outfits that were more like robes, flowing and capacious (to Marsalis, they looked more like dresses). 'I like shit that shines,' he said. His trumpets were matador red or bullfrog green, and he used them with a little microphone attached to the bell, so he could wander round the stage at will, taking the arm of a musician on a whim and walking them to the front, an instruction to solo – or maybe not. It depended. He hid his eyes behind outlandish dark glasses, and if he wanted to speak to us, he upturned the horn and raised the microphone to his lips. Sometimes he held up little placards with the names of the musicians on them, to acknowledge their efforts at the end of a set.

Davis was devastated by the death of Gil Evans in March 1988. Although he had not really worked with his old friend for many years, they never stopped talking to each other (which, in itself, was a rarity in Miles's circle). After an operation in March, Evans had gone down to Mexico to recuperate, but he never recovered. His own music had been feted in recent times – a seventy-fifth birthday concert in London the previous year had been a gala occasion, even though Gil looked all but worn out, and he had been leading a Monday night band in New York on a regular basis. The English trumpeter Henry Lowther had worked with him in his later years: 'Lovely man, charming guy, but disastrous. He didn't really care about mistakes and things like that. He was always looking for an atmosphere more than anything. There was a whole bar missing at the end of one of these things and he used to just say, "Oh, leave it out. It's not important." He was something else.'

Gil's death made Miles even more lonely, and though Jo Gelbard eventually became his partner, he withdrew further into painting and solitude: live performance was his only musical interest. Gelbard recalled that they never listened to music at home. At the end of 1988, though, he began work on another studio record, which would be his final collaboration with Marcus Miller. *Amandla* [6] was finished by January. Miller and Jason Miles used synthesizers again – it had only been a couple of years since [1], but the technology moved so fast that the new equipment was already a considerable advance on what they had used on that record – and LiPuma again controlled every step of the process. This time, the members of the Davis live band were involved rather more: Kenny Garrett figures on most of the tracks, Foley is on three and Ricky Wellman plays on two. There are a few other contributors, too: Joe Sample, a long-time member of the Crusaders, plays on one track, the extravagant fusion guitarist Jean-Paul Bourelly plays on two, and George Duke was again allotted one track which he wrote and produced. But the music is basically a continuation of the polished, careful grooves of [1], except this time the material is rather less ingratiating – it could use a few more hooks.

MILES DAVIS

A handful of idiosyncratic moments escape the spin-dried feel of the music, which is even more spick and span than [1] was. Davis interpolates a few twists in his first solo commentary on 'Big Time' which sound personal, and on the closing 'Mr Pastorius' he plays an open solo that has some of the immutable elegance of Davis in his prime, rather a poignant way for him and Miller to end their relationship. Otherwise, this is again a Marcus Miller–Tommy LiPuma record which Davis performs on, under orders. There has been much speculation as to why Warners didn't release any live material by the Davis touring band in his lifetime. The likeliest reason is that LiPuma just didn't like the idea.

The Other Records

1 *Tutu* (Warner Bros)
2 *Siesta* (Warner Bros)
3 *Live Around The World* (Warner Bros)
4 *From His Last Concert In Avignon* (Laserlight)
5 *Live Tutu* (Golden Age Of Jazz)
6 *Amandla* (Warner Bros)

They Offered Me
A Lot Of Money
1989–91

The *Amandla* sessions had been interrupted by Davis going into hospital with bronchial pneumonia. He recovered soon enough, but it was another illness visited on a body which was now ailing badly. The prescription drugs were debilitating him further, and his doctors even suggested that he retire from live playing altogether. But that was unthinkable. And by degrees, he got better. He spent more time in Malibu, was nursed by Jo Gelbard, and also had the regular company of his brother Vincent and his sister Dorothy. His youngest son Erin also grew closer to him (and Miles began giving Erin composer credits on some of his tunes, another means of keeping royalties away from his publishing deal). He had fresh management, under the lawyer Peter Shukat, and although he was not as wealthy as he might or should have been, money was not so much of a problem any longer.

As well as the release of *Amandla*, 1989 was also notable for the publication of *Miles: The Autobiography*. Davis would never have written a book on his own, but it was an as-told-to story completed in collaboration with Quincy Troupe, a journalist who had done a lengthy interview with Davis some years earlier and had earned his trust. The book is an often sensational read. It is scattered with pointless cruelties: he cites fellow musicians who became, like him, heroin users, and he goes through his many associations with women, rarely according any of them respect (when asked in 1985 if he intended to write an autobiography, his response was, 'The trouble with that is, I'd have to think about all of those bitches'). It is a sometimes comically unreliable memoir. But much of it does sound like the authentic Miles, throwaway one moment, coolly eloquent the next, and in its way it is a far more truthful and revealing portrait than the comparable book by Duke Ellington, *Music Is My Mistress*. Both men were good at masking their feelings, but Davis never had Ellington's genius for tactful evasion.

In 1990, the trumpeter was invited to be involved in two further film scores, neither of them exactly a predictable vehicle. *Dingo* [1] was a French–Australian collaboration, about a youth who plays trumpet and lives in the Australian outback. He dreams of meeting a famous jazz trumpeter, Billy Cross, and in the end does so, only to find that Cross has given up the horn. Dingo, the young man, encourages Billy to return to his trumpet. Davis actually took the part of Billy Cross and surprised everyone on the production with his amiability and professionalism. Michel Legrand, who had worked with Miles so many years earlier, scored the movie, and couldn't resist including pieces such as 'Concert On The Runway', which sounds like a clever rewrite of 'Milestones'. Although this was tantamount to Miles going back to an older style which he supposedly abhorred, he sounds remarkably strong on that and several other pieces on the record. The music emerges – as with so many soundtrack records – as a series of cues, and Miles was bolstered by the presence of another trumpeter, Chuck Findley, who plays many of the solo parts, but the record is curiously enjoyable. The film, alas, disappeared quickly and was barely given a full release.

The Hot Spot [2] was a film by Dennis Hopper. Jack Nitzsche directed the music and marshalled a band of New Orleans and blues veterans such as Earl

Palmer and Taj Mahal, with John Lee Hooker taking a vocal role. Davis came in and overdubbed some trumpet parts later in the proceedings. It was basically a cameo part, on a score that amounts to little, and the movie was another which didn't set the world alight. Davis had, in fact, been almost profligate in playing on other people's records in the later 1980s. He had not done any kind of 'sideman' work since the end of the 1950s, and it seemed strange to see him guesting on records by such unlikely bedfellows as Toto, Scritti Politti, Cameo and Chaka Khan. He also played on records by his own sidemen, Marcus Miller and Kenny Garrett, and was part of the all-star cast which made Quincy Jones's *Back On The Block*. But his most effective guest role was the final one he did, on the title track of Shirley Horn's *You Won't Forget Me* [3], from 1990. He and Horn had been close ever since he had insisted on the young singer taking a support slot at one of his Village Vanguard gigs in the early 1960s. Her own style was Milesian enough: slow, lagging behind the beat, parsing lines in unlikely yet natural ways, and swinging at the most trudging tempo. Davis plays a telling commentary on Horn's vocal which makes one wonder how he would have sounded in place of Clifford Brown, on one of the famous sessions where Brown played behind Sarah Vaughan and Dinah Washington.

It would surely have been better than the way he finally sounded with vocalists, on what turned out to be the last studio project with his name on it. In 1991, black music had moved rapidly on from fads such as go-go: rap and hip hop now ruled the scene, and as usual Davis wanted to be in on it. At first, the plan was for a grand overview of the vista of new black music: there would be rappers, singers, jazz, hip hop, anything that sounded of the moment and fitted in with Davis's perspective. The alliance with Prince was once again mooted, and the young maestro sent several tracks for Davis to play on. Chuck D and Flavor Flav from the leading rap band Public Enemy were involved at one point. Then Miles heard some tracks by a young rapper named Easy Mo Bee, and he took to his sound and style at once. Mo Bee (actually born Osten S. Harvey, Jr) and Davis hit it off easily, and the young man began putting tracks together for Davis to play over. It was summer in New York, and Miles was often tired:

every studio session was foreshortened because he would declare himself too fatigued to continue. But the tracks came together. Gordon Meltzer, the man now assigned the job of co-producer, had to walk warily between Davis, who wanted an extravagant double album involving all his ideas, and the Warners top brass, who didn't really want to hear of any such thing.

In the end, barely thirty minutes of music were finished in Miles's lifetime. When the record, *Doo Bop* [4], eventually came out, it was a cadaverous exercise: none of the Prince tracks were really completed (and in any case Prince himself

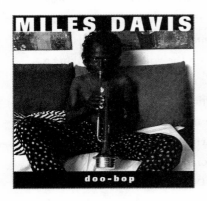

refused to allow any of them to be released), and Meltzer and Mo Bee had to go back to some of the pieces from the *Rubberband* sessions to salvage more music, and more Miles, to get the record up to a feasible length. One of them was a piece which ended up as 'High Speed Chase': a glib, nattily attired slice of cop-show music, it sounded almost nothing like what had been its original starting point, Mo Bee rebuilding it from the bottom up. Davis's crisp and punchy commentary on the

track, though, was one of the best things on the record. Little did any listener know that it was actually a solo he had played six years earlier.

The rest of the album was uneventful, a rote hip hop record which Davis often seems to have wandered into by accident. The raps are frequently as embarrassing as the lyrics to 'The Man With The Horn' were: 'The notes from his horn makes ladies get freaky like sex' ('Freaky') and 'Miles Davis's style is so different, you can't describe it as pacific/He rip, rage and roar, no time for watchin' Andy Griffith' ('The Doo-Bop Song') are about as immortal as they get. Phrase for phrase, Davis sounds like he's giving it his most serious attention. But no one can say how much of this is down to astute editing and overdubbing. When it was released in 1992 – the cover showing a very young-looking Miles – it won a Grammy, a posthumous and no doubt sentimental honour.

The spring had already been a busy season for Davis – bewilderingly busy, given his now parlous state of health. He was scheduled to do a North American tour, and would go to Europe in June. But the project which hovered around him, and which he kept trying to evade, was a re-creation of his old collaboration with Gil Evans, a gala concert at Montreux that would see him playing many of the original arrangements from the albums with Gil.

The Montreux Jazz Festival is one of the longest-serving events of its kind. Spread over some two weeks in July, it was first held in 1967, and is still convened on an annual basis. Its founder, Claude Nobs, has been involved with it throughout its history, although he handed over most of the programming to others in the 1990s. In its balmy Swiss location, it holds on to something of a village atmosphere, although for many years it was held in the decidedly unvillagelike atmosphere of the Montreux casino. In 1988, it shifted to two main locations, one named in honour of Igor Stravinsky, the other dedicated to Miles Davis. The trumpeter had been a regular at the event since the early 1980s, and Nobs prized his attendance there more than any other musician's.

In one way, it was singularly appropriate: just as Davis moved inexorably towards rock and popular music, so did the Montreux Jazz Festival. By the 1990s, there was at least as much rock as jazz at the event, and it was increasingly being annexed by major record companies, seeking showcases for their talent. Still, it has remained a prestigious event for jazz players. One of Nobs's shrewdest moves was to make sure every note at the Festival was recorded, with the Festival retaining the rights: as a result, every Davis performance at Montreux was preserved.

It's possible to see the release of *The Complete Miles Davis At Montreux 1973–1991* [5] as an act of atonement by Warners. Having shied away from offering anything bar a single CD of live highlights for years, they then issued this whopping nineteen-disc set in 2002. Featuring material from eight different Montreux appearances and one from Nice, it is at least a reasonable overview of the way Davis's approach to the concert stage evolved in his final period. The first set, from July 1973, is the odd one out, as well as being one of the best. In the notes to the set, Nobs relates that he had tried for years to get Davis to the Festival and finally made what he thought was a reasonable offer, only to be told, 'Your offer is an insult to my colour and my talent.' When a deal was eventually made, Davis then asked for the use of a Ferrari during his stay, only to be disappointed that the car provided was red rather than silver. Nobs confides that he also had to agree that the wife of the owner of the car, a chicken-farm owner, would be allowed to sell chickens at the concert. Such are the lengths some jazz promoters have to go to.

The 1973 band included Dave Liebman, Reggie Lucas, Pete Cosey, Michael Henderson, Al Foster and Mtume, and was in fiery and creative form. Davis plays long stretches on the opening material using his wah-wah pedal, and it is some of the most interesting extant work he did with that device, for once approaching a guitarist's ingenuity rather than trying to adapt his usual sound to the alien intrusion. The opening pieces, misidentified in the Montreux set as 'Miles In Montreux '73 #1' and '#2' and actually 'Turnaroundphrase' and 'Tune In Five', are juicy, pressure-cooker workouts around Henderson's dead-calm vamps, but the second half offers 'Ife' and 'Calypso Frelimo', humid and absorbing essays on the repertory of this not-overdocumented band, which in the context of the rest of the Montreux box-set only underline how powerful this line-up was, even on just another festival gig. The final piece, given the title 'Miles In Montreux '73, #3', is hard to identify and is possibly an improvisation, which Davis largely sits out until his final solo.

It would be eleven years before Miles played at Montreux again. The 1984 band was one of the best of that decade, with Bob Berg, John Scofield, Bobby Irving, Darryl Jones, Al Foster and Steve Thornton. They played one set in the afternoon and another in the evening and in total they run to well over three hours of music – Davis may have left his jazz club days behind him, but he was still used to playing long stretches of music in a single day's work. Both the afternoon and evening versions of 'Time After Time' are phrased and thought through with much refinement, even where the leader some-times almost wilfully cracks notes, and Bobby Irving's almost dapper use of synthesizers to underscore the trumpet playing is particularly agreeable. The strength of this band was its mix of individual excellence and easy passage into a collective will: it always feels like a band, even when some of the solos slip towards grandstanding. The move on from the 1973 band is startling when the discs are played end to end: Berg's sometimes faceless competence is less interesting than Dave Liebman's idiosyncratic virtuosity, but Scofield, while playing in an entirely different style to Pete Cosey, manages to subvert rock guitar from another direction. And the selfless Al Foster keeps guard of a good beat. The oddity is a piece in both sets called 'Lake Geneva': it sounds like a warm-up intro to 'Something's On Your Mind', running off some of the same chords, and that is what it eventually leads into.

The 1985 band was almost identical, bar the replacement of Al Foster by Vince Wilburn, and again the Davis band played lengthy sets in both the afternoon and the evening. *You're Under Arrest* was not long in the racks, and virtually all of the material from the record features across the two sets. In addition, the tribute tune 'Maze', 'Decoy', 'Hopscotch' and John McLaughlin's 'Pacific Express' make appearances. The afternoon set is sometimes marred by some very scrappy playing by Davis – 'Human Nature' is one clinker after another – and the evening assemblage is rather better in this regard. But both are played with brimming confidence and zeal by a band that was at its collective peak. Berg's muscular delivery on 'Ms Morrisine', Scofield's solid marriage of rock power and jazz harmony, the surprising and sometimes overlooked deftness of Irving and the tireless push and shove of the rhythm section give Davis a platform and a security blanket which elevate and protect him. Much of what this group did was, as with the other Davis groups to come, patterned after the routines and rituals of the rock concert, but since so many steps were also informed by improvisational excellence – the area where the later groups often fell down – that hardly seemed to matter then, and it has made the concert recordings endure very smartly.

These recordings cover the first ten discs of the Montreux set. At the 1986 Festival, the Davis band had a new guitarist, Robben Ford, and a second keyboard player, Adam Holzmann, to work alongside Irving. Ford was suggested by Tommy LiPuma, and was a guitarist who had recently signed a solo deal of his own with Warners, so it was a useful piece of cross-marketing for the label. He plays capably enough, although bringing little of the individuality which Scofield mustered. Some of the *Rubberband* material crops up in the set, as does music from the then forthcoming *Tutu*, and there are a couple of desultory guest appearances, by George Duke and by David Sanborn. From the customary opening of 'One Phone Call/Street Scenes', the band sounds supercharged, with even Davis, on open horn, playing with ferocious intensity. But it is drifting further from a jazz discipline and closer to the kind of almost hysterical licks-playing that Ford's approach exemplifies. The two-keyboard combination introduces some interesting new wrinkles, and at least Sanborn, one of the stars of crossover music, plays parts which fit plausibly into the group's language: Duke tends to merely noodle away while half the group take a breather.

The 1988 band was a settled outfit, with Kenny Garrett, Foley and Ricky Wellman, all regulars in Davis's later groups, each in place. As annoying as many of Foley's solos would be, he is a more temperate presence than Ford, and the clear mix of the Montreux music shows how inventive he could be as a rhythm player, quietly supportive and often building little internal dialogues with the rhythm section. Kenny Garrett, by contrast, is often flash and fire. Garrett is the only graduate of the final Miles Davis groups who has gone on to enjoy a significant jazz career, and his alto solos blend showmanship with a tough musical core better than any of his bandmates. Sometimes the showmanship does take over: he had begun to appropriate 'Human Nature' as a set-piece, and his solo here is a breathless extravagance. There are other concert concessions, too, such as a feature for Marilyn Mazur, shaking her ankles, and a drum solo by Wellman on 'Carnival Time' which merely fills up space. Davis, though, plays rather well, even if he is content to stand and listen much of the time.

One year later, Bobby Irving had departed and a new keyboard player, Kei

They Offered Me A Lot Of Money 1989–91

Akagi, took over. Holzmann had also been away, but had returned in time for the group's Montreux gig. Akagi brought a studious feel to the keyboard parts, although little he plays on this set makes much impression. Garrett was for some reason unavailable for the tour, and the tenor saxophonist Rick Margitza took his place. Margitza has made some admirable records under his own name since, but his rather thoughtful and undemonstrative approach didn't really suit this edition of the group, which underlines how much the Davis band had grown into a group based around oversized playing. Only when the group quietens around its leader on features such as 'New Blues' does it really sound like what one might expect from a Miles Davis ensemble. There is a bit of razzmatazz when Chaka Khan joined in for a guest vocal on 'Human Nature', although she fluffs several lines. Miles must have been really mellowing.

In 1990, Miles's son Erin had joined the group as a percussionist, Akagi was the sole keyboard player, and Richard Patterson was handling bass duties. This set feels even more pop-oriented, with a tune by Larry Blackmon of Cameo as well as the inevitable 'Human Nature' and 'Time After Time', here played back to back. Akagi, for one, was tiring of the routine, and decided to leave shortly after this European sojourn. There is nothing much wrong with the way the music is played, and Davis and Garrett have their expected moments, but a routine has been conferred on the set which suggests procedure has over-whelmed inspiration.

The final disc in the package offers a set played in Nice on 17 July 1991. The band is now down to a sextet: Garrett, Foley, Patterson, Wellman and a new keyboard player, Deron Johnson. Slimmed down to a six-piece, the music does have a leaner, sometimes even a muted feel, and on 'New Blues' it does sound as if things are starting to shift back towards jazz. But the set feels tired, as Miles must have been, and there is really no hint of what he might have toyed with next. Certainly there is nothing in it which reflects his ambitions as expressed by the music of [4]. As disc 20 in the package, it is something of an anti-climax, since it follows what should have been the real summation of the Montreux recordings, the concert of 1991.

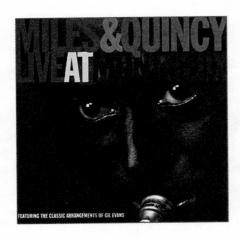

Miles Davis & Quincy Jones Live At Montreux

WARNER BROS

Boplicity; Introduction To *Miles Ahead* Medley; Springsville; Maids Of Cadiz; The Duke; My Ship; Miles Ahead; Blues For Pablo; Introduction To *Porgy And Bess* Medley; Orgone; Gone, Gone, Gone; Summertime; Here Come De Honey Man; Introduction To *Sketches Of Spain*; The Pan Piper; Solea.

Miles Davis (*t*); Wallace Roney (*t, flhn*); Kenny Garrett (*as*);

The Gil Evans Orchestra: Lew Soloff, Miles Evans (*t*); Tom Malone (*tb*); Alex Foster (*ss, as, f*); George Adams (*ts, f*); Gil Goldstein, Delmar Brown (*ky*); Kennwood Dennard (*d, perc*).

The George Gruntz Concert Jazz Band: Marvin Stamm, John D'Earth, Jack Walrath (*t, flhn*); John Clark, Tom Varner (*frhn*); Dave Bargeron, Earl McIntyre (*euph, tba*); Dave Taylor (*btb*); Howard Johnson (*bs, tba*); Sal Giorgianni (*as*); Bob Malach (*ts, cl, f*); Larry Schneider (*ts, ob, cl, f*); Jerry Bergonzi (*ts*); Mike Richmond (*b*); John Riley (*d*).

Additional musicians: Manfred Schoof, Benny Bailey, Ack van Rooyen (*t, flhn*); Conrad Herwig (*tb*); Alex Brofsky, Claudio Pontiggia (*frhn*); Roland Dahinden (*tb*); Anne O'Brien (*f*); Julian Cawdry, Hanspeter Frehner (*f, picc, af*); Michel Weber (*cl*); Christian Gavillet, Roger Rosenberg (*bcl, bs*); Tilman Zahn, Judith Wenziker (*ob*); Christian Rabe, Reiner Erb (*bsn*); Xenia Schindler (*hp*); Carles Benavent (*b*); Grady Tate (*d*).

8/7/91.

They Offered Me A Lot Of Money 1989–91

The impetus behind this occasion certainly didn't come from Davis himself. Given his fragile health, he could hardly have set himself a more onerous task, even if he had been inclined to begin revisiting some part of his illustrious past. Over and over again, ever since his return from the dark days of the late 1970s, Davis had insisted that there was no going back, that the 'old shit' should be left in the past, and that he wanted to concern himself with what was going on in the present. Sidemen were instructed not to even think about playing in four, or introducing old licks. 'Jazz' itself became a bad word. Davis gave every indication that he didn't want to know about anything other than the music he was playing now, something which in itself made him a sitting target for the adherents of the Wynton Marsalis doctrine.

Perhaps the only thing he might countenance, though, was the Gil Evans music. With Gil gone, there was no reason to suspect that the repertoire could be performed again, but Quincy Jones thought otherwise. In the sleevenotes to the resulting album – put together by Leonard Feather, his final act of devotion to his old friend – Jones claims that he had been talking to Davis 'for a long time' about performing some of the Evans scores. Since Jones was taking a hand in the programming at Montreux, this seemed like the perfect – and perhaps the last – opportunity. As Jones remembered it: 'At one point Claude [Nobs] came to New York and we sat with Miles and talked and talked, and finally he said, "Okay." But he said, "This stuff's gonna be expensive." I said, "What do you mean? The cost of the band can't be that much." "It ain't that, man," he said. "It's just that this shit is hard to play."'

Some romantic rumours circulated that the ghost of Gil Evans had spoken to Miles, and told him it was all right to play the music. But Miles wasn't into that kind of homage. What brokered it was the very large sum of money – the 'expensive' tag – Montreux paid him, probably in association with Warners, which would at least be assured a record out of it. When asked directly why he was effectively going back on his principles and playing the gig, Davis answered, 'In the first place, they offered me a lot of money.'

Davis had a strange relationship with money. He came from a comfortable home, and even when scuffling on the streets of Detroit during his junkie period, he never acted like a poor man. He loved shopping and spending money, and gave every impression that he wasn't interested in it for its own sake. But money stabilized him. He recognized its value in asserting his presence in a white society, and it bought much of what he prized most, the ability to withdraw and protect himself from the difficulties of being a public figure. So he agreed to the entreaties of Jones and Nobs.

The album's notes gloss over the circumstances, but the event almost didn't happen, and Davis played his role on a kind of autopilot. Jones elected to convene a band made up of two orchestras: the Gil Evans group, which Gil's son Miles had been leading in New York since his father's death, and the George Gruntz Concert Jazz Band, a rather jolly ensemble led by the genial Gruntz, who was a wizard at getting sponsorship for his groups and regularly managed to assemble and tour a group made up mostly of numerous American jazz stars. The keyboard player Gil Goldstein was assigned the task of transcribing some of Evans's orchestrations for the concert. Some rehearsals were held in New York prior to the trip to Europe, but Davis didn't show up for any of those. In Montreux, on 8 July, the band had already been through nine hours of rehearsals and there was still no sign of Davis. In his place, the young trumpeter Wallace Roney was playing his parts. At eleven that evening, having given everyone from Jones on down the runaround, Davis calmly arrived at the rehearsal and began unpacking his trumpet.

With hindsight, Jones must have been deluded in thinking that Davis would be able to carry off a major soloist's role, on a fearsomely difficult spread of music, across an entire evening, by himself. Goldstein had prepared everything from 'Boplicity', from *Birth Of The Cool*, to 'The Pan Piper' and 'Solea' from *Sketches Of Spain*, with a substantial helping of *Miles Ahead* and *Porgy And Bess* in between. To impose this on a man with a fragile lip, and obvious breathing

They Offered Me A Lot Of Money 1989–91

problems – the videotape of the concert suggests how frail Davis already was – was bordering on the absurd. In that light, the presence of Wallace Roney was a godsend. Davis himself listened appreciatively to Roney's handling of some of the more challenging parts at the rehearsal and assigned him the role of his understudy on the actual gig. On the record, Roney plays many of the open parts, covers the written passages, and leaves the decorative work with the Harmon mute to Miles. It was a watershed moment for Roney, to whom Davis later gave one of his trumpets, although it has been a mixed blessing: ever since, many commentators have seen Roney as little more than a Miles Davis impersonator.

The atmosphere of the recording is mainly good-natured, at times celebratory. Jones himself makes a cheery MC for the occasion, a somewhat jarring alternative to the silent Davis, and the orchestra plays its parts with professional finesse. Davis, for the most part, just about gets through it. On some pieces, he sounds weak and uncertain, fluffing notes and lagging behind both Roney and the ensemble: 'The Duke' is a particularly unfortunate example. He does well with 'My Ship', but any comparison with the lustrous original leaves one disappointed at the decline of a wonderful artist, and there is no compensating extra dimension, nothing that feels like some hard-earned wisdom gathered over the intervening years, the sort of autumnal spirit which attends the late work of many great artists.

It must have given Davis much pleasure to hear Evans's handsome music played again by a full orchestra. But he was not really able to fulfil the role which Jones and Nobs had been so thrilled at envisaging. This was hard music to play – probably too hard for someone who had spent the previous ten years working on groove tunes and backbeats. At any rate, despite all the talk of Miles beaming his satisfaction, thinking about taking the show out on tour and so forth, back at home he told Jo Gelbard that he hadn't enjoyed any of it.

There was, though, another engagement to fulfil in Europe. A mere two days after the Montreux concert, Davis played at a further gala event in Paris, headlined as 'Miles and Friends', where, as well as with his own band, he performed with groups drawn from different parts of his past: Wayne Shorter and Herbie Hancock were there, and so were Chick Corea, John Scofield and John McLaughlin, and Joe Zawinul and Dave Holland. Even Jackie McLean came over from New York. By the time of the finale, 'Jean Pierre', there were fifteen musicians playing on stage – an impromptu big band. Although an hour-long video of part of the concert has been issued, which portrays an event of good-humoured chaos, there has been no official release of any complete recording.

To many of those present, it seemed like Miles was offering a final bow. The young members of his current group looked around them in disbelief as one star sideman after another came into view. Pale and tired, the great man nevertheless roused himself to oversee all of the groups, dabbing in notes here and there, finishing a line or directing a soloist: a painter at his easel perhaps.

The Other Records

1 *Dingo* (Warner Bros)
2 *The Hot Spot* (Antilles)
3 Shirley Horn, *You Won't Forget Me* (Verve)
4 *Doo Bop* (Warner Bros)
5 *The Complete Miles Davis At Montreux 1973–1991* (Warner Bros)

Outro:
Goodbye, Miles

1991

Miles Davis's life came to an end faster than anyone expected, even though
most of those close to him – there were few enough of them – recognized
that his health was failing in a serious way. The Hollywood Bowl concert of
25 August, a track of which is preserved on *Live Around The World*, was the last
time he saw some of his sidemen and friends. Wayne Shorter visited backstage
and was shocked to see how much thinner he had become, even since the Paris
concert from a few weeks earlier.

Jo Gelbard was still with him. Their relationship, too, had become rocky:
she resented the frequent presence of his art dealer, Joanne Nerlino, who was
starting to seem like the Other Woman to Gelbard, and Davis had begun to
be violent towards her. He had always wanted Jo to move in with him in New
York, but 'I had a young son. I couldn't possibly think about bringing him into
Miles's home, because he was a maniac. I always left him by the time my son
came home from school, which was about five. And I always kept my handbag
by the door, and I was fast on my feet. And I got out of there the moment I
sensed anything coming.' But as her divorce finally went through, she went to
Europe with him, on the last tour of 1991, where he kept watch over her much
of the time.

Davis didn't play again after the Hollywood Bowl show. Over the Labor

Day weekend at the beginning of September, a public holiday in the US, he went into hospital, which was in itself nothing unusual after the many bouts of illness he had endured in recent years. This time, though, he was sinking rapidly, and literally raging as his life drew to a close, ripping out IV drips that were attached to his arms and stalking around his room. Then a stroke paralysed him, and he drifted into a coma, lingering for some weeks between life and death, still not quite letting go. He finally died on 28 September 1991. Although so much had been visited on his slim, slight frame over the years, in the end his cause of death was listed as respiratory failure and a stroke, complicated by pneumonia. He was buried in Woodlawn Cemetery in the Bronx, and on his gravestone is a line of music from 'Solar': ironically, it is one of the many compositions credited to Davis which may well have originated from another hand.

322

Considering his eminence, there was a strange stillness in the music world after his passing. Some of his former sidemen played a tribute concert or two, but there was no attempt to keep the Davis live band going, and even his record companies seemed slow in paying him any kind of homage: *Doo Bop* came out the following year, scarcely a worthy coda to his work, and it took Warners a further five years to release even *Live Around The World*. At the time of his death, the industry was enjoying a bonanza as the compact disc superseded the vinyl album as its chief sound-carrier, with millions replacing their old record collections with the new format. Artists with deep catalogues were also reaping the rewards. Over the next decade, the Davis catalogue would prove to be a small goldmine for Columbia Records, as records such as *Kind Of Blue* and *Sketches Of Spain* assumed a neo-classic status, finding fresh audiences by the thousand. How Miles would have regarded that, when any brand-new records he made would probably have enjoyed far more modest sales, one can only guess.

Similarly, it is impossible to say how he would have reacted to the one significant act of creative appropriation which has been inflicted on his output since his death. The bassist and record producer Bill Laswell was given the opportunity in 1998 to make *Panthalassa*, a record which consists of chunks of Davis's 1969–74 repertoire given a 'reconstruction and mix translation' by Laswell. Although he supposedly added no extra instrumental parts, instead using the remixer's arsenal of effects on pieces such as 'In A Silent Way', 'Black Satin', 'Rated X' and 'He Loved Him Madly', shifting parts around and altering the balance of much of the instrumentation, Laswell managed to make Davis's material sound very different. Whether it's better or worse is another matter. What Laswell mainly achieved was a more palatable spin on music which might otherwise be deemed long and rambling ('He Loved Him Madly', for instance, is shorn right back to a mere thirteen and a half minutes), its eccentricities traded for a more pointed result. 'Rated X' has its shocking organ dissonances emasculated in favour of a cleaner rhythm track (even though the original mix, as brightened on the *Complete Jack Johnson Sessions*, is far more effective). Laswell's perspective was that 'Macero and the other people who worked on these records were from a classical and jazz background. And I can't imagine people with a background like that having a clue what to do with the kind of stuff Miles was producing' – another instance of the many sour remarks Teo Macero has had to endure over the years. Most have said that *Panthalassa* is absolutely the kind of thing Miles would have wholeheartedly approved of. On the other hand, it is just as likely that the contrary Davis would have said 'Fuck you' to Laswell.

There were a handful of tribute projects. The trumpeter and film score composer Mark Isham released *Miles Remembered: The Silent Way Project*, a mild group record that touched on various aspects of Davis's electric period. Altogether more stormy was *Yo Miles!*, an album that paired the trumpeter Wadada Leo Smith and guitarist Henry Kaiser, in an energetic fusion set which actually treated some of Davis's electric material as repertory (Yo Miles! has since become a lasting band featuring the two principals). But no homage industry was spawned the way it was in the aftermath of Duke Ellington's death. Perhaps too many felt that the Davis legacy was untouchable.

Columbia, though, have addressed their enormous holdings of Davis material with a methodical and sometimes tiresomely fussy gatekeeper's approach. Beginning in 1996 with the Davis–Evans sessions, the original albums have been repackaged in elaborate multi-disc archives, with extravagant annotations, a mass of unissued takes – sometimes amounting to not much more than slivers of studio dialogue – and the kind of fanciful packaging which has been the major indulgence of the CD era, the discs sometimes hard to extricate from their folders and the notes often difficult to read (*The Complete In A Silent Way Sessions* in particular is a triumph of decoration over utilitarian values). And still they sit on tracts of live material that might at some time see the light of day. The emphasis on their prize artist, though, has if anything turned Columbia's jazz division into a Miles Davis division. In comparison, their other LP-era jazz artists have been neglected: Dave Brubeck, who at one time outsold Miles, has many out-of-print Columbia albums which have yet to see any kind of CD reissue.

Warner Brothers have been much more circumspect. A major multi-disc set was announced in 2001, *The Last Word: The Warner Bros Years*, which was to include all of the studio material, the various guest appearances and a smattering of live tracks. After numerous problems and track alterations, though, the project was abandoned altogether. Like Columbia, Warner Bros continue to hoard a considerable quantity of unreleased live material. In the meantime, the fifty-year copyright rule has meant that anything recorded more than a half-century ago is now fair game for independent reissue in Europe at least, and this has opened up plenty of early Davis to any interested party.

Whether the world *needs* any more Miles Davis music is debatable. It is certainly hard to imagine many lingering over the outtakes offered on *Miles Davis & Gil Evans: The Complete Columbia Studio Recordings*. Adopting the position of a vulture to pick over such bones is more tedious than enlightening: rare masterpieces reduced to the sweat of rehearsal and the indignity of false starts. It is hard to imagine Davis and Evans being pleased with such detritus becoming available.

But it does humanize Davis a little. His voice was regularly heard on his own records, rasping an instruction, a request to hear a playback, or something only he understood. One of the favourite descriptions of his playing is 'vulnerable', and whenever he cracks a note or otherwise displays some trait of mortal fallibility, it is regularly seized on as a virtue, as if he were godlike and we should treasure this descent into mere humanity. Since his death, the cult of Miles has grown ever more extravagant. Biographies compare him to every kind of musical genius, and other Olympian figures from every part of the arts. He was heroic, mystical: his presence itself seemed to fill up rooms, to dominate without anything being said, to leave observers wondering. Onlookers craved a word or some eye contact. Musicians who worked with him, however briefly, interviewed exhaustively, play their part in the mythology, perhaps not wanting to take a contrary position and make themselves seem like spoilers.

Against that, there is an alternative view: that Davis was a man small of stature, shy, reclusive; fascinated by the company of women, but mistrustful and abusive towards them whenever he felt like it; a former drug addict who struggled to escape the shadow it cast over most of his adult life; a sick man, plagued by illnesses that affected his mobility, his voice, his ability to simply play music; a man tormented by racism which he never felt able to escape, for all the wealth and respect and security he enjoyed.

But that is all gone now. All that is left is the records. It has become routine for the music industry to be pilloried by observers who feel that it has primarily exploited musicians, putting a distorted spin on the complexity of an artist's work. Miles grumbled unfailingly at the companies who preserved his playing over the years. But the labels who documented him fostered a unique portrait of an artist at work. Prestige recorded the greatest jazz small group of the 1950s in sessions which have an *audio vérité* quality – tense, volatile, fascinating in their flaws, incomparably vivid. The achievements of the later 1950s – the plush, sumptuous recordings with Gil Evans, and the riveting small-group dates of the period – were indulgently mothered by Columbia. Teo Macero ministered to Miles through the making of the vast archive of music he created in the 1960s and 1970s, a period when the label mostly adopted a position of remarkable patience with their maverick artist. And even in the final years, when Davis sometimes appeared to be a visitor on his own records, his producers were concerned to make him sound as good as possible.

Macero certainly deserves every recognition for his work. But there are others, usually cast as satellites in Miles's orbit, who actually effected much in the several revolutions accredited to the trumpeter: Gil Evans, Bill Evans, Wayne Shorter, Tony Williams, Joseph Zawinul, Chick Corea, Pete Cosey. And for every glittering moment which Davis himself contributes to the albums, there are indispensable contributions from so many other sidemen: John Coltrane, Cannonball Adderley, Red Garland, Ron Carter, Herbie Hancock, John McLaughlin, Michael Henderson, John Scofield. Who can imagine Miles's music without these men?

Davis himself certainly couldn't. As much as he enjoyed his personal limelight, he always acknowledged what his musicians brought. In the early days, he would sometimes be criticized for seemingly ignoring his sidemen, stalking offstage or smoking in the wings, yet always listening. In the video footage of his later concerts, the camera is frequently catching him calmly looking into space, head tilted back, lost in concentration – then abruptly deciding to signal a change.

The accepted wisdom is that change was a constant in Davis's life, but perhaps Miles himself didn't really change that much. Familiarity seemed to bore him, so his women, his cars, his style of clothes were all regularly shaken out. Music, which was more important to him than any of those other things, changed around him: no one figure can shift music by themselves, and coming from what was perceived – at least, in a late twentieth-century perspective – to be the marginal area of jazz, he tended to stand quietly in the eye of the storm and make small, telling adjustments. The modal advances of *Milestones* and *Kind Of Blue* weren't so much a revolution as a crystallization of many steps which had been taken in many parts of the music. The open-ended mystery of *In A Silent Way* feels like an assembling of numerous currents that were swirling inexorably towards a union. In a way, Davis was burdened with his role as an innovator: like Duke Ellington, he lived and performed for so long that his audience was often disappointed that he didn't start a fresh chapter every time. He may have disliked the term, but to the end he was a principled jazz musician: he knew that it was about a lifetime's work, a slow, patient unfolding.

In the past fifteen years, his legacy continues to haunt music, not always to music's advantage. Many bands and musicians have attempted to focus on some aspect of his electric period, and created miniatures that do little to flatter his achievements. Records such as *On The Corner*, once vilified, have been held up as harbingers of movements such as drum'n'bass, ambient music, anything where a dense beat and an abstracted surface makes up the substance of the sound. Where a post-bop jazz group once sought to emulate the dazzling conversations of the Miles Davis quintet, Nu Jazz ensembles try to copy the thick, impenetrable weave of the *Bitches Brew* era.

If we believe in Miles the magician, then we should imagine that he would have moved on again. In his acknowledgement in the notes to *Live At Montreux*, Quincy Jones trumpets: 'I love you. You really did revolutionize jazz five times.' (Only five, Quincy?) Tallying such securities, as if they were the wooden *Down Beat* plaques which Davis impassively hung on his wall, in the end means little. Better to say that we are fortunate we can go and put on *Miles Ahead* or *Birth Of The Cool*, *Steamin'* or *In A Silent Way*, and savour the immortal music he gifted us.

Acknowledgements

I am inevitably indebted to the several biographies of Davis which have previously appeared: Ian Carr, *Miles Davis The Definitive Biography* (HarperCollins); Jack Chambers, *Milestones* (Da Capo); Miles Davis and Quincy Troupe, *Miles: The Autobiography* (Simon & Schuster); Paul Tingen, *Miles Beyond: The Electric Explorations Of Miles Davis 1967–1991* (Billboard); George Cole, *The Last Miles* (Equinox); Ashley Kahn, *Kind Of Blue, The Making Of The Miles Davis Masterpiece* (Granta); and especially John Szwed's outstanding *So What: The Life Of Miles Davis* (Heinemann).

This book should really have been written by Angus MacKinnon, who was primarily responsible for making me into a music writer in the first place, and is a Davis scholar of the highest order. Angus's refusal to write about music any more is a great loss to everyone as far as I'm concerned, and he prevailed upon me to compile this book. It hardly needs saying that I will always be in his debt. Thanks Angus.

Bonnie Chiang was tolerant and kind about my usual hopelessness in meeting a deadline. Richard Marston did a fine job over design and pictures. My agent Anthony Goff is always a good guy. Peggy Sutton has been very helpful over records and pictures. And my wife, Lee Ellen, is my muse, as always.

RC, August 2005

References

Birth Of The Cool

p. 15: 'spent the better part of one winter' – sleevenotes to *Birth Of The Cool*.
p. 21: 'Miles didn't do it right' – Shearing interview with Andy Hamilton, *Jazz Review*.
p. 28: 'like a family' – *Miles: The Autobiography* (Simon & Schuster).

Steamin'

p. 38: 'One of the most dynamic' – Carr, *Miles Davis The Definitive Biography* (HarperCollins).

Like Nobody Else

p. 68: 'rich, fat brass with tuba' – notes to *Miles Davis & Gil Evans The Complete Columbia Studio Recordings*.
p. 74: 'the edited takes in mono' – notes to *Miles Davis & Gil Evans The Complete Columbia Studio Recordings*.
p. 75: 'If you want to drive yourself crazy' – notes to *Miles Davis & Gil Evans The Complete Columbia Studio Recordings*.
p. 75: 'Gil's understanding of Miles' – Art Pepper, *Straight Life* (Canongate).
p. 75: 'light imprisoned in a bright mineral cave' – Max Harrison, *A Jazz Retrospect* (Quartet).
p. 75: 'moony, saccharine' – Whitney Balliett, *A Journal Of Jazz 1954–2000* (Granta).
p. 75: 'great by example' – Danny Bank interview with Bob Rusch, *Cadence*, 1996.

Scales And Tones

p. 83: 'a spiritual awakening' – note to *A Love Supreme*.

So What?

p.105: 'I remember having to play Sam Woodyard's drums' – quoted in notes to *Jazz At The Plaza*.

p.114: 'Man, it *sounds* like Gil's stuff' – quoted in Ashley Kahn, *Kind Of Blue, The Making Of The Miles Davis Masterpiece* (Granta).

p.115: 'I thought that maybe' – quoted in Kahn, op cit.

I'm Going Out To Hear Miles

p.123: ' I played just over a week' – Nat Adderley, quoted in Chris Sheridan *Dis Here* (Greenwood).

p.125: 'I was drained' – quoted in *Miles: The Autobiography* (Simon & Schuster).

p.134: 'They'd take the same tunes' – quoted in Carr, op cit.

p.135: 'people from the black community' – Eddie Henderson, notes to *Friday Night At The Blackhawk*.

p.138: 'Eventually, the community' – Henderson, op cit.

All The Rockets Taking Off

p.154: 'After a few moments of silence' – Carter sleevenote to *My Funny Valentine*.

p.154: 'the acoustics were very weird' – quoted in notes to *'Four' And More*.

p.156: 'I gained a lot from being' Coleman quoted in Jack Chambers, *Milestones* (Da Capo).

p.158: 'he changed the sound' – Williams quoted in notes to *Miles In Tokyo*.

p.164: 'to hear all the train wrecks' – Carter quoted in notes to *The Complete Live At The Plugged Nickel*.

A Fine Madness

p.168: 'When we came off' – Shorter, quoted in John Szwed, *So What* (Heinemann).

A Portion Of The Music Inadvertently Gets Repeated

p.192: 'If you can hear a bass line' – quoted in Taylor, *Notes And Tones* (Quartet).

p.198: 'like trying to make conversation' – quoted in Chambers, op cit.

He Didn't Erase Anything

p.216: 'If anything sucked' – Belden, notes to *The Complete Bitches Brew Sessions*.

p.224: 'Some performances and compositions' – Belden, op. cit.

p.237: 'just got a hold of Steve' – Liebman, interview with Larry Nai, *Cadence*, 1999.

Dark, Dark

p. 255: 'That period was, like, chaotic' – Liebman, interview with Mark Gilbert, *Jazz Review*.

Tais-Toi Some Of This!

p. 273: 'He came to Seventh Avenue South' – Liebman, interview with Gilbert, op cit.
p. 282: 'No! Only thing is' – Davis, interview with author, 1985.

White, Yellow, Orange, Red...

p. 286: 'He'd overpaint' – Jo Gelbard, interview with Mick Brown, *Daily Telegraph*, 2005.
p. 292: 'This music will be like nothing' – Davis, interview with author, 1985.
p. 297: 'The music industry is political' – Hall, quoted in George Cole, *The Last Miles* (Equinox).
p. 301: 'I like shit that shines' – Davis, interview with author, 1985.
p. 301: 'Lovely man, charming guy, but disastrous' – Lowther, interview with Mark Gilbert, *Jazz Review*.

They Offered Me A Lot Of Money

p. 306: 'The trouble with that is' – Davis, interview with author, 1985.
p. 315: 'At one point Claude' – Jones, notes to *Miles Davis & Quincy Jones Live At Montreux*.
p. 316: 'In the first place' – Davis, interview with author, 1991.

Goodbye, Miles

p. 321: 'I had a young son' – Gelbard, op cit.
p. 323: 'Macero and the other people' – Laswell quoted in Paul Tingen, *Miles Beyond* (Billboard).

Discography

This is a listing of the official record releases involving Miles Davis as a leader, with a few of his selected sideman appearances also included. It is set out in a deliberately simple form: discography is the art of minutiae, and readers who want much more detailed information should consult either Jan Lohmann's *The Sound Of Miles Davis 1945–1991* (JazzMedia 1992), or Peter Losin's wonderful website dedicated to Davis' music, *www.plosin.com/milesAhead*. I am indebted to the research undertaken by both.

Charlie Parker, *The Complete Savoy And Dial Studio Recordings* (Savoy 91911-2)

Miles Davis (*t*); Charlie Parker (*as*); Dizzy Gillespie (*p*, *t*); Sadik Hakim (*p*); Curly Russell (*b*); Max Roach (*d*). 24 April 1945.

> **Billie's Bounce; Now's the Time; Thriving On A Riff; Meandering; Ko-Ko.**

Miles Davis (*t*); Charlie Parker (*as*); Lucky Thompson (*ts*); Dodo Marmarosa (*p*); Arvin Garrison (*g*); Vic McMillan (*b*); Roy Porter (*d*). 28 March 1945.

> **Moose The Mooche; Yardbird Suite; Ornithology; The Famous Alto Break; A Night In Tunisia.**

Miles Davis (*t*); Charlie Parker (*as*); Bud Powell (*p*); Tommy Potter (*b*); Max Roach (*d*). 4 May 1947.

> **Donna Lee; Chasing The Bird; Cheryl; Buzzy.**

Miles Davis (*t*); Charlie Parker (*as*); John Lewis (*p*); Nelson Boyd (*b*); Max Roach (*d*). 14 August 1947.

> **Milestones; Half Nelson; Little Willie Leaps; Sippin' At Bells.**

As above except Duke Jordan (*p*) and Tommy Potter (*b*) replace Lewis and Boyd. 28 October 1947.

> **Dexterity; Bongo Bop; Dewey Square; The Hymn; Bird of Paradise; Embraceable You.**

As above. 4 November 1947.

> **Bird Feathers; Klactoveesedstene; Scrapple From The Apple; Out Of Nowhere; Don't Blame Me.**

As above except add J. J. Johnson (*tb*). 17 December 1947.

> **Drifting On A Reed; Quasimado; Charlie's Wig; Bird Feathers; Crazeology; How Deep is The Ocean.**

As above except omit Johnson. 21 December 1947.

> **Another Hair-Do; Bluebird; Klaunstance; Bird Gets The Worm.**

Miles Davis (*t*); Charlie Parker (*as*); John Lewis (*p*); Curly Russell (*b*); Max Roach (*d*). 18 September 1948.

> **Barbados; Ah-Leu-Cha; Constellation.**

As above. 24 September 1948.

> **Perhaps; Marmaduke; Steeplechase; Merry-Go-Round.**

334 | *Birth Of The Cool* (Capitol 30117, RVG Edition)

Miles Davis (*t*); Kai Winding (*tb*); Junior Collins (*frhn*); Bill Barber (*tba*); Lee Konitz (*as*); Gerry Mulligan (*bs*); Al Haig (*p*); Joe Shulman (*b*); Max Roach (*d*). 21 January 1949.

> **Move; Jeru; Budo; Godchild.**

Miles Davis (*t*); J. J. Johnson (*tb*); Sandy Siegelstein (*frhn*); Bill Barber (*tba*); Lee Konitz (*as*); Gerry Mulligan (*bs*); John Lewis (*p*); Nelson Boyd (*b*); Kenny Clarke (*d*). 22 April 1949.

> **Venus De Milo; Rouge; Boplicity; Israel.**

Miles Davis (*t*); J. J. Johnson (*tb*); Gunther Schuller (*frhn*); Bill Barber (*tba*); Lee Konitz (*as*); Gerry Mulligan (*bs*); John Lewis (*p*); Al McKibbon (*b*); Max Roach (*d*); Kenny Hagood (*v*). 9 March 1950.

> **Deception; Rocker; Moon Dreams; Darn That Dream.**

Festival International Du Jazz 1949 (Columbia 32DP721)

Miles Davis (*t*); James Moody (*ts*); Tadd Dameron (*p*); Barney Spieler (*b*); Kenny Clarke (*d*). 8–15 May 1949

> **Rifftide; Good Bait; Don't Blame Me; Lady Bird; Wahoo; Wee; Embraceable You; Ornithology; All The Things You Are.**

Miles Davis And Horns (Prestige/Original Jazz Classics OJC 053)

Miles Davis (*t*); Bennie Green (*tb*); Sonny Rollins (*ts*); John Lewis (*p*); Percy Heath (*b*); Roy Haynes (*d*). 17 January 1951.

> **Morpheus; Down; Blue Room; Whispering.**

Miles Davis (*t*); Sonny Truitt (*ts*); Al Cohn, Zoot Sims (*ts*); John Lewis (*p*); Leonard Gaskin (*b*); Kenny Clarke (*d*). 19 February 1953.

> **Tasty Pudding; Floppy; Willie The Wailer; For Adults Only.**

Birdland 1951 (Blue Note 82-41779)

Miles Davis (t); J. J. Johnson (tb); Sonny Rollins (ts); Kenny Drew (p); Tommy Potter (b); Art Blakey (d); Symphony Sid Torin (announcer). 17 February 1951.

Out Of The Blue; Half Nelson; Tempus Fugit; Move.

Miles Davis (t); J. J. Johnson (tb); Sonny Rollins (ts); Kenny Drew (p); Tommy Potter (b); Art Blakey (d). 21 June 1951.

Move; Half Nelson; Down.

Miles Davis (t); Eddie 'Lockjaw' Davis, George 'Big Nick' Nicholas (ts); Billy Taylor (p); Charles Mingus (b); Art Blakey (d). 29 September 1951.

The Squirrel; Lady Bird.

Dig (Prestige/Original Jazz Classics OJC 005)

Miles Davis (t); Jackie McLean (as); Sonny Rollins (ts); Walter Bishop Jr (p); Tommy Potter (b); Art Blakey (d). 5 October 1951.

Out Of The Blues; Denial; Bluing; Dig; It's Only A Paper Moon.

Conception (Prestige/Original Jazz Classics OJC 1726)

Miles Davis (t); Lee Konitz (as); Sal Mosca (p); Billy Bauer (g); Arnold Fishkin (b); Max Roach (d) March 8, 1951

Odjenar; Hibeck; Yesterdays; Ezz-thetic.

Miles Davis (t); Jackie McLean (as); Sonny Rollins (ts); Walter Bishop Jr (p); Tommy Potter (b); Art Blakey (d). 5 October 1951.

Conception; My Old Flame.

Miles Davis: Volume 1 (Blue Note 36210)

Miles Davis (t); J. J. Johnson (tb); Jackie McLean (as); Gil Coggins (p); Oscar Pettiford (b); Kenny Clarke (d). 9 May 1952.

Dear Old Stockholm; Chance It; Donna; Woody 'N' You; Yesterdays; How Deep Is The Ocean?

Miles Davis (t); Horace Silver (p); Percy Heath (b); Art Blakey (d). 6 March 1954.

Take Off; Lazy Susan; The Leap; Well, You Needn't; Weirdo; It Never Entered My Mind.

Miles Davis: Volume 2 (Blue Note 36211)

Miles Davis (t); J. J. Johnson (tb); Jimmy Heath (ts); Gil Coggins (p); Percy Heath (b); Art Blakey (d). 20 April 1953.

Kelo; Enigma; Ray's Idea; Tempus Fugit; C.T.A.; I Waited For You.

Collectors' Items (Prestige/Original Jazz Classics OJC 071)

Miles Davis (t); Sonny Rollins, 'Charlie Chan' (Charlie Parker) (ts); Walter Bishop Jr (p); Percy Heath (b); Philly Joe Jones (d). 30 January 1953.

The Serpent's Tooth; Round Midnight; Compulsion.

Miles Davis (t); Sonny Rollins (ts); Tommy Flanagan (p); Paul Chambers (b); Art Taylor (d).
16 March 1956.
> **No Line; Vierd Blues; In Your Own Sweet Way.**

Blue Haze (Prestige/Original Jazz Classics OJC 245)

Miles Davis (t); John Lewis, Charles Mingus (p); Percy Heath (b); Max Roach (d). 19 May 1953.
> **When Lights Are Low; Tune Up; Miles Ahead; Smooch.**

Miles Davis (t); Horace Silver (p); Percy Heath (b); Art Blakey (d). 15 March 1954.
> **Four; That Old Devil Called Love; Blue Haze.**

Miles Davis (t); Davey Schildkraut (as); Horace Silver (p); Percy Heath (b); Kenny Clarke (d).
3 April 1954.
> **I'll Remember April.**

Walkin' (Prestige/Original Jazz Classics OJC 213)

Miles Davis (t); Davey Schildkraut (as); Horace Silver (p); Percy Heath (b); Kenny Clarke (d).
3 April 1954.
> **Solar; You Don't Know What Love Is; Love Me Or Leave Me.**

Miles Davis (t); J. J. Johnson (tb); Lucky Thompson (ts); Horace Silver (p); Percy Heath (b);
Kenny Clarke (d). 29 April 1954.
> **Blue 'N' Boogie; Walkin'.**

Bags' Groove (Prestige/Original Jazz Classics OJC 245)

Miles Davis (t); Sonny Rollins (ts); Horace Silver (p); Percy Heath (b); Kenny Clarke (d). 29 June 1954.
> **Airegin; Oleo; Doxy; But Not For Me.**

Miles Davis (t); Milt Jackson (vib); Thelonious Monk (p); Percy Heath (b); Kenny Clarke (d).
24 December 1954.
> **Bags' Groove.**

Miles Davis And The Modern Jazz Giants (Prestige/Original Jazz Classics OJC 347)

As above. 24 December 1954.
> **The Man I Love; Swing Spring; Bemsha Swing.**

Miles Davis (t); John Coltrane (ts); Red Garland (p); Paul Chambers (b); Philly Joe Jones (d).
26 October 1956.
> **Round Midnight.**

The Musings Of Miles (Prestige/Original Jazz Classics OJC 004)

Miles Davis (t); Red Garland (p); Oscar Pettiford (b); Philly Joe Jones (d). 7 June 1955.
> **Will You Still Be Mine?; I See Your Face Before Me; I Didn't; A Gal In Calico;**
> **A Night In Tunisia; Green Haze.**

Milt And Miles: All Star Quintet/Sextet (Prestige/Original Jazz Classics OJC 012)

Miles Davis (*t*); Jackie McLean (*as*); Ray Bryant (*p*); Milt Jackson (*vib*); Percy Heath (*b*); Art Taylor (*d*). 5 August 1955.

Dr Jackle; Bitty Ditty; Minor March; Changes.

'Round About Midnight (Columbia 519957)

Miles Davis (*t*); Zoot Sims (*ts*); Gerry Mulligan (*bs*); Thelonious Monk (*p*); Percy Heath (*b*); Connie Kay (*d*). 17 July 1955.

Round Midnight.

Miles Davis (*t*); John Coltrane (*ts*); Red Garland (*p*); Paul Chambers (*b*); Philly Joe Jones (*d*). 26 October 1955.

Ah-Leu-Cha; Two Bass Hit; Little Melonae; Budo.

As above. 18 February 1956.

Chance It; Walkin'; It Never Entered My Mind; Woody 'N' You; Salt Peanuts; The Theme.

As above. 5 June 1956

Bye Bye Blackbird; Tadd's Delight; Dear Old Stockholm.

As above. 10 September 1956

Round Midnight; All Of You; Sweet Sue, Just You.

Miles – The New Miles Davis Quintet (Prestige/Original Jazz Classics OJC 006)

As above. 16 November 1955.

Stablemates; How Am I To Know?; Just Squeeze Me; There is No Greater Love; S'Posin'; The Theme.

Workin' With The Miles Davis Quintet (Prestige/OJC 296)

As above. 11 May 1956.

In Your Own Sweet Way; Trane's Blues; Four; It Never Entered My Mind; The Theme 1; The Theme 2.

As above. 26 October 1956.

Ahmad's Blues; Half Nelson.

Relaxin' With The Miles Davis Quintet (Prestige/Original Jazz Classics OJC 190)

As above. 26 October 1956.

If I Were A Bell; You're My Everything; I Could Write A Book; Oleo; It Could Happen To You; Woody 'N' You.

Cookin' With The Miles Davis Quintet (Prestige/Original Jazz Classics OJC 128)

As above. 26 October 1956.

My Funny Valentine; Blues By Five; Airegin; Tune Up/When Lights Are Low.

Steamin' With The Miles Davis Quintet (Prestige/Original Jazz Classics OJC 391)

As above. 11 May 1956.
> **Diane; Something I Dreamed Last Night; Surrey With The Fringe On Top; When I Fall In Love; Salt Peanuts.**

As above. 26 October 1956.
> **Well, You Needn't.**

Gunther Schuller, *Music For Brass/Birth Of The Third Stream* (Columbia CK 64929)

Miles Davis (*t, flhn*); Joe Wilder, Bernie Glow, Arthur Statter, Joe Wilder, Mel Broiles, Carmine Fornarotto, Isidore Blank (*t*); Jimmy Buffington, Joe Singer, Ray Alonge, Art Sussman (*frhn*); J.J. Johnson, Urbie Green, John Clark (*tb*); Bill Barber (*tba*); Milt Hinton (*b*); Osie Johnson (*d*); Dick Horowitz (*perc*). 20 October 1956.
> **Three Little Feelings.**

As above. 23 October 1956.
> **Jazz Suite For Brass.**

Miles Ahead (Columbia CK 65121)

Miles Davis (*flhn*); Bernie Glow, Ernie Royal, Louis Mucci, Taft Jordan, John Carisi (*t*); Frank Rehak, Jimmy Cleveland, Joe Bennett (*tb*); Tom Mitchell (*btb*); Willie Ruff, Tony Miranda (*frhn*); Bill Barber (*tba*); Lee Konitz (*as*); Romeo Penque (*f, cl, bcl*); Sid Cooper (*f, cl*); Danny Bank (*bcl*); Paul Chambers (*b*); Art Taylor (*d*); Gil Evans (*arr, cond*). 6 May 1957.
> **The Maids Of Cadiz; The Duke.**

As above. 10 May 1957.
> **My Ship; Miles Ahead.**

As above, except Jimmy Buffington (*frhn*) replaces Miranda; add Wynton Kelly (*p*); Penque also plays oboe. 23 May 1957.
> **New Rhumba; Blues For Pablo; Springsville.**

As above except Tony Miranda (*frhn*) and Eddie Caine (*f, cl*) replace Buffington and Cooper. 27 May 1957.
> **I Don't Wanna Be Kissed; The Meaning Of The Blues; Lament.**

Ascenseur pour l'échafaud (Fontana 836305)

Miles Davis (*t*); Barney Wilen (*ts*); René Urtreger (*p*); Pierre Michelot (*b*); Kenny Clarke (*d*). 4 December 1957.
> **Générique; Florence sur les Champs-Elysées; Au bar du Petit Bac; Diner au motel; Sur l'autoroute; L'assassinat de Carala; Julien dans l'ascenseur; Chez le photographe du motel; Evasion de Julien; Visite du vigile.**

Cannonball Adderley, *Somethin' Else* (Blue Note 46338-2)

Miles Davis (*t*); Julian 'Cannonball' Adderley (*as*); Hank Jones (*p*); Sam Jones (*b*); Art Blakey (*d*).
9 March 1958.

Autumn Leaves; Love For Sale; Somethin' Else; One For Daddy-O; Alison's Uncle.

Milestones (Columbia CK 85203)

Miles Davis (*t*); Julian 'Cannonball' Adderley (*as*); John Coltrane (*ts*); Red Garland (*p*);
Paul Chambers (*b*); Philly Joe Jones (*d*). 4 February 1958.

Two Bass Hit; Billy Boy; Straight, No Chaser; Milestones.

As above. 4 March 1958.

Sid's Ahead; Little Melonae; Dr Jackle.

'58 Miles (Columbia CK 47825)

Miles Davis (*t*); Cannonball Adderley (*as*); John Coltrane (*ts*); Bill Evans (*p*); Paul Chambers (*b*);
Jimmy Cobb (*d*). 26 May 1958

On Green Dolphin Street; Fran-Dance; Stella By Starlight; Love For Sale.

As above. 9 September 1958.

Straight, No Chaser; The Theme; My Funny Valentine; Oleo.

At Newport 1958 (Columbia CK 85202)

As above. 3 July 1958.

**Ah-Leu-Cha; Straight, No Chaser; Fran-Dance; Two Bass Hit; Bye Bye Blackbird;
The Theme.**

Michel Legrand, *Legrand Jazz* (Philips 830074-2)

Miles Davis (*t*); Phil Woods (*as*); John Coltrane (*ts*); Jerome Richardson (*bs, bcl*); Herbie Mann (*f*);
Bill Evans (*p*); Eddie Costa (*vib*); Bary Galbraith (*g*); Betty Glamann (*hp*); Paul Chambers (*b*);
Kenny Dennis (*d*). 25 June 1958.

Wild Man Blues; Round Midnight; Jitterbug Waltz; Django.

Porgy And Bess (Columbia CK 65141)

Miles Davis (*t, flhn*); Ernie Royal, Johnny Coles, Bernie Glow, Louis Mucci (*t*); Joe Bennett,
Frank Rehak, Jimmy Cleveland (*tb*); Dick Hixon (*btb*); Willie Ruff, Julius Watkins,
Gunther Schuller (*frhn*); Bill Barber (*tba*); Cannonball Adderley (*as*); Phil Bodner, Romeo Penque (*f*);
Danny Bank (*bcl*); Paul Chambers (*b*); Philly Joe Jones (*d*); Gil Evans (*arr, cond*). 22 July 1958.

My Man's Gone Now; Gone; Gone, Gone, Gone.

As above except Jimmy Cobb (*d*) replaces Jones. 29 July 1958.

**Here Come De Honey Man; Bess, You Is My Woman Now; It Ain't Necessarily So;
Fisherman, Strawberry And Devil Crab.**

As above except Jerome Richardson (*f*) replaces Bodner. 4 August 1958.
> **Prayer (Oh Doctor Jesus); Bess, Oh Where's My Bess; Buzzard Song.**

As above. 14 August 1958.
> **Summertime; There's A Boat That's Leaving Soon For New York; I Loves You, Porgy.**

Jazz At The Plaza Vol. 1 (Columbia CK 85245)

Miles Davis (*t*); Cannonball Adderley (*as*); John Coltrane (*ts*); Bill Evans (*p*); Paul Chambers (*b*); Jimmy Cobb (*d*). 9 September 1958.
> **If I Were A Bell; Oleo; My Funny Valentine; Straight, No Chaser; The Theme.**

Kind Of Blue (Columbia CK 64935)

Miles Davis (*t*); Cannonball Adderley (*as*); John Coltrane (*ts*); Bill Evans, Wynton Kelly (*p*); Paul Chambers (*b*); Jimmy Cobb (*d*). 2 March 1959.
> **Freddie Freeloader; So What; Blue In Green.**

As above except omit Kelly. 22 April 1959.
> **Flamenco Sketches; All Blues.**

Sketches Of Spain (Columbia CK 65142)

Miles Davis (*t, flhn*); Ernie Royal, Bernie Glow, Taft Jordan, Louis Mucci (*t*); Dick Hixon, Frank Rehak (*tb*); Jimmy Buffington, John Barrows, Earl Chapin (*frh*); Jimmy McAllister (*tba*); Al Block, Eddie Caine (*f*); Romeo Penque (*ob*); Harold Feldman (*ob, cl*); Jack Knitzer (*bsn*); Janet Putnam (*hp*); Paul Chambers (*b*); Jimmy Cobb (*d*); Elvin Jones, Jose Manguel (*perc*); Gil Evans (*arr, cond*). 10, 15, 20 November 1959.
> **Concierto De Aranjuez.**

As above except Joe Singer (*frhn*), Tony Miranda (*frhn*), Johnny Coles (*t*), Danny Bank (*bcl*), Harold Feldman (*f*) replace Jordan, Barrows, Chapin and Caine. 10 March 1960.
> **Will O' The Wisp; The Pan Piper; Saeta; Solea.**

Someday My Prince Will Come (Columbia 466312)

Miles Davis (*t*); John Coltrane, Hank Mobley (*ts*); Wynton Kelly (*p*); Paul Chambers (*b*); Jimmy Cobb, Philly Joe Jones (*d*). 7–21 March 1961
> **Someday My Prince Will Come; Old Folks; Pfrancing; Drad-Dog; Teo; I Thought About You.**

In Person Friday Night At The Blackhawk (Columbia 87097)

Miles Davis (*t*); Hank Mobley (*ts*); Wynton Kelly (*p*); Paul Chambers (*b*); Jimmy Cobb (*d*). 21 April 1961.
> **Oleo; No Blues; Bye Bye (Theme); All Of You; Neo; I Thought About You; Bye Bye Blackbird; Walkin'; Love, I've Found You; If I Were A Bell; Fran-Dance; On Green Dolphin Street; The Theme.**

In Person Saturday Night At The Blackhawk (Columbia 87100)

As above. 22 April 1961.

**If I Were A Bell; So What; No Blues; On Green Dolphin Street; Walkin';
Round Midnight; Well, You Needn't; The Theme; Autumn Leaves; Neo;
Two Bass Hit; Bye Bye (Theme); Love, I've Found You; I Thought About You;
Someday My Prince Will Come; Softly As In A Morning Sunrise.**

At Carnegie Hall 1961 (Columbia CK 65027)

Miles Davis (*t*); Johnny Coles, Bernie Glow, Louis Mucci, Ernie Royal (*t*); Dick Hixon,
Jimmy Knepper, Frank Rehak (*tb*); Paul Ingraham, Bob Swisshelm, Julius Watkins (*frhn*);
Bill Barber (*tba*); Hank Mobley (*ts*); Danny Bank, Eddie Caine, Romeo Penque, Jerome Richardson,
Bob Tricarico (*reeds, woodwinds*); Janet Putnam (*hp*); Wynton Kelly (*p*); Paul Chambers (*b*);
Jimmy Cobb (*d*); Bobby Rosengarden (*perc*). 19 May 1961.

**So What; Spring Is Here; Teo; Walkin'; The Meaning Of The Blues; Lament;
New Rhumba; Someday My Prince Will Come; No Blues; Oleo; I Thought About You;
Concierto De Aranjuez.**

Quiet Nights (Columbia CK 65293)

Miles Davis (*t*); Ernie Royal, Bernie Glow, Louis Mucci, Harold 'Shorty' Baker (*t*); J.J. Johnson,
Frank Rehak (*tb*); Julius Watkins, Ray Alonge, Don Corrado (*frhn*); Bill Barber (*tba*); Steve Lacy (*ss*);
Jerome Richardson, Al Block (*f*); Ray Beckenstein (*f, reeds*); Bob Triscario (*bsn*); Garvin Bushell (*bsn,
cbsn*); Janet Putnam (*hp*); Paul Chambers (*b*); Jimmy Cobb (*d*); Willie Bobo (bgo); Elvin Jones (*perc*);
Gil Evans (*arr, cond*). 27 July 1962.

Aos Pes Da Cruz; Corcovado.

As above. 13 August 1962.

Song #1; Wait Till You See Her.

As above. 6 November 1962.

Song #2; Once Upon A Summertime.

Miles Davis (*t*); Dick Leith (*tb*); Richard Perissi, Bill Hinshaw, Arthur Maeba (*frhn*);
Paul Horn (*f, af, as*); Buddy Collette (*f, af, ts*); Gene Cipriano (*ob, af, ts*); Fred Dutton (*bsn*);
Marjorie Call (*hp*); Herbie Hancock (*p*); Ron Carter (*b*); Tony Williams (*d*); Gil Evans (*arr, cond*).
9 October 1963.

The Time Of The Barracudas.

Jingle Bell Jazz/Blue Christmas (Columbia CK 40166)

Miles Davis (*t*); Frank Rehak (*tb*); Wayne Shorter (*ts*); Paul Chambers (*b*); Jimmy Cobb (*d*);
Willie Bobo (*perc*); Bob Dorough (*v*). 21 August 1962.

Blue Christmas.

Seven Steps To Heaven (Columbia 466970)

Miles Davis (*t*); George Coleman (*ts*); Victor Feldman (*p*); Ron Carter (*b*); Frank Butler (*d*).
16–17 April 1963.

> Basin Street Blues; I Fall In Love Too Easily; Baby Won't You Please Come Home;
> So Near, So Far; Summer Night.

As above except Herbie Hancock (*p*) and Tony Williams (*d*) replace Feldman and Butler.
14 May 1963.

> Seven Steps To Heaven; So Near, So Far; Joshua.

Miles Davis In Europe (Columbia 519506)

Miles Davis (*t*); George Coleman (*ts*); Herbie Hancock (*p*); Ron Carter (*b*); Tony Williams (*d*).
27 July 1963.

> Autumn Leaves; Milestones; I Thought About You; Joshua; All Of You; Walkin'.

My Funny Valentine (Columbia 519503)

As above. 12 February 1964.

> My Funny Valentine; All Of You; Stella By Starlight; All Blues; I Thought About You.

'Four' And More (Columbia 519505)

As above. 12 February 1964.

> So What; Walkin; Joshua; Go-Go; Four; Seven Steps To Heaven;
> There Is No Greater Love; Go-Go.

Miles In Tokyo (Columbia 519508)

As above except Sam Rivers (*ts*) replaces Coleman. 14 July 1964.

> If I Were A Bell; My Funny Valentine; So What; Walkin'; All Of You; Go-Go.

Miles In Berlin (Columbia 519507)

As above except Wayne Shorter (*ts*) replaces Rivers. 25 September 1964.

> Milestones; Autumn Leaves; So What; Stella By Starlight; Walkin'; Go-Go.

E.S.P. (Columbia 467899)

As above. 20–22 January 1965.

> E.S.P.; Eighty-One; Little One; R.J.; Agitation; Iris; Mood.

The Complete Live At the Plugged Nickel (Columbia CXK 66955)

Miles Davis (*t*); Wayne Shorter (*ts*); Herbie Hancock (*p*); Ron Carter (*b*); Tony Williams (*d*).
22 December 1965.

> If I Were A Bell; Stella By Starlight; Walkin'; I Fall In Love Too Easily; The Theme;

Discography

My Funny Valentine; Four; When I Fall In Love; Agitation; Round Midnight;
Milestones; The Theme; All Of You; Oleo; I Fall In Love Too Easily; No Blues;
I Thought About You; The Theme.

As above. 23 December 1965.

If I Were A Bell; Stella By Starlight; Walkin'; I Fall In Love Too Easily;
The Theme; All Of You; Agitation; My Funny Valentine; On Green Dolphin Street;
So What; The Theme; When I Fall In Love; Milestones; Autumn Leaves;
I Fall In Love Too Easily; No Blues; The Theme; Stella By Starlight; All Blues;
Yesterdays; The Theme.

Miles Smiles (Columbia CK 65683)

As above. 24–25 October 1966.

Circle; Orbits; Dolores; Freedom Jazz Dance; Gingerbread Boy; Footprints.

Sorcerer (Columbia CK 65680)

As above. 16–24 May 1967.

Limbo; Vonetta; Masqualero; The Sorcerer; Prince Of Darkness; Pee Wee.

Nefertiti (Columbia CK 65681)

As above. 7–23 June 1967.

Nefertiti; Fall; Hand Jive; Madness; Riot; Pinocchio.

Miles In The Sky (Columbia CK 65684)

As above except add George Benson (*g*). 16 January 1968.

Paraphernalia.

As above except omit Benson. 15–17 May 1968.

Stuff; Black Comedy; Country Son.

Filles de Kilimanjaro (Columbia CK 46116)

Miles Davis (*t*); Wayne Shorter (*ts*); Chick Corea (*p*); Dave Holland (*b*); Tony Williams (*d*).
19 June 1968

Petits machins (Little Stuff).

As above except Herbie Hancock (*p*) and Ron Carter (*b*) replace Corea and Holland.
20–21 June 1968.

Tout de suite; Filles de Kilimanjaro.

As above except Corea and Holland return. 24 June 1968.

Frelon brun; Mademoiselle Mabry.

Water Babies (Columbia 86557)

Miles Davis (*t*); Wayne Shorter (*ts*); Herbie Hancock (*p*); Ron Carter (*b*); Tony Williams (*d*). 7–23 June 1967.

Water Babies; Capricorn; Sweet Pea.

Miles Davis (*t*); Wayne Shorter (*ts*); Herbie Hancock, Chick Corea (*p*); Dave Holland (*b*); Tony Williams (*d*). 1–12 November 1968.

Two Faced; Dual Mr Anthony Tillmon Williams Process; Splash.

In A Silent Way (Columbia 450982)

Miles Davis (*t*); Wayne Shorter (*ts*); Josef Zawinul (*p, org*); Herbie Hancock, Chick Corea (*p*); John McLaughlin (*g*); Dave Holland (*b*); Tony Williams (*d*). 18 February 1969.

Shhh/Peaceful; In A Silent Way/It's About That Time.

The Complete In A Silent Way Sessions (Columbia C3K 65362)

Miles Davis (*t*); Wayne Shorter (*ts*); Chick Corea, Herbie Hancock (*p*); Joe Zawinul (*org*); Dave Holland (*b*); Tony Williams (*d*). 25 November 1968.

Splashdown.

As above except Jack DeJohnette (*d*) replaces Williams. 27 November 1968.

Ascent; Directions I; Directions II.

As above except add John McLaughlin (*g*), and Joe Chambers (*d*) replaces DeJohnette. 20 February 1969.

The Ghetto Walk; Early Minor.

[In addition to the above, this set also includes portions of *Filles de Kilimanjaro* and *Water Babies*, as well as all of *In A Silent Way*, including extended versions of the material from the last-named.]

Bitches Brew (Columbia 460602)

Miles Davis (*t*); Wayne Shorter (*ss*); Bennie Maupin (*bcl*); Chick Corea, Larry Young, Joe Zawinul (*p*); John McLaughlin (*g*); Dave Holland, Harvey Brooks (*b*); Jack DeJohnette, Lenny White, Don Alias (*d*); Jim Riley (*perc*). 19–21 August 1969.

Pharaoh's Dance; Bitches Brew; Spanish Key; John McLaughlin; Miles Runs The Voodoo Down; Sanctuary.

Big Fun (Columbia C2K 63973)

Miles Davis (*t*); Steve Grossman (*ss*); Bennie Maupin (*bcl*); John McLaughlin (*g*); Khalil Balakrishna, Bihari Sharma (*sitar, tambura*); Herbie Hancock, Chick Corea (*p*); Ron Carter, Harvey Brooks (*b*); Billy Cobham (*d*); Airto moreira (*perc*). 19 November 1969.

Great Expectations; Yaphet.

As above except Larry Young (*org, cel*), Dave Holland (*b*), Jack DeJohnette (*d*) added, Carter out. 28 November 1969.

Trevere; The Little Blue Frog.

Miles Davis (*t*); Steve Grossman (*ss*); Bennie Maupin (*bcl*); Joe Zawinul, Chick Corea (*p*);
John McLaughlin (*g*); Khalil Balakrishna (sitar); Dave Holland (*b*); Billy Cobham,
Jack DeJohnette (*d*); Airto Moreira (*perc*). 27 January 1970.

> **Lonely Fire.**

Miles Davis (*t*); Wayne Shorter (*ss*); John McLaughlin (*g*); Joe Zawinul, Chick Corea (*p*);
Dave Holland (*b*); Jack DeJohnette (*d*); Billy Cobham, Airto Moreira (*perc*). 6 February 1970.

> **Recollections.**

Miles Davis (*t*); Steve Grossman (*ss*); John McLaughlin (*g*); Dave Holland (*b*); Jack DeJohnette (*d*).
3 March 1970.

> **Go Ahead John.**

Miles Davis (*t*); Carlos Garnett (*ss*); Bennie Maupin (*cl, f*); Lonnie Smith, Harold I. Williams (*p*);
Michael Henderson (*b*); Al Foster, Billy Hart (*d*); Badal Roy, Mtume (*perc*). 12 June 1972.

> **Ife.**

The Complete Bitches Brew Sessions (Columbia C4K 65570)

Miles Davis (*t*); Steve Grossman (*ss*); Bennie Maupin (*bcl*); John McLaughlin (*g*); Khalil Balakrishna,
Bihari Sharma (*sitar, tambura*); Herbie Hancock, Chick Corea (*p*); Ron Carter, Harvey Brooks (*b*);
Billy Cobham (*d*); Airto Moreira (*perc*). 19 November 1969.

> **Orange Lady; Corrado.**

As above except Larry Young (*org, cel*), Dave Holland (*b*), Jack DeJohnette (*d*) added, Carter and
Hancock out. 28 November 1969.

> **The Big Green Serpent; The Little Blue Frog (alternate).**

Miles Davis (*t*); Steve Grossman (*ss*); Bennie Maupin (*bcl*); Joe Zawinul, Chick Corea (*p*);
John McLaughlin (*g*); Khalil Balakrishna (*sitar*); Dave Holland (*b*); Billy Cobham,
Jack DeJohnette (*d*); Airto Moreira (*perc*). 27 January 1970.

> **Guinnevere.**

As above except omit Balakrishna. 28 January 1970.

> **Feio; Double Image.**

Miles Davis (*t*); Wayne Shorter (*ss*); John McLaughlin (*g*); Joe Zawinul, Chick Corea (*p*);
Dave Holland (*d*); Jack DeJohnette (*d*); Billy Cobham, Airto Moreira (*perc*). 6 February 1970.

> **Take It Or Leave It.**
> [In addition to the above, this set also includes all of *Bitches Brew* and portions of *Live–Evil*
> and *Big Fun*.]

Jack Johnson (Columbia 519264)

Miles Davis (*t*); Steve Grossman (*ss*); Herbie Hancock (*org*); John McLaughlin (*g*);
Michael Henderson (*b*); Billy Cobham (*d*). 7 April 1970.

> **Right Off; Yesternow.**

The Complete Jack Johnson Sessions (Columbia 86359)

Miles Davis (*t*); Steve Grossman (*ss*); John McLaughlin (*g*); Dave Holland (*b*); Jack DeJohnette (*d*).
27 February 1970

Willie Nelson; Johnny Bratton.

As above. 3 March 1970.

Archie Moore; Go Ahead John.

Miles Davis (*t*); Wayne Shorter (*ss*); Bennie Maupin (*bcl*); John McLaughlin (*g*); Dave Holland (*b*);
Billy Cobham (*d*). 17 March 1970.

Duran.

As above except Steve Grossman (*ss*) and Lenny White (*d*) replace Shorter and Cobham, Maupin
out. 20 March 1970.

Sugar Ray.

Miles Davis (*t*); Steve Grossman (*ss*); Keith Jarrett (*p*); Herbie Hancock (*org*); John McLaughlin (*g*);
Michael Henderson, Gene Perla (*b*); Billy Cobham (*d*); Airto Moreira (*perc*). 19 May 1970.

Honky Tonk; Ali.

Miles Davis (*t*); Keith Jarrett (*p*); John McLaughlin (*g*); Jack DeJohnette (*d*); Airto Moreira (*perc*).
21 May 1970.

Konda.

Miles Davis (*t*); Keith Jarrett (*p*); Herbie Hancock (*org*); John McLaughlin (*g*); Michael
Henderson (*b*); Airto Moreira (*perc*); Hermeto Pascoal (*v*). 27 May 1970.

Nem Um Talvez.

Miles Davis (*t*); Steve Grossman (*ss*); Chick Corea (*org*); Keith Jarrett, Herbie Hancock (*p*);
Ron Carter (*b*); Jack DeJohnette (*d*); Airto Moreira (*perc*); Hermeto Pascoal (*v*). 3 June 1970.

Little High People; Nem Um Talvez; Selim.

Miles Davis (*t*); Steve Grossman (*ss*); Chick Corea, Keith Jarrett (*p*); Herbie Hancock (*org*);
John McLaughlin (*g*); Dave Holland (*b*); Jack DeJohnette (*d*); Airto Moreira (*perc*);
Hermeto Pascoal (*v*). 4 June 1970.

The Mask Parts 1 & 2; Little Church.

[In addition to the above, this set also includes all of *Jack Johnson* and portions of *Live–Evil*,
Big Fun and *Get Up With It*.]

Live At The Fillmore East (March 7 1970): It's About That Time (Columbia C2K 85191)

Miles Davis (*t*); Wayne Shorter (*ss*, *ts*); Chick Corea (*p*); Dave Holland (*b*); Jack DeJohnette (*d*);
Airto Moreira (*perc*). 6 March 1970.

**Directions; Spanish Key; Masqualero; It's About That Time; The Theme; Directions;
Miles Runs The Voodoo Down; Bitches Brew; Spanish Key; It's About That Time/
Willie Nelson.**

Live–Evil (Columbia C2K 65135)

Miles Davis (*t*); Wayne Shorter (*ss*); John McLaughlin (*g*); Joe Zawinul, Chick Corea (*p*);
Dave Holland (*d*); Jack DeJohnette (*d*); Billy Cobham, Airto Moreira (*perc*). 6 February 1970.
> **Gemini; Double Image.**

Miles Davis (*t*); Steve Grossman (*ss*); Chick Corea (*org*); Keith Jarrett, Herbie Hancock (*p*);
Ron Carter (*b*); Jack DeJohnette (*d*); Airto Moreira (*perc*); Hermeto Pascoal (*v*). 3 June 1970.
> **Nem Um Talvez; Selim.**

Miles Davis (*t*); Steve Grossman (*ss*); Chick Corea, Keith Jarrett (*p*); Herbie Hancock (*org*);
John McLaughlin (*g*); Dave Holland (*b*); Jack DeJohnette (*d*); Airto Moreira (*perc*);
Hermeto Pascoal (*v*). 4 June 1970.
> **Little Church.**

Miles Davis (*t*); Gary Bartz (*ss, as*); Keith Jarrett (*p, org*); John McLaughlin (*g*); Michael
Henderson (*b*); Jack DeJohnette (*d*); Airto Moreira (*perc*); Conrad Roberts (*v*). 19 December 1970.
> **Sivad; What I Say; Funky Tonk; Inamorata.**

Black Beauty (Columbia C2K 65138)

Miles Davis (*t*); Steve Grossman (*ss*); Chick Corea (*p*); Dave Holland (*b*); Jack DeJohnette (*d*);
Airto Moreira (*perc*). 10 April 970.
> **Directions; Miles Runs The Voodoo Down; Willie Nelson; I Fall In Love Too Easily;
> Sanctuary; It's About That Time; Bitches Brew; Masqualero; Spanish Key/
> The Theme.**

At Fillmore (Columbia C2K 65139)

As above except add Keith Jarrett (*org*). 17–20 June 1970.
> **Directions; Bitches Brew; The Mask; It's About That Time; Bitches Brew/
> The Theme; Directions; The Mask; It's About That Time; It's About That Time;
> I Fall In Love Too Easily; Sanctuary; Bitches Brew/ The Theme; It's About That Time;
> I Fall In Love Too Easily; Sanctuary; Bitches Brew/Willie Nelson/The Theme.**

On The Corner (Columbia CK 63980)

Miles Davis (*t*); Dave Liebman, Carlos Garnett (*ss*); Bennie Maupin (*bcl*); Herbie Hancock,
Chick Corea, Harold Williams (*ky*); John McLaughlin, David Creamer (*g*); Collin Walcott,
Khalil Balakrishna (*sitar*); Michael Henderson (*b*); Billy Hart, Jack DeJohnette, Al Foster (*d*);
Badal Roy (*perc*). 1 June–7 July 1972.
> **On The Corner; New York Girl/Thinkin' Of One Thing And Doin' Another/
> Vote For Miles; Black Satin; One And One; Helen Butte/Mr Freedom X.**

In Concert: Live At Philharmonic Hall (Columbia C2K 65140)

Miles Davis (*t*); Carlos Garnett (*ss, ts*); Cedric Lawson (*ky*); Reggie Lucas (*g*); Khalil
Balakrishna (*sitar*); Michael Henderson (*b*); Al Foster (*d*); Badal Roy, Mtume (*perc*).
29 September 1972.
> **Rated X; Honky Tonk; Theme From Jack Johnson; Black Satin/The Theme; Ife;
> Right Off/The Theme.**

Dark Magus (Columbia C2K 65137)

Miles Davis (*t, org*); Dave Liebman (*f, ss, ts*); Azar Lawrence (*ts*); Reggie Lucas, Pete Cosey, Dominique Gaumont (*g*); Michael Henderson (*b*); Al Foster (*d*); Mtume (*perc*). 30 March 1974.
   Moja; Wili; Tatu; Nne.

Get Up With It (Columbia C2K 63970)

Miles Davis (*t*); Steve Grossman (*ss*); Keith Jarrett (*p*); Herbie Hancock (*org*); John McLaughlin (*g*); Michael Henderson, Gene Perla (*b*); Billy Cobham (*d*); Airto Moreira (*perc*). 19 May 1970.
   Honky Tonk.

Miles Davis (*t*); Wally Chambers (*hmca*); Cornell Dupree (*g*); Michael Henderson (*b*); Al Foster, Bernard Purdie (*d*); Mtume (*perc*). 9 March 1972.
   Red China Blues.

Miles Davis (*org*); Cedric Rhodes (*p*); Reggie Lucas (*g*); Khalil Balakrishna (*sitar*); Michael Henderson (*b*); Al Foster (*d*); Mtume, Badal Roy (*perc*). 6 September 1972.
   Rated X.

As above except Davis plays trumpet, add Carlos Garnett (*ss*). 8 December 1972.
   Billy Preston.

Miles Davis (*t, p, org*); Dave Liebman (*f*); John Stubblefield (*ss*); Pete Cosey, Reggie Lucas (*g*); Michael Henderson (*b*); Al Foster (*d*); Mtume (*perc*). 17 September 1973.
   Calypso Frelimo.

Miles Davis (*t*); Dave Liebman (*af*); Pete Cosey, Reggie Lucas, Dominique Gaumont (*g*); Michael Henderson (*b*); Al Foster (*d*); Mtume (*perc*). 19–20 June 1974.
   He Loved Him Madly.

As above except Sonny Fortune (*f*) replaces Liebman. 7 October 1974.
   Maiysha; Mtume.

Agharta (Columbia 467897)

Miles Davis (*t, org*); Sonny Fortune (*ss, as, f*); Pete Cosey (*g, syn, perc*); Reggie Lucas (*g*); Michael Henderson (*b*); Al Foster (*d*); Mtume (*perc*). 1 February 1975.
   Prelude; Maiysha; Interlude; Theme From Jack Johnson.

Pangaea (Columbia 467087)

As above. 1 February 1975.
   Zimbabwe; Gondwana.

The Man With The Horn (Columbia 468701)

Miles Davis (*t*); Bill Evans (*ss, f*); Robert Irving III (*ky*); Randy Hall (*g, ky, v*); Felton Crews (*b*); Vincent Wilburn Jr (*d*); Angela Bofill (*v*). May 1980.
   The Man With The Horn.

Miles Davis (*t*); Bill Evans (*ss, ts, f*); Barry Finnerty (*g*); Marcus Miller (*b*); Al Foster (*d*); Sammy Figueroa (*perc*). January 1981.

Back Seat Betty. Aida; Ursula.

As above except Mike Stern (*g*) replaces Finnerty. March 1981.

Fat Time.

Miles Davis (*t*); Bill Evans (*ss, ts, f*); Robert Irving III, Randy Hall (*ky*); Barry Finnerty (*g*); Felton Crews (*b*); Vincent Wilburn (*d*); Sammy Figueroa (*perc*). 6 May 1981.

Shout.

We Want Miles (Columbia 469402)

Miles Davis (*t*); Bill Evans (*ss, ts, f, p*); Mike Stern (*g*); Marcus Miller (*b*); Al Foster (*d*); Mino Cinelu (*perc*). 27 June–4 October 1981.

Fast Track; My Man's Gone Now; Kix; Back Seat Betty; Jean Pierre.

Miles! Miles! Miles! (Columbia SRCS 6513/4)

As above. 4 October 1981.

Back Seat Betty; Ursula; My Man's Gone Now; Aida; Fat Time; Jean Pierre.

Star People (Columbia 25395)

Miles Davis (*t, ky*); Bill Evans (*ss, ts, f, p*); Mike Stern (*g*); Marcus Miller (*b*); Al Foster (*b*); Mino Cinelu (*perc*). August–September 1982.

Star On Cicely; Come Get It; Star People; U'n'I.

As above except add John Scofield (*g*), Tom Barney (*b*). January–February 1983.

It Gets Better; Speak.

Decoy (Columbia 468702)

Miles Davis (*t, ky*); Bill Evans (*ss, ts, f, p*); Branford Marsalis (*ss*); Robert Irving III (*ky*); John Scofield (*g*); Darryl Jones (*b*); Al Foster (*d*); Mino Cinelu (*perc*). June–September 1983.

What It Is; That's What Happened; Robot 415; Decoy; Code M.D.; That's Right; Freaky Deaky.

You're Under Arrest (Columbia 468703)

Miles Davis (*t, ky, v*); Bob Berg (*ss*); Robert Irving III (*ky*); John Scofield, John McLaughlin (*g*); Darryl Jones (*b*); Al Foster, Vincent Wilburn Jr (*d*); Steve Thornton (*perc*); Marek Olko, Sting, James Prindiville (*v*). January 1984; December 1984–January 1985.

One Phone Call/Street Scenes; Human Nature;
Intro: MD 1/Something's On Your Mind/MD 2; Ms Morrisine;
Katia Prelude; Katia; Time After Time; You're Under Arrest;
Medley: Jean Pierre/You're Under Arrest/Then There Were None.

Aura (Columbia CK 63962)

Miles Davis (*t*); Palle Mikkelborg, Benny Rosenfeld, Palle Bolvig, Jens Winther, Perry Knudsen, Idrees Sulieman (*t, flhn*); Vincent Nilsson, Jens Engel, Ture Larsen (*tb*); Ole Kurt Jensen (*btb*); Axel Windfeld (*btb, tba*); Jesper Thilo, Per Carsten, Uffe Karskov, Bent Jaedig, Flemming Madsen (*saxes*); Niels Eje (*ob, cor*); Thomas Clausen, Ole Koch-Hansen, Kenneth Knudsen (*ky*); Lillian Toernqvist (*hp*); John McLaughlin, Bjarne Roupe (*g*); Bo Stief, Niels-Henning Ørsted Pedersen (*b*); Lennart Gruvstedt (*d*); Marilyn Mazur, Ethan Weisgaard (*perc*); Vincent Wilburn (*elec d*); Eva Thaysen (*v*). January 1985.

> **Intro; White; Yellow; Orange; Red; Green; Blue; Electric Red; Indigo; Violet.**

Tutu (Warner Bros 925490)

Miles Davis (*t*); Marcus Miller (*bcl, ky, g, b, d*); Adam Holzmann, George Duke (*ky*); Omar Hakim, Paulinho da Costa (*perc*); Michael Ualaniak (*v*). February–March 1986.

> **Tutu; Portia; Tomaas; Backyard Ritual; Splatch; Perfect Way; Don't Lose Your Mind; Full Nelson.**

Music From Siesta (Warner Bros 925655)

Miles Davis (*t*); Marcus Miller (*bcl, ky, g, b, d*); James Walker (*f*); Earl Klugh (*g*). March 1987.

> **Lost In Madrid Part 1; Siesta-Kitt's Kiss–Lost In Madrid Part II; Theme For Augustine–Wind-Seduction–Kiss; Submission; Lost In Madrid Part III; Concita–Lament; Lost In Madrid Part IV–Rat Dance–The Call; Claire–Lost In Madrid Part V; Afterglow; Los Feliz.**

Amandla (Warner Bros 925873)

Miles Davis (*t*); Marcus Miller (*ss, bcl, ky, g, b, d*); Kenny Garrett (*ss*); Rick Margitza (*ts*); George Duke, Joey DeFrancesco (*ky*); Joe Sample (*p*); Billy Paterson, Foley McCreary, Michael Landau, Jean-Paul Bourelly (*g*); Ricky Wellman, Omar Hakim (*d*); Mino Cinelu, Bashiri Johnson, Don Alias (*perc*). September 1988–January 1989.

> **Catembe; Cobra; Big Time; Hannibal; Jo-Jo; Amandla; Jilli; Mr Pastorius.**

Dingo (Warner Bros 7599-26438-2)

Miles Davis (*t*); orchestra conducted by Michel Legrand. May 1990.

> **Kimberley Trumpet; The Arrival; Concert On The Runway; The Departure; Dingo Howl; Letter As Hero; Trumpet Cleaning; the Dream; Paris Walking I; Paris Walking II; Kimberley Trumpet In Paris; The Music Room; Club Entrance; The Jam Session; Going Home; Surprise!**

The Hot Spot (Antilles 422-846813-2)

Miles Davis (*t*); John Lee Hooker, Taj Mahal (*g, v*); Roy Rogers (*g*); Bradford Ellis (*ky*); Tim Drummond (*b*); Earl Palmer (*d*). May 1990.

> **Coming To Town; Empty Bank; Harry's Philosophy; Dolly's Arrival; Harry And Dolly;**

Sawmill; Bank Robbery; Moanin'; Gloria's Story; Harry Sets Up Button; Murder; Blackmail; End Credits.

Live Around The World (Warner Bros 7599-25490-2)

Miles Davis (*t*); Kenny Garrett (*ss, as, f*); Adam Holzmann, Robert Irving III (*ky*); Foley McCreary, Benny Rietveld (*b*); Ricky Wellman (*d*); Marilyn Mazur (*perc*). 7 August 1988.

Full Nelson.

As above. 14 August 1988.

Star People.

As above except Joey DeFrancesco (*ky*) replaces Irving. 1 November 1988.

Human Nature.

As above. 17 December 1988.

In A Silent Way; Intruder.

As above except Kei Akagi, John Beasley (*ky*) replace deFrancesco and Holzmann, Munyungo Jackson (*perc*) replaces Mazur. 12 April 1989.

Mr Pastorius.

As above. 5 June 1989.

Time After Time.

As above. 26 July 1989.

Amandla.

Miles Davis (*t*); Kenny Garrett (*as, f*); Kei Akagi (*ky*); Foley McCreary, Richard Patterson (*b*); Ricky Wellman (*d*); Erin Davis (*perc*). 20 July 1990.

Star On Cicely; Tutu.

As above except Deron Johnson (*ky*) replaces Akagi, Erin Davis out. 25 August 1991.

Hannibal.

Miles Davis & Quincy Jones Live At Montreux (Warner Bros 45221)

Miles Davis (*t*); Wallace Roney (*t, flhn*); Kenny Garrett (*as*); The Gil Evans Orchestra: Lew Soloff, Miles Evans (*t*); Tom Malone (*tb*); Alex Foster (*ss, as, f*); George Adams (*ts, f*); Gil Goldstein, Delmar Brown (*ky*); Kennwood Dennard (*d, perc*).

The George Gruntz Concert Jazz Band: Marvin Stamm, John d'Earth, Jack Walrath (*t, flhn*); John Clark, Tom Varner (*frhn*); Dave Bargeron, Earl McIntyre (*euph, tba*); Dave Taylor (*btb*); Howard Johnson (*bs, tba*); Sal Giorgianni (*as*); Bob Malach (*ts, cl, f*); Larry Schneider (*ts, ob, cl, f*); Jerry Bergonzi (*ts*); Mike Richmond (*b*); John Riley (*d*). Additional musicians: Manfred Schoof, Benny Bailey, Ack van Rooyen (*t, flhn*); Conrad Herwig (*tb*); Alex Brofsky, Claudio Pontiggia (*frhn*); Roland Dahinden (*tb*); Anne O'Brien (*f*); Julian Cawdry, Hanspeter Frehner (*f, picc, af*); Michel Weber (*cl*); Christian Gavillet, Roger Rosenberg (*bcl, bs*); Tilman Zahn, Judith Wenziker (*ob*); Christian Rabe, Reiner Erb (*bsn*); Xenia Schindler (*hp*); Carles Benavent (*b*); Grady Tate (*d*). 8 July 1991.

Boplicity; Introduction To *Miles Ahead* Medley; Springsville; Maids Of Cadiz; The Duke; My Ship; Miles Ahead; Blues For Pablo; Introduction To *Porgy And Bess* Medley; Orgone; Gone, Gone, Gone; Summertime; Here Come De Honey Man; Introduction To *Sketches Of Spain*; The Pan Piper; Solea.

The Complete Miles Davis At Montreux 1973–1991
(Warner Bros 0927-41836-2)

Miles Davis (*t, org*); Dave Liebman (*ss, ts f*); Reggie Lucas, Pete Cosey (*g*); Michael Henderson (*b*); Al Foster (*d*); Mtume (*perc, ky*). 8 July 1973.

> **Miles In Montreux '73 #1; Miles In Montreux '73 #2; Ife; Calypso Frelimo; Miles In Montreux '73 #3.**

Miles Davis (*t*); Bob Berg (*ss, ts*); Robert Irving III (*ky*); John Scofield (*g*); Darryl Jones (*b*); Al Foster (*d*); Steve Thornton (*perc*). 8 July 1984.

> **Speak/That's What Happened; Star People; What It Is; It Gets Better; Something's On Your Mind; Time After Time; Hopscotch/Star On Cicely; Bass Solo; Jean Pierre; Lake Geneva; Something's On Your Mind; Speak/ That's What Happened; Star People; What It Is; It Gets Better; Something's On Your Mind; Time After Time; Hopscotch/Star On Cicely; Bass Solo; Jean-Pierre; Lake Geneva; Something's On Your Mind; Code M.D.**

As above except Vincent Wilburn (*d*) replaces Foster. 14 July 1985.

> **Theme From Jack Johnson/One Phone Call/Street Scenes/That's What Happened; Star People; Maze; Human Nature; MD1/Something's On Your Mind; Time After Time; Ms Morrisine; Code M.D.; Pacific Express; Katia; Hopscotch; You're Under Arrest; Jean Pierre/You're Under Arrest/Then There Were None; Decoy; Theme From Jack Johnson/One Phone Call/Street Scenes/That's What Happened; Star People; Maze; Human Nature; MD1/ Something's On Your Mind/MD 2; Time After Time; Ms Morrisine; Code M.D.; Pacific Express; Katia; Hopscotch; You're Under Arrest; Jean Pierre/You're Under Arrest/Then There Were None; Decoy.**

Miles Davis (*t*); Bob Berg (*ss, ts*); Adam Holzmann, Robert Irving III (*ky*); Robben Ford (*g*); Felton Crews (*b*); Vincent Wilburn (*d*); Steve Thornton (*perc*). 17 July 1986.

> **Theme from Jack Johnson/One Phone Call/Street Scenes/ That's What Happened; New Blues; Maze; Human Nature; Wrinkle; Tutu; Splatch; Time After Time; Al Jarreau; Carnival Time; Burn; Portia; Jean-Pierre.**

Miles Davis (*t*); Kenny Garrett (*ss, as, f*); Adam Holzmann, Robert Irving III (*ky*); Foley McCreary, Benny Rietveld (*b*); Ricky Wellman (*d*); Marilyn Mazur (*perc*). 7 July 1988.

> **In A Silent Way; Intruder; New Blues; Perfect Way; The Senate/Me & U; Human Nature; Wrinkle; Tutu; Time After Time; Movie Star; Splatch; Heavy Metal Prelude; Heavy Metal; Don't Stop Me Now; Carnival Time; Jean-Pierre; Tomaas.**

As above except Rick Margitza (*ss, ts*), Kei Akagi (*ky*) and Munyungo Jackson (*perc*) replace Garrett, Irving and Mazur. 21 July 1989.

> **Intruder; New Blues; Perfect Way; Hannibal; Human Nature; Mr Pastorius; Tutu; Jilli; Time After Time; Jo Jo; Amandla; The Senate/Me & U; Wrinkle; Portia.**

As above except Kenny Garrett (*ss, as, f*), Richard Patterson (*b, v*), Erin Davis (*perc*) replace Margitza, Rietveld and Jackson, Holzmann out. 20 July 1990.

> **Perfect Way; New Blues; Hannibal; The Senate/Me & U; In The Night; Human Nature; Time After Time; Wrinkle; Tutu: Don't Stop Me Now; Carnival Time.**

As above except Deron Johnson (*ky*) replaces Akagi, Erin Davis out. 17 July 1991.

> **Perfect Way; New Blues; Hannibal; Human Nature; Time After Time; Wrinkle.**
>
> [This set also includes all of *Miles Davis & Quincy Jones Live At Montreux*.]

Doo Bop (Warner Bros 26938)

Miles Davis (*t*); Deron Johnson (*ky*); Easy Mo Bee, J.R., A. B. Money (*v*); others unlisted. 1991.

> **Mystery; The Doo-Bop Song; Freaky; Chocolate Chip; High Speed Chase; Blow; Sonya; Fantasy; Duke Booty; Mystery (Reprise).**

Index of Recordings

1969 Miles – Festiva De Juan Pins, 211, 229
'58 Miles, 96, 103

Agharta, 257–60, 265, 266
Agharta Prelude, 258
Agitation, 161, 163, 166, 172, 190, 196
Ah-Leu-Cha, 48, 57, 66, 98
Ahmad's Blues, 52, 53
Aida, 266
Airegin, 39
Ali, 238
Alison's Uncle, 93
All About Rosie, 94
All Blues, 111, 116, 117, 118, 129, 130, 149, 163, 197
All God's Chillun Got Rhythm, 12
All Of Me, 79, 106
All Of You, 56, 106, 108, 127, 129, 133, 135, 151, 155, 157, 160, 163, 170
All Stars Recordings, 24, 25, 29
Alone Together, 114
Amandla, 301–2, 303, 305
Amandla, 300
America Today (Curtis Mayfield), 282
Another 1969 – Miles Vol. 2, 213, 229
Another 1969 – Miles Vol. 3, 213, 229
Another Bitches Brew, 254, 260
Aos Pes da Cruz, 141

Archie Moore, 233
Ascension, 256
Ascent, 203
At Carnegie Hall, 139, 143
At Last!, 35, 59
Atmosphere: Live In Tokyo, 274, 282
Au bar du Petit Bac, 81
Aura, 287–92, 293, 299
Autumn Leaves, 92, 129, 134, 151, 161, 163

Baby Won't You Please Come Home, 146
Back On The Block (Quincy Jones), 307
Back Seat Betty, 266, 267, 269
Backyard Ritual, 295
Bags' Groove, 39, 41, 59
Bags' Groove, 41, 108
Bangoon, 93
Basin Street Blues, 146, 148
Bemsha Swing, 41
Bess You Is My Woman Now, 100, 101
Bess, Oh Where's My Bess, 100, 101
Big Fun, 222, 223, 224, 229, 232, 250, 260
Big Green Serpent, The, 224
Big Time, 302
Billie's Bounce, 10–11
Billy Boy, 85, 86, 89
Billy Preston, 252

Bird Gets The Worm, 12
Birdland 1951, 26, 29
Birth Of The Cool, 6, 13–23, 38, 48, 56, 251, 327
Bitches Brew, 6, 190, 214–21, 222, 224, 227, 228, 232, 239, 258, 260, 327
Bitches Brew, 213, 214, 216, 218, 240
Bitches Brew Live, 209, 213, 229
Bitty Ditty, 46
Black Beauty, 237, 261
Black Comedy, 194
Black Satin, 248, 249, 323
Blue, 287, 291
Blue By Five, 51
Blue Christmas, 142, 143
Blue Christmas, 142
Blue Haze, 34, 37, 59
Blue Haze, 37
Blue In Green, 111, 112, 114
Blue Moods, 45, 59
Blue 'N' Boogie, 38, 81
Blue Room, 26
Blues For Pablo, 67, 69, 71, 73, 77, 119, 314
Blues In The Closet, 94
Blues No. 2, 131, 132
Bluing, 27
Boplicity, 14, 20, 314, 316
Brubeck Plays Brubeck (Dave Brubeck), 69
Budo, 13, 17, 19, 48
Buzzard Song, 100, 101, 103
Bye Bye (The Theme), 133, 134, 151
Bye Bye Blackbird, 45, 55, 78, 94, 98, 106, 107, 127, 133, 136, 151, 183

Call It Anythin', 242
Call It What It Is, 254, 260
Calypso Frelimo, 253, 310
Can I Play With U?, 295
Capricorn, 184–5
Carnival Time, 312
Circle, 176
Circle In The Round, 190, 192, 209, 224, 229, 264
Circle In The Round, 190
Code M.D., 275
Collector, The, 193

Collectors' Items, 31, 59, 62, 81
Come Get It, 272
Complete Amsterdam Concert, The, 79, 81
Complete Bitches Brew Sessions, The, 216, 218, 221, 222, 223, 229, 234
Complete Columbia Studio Recordings, The, 152
Complete Concert, The, 153
Complete In A Silent Way Sessions, The, 203, 208, 209, 324
Complete Jack Johnson Sessions, The, 232, 233, 236, 238, 239, 261, 323
Complete Live At The Plugged Nickel, The, 163–70
Complete Miles Davis At Montreux 1973–1991, The, 309–14, 318
Complete Savoy And Dial Recordings, The (Charlie Parker), 11, 29
Complete Sessions, 28, 29
Complete Studio Recordings of the Miles Davis Quintet 1965–1968, 190, 191, 196, 209
Compulsion, 32
Conception, 26, 29
Conception, 24, 27, 28
Concert On The Runway, 306
Concerto For Billy The Kid, 94
Concierto de Aranjuez for guitar and orchestra, 124, 139
Conference Of The Birds (Dave Holland), 242
Confirmation, 28
Cookin, 51, 52, 59
Cool Boppin, 17, 29
Copenhagen 1960, 128, 143
Corcovado, 141
Corrado, 223
Côte Blues, 150, 151, 173
Country Son, 194
C.T.A., 34
Curried Jazz, 222

Dancing In The Dark, 93
Dark Magus, 254, 261
Dark Star (Grateful Dead), 205
Darn That Dream, 21
Dear Old Stockholm, 29, 55

Deception, 21, 24
Decoy, 275–6, 278, 282, 286
Decoy, 275, 311
Devil May Care, 142
Diane, 47, 49
Dig, 26, 29
Dingo, 306, 318
Directions, 178, 187, 238, 261, 264
Directions, 203, 204, 243, 244
Django, 96, 97
Dr Jackle, 46, 85, 90
Dolores, 176
Doo Bop, 308, 314, 318, 322
Doo-Bop Song, The, 308
Double Image, 225
Down, 26
Doxy, 39
Drad-Dog, 131
Dream Of You (Gil Evans and Helen Merrill),
66
Dual Mr Anthony Tillmon Williams Process,
201, 202
Duke, The, 67, 69, 71, 119, 314, 317

E.S.P., 161–2, 173, 179
E.S.P., 161, 162
Early Minor, 208
Eighty-One, 161, 162
El Toro, 159
Electric Red, 287, 291
Enigma, 33
Everybody Digs Bill Evans (Bill Evans), 111
Ezz-Thetic (Lee Konitz), 26, 29
Ezz-Thetic, 26

Fall, 180, 182
Falling Water, 195, 196
Fast Track, 269
Fat Time, 266, 267
Feio, 225
Festival International de Jazz Paris 1949, 24, 29
Filles de Kilimanjaro, 196–9, 204, 208, 209
Filles de Kilimanjaro, 197
Fisherman, Strawberry And Devil Crab, 100,
101

Flamenco Sketches, 111, 112, 115–16, 118, 131
Footprints, 176–7, 178
Forest Flower (Charles Lloyd), 200
'Four' And More, 6, 153, 155–6, 173
Four, 36, 65, 79, 94, 156, 163, 167
Four-Play, 106
Fran-Dance, 95, 98, 111, 133, 136
Freaky, 308
Freaky Deaky, 275
Freddie Freeloader, 111, 112
Free Trade Hall Vols. 1 & 2, 129, 143
Freedom Jazz Dance, 175, 177
Frelon brun, 198
From His Last Concert In Avignon, 299, 303
Fun, 192
Funky Tonk, 244

Gal In Calico, A, 43
Get Up With It, 238, 250, 253, 255, 256, 261
Ghetto Walk, The, 207
Giant Steps (John Coltrane), 79
Gingerbread Boy, 175, 177
Go Ahead John, 232
Godchild, 13, 17, 19
Gone, 100, 101, 102, 103
Gone, Gone, Gone, 100, 101, 102, 314
Great Expectations, 222, 223
Green, 287, 291
Guinnevere, 224

Hackensack, 44
Half Nelson, 12
Hallucinations, 19
Hand Jive, 180, 181
Hannibal, 300
He Loved Him Madly, 255, 323
Helen Butte, 248
Here Come De Honey Man, 100, 314
High Speed Chase, 308
Honky Tonk, 238, 243
Hopscotch, 311
Hot Spot, The, 306–7, 318
Hotel Me, 153
How Deep Is The Ocean, 29
How High The Moon, 65

Human Nature, 277, 280, 281, 299, 311, 312, 313

I Didn't, 43
I Don't Wanna Be Kissed, 68, 69, 72
I Fall In Love Too Easily, 146, 163, 163, 170, 185, 190, 213, 218, 237, 240
I Got Plenty Of Nuttin', 101
I Have A Dream, 196
I Loves You Porgy, 100, 103
I Thought About You, 132, 133, 134, 136, 137, 149–150, 151, 155, 163, 170
I Waited For You, 34
I'll Remember April, 37
If I Were A Bell, 105–6, 130, 133, 134, 136, 151, 157, 163
Ife, 250, 254, 258, 310
In A Sentimental Mood, 167
In A Silent Way, 180, 201, 204–8, 209, 211, 245, 326, 327
In A Silent Way, 201, 205, 206, 208, 226, 323
In Concert: Live At Philharmonic Hall, 251, 261
In Person Friday Night At The Blackhawk, 133–6, 140
In Person Saturday Night At The Blackhawk, 134, 136–8, 140
In Your Own Sweet Way, 52, 62
Inamorata, 244
Indigo, 287, 291
Interlude, 257
Intro, 287, 289, 290
Intro: MD 1/Something's On Your Mind/MD 2, 277
Introduction To *Miles Ahead* Medley, 314
Introduction To *Porgy and Bess* Medley, 314
Introduction To *Sketches Of Spain*, 314
Irene, 161, 162
Israel, 14, 16, 20, 69
It Ain't Necessarily So, 100, 103
It Gets Better, 272, 274
It Never Entered My Mind, 36, 61, 78
It's About That Time, 201, 205, 228, 240, 241, 244
It's Magic, 62
It's Only A Paper Moon, 27

Jack Johnson, 232, 234–6, 260, 261, 279
Jazz At the Plaza Vol. 1, 105
Jazz Samba (Stan Getz), 140
Jazz Suite For Brass, 64
Jazz Track, 96, 118
Jazz Workshop (Hal McKusick), 72
Jean Pierre, 269–70, 274, 277, 281, 318
Jeru, 13, 17, 18–19
Jitterbug Waltz, 96, 97
John McLaughlin, 214, 216, 218
Johnny Bratton, 232
Joshua, 149, 151, 160
Julien dans l'ascenseur, 81
Just Squeeze Me, 51

Katia, 277, 280
Katia Prelude, 277, 280
Kind Of Blue, 1, 4, 111–19, 124, 130, 138, 189, 214, 293, 322, 326
Kix, 269
Klaunstance, 12
Konda, 238

La Paloma (Claude Thornhill), 14, 15
Lady Be Good, 65
Lady Bird, 12
Lake Geneva, 311
Lament, 68, 69, 72
L'Ascenseur pour l'échafaud (*Lift To The Scaffold*), 80–1, 96
Last Word, The: The Warner Bros Years, 324
Leap, The, 36
Legendary Performance In New York 1959, 79, 81, 119
Legrand Jazz (Michel Legrand), 96–7, 103
Lester Leaps In, 65
Lester Left Town, 159
Limbo, 178
Little Blue Frog, The, 224
Little Church, 239
Little High People, 239
Little Melonae, 48, 85, 90
Little One, 162
Little Stuff, 197
Little Willie Leaps, 12

Live Around The World, 298, 300, 303, 321, 322
Live At The Fillmore East (March 7, 1970):
    It's About That Time , 227, 229, 237
Live At Newport 1958, 98, 103
Live Dead (Grateful Dead), 205
Live–Evil, 225, 229, 239, 243, 244, 261
Live In Holland, 128, 143
Live In New York, 94, 103
Live In Sindelfingen 1964, 160–1, 173
Live In St Louis And Paris 1963, 149, 150, 173
Live In Stockholm 1960, 127, 130, 143
Live Tutu, 299, 300, 303
Lonely Fire, 224
Love For Sale, 93, 96
Love Supreme, A (John Coltrane), 83
Love, I've Found You, 133, 134, 136

Mademioselle Mabry, 198, 199
Madness, 180, 181
Maids of Cadiz, The, 67, 69, 77, 314
Maiysha, 256, 257, 258
Man I Love, The, 40
Man With The Horn, The, 266–8, 269, 273, 275, 282, 294, 295
Man With The Horn, The, 266, 308
Mask, The, 239
Masqualero, 179, 185, 228
Max Is Making Wax, 61, 62
Maze, 294, 311
Meaning Of The Blues, The, 68, 69, 72
Mercy Mercy Mercy, 202
Message To Love: The Isle Of Wight Festival, 242, 261
Miles – The New Miles Davis Quintet, 50, 59
Miles Ahead, 5, 67–77, 78, 99, 101, 102, 117, 118, 119, 125, 142, 214, 278, 279, 316, 327
Miles Ahead, 34, 67, 68, 69, 71, 75, 314
Miles Davis, 213, 229
Miles Davis, 289, 290, 291
Miles Davis: Volume 1, 28, 29
Miles Davis: Volume 2, 28, 29, 33, 35, 59
Miles Davis All Stars, 107
Miles Davis & Gil Evans: The Complete Columbia Studio Recordings, 73–4, 81, 173, 195, 209, 324

Miles Davis And Horns, 25, 29, 33, 59
Miles Davis + Keith Jarrett Live, 246
Miles Davis And Quincy Jones Live At Montreux, 314–18, 327
Miles Davis And The Modern Jazz Giants, 40, 41, 59
Miles Davis At Fillmore, 240, 261
Miles Davis In Europe, 150, 173
Miles Davis Quintet At Peacock Alley, The, 65–6, 81
Miles In Berlin, 159, 173
Miles In Montreux '73 #1, 310
Miles In Montreux '73 #2, 310
Miles In Montreux '73 #3, 310
Miles In The Sky, 192, 193–4, 198, 200, 209
Miles In Tokyo, 157, 173
Miles Remembered: The Silent Way Project (Mark Isham), 323
Miles Runs The Voodoo Down, 208, 213, 214, 218
Miles Runs The Voodoo Down At Central Park, 211, 229
Miles Smiles, 175–7, 179, 185, 187, 194
Miles! Miles! Miles!, 270, 282
Milestones, 85–91, 92, 95, 100, 118, 124, 200, 326
Milestones (1947), 12, 34, 86
Milestones (1958), 85, 86, 88–9, 90, 94, 95, 103, 109, 116, 148, 151, 160, 163, 306
Milt and Miles: All Star Quintet/Sextet, 46, 59
Miscellaneous Davis 1955–57, 59, 65, 79, 81
Mr Pastorius, 300, 302
Molester, The, 249
Mood, 162
Moon Dreams, 21–2
More Live At Fillmore East, 227, 229
Morpheus, 26
Move, 13, 17–18, 26
Ms Morrisine, 277, 280, 291, 311
Mtume, 256
Music For Brass/Birth Of The Third Stream, 63, 67, 81
Music Forever And Beyond: The Selected Works Of Chick Corea 1964–1996, 211, 229
Musings of Miles, The, 42, 59
My Funny Valentine, 153–4, 173

My Funny Valentine, 3, 106, 154–5, 157–8, 163, 166, 167, 183, 251, 260, 281
My Man's Gone Now, 100, 101, 269
My Old Flame, 27
My Ship, 67, 69, 71, 314, 317

Naima, 200
Nefertiti, 180–4, 185, 189, 194, 213
Nefertiti, 180, 182, 184, 196
Nem Um Talvez (Not Even A Maybe), 238–9
Neo, 133, 134, 135–6, 137
New Blues, 299, 313
New Jazz Conceptions (Bill Evans), 93
New Rhumba, 67, 69, 72, 119
Night in Tunisia, A, 11, 43
No Blues, 185, 187, 190, 209
No Blues, 133, 134, 135, 150, 159, 160, 163, 170, 185
No Line, 62
No (More) Blues, 172, 173
Nothing Like You, 142, 178
Now's The Time, 10, 44, 88

O Sole Mio (Claude Thornhill), 14
Odds 'N' Ends 1969–73, 211, 229
Old Folks, 131
Oleo, 39, 40, 51, 66, 105, 106, 127, 133, 161, 163, 170
Olympia, 11 juillet 1973, 252, 261
On Green Dolphin Street, 95, 111, 127, 128, 133, 134, 136, 163, 185, 190
On The Corner, 5, 247–9, 250, 251, 252, 254, 261, 327
Once Upon A Summertime, 141
One And One, 248
One For Daddy-O, 93
One Phone Call/Street Scenes, 277, 279, 312
Orange, 287, 288, 290
Orange Lady, 223
Orgone, 314
Out Of The Cool (Gil Evans), 22
Out Of This World, 71

Pacific Express, 311
Palais des Sports, Paris 1973, 254, 261
Pan Piper, The, 124, 126, 314, 316

Pangaea, 257, 259, 261
Panthalassa: The Remixes, 208, 209, 323
Paraphernalia, 192, 193, 194
Paris, France, 160, 173
Paris Jazz Concert, 126, 129, 143
Peace Piece, 111, 115
Pee Wee, 178, 179
Perfect Way, 296
Pet Sounds (Beach Boys), 186
Petits machins, 197
Pfrancing, 131, 135
Pharaoh's Dance, 214, 216
Pinocchio, 180, 182
Pop Goes The Weasel (Claude Thornhill), 14
Porgy And Bess, 99–103, 117, 124, 125, 142, 189, 269, 316
Portia, 296
Prayer (Oh Doctor Jesus), 100, 102
Prelude, 254, 257
Prince Of Darkness, 179
Put Your Little Foot Right Out, 95

Quantum Physics (Can), 289
Quiet Nights, 140–1, 147, 149

Ramblin', 177
Rare Live, 65, 81
Rare Unissued Broadcasts, 61, 81
Rarities From Private Collections, 65, 78, 81
Rated X, 250–1, 253, 258, 323
Re-Birth Of The Cool (Gerry Mulligan), 15
Recollections, 225
Red, 287, 290
Relaxin, 50, 51, 52, 59
Right Off, 235, 258, 279
Riot, 180, 181–2, 185
Robot 415, 275
Rocker, 21
Rouge, 14, 19, 20
'Round About Midnight, 47, 57, 59, 62, 67
Round Midnight, 32, 34, 44, 56, 57, 62, 80, 97, 106, 127, 134, 137, 163, 185, 196
Royal Garden Blues (Claude Thornhill), 14
Saeta, 124, 126
Salt Peanuts, 47, 62

359

San Francisco (Scott Mackenzie), 186
Sanctuary, 192, 208, 214, 216, 218, 221, 237, 240, 244
Secret Love, 106
Selim, 239
Sgt Pepper's Lonely Hearts Club Band (Beatles), 186
Serpent's Tooth, The, 32
Seven Steps To Heaven (authorized), 146–50, 161, 173
Seven Steps To Heaven (unauthorized), 161, 173
Seven Steps To Heaven, 148–9, 150–1
Sextet With Jackie McLean, 28, 29
Shaft (Isaac Hayes), 205
Shhh/Peaceful, 201, 205, 206, 208, 236
Shout, 266, 267
Sid's Ahead, 36, 85, 86, 89–90, 106, 107
Sid's Delight, 55
Side Car I, 193
Side Car II, 192
Siesta, 297–8, 303
S'il vous plait, 17
Sincerely Diana, 159
Sippin' At Bells, 12
Sivad, 243
Sketches Of Spain, 69, 124–6, 143, 185, 293, 298, 316, 322
Sleeping Dancer Sleep On, 159
Smooch, 34
So Near, So Far, 147
So What, 111, 113–14, 117, 119, 127, 128, 134, 140, 149, 150, 151, 155, 157–8, 160, 163, 258
Softly As In A Morning Sunrise, 134, 137
Solar, 37, 322
Solea, 124, 126, 314, 316
Some Other Time, 112
Someday My Prince Will Come, 130–2, 143, 179
Someday My Prince Will Come, 134, 137
Somethin' Else (Cannonball Adderely), 92, 96, 103
Somethin' Else, 93
Something I Dreamed Last Night, 47, 53
Something's On Your Mind, 280–1, 311
Song #1, 141
Song #2, 141

Sorcerer, 142, 178–9, 187
Sorcerer, The, 179
Spanish Key, 213, 214, 216, 217–18, 228, 246
Speak, 272, 273, 279
Speak Like A Child (Herbie Hancock), 181
Speak Like A Child, 196
Splash, 202–3
Splashdown, 203
Splatch, 296
Spring Is Here, 140
Springsville, 67, 69, 70, 314
Stablemates, 51
Star On Cicely, 272
Star People, 271–3, 279, 282
Star People, 272, 274
Steamin' With The Miles Davis Quintet, 47, 49, 53–4, 327
Stella By Starlight, 96, 150, 155, 160, 163, 172
Straight, No Chaser, 85, 86, 87, 98, 106, 108
Stuff, 194, 198
Sugar Ray, 233
Summer Night, 147
Summertime, 100, 101, 314
Sunken Treasure, 22
Super Nova (Wayne Shorter), 184
Sur l'autoroute, 81
Surrey With The Fringe On Top, 47, 54
Sweet Pea, 185
Sweet Sue, Just You, 56, 57
Swing Spring, 41

Tadd's Delight, 55
Take It Or Leave It, 226
Take Off, 36
Takin' Off (Herbie Hancock), 149
Tatu, 258
Tempus Fugit, 33
Teo, 131, 139
Teo's Bag, 193
That Old Devil Called Love, 36
That's Right, 275–6
That's What Happened, 275
Theme, The, 51, 53, 98, 133, 134, 163, 170, 228, 240
Theme From Jack Johnson, 257
Then There Were None, 277, 279

Index of Recordings

There Is No Greater Love, 51

There's A Boat That's Leaving Soon For New York, 100, 101–2

Three Little Feelings, 63

Thriller (Michael Jackson), 280

Time After Time, 3, 277, 278, 280, 281, 288, 300, 310, 313

Times They Are A-Changing, The (Bob Dylan), 279

Tout de suite, 196–7

Trane's Blues, 53

Tune In Five, 310

Tune Up, 34, 36, 65

Turnaroundphase, 310

Tutu, 295–7, 302, 303, 312

Tutu, 296, 299, 300

Two Bass Hit, 48, 85, 86, 98, 134

Two Faced, 201–2

U 'n' I, 272

Ursula, 266

Venus De Milo, 14, 19

Vierd Blues, 62

Violet, 287, 291

Vonetta, 179

Wait Till You See Her, 141

Walkin', 37, 59

Walkin', 36, 38, 45, 62, 65, 66, 80, 86, 94, 106, 108, 127, 129, 133, 134, 136, 139, 151, 155, 157, 158, 160, 161, 163, 166, 185–6, 190

Walkin' Shoes, 19, 90

Waltz For Debby, 93

Water Babies, 184, 187, 202, 209

Water Babies, 184

Water On The Pond, 191–2

Watermelon Man, 149

We Want Miles, 268–9, 273, 282

Wee Dot, 28

Weirdo, 36, 85

Well, You Needn't, 32, 36, 43, 47, 53, 54, 66, 80, 134, 137

What I Say? Vol. 1, 246

What I Say? Vol. 2, 243, 244, 261

What I Say, 243, 244

What It Is, 275

What's Going On (Marvin Gaye), 282

What's Love Got To Do With It (Tina Turner), 278

What's New, 65, 80

When I Fall In Love, 47, 53, 163

When Lights Are Low, 34

Whispering, 26

White, 287, 289, 291

Why Do I Love You, 17

Wild Man Blues, 96, 97

Wili, 258

Wili, Part 2, 254

Will O' The Wisp, 124, 126

Willie Nelson, 232, 236, 240

Willow Weep For Me, 127

Winelight (Grover Washington), 266

With A Song In My Heart, 114

Woody 'N' You, 50, 51, 62

Workin' With The Miles Davis Quintet, 49, 52, 59

Wrinkle, 300

Yaphet, 223

Yellow, 287, 288, 290

Yesterdays, 29, 80, 163

Yesternow, 236

Yo Miles! (Wadada Leo Smith and Henry Kaiser), 323

You Don't Know What Love Is, 37

You Make Me Feel Like A Natural Woman (Aretha Franklin), 196

You Won't Forget Me (Shirley Horn), 307, 318

You're My Everything, 52

You're Under Arrest, 5, 120, 277–82, 291, 294, 296, 311

You're Under Arrest, 277, 280, 281

Zawinul (Joe Zawinul), 205

Zimbabwe, 254

361

General Index

Adams, George, 314
Adderley, Alison, 93
Adderley, Julian 'Cannonball', 31, 79, 128, 137, 145, 147, 297, 326; plays on *Milestones*, 85–8, 90; with Davis sextet, 91–2, 95, 98, 106–9, 111, 113–16, 118–19; *Somethin' Else*, 92–3; plays on *Porgy And Bess*, 100; pursues own career, 107–8, 119, 123; plays on *Kind Of Blue*, 111, 113–16, 118; leaves Davis band, 123; stage presence, 183; uses Zawinul as pianist, 191, 202; blues playing, 271
Adderley, Nat, 79, 92–3, 123, 208
African Research Foundation, 139
Akagi, Kei, 299, 313
Alias, Don, 214–15, 218, 245
Allen, Steve, 61
Alpert, Herb, 268, 280
'American songbook' repertoire, 43
Ammons, Gene, 24
amplification, 243
Amsterdam, 79, 80
Anderson, Peter, 271
Antibes Festival, 150
Armstrong, Louis, 2, 31, 48, 61, 73; 'Wild Man Blues', 96, 97; *Porgy And Bess*, 99; elder of jazz, 220
Atlantic Records, 107, 108, 109, 123, 143

Avakian, George, 44, 47, 55–7, 66–8, 73–4, 76; joins Warner Brothers, 99
Ayler, Albert, 143, 183, 220

Bailey, Benny, 314
Baker, Chet, 15, 35, 91, 114
Balakrishna, Khalil, 222, 224–5, 250
Balliet, Whitney, 75
Bandstand USA, 65, 106, 108
Bank, Danny, 67, 70, 75, 100
Barber, Bill, 13, 14, 67, 100, 103
Barboza, Anthony, 281
Bargeron, Dave, 314
Barney, Tom, 273
Bartz, Gary, 242–4, 246, 258, 267
Basie, Count, 16, 31, 44, 65
Battle, Jackie, 252
Beach Boys, 186
Beatles, 153, 186, 222
Beck, Jeff, 233
Beck, Joe, 190–2, 196
Beethoven, Ludwig van, 281
Belden, Bob, 216, 224
Benavent, Carles, 314
Bennett, Joe, 67, 100
Benson, George, 192–4
Berg, Bob, 277–8, 280, 297, 310–11

Bergonzi, Jerry, 314
Bernstein, Leonard, 56–7, 102
Best Denzil, 17
Bethlehem label, 99
Billboard chart, 211
Bishop, Walter, 26, 32
Black Sabbath, 243
Blackmon, Larry, 313
Blakey, Art, 26–7, 33, 35, 37, 54; Jazz
     Messengers, 91, 128, 130, 276; plays on
     Somethin' Else, 92; his band, 142, 143, 157,
     159, 242–3
Blank, Lester and Jerry, 285
Blue Note, 105, 207; Davis sessions, 28–9, 33–4,
     40, 55, 86; Adderley's *Somethin' Else*, 92;
     Mobley recordings, 130; Hancock record-
     ings, 149, 181, 198; Shorter recordings, 162,
     183, 184
Blumenthal, Bob, 114
Bobo, Willie, 142
Bodner, Phil, 100
Bolden, Buddy, 220
Bolvig, Palle, 287
Bourrelly, Jean-Paul, 302
Boyd, Nelson, 14
Brass Ensemble of the Jazz and Classical
     Music Society, 63
Brofsky, Alex, 314
Brooks, Harvey, 214–16
Broom, Bobby, 297
Brown, Clifford, 91, 307
Brown, Delmar, 314
Brown, James, 231, 247
Brown, Ray, 235
Brubeck, Dave, 84, 132, 293, 324; signs to
     Columbia, 44; 'In Your Own Sweet Way', 52,
     62; 'The Duke', 69, 71; as band leader, 91;
     record sales, 105
Bruce, Jack, 247
Bryant, Ray, 45
Buckmaster, Paul, 247–50, 264
Buffington, Jimmy, 67–8
Bullock, Hiram, 297
Burton, Gary, 186
Butler, Frank, 145–7

Butler, George, 264–5, 277, 279, 293–4
Byrd, Donald, 149
Byrds, 186

Cage, John, 219
Caine, Eddie, 68
Camelot, 195
Cameo, 307, 313
Can, 289
Capitol Records, 16, 17, 19–20, 23–4, 38, 70, 77
Carisi, John, 16, 20, 67, 69, 70
Carle, Frankie, 96
Carr, Ian, 38, 134, 221, 245
Carsten, Per, 287
Carter, Benny, 11, 34
Carter, Elliot, 219
Carter, Ron, 178, 213, 223, 234, 326; with Davis
     quintet, 145–54, 156, 160–5, 167–9, 186, 191;
     session work, 172, 190; contributions to
     Miles Smiles, 176–7; plays on *Sorcerer*, 179;
     plays on *Nefertiti* sessions, 180–2, 185; plays
     on *Miles In The Sky*, 193–4; plays electric
     bass, 193, 196–7; plays on *Filles de
     Kilimanjaro*, 196–7; plays on *Bitches Brew*
     sessions, 222
Cawdry, Julian, 314
CBS, 119, 131, 215
Chambers, Joe, 207
Chambers, Paul, 146, 235; with Davis quintets,
     45, 47, 49, 51–2, 54–5, 62, 65, 78, 126–7, 131, 133,
     137; heavy drinking, 57–8; plays on *Miles
     Ahead*, 67, 70–2; plays on *Milestones*, 85–90;
     with Davis sextet, 95–6, 106, 119; plays on
     Legrand Jazz, 97; plays on *Porgy And Bess*,
     100; plays on *Kind Of Blue*, 111, 113–16; plays
     on *Sketches Of Spain*, 126; plays on
     Someday My Prince Will Come, 131; plays on
     Blackhawk recordings, 133, 137; leaves Davis
     band, 142
Chancler, Leon 'Ndugu', 245–6
Chapman, Harold, 86
Charles, Ray, 298
Charles, Teddy, 45
Cherry, Don, 290
Chess label, 252

363

Chicago Symphony Orchestra, 149
Chuck D, 307
Cinelu, Mino, 269
Circle, 242
clark, John, 314
Clarke, Kenny, 9, 14, 28, 33, 37, 39–41, 79–80
Clausen, Thomas, 287, 291
Cleveland, Jimmy, 67, 100
Clinton, George, 260
Cobb, Jimmy, 95–6, 98, 105; plays on *Porgy And Bess*, 100; plays on *Kind Of Blue*, 111, 114–15, 118; plays on *Sketches Of Spain*, 126; with Davis quintets, 126–7, 131, 133–4, 137, 147; plays on *Someday My Prince Will Come*, 131; plays on Blackhawk recordings, 133–4, 137; leaves Davis band, 142
Cobham, Billy, 222–5, 235, 238, 267
Coggins, Gil, 28, 33, 34
Cohn, Al, 33
Cole, Nat, 76
Coleman, George, 124, 145, 147, 149–52, 155, 156–7, 159
Coleman, Ornette, 31, 109–10, 119, 142–3, 177, 219
Coles, Johnny, 100
Collins, Junior, 13
Coltrane, John, 4, 137, 152–3, 159–60, 253, 297, 326; with Davis quintets, 46–52, 54–8, 62, 123–4, 126–8; drug addiction, 57–8, 66, 83–4, 200; fired by Davis, 66; plays with Monk, 66, 78, 83–4; *Giant Steps*, 79, 109; rejoins Davis band, 83–4; *A Love Supreme*, 83; plays on *Milestones*, 85–90; with Davis sextet, 91, 94–6, 98, 103, 106, 108–9, 120; plays on *Legrand Jazz*, 97; pursues own career, 107–9, 119, 123–4, 126, 128, 143; plays on *Kind Of Blue*, 111–12, 114–16; leaves Davis band, 128–30; plays on *Someday My Prince Will Come*, 131–2, 136; quartet, 168; death, 200
Columbia Records, 6, 44, 66, 124, 132, 194; Davis recordings, 47–8, 51, 55, 57, 61–2, 67–8, 96, 150, 159, 178, 190, 207–8, 211, 213, 236–7, 240, 242–3, 248–9, 254, 256–8, 268, 325; Third Stream recordings, 63; recording and promotion of *Miles Ahead*, 73–7; dealings

with Davis, 84, 189, 226, 264, 292–3, 298; recording of *Milestones*, 85–6; *Porgy And Bess* recording, 99, 101, 102; promotional concert, 105; recording and marketing of *Kind Of Blue*, 110, 114, 117–18; Blackhawk recordings, 133–5, 137; Carnegie Hall recording, 139–40; Christmas record, 142; Hollywood studios, 153; Philharmonic Hall recordings, 154–6; Plugged Nickel recordings, 164, 170; Los Angeles studio, 178; difficulties with Davis; New York studio, 190, 204; and *Bitches Brew*, 221, 223, 224, 228, 250; blocks release of 'Rated X', 251; signs Marsalis brothers, 276, 293; Davis leaves, 292–3; profits from Davis back catalogue, 322–4
Concord label, 12
Contemporary label, 109
Cooper, Sid, 67–8
Copenhagen, 128, 213, 286, 292
Corea, Chick, 198–9, 203, 208, 213, 255, 326; plays on *In A Silent Way*, 201, 205–6; reputation, 211; plays on *Bitches Brew* sessions, 214–15, 218, 223–4; with Davis electric bands, 227, 232, 234, 237, 239, 241–2, 246, 248; joins Circle, 242, 245; with Return To Forever, 265; appears at Paris gala, 318
Coryell, Larry, 264
Cosey, Pete, 252–4, 257–9, 326, 310–11
Crombie, Tony, 147
Crosby, David, 224
Cross, Billy, 306
Crusaders, 302

D Train, 280
Dahinden, Roland, 314
Dameron, Tadd, 12, 19, 23, 24, 55
Danish Radiojazzgruppen, 288
Davis, Cheryl, 10
Davis, Clive, 189, 211, 228, 232
Davis, Dorothy, 252, 305
Davis, Eddie 'Lockjaw', 26
Davis, Erin, 221, 246, 305, 313
Davis, Gregory, 257
Davis, Irene (common-law wife), 10, 35, 110, 132

Davis, Miles: background, 2; physical appearance, 2, 24, 77, 300–1; fitness, 2, 157; dress sense, 2, 77, 208–9, 300; relationships with women, 2, 95, 157, 179, 195, 221, 270, 274, 286, 298, 305, 325; violence, 2, 157, 249, 270, 298, 325; musical education, 2, 9, 10, 94; diet, 2, 221, 270; drinking, 3, 24, 257, 263, 270; drug use, 3, 24, 25, 28, 29, 35, 57, 84, 140, 157, 172, 221–2, 246, 249, 252, 257, 263, 270, 274, 325; sex addiction, 3, 263; style and technique, 3, 9, 23, 24, 48, 241; health, 3, 140, 142, 156–7, 162, 179, 246, 255, 257, 263, 267, 270, 285, 305, 309, 315, 317, 325; disdain for jazz, 3, 6, 231, 298, 315; quotable quotes, 4, 282; association with Parker, 9–12, 19, 23–5, 31–2, 88; domestic arrangements, 10, 35, 120; first recording, 10; records Birth Of The Cool, 13–23, 24; visits Europe, 23–4, 58, 64–5, 79–80, 126–30, 150, 159–61, 185–6, 189–90, 211, 213, 245, 252–2, 254, 270–1, 274, 286, 298, 309, 317, 321; career difficulties, 25–6, 28–9, 31–2, 35, 142–3; arrests, 25, 120, 123, 252; recordings for Prestige, 25–7, 32–43, 45–55, 57, 61–2, 86, 90, 106, 132; pimping, 28, 286; Blue Note sessions, 28–9, 33–4, 40, 55, 86; cold turkey treatment, 35, 84; attitude to blues playing, 41–2, 271–2; starts to play standards, 43; appears at Newport Jazz Festival, 43–4, 98, 172; acoustic quintets, recordings and concerts, 46–58, 61–2, 65–6, 78–9, 83, 86, 92, 106, 123–4, 126–32, 145–86, 190–1, 327; signs to Columbia, 47; self-promotion, 47; ballad playing, 53, 64, 70; throat operation and rasping voice, 61–2; plays on Third Stream record, 62–3; records Miles Ahead, 68–77, 214; celebrity, 76–7, 84, 109, 132, 285; records film music, 80–1, 306–7; and racism, 84, 94, 298, 325; and money, 84, 112, 132, 246, 264, 285, 293–4, 305, 315–16; records Milestones, 85–91; sextet recordings and concerts, 92–6, 98–9, 105–9, 110–20, 123; impact of sextet, 90–2; plays on Adderley's record, 92–3; plays on Legrand Jazz, 96–7; records Porgy And Bess, 99–103; record sales, 105, 189, 211, 228, 232, 248, 285, 296, 322; dislike of rehearsals, 107, 299; records Kind Of Blue, 110–19, 214; attitudes to recording, 107, 117, 240, 275; stage demeanour, 123, 129, 133, 157, 271; records Sketches Of Spain, 124–6; records Someday My Prince Will Come, 130–2; marriage to Frances Taylor, 132, 179; Blackhawk recordings, 133–8, 140; Carnegie Hall concert, 138–40, 142, 196; Quiet Nights sessions, 140–2; Philharmonic Hall concert, 153–6, 157; Plugged Nickel concerts, 164–70, 175, 228, 299; records Nefertiti, 180–4; faces musical crossroads, 186–7, 201; electric bands, 190–208, 211–13, 224, 226–8, 232–46, 250, 297–9; marriage to Betty Mabry, 199, 221; records In A Silent Way, 204–8; Bitches Brew sessions, 214–26; favourite term for women, 221; involved in shooting, 222; Fillmore East concerts, 227–8, 231–2, 240–1; mellowing, 232, 271; records Jack Johnson, 234–6; records On The Corner, 247–9; car accidents, 249, 252, 257; his home, 252, 263–4, 285; tours South America, 255; records Agharta, 257–9; stops playing, 260, 263–5; supports Hancock, 263; records The Man With The Horn, 266–8; comeback, 268–70; marriage to cicely Tyson, 270, 286; suffers stroke, 270; records Star People, 271–3; album covers, 273–4; ends relationship with Macero, 274–5; records Decoy, 275–6; records You're Under Arrest, 277–82; painting, 285–6, 301; makes commercials, 286; records Aura, 287–92; influence on European trumpeters, 288; joins Warner Brothers, 292–4; Rubberband project, 294–5, 297, 300, 308, 312; records Tutu, 295–7; final live appearance, 300; relationship with Jo Gelbard, 301, 321; records Amandla, 301–2; publishes autobiography, 305–6; guests on others' records, 307; Montreux appearances, 309–18; death, 321–2; re-releases, 322–5; growth of cult, 325

Davis, Richard, 172

Davis, Vincent, 305

Day, Doris, 69

de Falla, Manuel, 71, 124

Dearie, Blossom, 78
D'Earth, John, 314
DeBarge, 278
Debussy, Claude, 160
Debut label, 45
DeFrancesco, Joey, 299
DeJohnette, Jack, 200, 203–4, 208, 211, 222, 253;
    plays on *Bitches Brew* sessions, 214–15, 223–
    5; with Davis electric bands, 227, 232–3, 237,
    239–40, 244, 248; leaves Davis band, 245–6
Delibes, Leo, 69
Denmark, 127, 286
Dennard, Kennwood, 314
Denny, Martin, 141
Desmond, Paul, 92
Dial label, 11
Dingo (film), 306
DJ Cam, 208
Doctor Doolittle, 195
Dolphy, Eric, 110
Donaldson, Lou, 92
Dorough, Bob, 141–2, 157, 178
Down Beat, 44, 98, 228, 245, 327
Drew, Kenny, 26
Duke, George, 294–5, 302, 312
Dylan, Bob, 187, 292

Easy Mo Bee (Osten S. Harvey Jr), 307–8
Eckstine, Billy, 9–10, 11, 21, 25
ECM label, 242, 246, 290
Edelhagen, Kurt, 65
Eje, Niels, 287, 289
Ellington, Duke, 45, 51, 98, 105, 167, 185, 244,
    295; recorded output, 6; orchestra, 31;
    featured in *Time* magazine, 84; elder of
    jazz, 220, 327; death, 255, 323; autobiog-
    raphy, 306
Emarcy label, 91, 107
Engel, Jens, 287
Erb, Reiner, 314
Eskridge, Marguerite, 221–2, 246
Evans, Anita, 114
Evans, Bill, 152, 197, 326; with Davis sextet, 93–
    5, 97–9, 106–8, 110; and *Kind Of Blue*, 111–16;
    Village Vanguard recordings, 135; trio, 143

Evans, Bill (saxophonist), 265–7, 269, 272, 278
Evans, Gil, 97, 155, 170, 179, 203, 286, 297, 309;
    early collaborations, 14–17, 20–2; and *Miles
    Ahead*, 56, 64, 66–75, 77; and *Porgy and
    Bess*, 99–103; and 'So What', 114; and
    Sketches Of Spain, 124–6; Carnegie Hall
    concert, 138–40; final collaborations with
    Davis, 140–2, 153, 189, 194–6, 198–9; and Jimi
    Hendrix, 195, 245; visits Davis, 264; contri-
    bution to *Star People*, 272; and *You're Under
    Arrest*, 278; influence on *Aura*, 288, 291;
    death, 301, 315; orchestra, 314, 316–17;
    re-releases, 324; legacy, 325–6
Evans, Miles, 314, 316
Exodus (film), 177

Fabian, 187
Farmer, Art, 72, 91, 97–8, 145
Feather, Leonard, 270–1, 315
Feldman, Victor, 146–9
Ferguson, Maynard, 159
Fields, Herbie, 10
Figueroa, Sammy, 266
Findley, Chuck, 306
Finnerty, Barry, 266–7
Fitzgerald, Ella, 99
Flanagan, Tommy, 62, 78–9
Flavor Flav, 307
Ford, Robben, 297, 311
Foreman, James 'Mtume', 245–6, 250, 257, 310
Forrest, Jimmy, 28
Fortune, Sonny, 256–9, 267
Foster, Al, 248, 250, 253, 255; plays on *Agharta*,
    257; rejoins Davis, 266–7, 269, 272, 275–6;
    plays on *You're Under Arrest*, 277, 279–80;
    plays at Montreux, 310–11
Foster, Alex, 314
France, 127
Franklin, Aretha, 196
Franklin, David, 285, 293
Frehner, Hanspeter, 314
Freiburg, 65

Garland, Red, 42–3, 152, 326; with Davis
    quintet, 45, 47, 49–52, 54–6, 78; plays on

Milestones, 85–90; leaves Davis band, 89, 90, 93–4; rejoins Davis band, 106–8, 110

Garnett, Carlos, 248, 250–1

Garrett, Kenny, 297, 302, 307, 312–14

Gaskin, Leonard, 33

Gaumont, Dominique, 254, 256

Gavillet, Christian, 314

Gaye, Marvin, 247, 282

Gelbard, Jo, 286, 301, 305, 317, 321

Gershwin, George, 99–101, 125, 126

Getz, Stan, 12, 24, 25, 29, 55, 140

Gillespie, Dizzy, 5, 9–11, 44, 46, 48, 56, 77, 79

Gilmore, John, 46

Giorgianni, Sal, 314

Gitler, Ira, 32, 34, 87

Giuffre, Jimmy, 110

Gleason, Jackie, 77

Gleason, Ralph, 133

Glow, Bernie, 67, 100

Goldstein, Gil, 314, 316

Golson, Benny, 51

Goodman, Benny, 31

Gordon, Dexter, 79

Gordon, Max, 164

Gordy, Berry, 226

Graham, Bill, 226, 227, 232

Grammy Awards, 228, 309

Granz, Norman, 25, 126, 128

Grateful Dead, 186, 204

Green, Bennie, 25, 26

Griffin, Johnny, 41

Grossman, Steve, 222, 232–3, 237–42

Gruntz, George, 314, 316

Gruvstedt, Lennart, 287

Hackett, Bobby, 77

Hagood, Kenny, 14, 17, 21

Haig, Al, 13

Hall, Jim, 110, 145

Hall, Randy, 266–7, 294–5, 297

Hamilton, Chico, 79

Hammond, Johnny, 183

Hancock, Herbie, 211, 213, 245, 255, 293, 326; with Davis quintet, 148–52, 157, 160, 162–3, 165, 167–8, 170; Philharmonic Hall concert, 154–6; plays on *Miles Smiles*, 175–7; plays on *Sorcerer*, 178–9; plays on *Nefertiti* sessions, 180–2, 184–5; plays celeste, 190; plays electric piano, 191–3, 196–7; plays on *Miles In The Sky*, 193–4; plays on *Filles de Kilimanjaro*, 196–7; career aspirations, 198; plays on *In A Silent Way*, 201, 204; rejoins Davis, 222; plays on *Bitches Brew* sessions, 223; plays with Davis electric bands, 235, 238–9; success with Headhunters, 263; appears at Paris gala, 318

Handy, W. C., 146

Harris, Eddie, 175, 177

Harrison, Max, 71, 75, 97

Hart, Lorenz, 141

Hawkins, Coleman, 38, 53

Hawkins, Doug, 33

Hayes, Isaac, 205

Haynes, Roy, 25

Headhunters, 263

Heath, Jimmy, 24, 33–5, 119, 128, 175, 264

Heath, Percy, 25, 32–5, 37, 39–41, 44, 46, 52

Henderson, Eddie, 135, 137–8

Henderson, Joe, 177

Henderson, Michael, 238, 242, 244, 246, 248, 250, 326; plays on *Jack Johnson*, 234–6; plays on *Agharta*, 257–8; plays at Montreux, 310

Hendrix, Jimi, 195, 200, 220, 231, 235, 260; Davis and, 187, 245, 247; recordings, 218; death, 245

Hentoff, Nat, 89, 103

Herman, Woody, 13, 149

Herridge, Robert, 119

Herwig, Conrad, 314

Hines, Earl, 48

Hinton, Milt, 63

Hixon, Dick, 100

Hodeir, André, 71, 73

Hodges, Johnny, 46, 93

Holland, 127

Holland, Dave, 197–9, 208, 211, 222; plays on *In A Silent Way*, 201, 205; plays on *Bitches Brew* sessions, 214, 223–5, 228; with Davis electric bands, 232–4, 237, 239–40, 242; joins Circle,

242; appears at Paris gala, 318
Holliday, Billie, 25, 105
Holzmann, Adam, 297, 299, 300, 312–13
Hooker, John Lee, 307
Hopper, Dennis, 306
Horn, Shirley, 146, 307
Horowitz, Dick, 63
Hot Spot, The (film), 306
Hubbard, Freddie, 266

Irving, Robert, 275–8, 297, 299, 313, 310–12
Isham, Mark, 323
Isle Of Wight Rock Festival, 242

Jackson, Michael, 280
Jackson, Milt, 38, 40–2, 45, 108
Jackson, Munyungo, 300
Jaedig, Bent, 287
Jamal, Ahmad, 43, 52, 54, 69, 72, 85, 89, 95
Jamerson, James, 235
James, Bob, 295
Jankowski, Horst, 80
Japan, 165, 237, 254, 257, 260, 263, 270, 274, 298
Jarreau, Al, 294
Jarrett, Keith, 200, 211, 248, 255; with Davis
    electric bands, 237–8, 241–2, 244, 246
Jaspar, Bobby, 78–9
'Jazz For Moderns' tour, 79
Jazz Messengers, 31, 91, 128, 130, 276
Jefferson Airplane, 200
Jenkins, Gordon, 77
Jensen, Ole Kurt, 287
Johnson, Deron, 313
Johnson, Howard, 314
Johnson, J. J., 14, 21, 24–6, 28, 33, 37–8, 78; as
    composer, 63–4, 69
Johnson, Jack, 234, 236
Johnson, Osie, 63
Jones, Darryl 'The Munch', 274–5, 277, 279–80,
    310
Jones, Elvin, 45, 126
Jones, Hank, 92–3
Jones, Philly Joe, 32, 35, 43; with Davis quintet,
    45–7, 49, 51–2, 54–6; drug addiction, 57–8,
    95; fired by Davis, 66; rejoins Davis band,

78; plays on *Milestones*, 85, 87–9; the 'Philly
lick', 87; leaves Davis band, 95, 98; plays on
Porgy And Bess, 100–3; plays on *Someday
My Prince Will Come*, 131–2
Jones, Quincy, 280, 307, 315–17, 327
Jones, Sam, 92
Jones, Thad, 41, 46
Jordan, Taft, 67

Kaiser, Henry, 323
Kaper, Bronisław, 95
Karlsruhe, 190
Karskov, Uffe, 287
Kay, Connie, 44
Keepnews, Peter, 180
Kelly, Wynton, 69, 152; with Davis sextet, 110–
    13, 118, 126–7; plays on *Someday My Prince
    Will Come*, 131; plays on Blackhawk record-
    ings, 133, 136–7; forms Trio, 142
Kenton, Stan, 13, 37, 70
Kern, Jerome, 125
Kershaw, Nik, 278
Khachaturian, Aram, 94
Khan, Chaka, 294, 307, 313
King, Albert, 149
Klarwein, Mati, 220
Klugh, Earl, 295
Knudsen, Perry, 287
Koch-Hansen, Ole, 287
Konitz, Lee, 13, 14, 17–22, 26, 92; plays on *Miles
    Ahead*, 67, 69

LaFaro, Scott, 143
Lampley, Calvin, 99
Land, Harold, 198
Larsen, Ture, 287
Laswell, Bill, 294, 322–3
Lauper, Cyndi, 280, 281
Lawrence, Azar, 254
Lawson, Cedric, 250
Legrand, Michel, 96–7, 306
Lehn, Erwin, 80
Levy, Morris, 64
Lewis, John, 12, 36, 85–6, 91; with Davis nonet,
    14–17, 19, 22–3, 48; on Prestige recordings,

25–6, 33–4; and Third Stream music, 63; 'Django', 96, 97
Lieberson, Goddard, 131
Liebman, Dave, 252–5, 258, 265, 273; on Steve Grossman, 237; plays on *On The Corner*, 247–8; plays at Montreux, 310–11
Lifetime, 204, 205, 245
Lighthouse club, 35
Lion, Alfred, 92, 207
LiPuma, Tommy, 294–6, 302, 312
Little, Booker, 110
Lloyd, Charles, 200–1, 203, 237–8
London, Julie, 69
Lookout Farm, 255
Lorman, Ronald, 279
Los Angeles Jazz Festival, 128
Louisiana, 154
Love, 186
Lovett, Harold, 108
Lowther, Henry, 301
Lucas, Reggie, 250, 257, 259, 310
Lund, Henrik, 292
Lund, Niels Erik, 292
Lundvall, Bruce, 264

Mabern, Harold, 145–7
Mabry, Betty, 199, 215, 221
McCoy, Corky, 251
McCreary, Joe (Foley), 297, 299–300; plays at Montreux and Nice, 312–13
McDuff, Jack, 183
Macero, Teo, 56, 114, 124, 294; as Davis's regular producer, 131, 164, 177–8, 184, 189, 195 199, 211, 232–3, 235–6, 240–4, 247, 249, 251; difficulties with Davis, 139, 141, 149, 161; tape editing, 190, 201–2, 205–8; records *In A Silent Way*, 201–2, 205–8; records *Bitches Brew*, 215–21, 223, 228; use of effects, 233, 255; and Columbia CD releases, 236–7; compilation records, 260; and Davis comeback recordings, 265–6, 268, 271–2; end of relationship with Davis, 274–5; criticisms and legacy, 323, 325–6
McGregor, Chummy, 21
McIntyre, Early, 314

McKenzie, Scott, 186
McKibbon, Al, 14
McKnight, Dwayne, 297
McKusick, Hal, 70, 72
McLaughlin, John, 232–3, 238–9, 243–4, 326; plays on *In A Silent Way*, 201, 205–6; with Lifetime, 204, 205; with Mahavishnu Orchestra, 205, 233, 245; plays on *Bitches Brew* sessions, 214, 217, 223–5; plays on *Jack Johnson*, 235–6; plays on *On The Corner*, 248–9; career aspirations, 250; visits Davis, 264; plays on *You're Under Arrest*, 277, 280; plays on *Aura*, 287, 289–91; 'Pacific Express', 311; appears at Paris gala, 318
McLean, Jackie, 24, 26–8, 45, 48, 92, 147, 215; 'Dr Jackle', 85, 90; appears at Paris gala, 318
Madsen, Flemming, 287
Mahavishnu Orchestra, 205, 245
Maher, Jack, 52
Malach, Bob, 314
Malle, Louis, 80
Malone, Tom, 314
Manguel, Jose, 126
Mann, Herbie, 97
Manne, Shelly, 23, 35
Mantovani, 96
Margitza, Rick, 299, 313
Marmarosa, Dodo, 11
Marsalis, Branford, 276, 293
Marsalis, Wynton, 276, 293, 298, 301, 315
Mathis, Johnny, 66, 292
Maupin, Bennie, 214–15, 223–5, 232–3
May, Billy, 77
Mayfield, Curtis, 282
Maze, 294
Mazur, Marilyn, 287, 290, 299, 312
Melody Maker, 120, 249
Meltzer, Gordon, 300, 308
Merrill, Helen, 66
Messiaen, Olivier, 289, 291
Miami Vice, 286
Michelot, Pierre, 79, 81
Mikkelborg, Palle, 287–92
Miles, Buddy, 235
Miles, Jason, 295, 301

Milestone label, 242

Miley, Bubber, 244

Miller, Glenn, 21

Miller, Marcus, 266–7, 269, 272, 274, 300;
    works on *Tutu*, 295–7; works on *Amandla*,
    301–2; Davis guests on record, 307

Miller, Steve, 226, 227

Mingus, Charles, 11, 26, 34–5, 45, 94, 168

Miranda, Tony, 67–8

Mitchell, Blue, 198

Mitchell, Tom, 67

Mobley, Hank, 130–3, 135–7, 142, 152, 159

Modern Jazz Quartet, 31, 39, 63–5, 91

Monk, Thelonious, 9, 12, 40–2, 44, 61, 143;
    'Well, You Needn't', 32, 36, 43, 54; 'Round
    Midnight', 44, 56; works with Coltrane, 66,
    78; 'Straight, No Chaser', 85, 87, 106; plays in
    Europe, 186

Monterey Rock Festival, 201

Montgomery, Wes, 266

Montreal Jazz Festival, 275, 309-18

Moreira, Airto, 222, 223–5, 238–41, 245–6

Morton, Brian, 138

Moselholm, Erik, 286

Mothers Of Invention, 245

Motian, Paul, 143

Motown, 187, 226, 235

Mozart, Wolfgang Amadeus, 149

Mucci, Louis, 67, 100, 102

Mulligan, Gerry, 13–23, 35, 44, 79, 90–1, 143

Murray, Sunny, 148

NAACP (National Association for the
    Advancement of Coloured People), 154

Navarro, Fats, 19, 25

Nerlino, Joanne, 321

New Orleans, 218, 220, 276, 306

New York: Juilliard College, 2, 10; 52nd Street,
    10, 24, 197; Harlem, 10; Royal Roost, 16, 17,
    18; Birdland, 24, 25, 26, 28, 79, 108, 119–20,
    123; Bop City, 24; jazz scene, 43, 44, 84, 109–
    10, 157, 162, 207; Café Bohemia, 45, 46, 58,
    65–6, 78, 91, 93, 94; Five Spot Café, 78, 119;
    Carnegie Hall, 79, 138, 142, 164, 196, 254;
    Plaza Hotel, 105; Apollo Theater, 108; Jazz

Gallery, 128; Village Vanguard, 135, 164, 165,
    172, 307; Philharmonic Hall, 153, 154, 157, 166,
    251; session scene, 172, 267; Columbia
    studio, 190, 204; Village Gate, 197, 208; Blue
    Coronet Club, 208; Central Park, 211;
    Fillmore East, 226, 231–2, 240–1; annual
    festival, 268; Avery Fisher Hall, 269;
    Woodlawn Cemetery, 322

New York Times, 180

Newark, New Jersey, 158

Newport All Stars, 186

Newport Jazz Festival, 43–4, 98, 132, 172; In
    Europe, 186, 189

Nicholas, Big Nick, 26

Nilsson, Vincent, 287

Nisenson, Eric, 264

Nitzsche, Jack, 306

Nobs, Claude, 309–10, 315–17

Norman, Gene, 62

Nucleus, 245

O'Brien, Anne, 314

Oklahoma, 54

Olko, Marek, 277, 279

Ørsted Pedersen, Niels-Henning, 287, 291

Palmer, Earl, 307

Paris, 23, 78, 79, 150, 160, 185, 190, 254;
    Olympia, 126–7, 129, 130, 253; 'Miles and
    Friends' gala, 317–18

Parker, Charlie, 5, 36, 48, 61–2, 66, 129, 237;
    Davis's association with, 9–12, 19, 23–5, 31–2,
    88; substance abuse, 2, 10, 24, 32, 42;
    difficult behaviour, 10, 23; plays tenor
    saxophone, 12, 32, 62; death, 42; Adderley
    compared to, 91

Pascoal, Hermeto, 239, 244

Patterson, Don, 183

Patterson, Richard, 313

Peacock, Gary, 172

Penque, Romeo, 67, 72, 100

Pepper, Art, 75, 92

Perla, Gene, 238

Peters, Brock, 236

Pettiford, Oscar, 28, 43, 91

Pickett, Wilson, 187
Plaut, Fred, 115, 124, 125
Pontiggia, Claudio, 314
Porcaro, Steve, 294
Porgy And Bess, 69
Porter, Cole, 56
Potter, Tommy, 26
Powell, Bud, 5, 12, 19, 33, 41
Prestige Records, 6, 22, 28, 107; Davis record-
    ings, 25–7, 32–43, 45–55, 57, 61–2, 67, 73, 81,
    86, 90, 106, 132, 166, 325
Prince, 294–5, 307–8
Prindiville, James, 277
Pryor, Richard, 275
Public Enemy, 307

Rabe, Christian, 314
Ramey, Gene, 24
Ravel, Maurice, 94
recording: techniques, 27, 52, 73–4, 218; stereo,
    74; editing, 205–7; technology, 265, 268, 271;
    remixes, 267–8
Redding, Otis, 187
Rehak, Frank, 67, 100, 142
Return To Forever, 31, 265
Richardson, Jerome, 100
Richmond, Mike, 314
Rietveld, Benny, 300
Riley, Jim, 214–15
Riley, John, 314
Rivers, Sam, 157-8, 159
Rivers, Walter, 22
Riverside label, 93, 94, 107, 111
Roach, Max, 13–14, 18, 21, 24, 34–5, 91; protest
    at Carnegie Hall, 139; his band, 143, 242–3
Roberts, Conrad, 244
Robeson, Paul, 244
Robin, Leo, 43
Rodgers, Richard, 141, 167
Rodrigo, Joaquin, 124, 125, 139
Rogers, Shorty, 23, 35
Rollins, Sonny, 91, 130, 152, 242; plays with
    Davis, 24–7, 32, 36, 58, 78; 'Oleo', 39, 40, 51;
    contrary behaviour, 45–6; contrasted with
    Coltrane, 48–9; Prestige recordings, 62;

leaves jazz scene, 109; re-emergence, 143;
    calypsos, 192
Roney, Wallace, 314, 316–17
Rosenberg, Roger, 314
Rosenfeld, Benny, 287
Rothbaum, Mark, 285
Roulette label, 64
Roupe, Bjarne, 287
Rouse, Charlie, 143
Roy, Badal, 248, 250
Royal, Ernie, 67, 72, 100, 102–3, 125
Ruff, Willie, 67, 100
Rugolo, Pete, 17
Rushing, Jimmy, 105
Russell, George, 72, 26, 94, 109, 195
Rutgers University, 211
Rypdal, Terje, 290

Sample, Joe, 302
Sanborn, David, 312
Sanders, Pharoah, 143, 183
Sandpipers, 294
Saturn label, 110
Savoy label, 11, 12, 25, 38, 91
Schaap, Phil, 74
Schildkraut, Davey, 37
Schindler, Xenia, 314
Schneider, Larry, 314
Schoof, Manfred, 314
Schuller, Gunther, 14, 63, 68, 100
Schwartz, Arthur, 43
Scofield, John, 272–7, 280, 326, 310–12, 318
Scritti Politti, 296, 307
Shankar, Ravi, 222
Sharma, Bihari, 222
Sharrock, Sonny, 232
Shearing, George, 21, 24, 27, 79
Shepp, Archie, 183, 186
Sheridan, Chris, 92, 93
Shorter, Wayne, 128, 222, 237, 253, 321, 326;
    with Blakey's band, 142, 157, 159; with Davis
    quintet, 158–60, 162–3, 165, 167–9, 185, 191–3,
    198, 202–3, 208, 213; plays on *Miles Smiles*,
    175–6; plays on *Sorcerer*, 178–9; plays on
    Nefertiti sessions, 180–4, 213; plays on *Filles*

de Kilimanjaro, 196–7; plays on *In A Silent Way*, 201, 206; plays soprano saxophone, 203; plays on *Bitches Brew* sessions, 214, 217–18, 221, 224–5; last gigs with Davis, 228; with Davis electric bands, 233; joins Weather Report, 234, 245; appears at Paris gala, 318
Shukat, Peter, 305
Shulman, Joe, 13
Siegelstein, Sandy, 14
Siesta (film), 297
Silver, Horace, 35–7, 39, 91–2, 215
Sims, Zoot, 33, 44
Sinatra, Frank, 77, 146
Sindelfingen, 160
Sly And The Family Stone, 246
Smith, Charles Edward, 102
Smith, Jimmy, 183
Smith, Lonnie, 250, 252
Smith, Louis, 92
Smith, Wadada Leo, 323
Smythe, Pat, 197
Snow White, 131
Soft Machine, 245
Soloff, Lew, 314
Sonning, Léonie, Music Award, 286, 290
Sound of Jazz broadcast, 119
Spivak, Charlie, 21
Springsteen, Bruce, 292
Stamm, Marvin, 314
Stern, Mike, 266–7, 269–70, 272–4
Stief, Bo, 287, 291
Sting, 277, 279
Stinson, Albert, 177
Stitt, Sonny, 20, 92, 128–30, 256
Stockhausen, Karlheinz, 247
Stockholm, 127, 130, 213
Stone, Sly, 231, 235, 246–7, 260
Stordahl, Axel, 77
Stravinsky, Igor, 309
Strayhorn, Billy, 185
Strozier, Frank, 145–7
Stubblefield, John, 253
Sulieman, Idrees, 287
Sun Ra, 46, 110

Superfly, 244
Swift, Tom, 279
Szwed, John, 38

Taj Mahal, 307
Tate, Grady, 314
Taylor, Art, 46, 62, 67, 70–1, 78, 192
Taylor, Billy, 26
Taylor, Cecil, 109
Taylor, Dave, 314
Taylor, Frances, 95, 99, 124, 132, 157, 179, 195, 298
Terry, Clark, 9, 28, 219
Thaysen, Eva, 291
Thilo, Jesper, 287
Third Stream music, 63–4
Thomas, Gary, 297
Thompson, Lucky, 11, 37
Thornhill, Claude, 14–15, 16, 21–2, 68–9
Thornton, Steve, 277, 279, 310
Time magazine, 84
Time Of The Barracudas (play), 153
Toernqvist, Lillian, 287
Tokyo, 157, 269, 270
Tormé, Mel, 99
Tosca (Puccini), 195
Toto, 294, 307
Townsend, Irving, 116, 161
Tristano, Lennie, 18
Troup, Bobby, 69
Troupe, Quincy, 305
Truitt, Sonny, 33
Turner, Tina, 278
Tyner, McCoy, 254, 273
Tyson, Cicely, 179, 199, 263–4, 270, 285, 298

Urtreger, René, 64–5, 79

Van Gelder, Rudy, 22, 27, 33, 35, 37, 40, 46
van Rooyen, Ack, 314
Vancouver Festival, 298
Varner, Tom, 314
Vaughan, Sarah, 186, 307
Vee, Bobby, 187
Vee Jay label, 159

Ventura, Charlie, 13
Verve Records, 99
Vinson, Eddie 'Cleanhead', 36
Vitous, Miroslav, 197
Voice Of America, 44

Walcott, Collin, 248
Walker, T-Bone, 157
Waller, Fats, 96
Wallington, George, 19
Walrath, Jack, 314
Warner Brothers, 6, 298, 302, 308, 309, 312, 315;
    Davis signs to, 292–4; attitude to Davis
    catalogue, 322, 324
Warwick, Dionne, 278
Washington, Dinah, 307
Washington, Grover, 265–6
Watkins, Julius, 100
Watts, Michael, 249
Weather Report, 31, 203, 223, 234, 238, 245, 293
Weber, Michael, 314
Webster, Ben, 53, 97, 281
Webster, Freddie, 11
Weill, Kurt, 69
Wein, George, 43–4, 186, 268
Weinstock, Bob, 25, 27–8, 31, 33, 36, 40, 42, 45,
    47, 50
Weisgaard, Ethan, 287
Wellman, Ricky, 299–300, 302, 312–13
Wenziker, Judith, 314
White, Lenny, 214–15, 222, 233
Whittemore, Jack, 108
Who, 243
Wilburn, Vincent, 264–5, 275, 277–8, 299, 287,
    292, 311
Wilen, Barney, 79–81

Williams, 'Rubberlegs', 10
Williams, Buster, 177
Williams, Martin, 206
Williams, Tony, 202, 207, 211, 213, 215, 227, 326;
    with Davis quintet, 147–53, 153, 160–1, 163,
    165, 167, 169–70, 172, 185, 190–4, 202–3;
    Philharmonic Hall concert, 155–6; brings
    Rivers into Davis band, 157–8; plays on
    Miles Smiles and Sorcerer, 176–9; plays on
    Nefertiti, 180–2; plays on Filles de
    Kilimanjaro, 196–7; plays on In A Silent
    Way, 201, 205; career aspirations, 203–4;
    with Lifetime, 204, 245
Windfeld, Axel, 287
Winding, Kai, 13
Winther, Jens, 287
Wonder, Stevie, 234, 260
Woodman, Britt, 45
Woods, Phil, 92, 97
Woodyard, Sam, 105
WOR Studios, 33
World Series Of Jazz, 177

Yo Miles!, 323
Young, Larry, 204, 214, 223
Young, Lester, 64–5
Young, Neil, 226, 227

Zahn, Tilman, 314
Zappa, Frank, 245
Zawinul, Joe, 191, 202–3, 208, 211, 222, 326;
    plays on In A Silent Way, 201, 204–6; plays
    on Bitches Brew sessions, 214, 216, 219, 223–
    6; joins Weather Report, 234, 245; appears
    at Paris gala, 318
Zwerin, Michael, 17

373